OVERLY
ON
ELECTRONIC EVIDENCE IN CALIFORNIA

Michael R. Overly

Foley & Lardner
Los Angeles, California

THE EXPERT SERIES

D1457886

SO-BUB-687

 WEST GROUP

San Francisco

St. Paul

1999

ISBN 0-314-23371-7

West's Commitment to the Environment

In 1906, West Publishing Company began recycling materials left over from the production of books. This began a tradition of efficient and responsible use of resources. Today, 100% of our legal bound volumes and college texts are printed on acid-free, recycled paper consisting of 50% new paper pulp and 50% paper that has undergone a de-inking process. We also use vegetable-based inks to print many of our books. West Group recycles nearly 30,000,000 pounds of scrap paper annually—the equivalent of 300,000 trees. Since the 1960s, West has devised ways to capture and recycle waste inks, solvents, oils, and vapors created in the printing process. We also recycle plastics of all kinds, wood, glass, corrugated cardboard, and batteries, and have eliminated the use of styrofoam book packaging. We at West Group are proud of the longevity and the scope of our commitment to the environment.

Copyright © 1999

WEST GROUP
610 Opperman Drive
P.O. Box 64526
St. Paul, MN 55164-0526
1-800-328-9352

ISBN 0-314-23371-7

Library of Congress Cataloging-in-Publication Data

Overly, Michael R.
    Overly on electronic evidence in California / Michael R. Overly.
        p. cm. — (The expert series)
    Includes index.
    ISBN 0-314-23371-7 (alk. paper)
        1. Evidence, Documentary—California.   2. Computer files—Law and
legislation—California.   I. Title.   II. Series: Expert series (San Francisco, Calif.)
    KFC1038.094   1999   98-55952
        347.794'064—dc21   CIP

Michael R. Overly is special counsel to the Information Technology Department in the Los Angeles office of Foley & Lardner. His practice focuses on counseling clients regarding technology licensing, copyright law, electronic commerce, and Internet and multimedia law. Foley & Lardner has 14 offices nationwide with six firm-wide departments, including business law, health law, intellectual property, and litigation.

Mr. Overly is a 1989 graduate of Loyola Law School in Los Angeles, where he was articles editor of the Loyola Law Review and elected to the Order of the Coif. Prior to becoming an attorney, Mr. Overly worked as a research engineer in the Space and Technology Division of TRW, Inc. He received his MS and BS in Electrical Engineering from Texas A&M University.

Mr. Overly writes and speaks frequently on the legal issues of doing business on the Internet, technology in the workplace, e-mail, and electronic evidence. He has written numerous articles on these subjects for legal and technical periodicals, has authored a corporate guide for computer, e-mail, and Internet policies, and has contributed chapters for several treatises, including a chapter on the Internet and online transactions in *California Transactions Forms* from West Group.

WEST GROUP

50 California Street
19th Floor
San Francisco, California 94111

Publisher's Editorial Staff

ROBIN KOJIMA, ESQ.

ERIN MILNES

JEFFREY SHEA, ESQ.

ROBERT THOMPSON

Production Services
ImageInk, San Francisco

*This book is dedicated to Amy and Emma,
for their constant love and support.*

The almost ubiquitous presence of computers in our personal and business lives has resulted in a sea change in the way evidence is discovered and introduced at trial. To keep up with this growing use of technology to create, store, and transmit information, attorneys must learn to identify and exploit evidence that may be stored electronically. The potential sources of this new form of evidence change almost minute-to-minute as technology advances. Yesterday, the primary source of electronic evidence was a mainframe computer, and the Internet was just a glimmer in an engineer's eye. Today, electronic evidence is generally found on file servers and personal computers, and the Internet provides a vital means for conducting business. Tomorrow, relevant information will be stored on pocket-sized personal digital appliances that communicate with the Internet via cellular or microwave links.

Already, electronic evidence has proven the smoking gun in a broad range of actions, including breach of contract, theft of trade secrets, copyright infringement, sexual harassment, and racial discrimination. Attorneys that neglect this new form of evidence do so at their own peril.

This book was prepared with three goals in mind. First, to provide practitioners with a working knowledge of relevant computer concepts essential to discovering and using electronic evidence. Second, to provide an extensive catalog of the types and sources of electronic evidence. Finally, to provide guidance in the introduction and use of electronic evidence at trial. In furtherance of these goals, the text includes numerous checklists, example forms, and sample examinations.

Because technology is evolving almost daily, the discovery and use of electronic evidence is constantly changing. Consequently, this book must be read as a work in progress. If you have any questions, comments, or suggestions for future revisions, please feel free to contact me at *moverly@foleylaw.com*.

Michael R. Overly
Los Angeles, California
February 1999

COORDINATED RESEARCH IN CALIFORNIA FROM WEST GROUP

WITKIN TREATISES
Summary of California Law, 9th
California Procedure, 4th
California Evidence, 3rd
California Criminal Law, 2d (with Norman Epstein)
[Also available on CD-ROM]

CALIFORNIA JURISPRUDENCE (3D)
[Also available on CD-ROM]

JURY INSTRUCTIONS
California Jury Instructions—Civil (BAJI), 8th
California Jury Instructions—Criminal (CALJIC), 6th
[Also available in computer disk and looseleaf formats]

CALIFORNIA CIVIL PRACTICE
Business Litigation
Civil Rights Litigation
Employment Litigation
Environmental Litigation
Family Law Litigation
Probate and Trust Proceedings
Procedure
Real Property Litigation
Torts
Workers' Compensation
[Also available on CD-ROM]

CALIFORNIA LITIGATION AND TRANSACTIONS FORMS
West's California Litigation Forms: Civil Procedure Before Trial
West's California Litigation Forms: Civil Trials and Evidence
West's California Litigation Forms: Civil Appeals and Writs
California Transactions Forms: Business Entities
California Transactions Forms: Business Transactions
California Transactions Forms: Family Law
[Also available on CD-ROM]

CALIFORNIA PRACTICE GUIDES AND HANDBOOKS
California Affirmative Defenses 2d
Ann Taylor Schwing
California Community Property Law 3d
William W. Bassett
California Insurance Law 4th Desk Reference
Bruce Cornblum
California Insurance Law Handbook
John K. DiMugno and Paul E. B. Glad
California Insurance Law Reporter
California Legal Filing Directory
Patricia A. Britton
California Medical Malpractice
George McDonald
California Prejudgment Money Remedies
Justice John Zebrowski, Barry Adler, and Paul S. Malingagio
California Premises Liability Law and Practice
Michael Thomas, Mark Kelegian, and Paul Gutierrez
California Subpoena Handbook
John M. Sink
California Tort Reporter
California Family Law Practice Library on CD-ROM
California Personal Injury Practice Library on CD-ROM

———————

THE EXPERT SERIES
Cohelan on California Class Actions by Timothy D. Cohelan
Dunne on Depositions by Kevin J. Dunne
Overly on Electronic Evidence in California by Michael R. Overly
Simons on California Evidence by Judge Mark B. Simons
Younger on California Motions by Judge Eric E. Younger (ret.)

———————

REAL ESTATE PRACTICE
California Real Estate 2d by Harry Miller and Marvin Starr
California Real Estate Forms by Alexander Hamilton
California Real Property Digest
Real Estate NewsAlert
[Also available on CD-ROM]
California Construction Law Manual 5th by James Acret
California Construction Law Reporter
California Land Use Procedure by J. R. Ramos
California Foreclosure by Margaret Sheneman
California Real Estate Practice Library on CD-ROM

CRIMINAL PRACTICE
West's California Criminal Law
Douglas Dalton
West's California Criminal Procedure
Laurie L. Levenson
California Criminal Trialbook
Harry M. Caldwell, Sue Steding and Gary Nichols
California Criminal Forms and Instructions 2d
Edward A. Rucker and Mark E. Overland
California Drunk Driving Defense 2d
Lawrence Taylor
California Criminal Practice Library on CD-ROM

JURY SELECTION PRACTICE BOOKS
**Bennett's Guide to Jury Selection and Trial Dynamics:
California Criminal Litigation
Bennett's Guide to Jury Selection and Trial Dynamics:
California Civil Litigation**
By Cathy E. Bennett, Robert B. Hirschhorn and Dr. Jo-Ellan Dimitrius

---

WEST'S CALIFORNIA CODE FORMS
Business and Professions by Joel S. Primes
Civil by Jeanne P. Robinson
Civil Procedure by Gregory L. Ogden and Daryl Fisher-Ogden
Commercial by Stephen N. Hollman and Ray D. Henson
Corporations by Janet E. Kerr
Education by Jay E. Grenig
Elections, Fish & Game, Food & Agricultural, Insurance by Susan J. Orton
Family by Margaret McAllister
Government by Jay E. Grenig
Probate by Ann E. Stodden and Timothy A. Whitehouse
Public Utilities by Boris H. Lakusta
Revenue and Taxation by Anthony X. McDermott

RUTTER PRACTICE GUIDES
Alternative Dispute Resolution
Civil Appeals and Writs
Civil Procedure Before Trial
Civil Trials and Evidence
Corporations
Enforcing Judgments and Debts
Family Law
Federal Civil Procedure Before Trial
Federal Ninth Circuit Civil Appellate Practice
Insurance Litigation

Landlord-Tenant
Law Practice Management
Personal Injury
Probate
Professional Responsibility
Real Property Transactions
[*Also available on CD-ROM*]

WEST'S ANNOTATED CALIFORNIA CODES
[*Also available on CD-ROM*]

BARCLAY'S OFFICIAL CALIFORNIA CODE OF REGULATIONS
[*Also available on CD-ROM*]

CALIFORNIA OFFICIAL REPORTS
[*Also available on CD-ROM*]

CALIFORNIA DIGEST OF OFFICIAL REPORTS 3D
[*Also available on CD-ROM*]

WEST'S CALIFORNIA REPORTER
[*Also available on CD-ROM*]

WEST'S CALIFORNIA DIGEST 2D
[*Also available on CD-ROM*]

WEST GROUP'S CALIFORNIA DESKTOP CODES
Unannotated Desktop Codes
California Civil Code
California Code of Civil Procedure
California Corporations Code
California Education Code
California Evidence Code
California Insurance Code
California Penal Code
California Probate Code
California Revenue and Taxation Code
California Vehicle Code
California Water Code
California Business Statutes
California Employment Laws
California Environmental Laws
California Family Laws and Rules
California Juvenile Laws and Rules

Annotated Desktop Codes
California Civil Practice Statutes and Rules
Blumberg California Family Code Annotated
California Commercial Code Annotated
DiMugno & Glad California Insurance Laws Annotated
Dwyer & Bergsund California Environmental Laws Annotated
Imwinkelreid & Hallahan California Evidence Code Annotated
McGovern California Probate Code Annotated
Miller and Starr Real Estate Laws Annotated

Court Rules
California Rules of Court—State and Federal
Northern California Local Court Rules—Superior and Municipal Courts
Bay Area Local Court Rules—Superior and Municipal Courts
Central California Local Court Rules—Superior and Municipal Courts
Southern California Local Court Rules—Superior and Municipal Courts
Los Angeles County Court Rules—Superior and Municipal Courts

JUDICIAL COUNCIL FORMS
California Judicial Council Forms (Official Publisher)
Legal Solutions Judicial Council and local forms disk products (DOS and Windows)
See the Judicial Council Forms provided by West Group
on the Internet at *www.courtinfo.ca.gov/forms*.

INTERNET
Visit West Group's online store on the World Wide Web at *http://www.westgroup.com*.

For more information about West Group's California practice tools, please call your West Group Representative or West Group Customer Service at 1-800-328-9352. You may also fax inquiries to 1-800-340-9378 (WEST). If you have research questions concerning WESTLAW® or West Group Publications, please call the West Reference Attorneys at 1-800-733-2889.

WESTLAW® ELECTRONIC RESEARCH GUIDE

WESTLAW, Computer Assisted Legal Research

WESTLAW is part of the research system provided by West Group. With WESTLAW, you find the same quality and integrity that you have come to expect from West books. For the most current and comprehensive legal research, combine the strengths of West books and WESTLAW.

WESTLAW Adds to Your Library

Whether you wish to expand or update your research, WESTLAW can help. For instance, WESTLAW is the most current source for case law, including slip opinions and unreported decisions. In addition to case law, the online availability of statutes, statutory indexes, legislation, court rules and orders, administrative materials, looseleaf publications, texts, periodicals, news, and business information makes WESTLAW an important asset to any library. Check the online WESTLAW Directory or the print WESTLAW Database Directory for a list of available databases and services. Following is a brief description of some of the capabilities that WESTLAW offers.

Natural Language Searching

You can now search most WESTLAW databases using WIN®, the revolutionary Natural Language search method. As an alternative of formulating a query using terms and connectors, you simply enter a description of your research issue:

> What is the government's obligation to warn military personnel of the danger of past exposure to radiation?

WESTLAW then retrieves the set of documents that has the highest statistical likelihood of matching your description.

Retrieving a Specific Document

When you know the citation to a case, statute, or Constitution section that is not in your library, use the Find service to retrieve the document on WESTLAW. Access Find and type a citation like the following:

find 639 p2d 939
find ca elec s 7559
find ca const art 12 s 1

Updating Your Research

You can use WESTLAW to update your research in many ways:

- Retrieve cases citing a particular statute or Constitution section.

- Update a state statute or Constitution section by accessing the Update service from the displayed statute or Constitution section using the Jump marker.

- Retrieve newly enacted legislation by searching in the appropriate legislative service database.

- Retrieve cases not yet reported by searching in case law databases.

- Read the latest U.S. Supreme Court opinions within an hour of their release.

- Update West digests by searching topic and Key Numbers.

Determining Case History and Retrieving Citing Cases

KeyCite™, the new citation research service developed by West Group and made available through the WESTLAW computer-assisted legal research service, integrates all the case law on WESTLAW, giving you the power to

- trace the history of a case;

- retrieve a list of all cases on WESTLAW that cite a case; and

- track legal issues in a case.

Citing references from the extensive library of secondary sources on WESTLAW, such as ALR® annotations and law review articles, are covered by KeyCite as well. You can use these citing references to find case discussions by legal experts.

In additioin, KeyCite is completely integrated with West's Key Number System so that is provides the tools for navigating the case law databases on WESTLAW. Only KeyCite combines the up-to-the-minute case-verification functions of an online citator service with the case-finding tools needed to find relevant case law.

Additional Information

For more detailed information or assistance, contact your WESTLAW Account Representative or call 1–800–REF–ATTY (1–800–733–2889).

[February 1999]

SUMMARY TABLE OF CHAPTERS

DETAILED TABLE OF CONTENTS

Sec.

PART III APPENDICES

PART I

DISCOVERY OF ELECTRONIC EVIDENCE

OVERVIEW

The vast majority of business documents are created on or pass through a computer. When such electronic information is relevant to issues in a litigation, questions arise regarding where the data is located, how to access it through discovery procedures, how to limit discovery of privileged or protected data, and how to introduce discovered electronic evidence at trial. Part I reviews sources of electronic evidence and how to obtain it. The glossary of essential computer terms in Chapter 1 and the electronic sources described in Chapter 2 provide a good starting point for attorneys who are not experienced in crafting requests and responses for such information. The forms in Chapter 3 provide a selection of discovery tools for seeking electronic evidence, while illustrating the appropriate level of detail for these methods. When responding to requests for electronic discovery, attorneys must carefully consider potential limitations on discovery, including privilege, privacy, and the effects of copyright and trade secret restrictions, as discussed in Chapters 5 and 7. Each party to a litigation must be ever vigilant to preserve evidence, as discussed in Chapter 6.

1 INTRODUCTION

§ 1.01 What Is Electronic Evidence?

Almost every aspect of business now revolves around the computer. Moreover, the very role of computers in business is changing from being merely an efficient repository and processor of information to an effective means of communicating and conducting business online. It is difficult to identify any business transaction that is not created on or passed through a computer. Many personal transactions are also conducted electronically. In particular, millions of individuals now use e-mail as one of their primary means of communication. Each contact with a computer may, and likely will, result in the creation of "electronic evidence." In its broadest form, electronic evidence is defined as information stored in electronic form (for example, on a computer hard disk or floppy disk) that is relevant to the issues in a particular litigation.

> **Example:** A seller creates an invoice with a popular word processing program and then transmits the invoice to a buyer over the Internet using e-mail. This simple transaction has created a number of pieces of electronic evidence: (1) a copy of the invoice will be stored by the word processing program on the seller's hard disk; (2) if the invoice was revised several times before being sent, the word processing program may have recorded the dates and times of the revisions and the names of each employee who edited the file; (3) a copy of the invoice may exist on a backup tape created on the seller's network; (4) a copy of the invoice along with the e-mail transmittal letter will be stored in the "sent" box in the seller's e-mail program; (5) a copy of the e-mail with the attached invoice will be stored on the backup tapes of the seller's Internet service provider; (6) a copy of the e-mail with the attached invoice will be stored on the backup tapes of the buyer's Internet service provider; (7) a copy of the invoice may exist on a backup tape created on the buyer's network; (8) a copy of the e-mail will exist on the hard disk of the employee's computer who receives it; and (9) if the employee forwards the e-mail to anyone else at the buyer, copies of the e-mail will exist on their individual hard disks.

The nature of electronic evidence poses unique challenges to both the discovery and admissibility of such evidence. As the foregoing example illustrates, simply identifying all of the potential sources of relevant electronic evidence may present a considerable challenge. Once located and produced, the admissibility of electronic evidence is complicated by the fact that information stored in electronic form is relatively easy to alter or modify. In many instances, such alterations or modifications cannot be detected, even with sophisticated forensic techniques. For example, the return address on an e-mail can be easily altered to make it appear as though the message was sent by a completely different sender. (See, e.g., *People v. Lee* (San Mateo County Sup. Ct. 1/30/97) (former employee falsified an e-mail from her supervisor to support her claim of wrongful termination).)

The volume of potentially relevant electronic documents that may have to be reviewed in order to respond to a discovery request or may have to be reviewed by the requesting party after a production can be daunting. As the following table illustrates, thousands, if not millions, of pages of documents may have to be reviewed.

Type of Storage Medium	Approximate Number of Text Pages
Floppy disk (5 ¼")	180
Floppy disk (3 ½")	720
CD ROM (650 megabytes)	325,000
Laptop hard disk (2 gigabytes)	1,000,000
PC hard disk (4 gigabytes)	2,000,000
Network hard disk (40 gigabytes)	20,000,000

▶ **COMMENT**

The totals above assume there are approximately 2,000 bytes per page. The actual storage required per page will vary depending on the program used to create the document. Graphics (Windows) based word processors require more storage space for documents than text (DOS) based word processors.

One of the primary reasons so many documents are stored electronically is that the price of computer storage space has decreased dramatically in recent years: In 1963, 1 megabyte of hard disk storage cost approximately $2,000.00. Today, the same amount of storage costs less than $1.00. Because storage space is so inexpensive, many businesses simply choose to never delete documents or e-mail. They prefer to simply keep everything online for ready retrieval in the event something is needed.

One of the benefits of storing documents electronically is that they can be searched automatically using commercially available software for the occurrence of specified key words or phrases. Such search programs can greatly reduce the time required to review electronic documents in preparation for production. This benefit to the producing party, however, can also be exploited by the requesting party. A growing number of production demands request production in electronic form so that search software can be used to expedite review of the documents.

§ 1.02 Use of Forensic Experts

[A] Services Experts Can Provide

Because of the complex nature of computer systems, it is frequently necessary to seek the assistance of experts when dealing with electronic evidence. Such assistance generally falls into three categories.

Planning and Conducting Discovery. Experts can provide valuable guidance in identifying potential sources of electronic evidence and in drafting appropriate discovery requests to elicit that evidence. The presence of experts at the depositions of technical witnesses can also be useful to the examining attorney to obtain real-time guidance on particular areas of inquiry. If a technical issue arises during the witness's testimony that is unfamiliar to the examining attorney, the expert can provide immediate assistance regarding the issue— obviating the potential need for later discovery to follow up on the testimony.

Analyzing the Evidence. If evidence is produced in electronic form (for example, on a hard disk or magnetic tape), an expert can perform the following functions: (1) retrieve and sort the information and perform searches for specific keywords; (2) recover previously deleted or erased files; (3) scan the electronic media for potential viruses or other harmful programs; (4) bypass or defeat passwords; (5) decode encrypted files; (6) identify the electronic format in which evidence is stored; and (7) ensure the evidence is properly preserved for use at trial. The most common function served by experts in analyzing electronic evidence is to perform searches on the evidence. Experts can provide specialized software for rapidly searching enormous amounts of electronically stored data. For example, an expert could quickly search thousands of pieces of e-mail for every reference to particular keywords describing a relevant event or occurrence. The use of automated search software can save many hours of attorney time in reviewing printouts of the messages.

Trial Preparation and Testimony. The expert can assist in preparing direct and cross-examination for technical witnesses. They can also be useful in anticipating and preparing for potential objections to computer-related evidence. The trial testimony of experts may be required to establish how electronic evidence was preserved and the nature of the evidence and to explain technical matters (for example, the operation of a computer system) to the trier of fact.

[B]   Finding an Expert

Computer forensics experts are found in much the same way as any other type of expert. Professional computer organizations, universities, industry trade organizations, and expert services (for example, Martindale-Hubbell's Buyer's Guide, Technical Advisory Service for Attorneys (TASA), and the Los Angeles County Bar Association's Directory of Experts and Consultants) are all valuable sources of potential experts. Another potential source of experts is product user groups. The users of many popular software applications and items of computer hardware frequently band together to establish (usually with the assistance/encouragement of the software or hardware vendor) user groups. Such groups are formed to allow users to exchange information and ideas about certain products. For example, they may share information about potential bugs or new ways to use a piece of hardware. Monitoring these groups may assist in identifying consultants who are experts with the particular software or hardware that is the subject of the user group.

Before beginning a search for an expert, it is important to learn as much as possible about the computer hardware, software, and file types at issue. This information will be essential in identifying the expert that is best for a particular litigation. It should be kept in mind that not all computer consultants are experts with every system. Indeed, most consultants restrict their efforts to particular hardware platforms and software applications.

▶ **COMMENT**

The Internet provides an excellent starting point for locating an expert. Typing the terms "computer forensic discovery" into a variety of Internet search engines will yield a number of potential businesses that focus on providing forensic computer services to attorneys.

For a list of federal experts for computer crime investigations, see Appendix E.

§ 1.03 An Introduction to Computers and Computer Networks

[A] Computer System Components

Although computer systems can be configured in an unlimited number of ways, every system will contain certain common components. A basic understanding of these components is essential for working with and discovering electronic evidence.

Component	Description
CPU	Central processing unit. CPUs can exist in a stand-alone configuration (for example, a typical desktop computer or workstation) or networked together (see § 2.02). CPUs can also be combined within a single computer; multiple CPUs are growing common in, for example, file servers.
storage device	A piece of computer hardware used to store data and programs. Examples include hard disks, floppy disks, optical disks, and magnetic tape drives. The capacity of such storage devices is generally measured in multiples of one of the following units: Kilobyte (1,000 bytes) Megabyte (1,000,000 bytes) Gigabyte (1,000,000,000 bytes) For example, the hard disk in a personal computer may have a 3 gigabyte capacity. The floppy disk in the same computer may have a 1.44 megabyte capacity.
input/output device	Computer hardware used to send and receive information to a computer. Common input devices include keyboards, mice, and scanners. Output devices include video monitors and printers.
communications devices	Methods by which the computer communicates with the outside world, usually over a telephone line. A modem is a typical communications device.
software	Programs or instructions used to operate the computer. Software includes system programs that control the internal operation of the computer (that is, the operating system for the computer) and application programs used to produce work (for example, word processing and spreadsheet programs).
documentation	Documents that describe how a computer system or piece of software operates.

[B] Glossary of Essential Computer Terms

anonymous remailer   A mail server that is designed to take an e-mail message sent to it, strip off all the identifying information in the header, replace the identifying data with anonymous information, and then forward the message on to its intended destination.

ASCII   An acronym for American Standard Code for Information Interchange. An almost universally accepted format for exchanging text-based information. ASCII format is, however, limited in that it does not preserve the formatting of the text or any special characteristics of the document (for example, footnotes, tables, and bullet points).

asymmetric encryption   A method of encryption in which every user has two passwords: one private, the other public. The public passwords are exchanged freely and are frequently listed in public directories on the Internet. In contrast, the private password is known only to its owner and is never shared with anyone else. The public and private passwords are related by a complex mathematical formula, which prevents one password from being deduced from the other. The public password can be widely disseminated without compromising security. Asymmetric encryption is also known as public key encryption. It is the most common form of encryption used in online communications and transactions.

audit trail   An automatic feature of computer operating systems or certain programs that creates a record of transactions relating to a file, piece of data, or particular user.

BBS   Acronym for electronic bulletin board services. A BBS is a computer set up to provide the electronic equivalent of a common bulletin board. Users use the board to post and read messages. A BBS may also permit users to exchange e-mail, to "chat" electronically online (the users talk in real-time by typing messages to each other using their keyboards), and to upload and download files. A "sysop" (system operator) runs the BBS.

bit   The smallest unit of data. A bit can have only one of two values: "1" or "0." See **byte**.

byte   A basic unit of data. A byte consists of eight bits and can represent a single character such as a letter or number. A "megabyte" refers to a million bytes of information. A "gigabyte" refers to a billion bytes of information.

cache   Memory used to store frequently used data. With regard to the Internet, caching refers to the process of storing popular or frequently visited Web sites on a hard disk or in RAM so that the next time the site is accessed it is retrieved from memory rather than from the Internet. Caching is used to reduce traffic on the Internet and to vastly decrease the time it takes to access a Web site.

central processing unit Abbreviated "CPU." The portion of a computer that controls the processing and storage of data.

ciphertext The encrypted version of a message or data file.

client computer A personal computer or workstation connected to a network file server. See **file server**.

client-server network A type of network in which server computers provide files to client computers. See **client computer** and **file server**.

compressed files A file whose contents have been "compressed" using specialized software so that it occupies less storage space than in its uncompressed state. Files are typically compressed to save disk storage space or to decrease the amount of time required to send them over a communications network such as the Internet.

cookie A cookie is a small data file that a Web site can store on a visitor's computer. If the visitor returns to the Web site, the cookie can be used to identify the visitor and to provide personalized information to the visitor. Cookies are used by the operators of Web sites as marketing tools to gain information about their visitors and to track their movements on the site. Web browsers can be configured to reject cookies when they are offered.

CPU Acronym for Central Processing Unit. See **central processing unit**.

Data Encryption Standard Abbreviated "DES." One of the most popular forms of private key encryption. DES was developed by IBM in the late 1970's.

DES Acronym for Data Encryption Standard. See **Data Encryption Standard**.

disk mirroring A method of protecting data from a catastrophic hard disk failure. As each file is stored on the hard disk, an identical, "mirror" copy is made on a second hard disk or on a different partition of the same disk. If the first disk fails, the data can be recovered instantly from the mirror disk. Mirroring is a standard feature in most network operating systems.

EDI Acronym for Electronic Data Interchange. See **Electronic Data Interchange**.

Electronic Data Interchange Abbreviated "EDI." A method of electronically communicating standard business documents (for example, purchase orders, invoices, and shipping receipts) between the computer systems of businesses, government organizations, and banks. EDI was developed in the 1960's as a means of accelerating the movement of standard documents related to the shipment and transportation of goods.

encryption   A method of using mathematical algorithms to encode a message or data file so that it cannot be understood without a password.

extranet   An extension of the corporate intranet over the Internet so that vendors, business partners, customers, and others can have access to the intranet. See **intranet** and **Internet**.

FAT   Acronym for file allocation table. See **file allocation table**.

field(s)   Individual entries or groups of entries within a file relating to the same subject. For example, a litigation support database may have fields for the creator and recipient of a document and its subject.

file   A collection of data or information stored under a specified name on a disk. Examples of files are programs, data files, spreadsheets, databases, and word-processing documents.

file allocation table   Abbreviated "FAT." A table used by a computer's operating system to track the used and unused portions of a disk. Because files are typically not stored in consecutive areas on a disk, the FAT also keeps track of where the parts of a file are stored on the disk. By editing the FAT, deleted files can sometimes be recovered.

file server   A central computer used to store files (for example, data, word-processing documents, programs) for use by client computers connected to a network. Most file servers run special operating systems known as "network operating systems (NOS)." Novell Netware and Windows NT are common NOS. See **client computer** and **client-server network**.

GIF   Acronym for Graphics Interchange Format. A graphics file format used to exchange images on the Internet.

hard disk   A storage device based on a fixed, permanently mounted disk drive. Hard disks can be either internal or external to the computer.

hash function   A mathematical method of generating a unique number to represent the content of a message or document. Any change to the message or document will cause the hash function to change. Hash functions are used to authenticate information to ensure that it has not been modified or tampered with in any way. Hash functions are commonly used in digital signatures and public key encryption.

HTML Acronym for Hypertext Markup Language. The formatting and layout language used to create documents for viewing on the World Wide Web. HTML tells Web browsers how documents on the Web are to be displayed.

home page Generally the first of a collection of HTML pages, collectively forming a Web site. See **HTML** and **Web site**.

Internet A global collection of interconnected computers and networks that use TCP/IP (Transmission Control Protocol/Internet Protocol) to communicate with each other. At one time, the term "Internet" was used as an acronym for "interconnected networks."

intranet A computer network designed to be used within a business or company. An intranet is so named because it uses much of the same technology as the Internet. Web browsers, e-mail, newsgroups, HTML documents, and Web sites are all found on intranets. In addition, the method for transmitting information on these networks is TCP/IP. See **Internet**.

ISP Acronym for Internet service provider.

JPEG Acronym for Joint Photographic Experts Group. A standard file format for storing images in a compressed form.

key In the context of encryption, a key is a more general form of a password. Passwords are ordinarily thought of as a brief series of characters that a user commits to memory. In contrast, a key is usually a small computer file consisting of 56 or more random characters. Typical key lengths for symmetric encryption systems are 56 or 128 bits. Asymmetric systems have key lengths of a thousand or more bits.

LAN Acronym for local area network. See **local area network**.

listserv An online discussion group. Messages are disseminated to the subscribers to the listserv by e-mail. When a subscriber desires to post a message to the discussion group, he or she e-mails the message to a special address for the group. The listserv software then forwards the message and any replies to all of the members of the group.

local area network Abbreviated "LAN." A network of computers and other devices generally located within a relatively limited area (for example, within a particular office, building, or group of buildings).

log file A record of activity or transactions that occur on a particular computer system.

MIS Management Information Services. The department within a business assigned the task of operating and maintaining its computer resources.

modem A device used to change a stream of data from a computer into audio tones for transmission over a telephone line. Originally a concatenation of modulator-demodulator.

MPEG Acronym for Moving Pictures Experts Group. A standard file format for storing compressed versions of audio and video files.

network map A graphical depiction of the way in which the various computers, file servers, and peripherals on a network are inter-connected. The map typically identifies the type and speed (bandwidth) of the connections.

Newsgroup See **Usenet**.

NOS Acronym for network operating system. See **file server**.

object code The machine readable version of a computer program. See **source code**.

operating system Abbreviated "OS." A program used to control the basic operation of a computer (for example, storing and retrieving data from memory, controlling how information is displayed on the computer monitor, operating the central processing unit, and communicating with peripherals).

PC Acronym for personal computer.

partition A region of a hard disk treated by the computer's operating system as a separate drive. Through the use of partitions, a computer with a single hard disk can appear to have two or more drives.

PCMCIA Acronym for "Personal Computer Memory Card International Association." A standard for laptop and PDA-based peripherals (for example, memory cards and modems) and the slots that hold them. See **personal digital assistants**.

peer-to-peer network A type of network in which a group of personal computers is interconnected so that the hard disks, CD ROMS, files, and printers of each computer can be accessed from every other computer on the network. Peer-to-peer networks do not have a central file server and are used when fewer than a dozen computers will be networked together.

peripherals   A device, such as a printer, mouse, or disk drive, that is connected to a computer and controlled by its microprocessor.

personal digital assistants   Abbreviated "PDA." PDAs range from compact personal electronic organizers (for example, calendars, phone lists, brief notes) to the new breed of palm-sized computers that are capable of running full-featured word processing programs and spreadsheets and of browsing the Internet and sending and receiving e-mail. These devices can hold hundreds, and will soon be able to store thousands, of pages of information.

plaintext   The version of a message or data file before it is encrypted.

private-key encryption   See **symmetric encryption**.

proxy server   A server used to manage Internet-related traffic coming to and from a local area network that can provide certain functionality (for example, access control and caching of popular Web sites).

RAM   Acronym for random access memory. See **random access memory**.

random access memory   Abbreviated "RAM." An integrated circuit into which data can be read or written by a microprocessor or other device. The memory is volatile and will be lost if the system is disconnected from its power source.

read only memory   Abbreviated "ROM." An integrated circuit into which information, data, and/or programs are permanently stored. The absence of electric current will not result in loss of memory.

ROM   Acronym for read only memory. See **read only memory**.

ROT13   A simple, yet popular, form of encryption used primarily on Internet newsgroups. ROT13 is a "substitution cipher" in which each letter of a message is replaced by the letter 13 places away from it in the alphabet.

RSA   The most popular form of public key encryption.

scanner   A piece of computer hardware used to scan text and/or images into the memory of a computer system.

software   A series of prerecorded commands issued to a computer to accomplish a particular task.

source code   The version of a computer program that can be read by humans. The source code is translated into machine readable code by a program called a "compiler." Access to the source code is required to understand how a computer program works or to modify the program. See **object code**.

stand-alone computer   A personal computer that is not connected to any other computer or network, except possibly through a modem.

swap files   Hidden areas on a hard disk used by the computer's operating system to temporarily store programs and data. The operating system "swaps" information as needed between RAM and the hard disk. Swap files are a form of virtual memory. See **virtual memory**.

symmetric encryption   A method of encryption that uses the same key to encrypt and decrypt a message. The most common form of symmetric encryption is the password function provided in most word processing and spreadsheet programs. Symmetric encryption is also known as private-key encryption.

temporary files   A file that is temporarily created, either in RAM or on disk, for purposes of a particular computer session and then automatically deleted. If a computer session is terminated prematurely (by a system failure or by turning the power off or rebooting the computer, for example), these files might not be deleted and can be recovered.

Unix   A multi-user operating system developed at Bell Laboratories in the late 1960's for use on minicomputers.

URL   Acronym for Uniform Resource Locator. URLs are used by Web browsers to locate sites on the Internet.

Usenet   A collection of thousands of discussion groups on the Internet, each devoted to a single topic or issue. Users can post messages of their own and read messages left by others. The Usenet predates the establishment of the Internet.

VAN   Acronym for value added network. See **value added network**.

value added network   Abbreviated "VAN." A computer communications network commonly used by businesses to exchange EDI documents.

virtual memory   The ability of a computer operating system to make RAM appear larger than it really is by storing programs and data temporarily on the hard disk. See **swap files**.

WAN   Acronym for wide area network. See **wide area network**.

wide area network   Abbreviated "WAN." A network of computers and other devices distributed over a broad geographic area.

Web   See **World Wide Web**.

Web browser   A program used to view HTML pages on the World Wide Web.

Web server   A computer on which a Web site is stored.

Web site   A collection of related HTML documents stored on the same computer and accessible to users of the Internet. See **home page**.

workstation   A personal computer connected to a network. A workstation can also refer to a high performance computer used for intensive graphics or numerical calculations.

World Wide Web   Abbreviated "WWW" or the "Web." A user friendly, graphical interface to the Internet. Documents, sometimes called "pages," on the Web are created using the Hypertext Markup Language (HTML). Documents are connected to one another on the Web through the use of hyperlinks. A hyperlink is a highlighted word, phrase, or graphic image that when selected by pressing a key or clicking a mouse will automatically transfer the user from one page on the Web to another. Web pages are transmitted over the Internet using the Hypertext Transfer Protocol (HTTP).

WWW   Acronym for World Wide Web. See **World Wide Web**.

2 SOURCES OF ELECTRONIC EVIDENCE

A. Text

§ 2.01 Overview

To conduct effective discovery of electronic evidence, attorneys must possess a basic understanding of computers and computer networks, knowledge of the various locations where electronic evidence can be found, and a little creativity. This chapter catalogs a wide range of potential sources of electronic evidence. Each of these sources should be considered in creating a discovery plan. The assistance of a skilled computer forensics expert can be invaluable in identifying additional sources of information and refining discovery requests for particular computer systems.

§ 2.02 Networks and Workstations

[A] Stand-Alone Versus Networked Computers

A threshold question in discovering electronic evidence is whether the information sought exists on a stand-alone computer, a workstation, or a network of computers. Stand-alone computers are not connected to any other computers, except possibly through the use of a modem. Stand-alone computers can be traditional desktop computers, laptop computers (see § 2.15), or Personal Digital Assistants (see § 2.16). There are two primary sources of evidence on stand-alone computers: the internal hard disk and any floppy disks that can be located. The internal random access memory (RAM) of the computer can also be searched, but will probably not be availing because this memory is "volatile" (i.e., it is erased every time the computer is turned off or rebooted).

Few businesses use their computers in stand-alone mode. Instead, they connect their computers together to form a computer network. When a stand-alone computer is attached to a network, it is frequently referred to as a workstation. Networks are advantageous because, among other things, they allow peripherals, hard disks, and other resources to be shared by all users and provide group scheduling and messaging capabilities. There are two basic ways in which computers can be networked (network topographies): peer-to-peer and client-server.

[B] Peer-to-Peer Networks

Peer-to-peer networks are constructed by connecting each computer to every other computer in the network. There is no central or independent file storage. Files are stored on the individual hard disks of the networked computers. Peripherals, such as printers and CD ROM drives, are shared. A user without a printer on his or her particular computer can use the printer attached to another user's computer.

Peer-to-peer networks are generally used to connect only a few computers and are popular in small businesses because they are relatively inexpensive to construct. Because there is no central file storage, discovery of a peer-to-peer network will require examination of the hard disks on each workstation connected to the network.

[C] Client-Server Networks

The vast majority of networks used in business are of the client-server variety. In these networks, each user's desktop computer is a "client" of a central "server" computer. All of the files on the network are stored on the server, which typically has substantial hard disk space. Files may also be stored on the hard disks of the individual client computers, but that practice is usually discouraged because other users may not be able to access the files. This is one of the primary distinctions between peer-to-peer networks, in which users have access to each other's hard disks, and client-server networks, in which users share files stored in a central location and generally cannot access the files on other user's hard disks. This distinction, however, is blurring as network software evolves.

Discovery on a client-server network should include, at a minimum, an examination of the server's hard disk and the client hard disks of relevant employees. The computer manager or system operator should also be deposed, among other things, regarding system topology and maintenance, location of files, instances of unauthorized access to the network (hacking), incidents when data has been lost, recent occurrences of viruses, and policies regarding the periodic deletion of files (file retention). These potential topics for deposition are explored further in Chapter 3.

▶ COMMENT

It is important to keep in mind that client computers and servers can each have more than one hard disk. Servers, in particular, usually have several internal hard disks. Each hard disk in each computer may contain relevant evidence. Computers that are no longer in service and hard disks that have been removed from computers because of service problems may also contain relevant evidence.

---

§ 2.03 Removable Disks

Until recently, the most common form of removable computer storage was the floppy disk. There are two common types of floppy disks: the older 5 ¼" inch disk and the newer 3 ½" disk. The 5 ¼" disk consists of a round flexible plastic film capable of holding a magnetic field encased in a flexible plastic jacket with a large hole in the center. These disks were capable of storing several hundred thousand bytes of information. The 3 ½" disks are encased in rigid plastic and are capable of storing over a million bytes. A typical business may have thousands of floppy disks scattered around its office, carried with laptop computers, or at the homes of its employees. Each of those disks may contain documents or fragments of documents that may be relevant to a litigation.

In addition to the traditional types of floppy disks discussed above, many businesses are now using special high density removable disks. The most popular type of high density disk, the Iomega Zip disk, is approximately the same size as a 3 ½" disk, but twice the thickness and capable of storing nearly one hundred times more information. Other high density disks resemble an 8 track tape and are capable of storing nearly a thousand times more information than a 3 ½" disk.

§ 2.04 Temporary Files

Temporary or transitory files are created for purposes of a particular computer session and then automatically deleted when that session is completed. For example, opening a document with a word-processing program usually causes a copy of the document to be stored in a backup file and certain temporary editing, cutting and pasting, and printing files to be created. When editing is completed and the document saved to disk, the temporary files are automatically deleted. If there is a system failure while the document is open, the temporary files are not deleted. Instead, they can be used to recover the document without losing the revisions made during the session.

Because many computer sessions are terminated improperly (that is, exiting a program without saving open files, system failure, or power loss), a wide variety of temporary files may exist on a user's hard disk or on the network hard disk. These files will not be automatically deleted because the computer session with which they were associated was not properly completed. Discovery of these files may reveal copies of documents, e-mail, or spreadsheets that would otherwise not be obtainable from any other source.

§ 2.05 Swap Files

Because computers have a limited amount of RAM in which to execute programs and store data, computer operating systems frequently use portions of the hard disk as virtual memory. These areas of the hard disk are sometimes referred to as "swap files" because the operating system swaps data as needed between RAM and the hard disk. Depending on how the system is configured, swap files may take up 40 or more megabytes of hard disk space. These files can contain fragments of e-mail, spreadsheets, word processing documents, and information relating to recent Internet activity.

☀ WARNING

The information contained in temporary and swap files will likely be irretrievably lost if the computer is operated without first making an image copy of the hard disk. (See § 2.19[B].) A computer forensics expert should be used to preserve this source of evidence.

---

§ 2.06 Mirror Disks

Mirroring is a means of providing fault tolerance to critical systems. For example, most network operating systems allow specified areas of a hard disk or a separate hard disk to be designated as a mirror or "shadow" disk. When information is saved to the network's primary hard disk, a copy of the information is automatically stored on the mirror disk. If the primary disk fails, the network will immediately switch to the mirror disk without loss of data. Most users will not even be aware that a disk failure has occurred.

The existence of a mirror disk should always be investigated when a responding party claims its hard disk has "crashed" and cannot be accessed. In many instances, the information sought will be stored on the mirror disk.

§ 2.07 Program Files

Another area of inquiry is the type of program that created a particular electronic document. For example, if a critical memorandum is in issue, it may be important to know that most word processing programs make automatic backup copies of the last revision of a document. In addition, word processing programs are often configured to track the creator of a document, the date and time of creation, the last person to edit the document, and the date and time of the last edit. This information may be crucial in constructing the history of the document.

Discovery requests should be tailored to identify the program used to create the evidence, the author or developer of the program, the version number of the program, whether the program has been modified in any way by the responding party, and whether the program is located on the file server or on the client computer. When two or more word processing files are discovered that appear identical, a simple redlining or compare program can be used to quickly identify any differences.

§ 2.08 Embedded Information

Embedded information is information about a document, spreadsheet, or other type of file that is not normally visible when the document is printed. If only the printed version of the document is produced during discovery, this type of information will be overlooked. There are two types of embedded information that may be of particular interest in discovery: file editing history and embedded comments.

Many types of programs, including most wordprocessors and spreadsheets, automatically track information relating to the editing history of the files they create. This history normally includes the name of the person who created the document, the date and time it was created, how many times it has been edited, the name of the last person to edit the document, and the date and time of the last revision.

In addition to the editing history, documents and spreadsheets may also contain comments by the various users who have worked on them. Although the majority of comments are entered in text, much like a footnote, newer programs also allow spoken comments to be digitally recorded and added to the document using a microphone connected to the computer.

When they exist, editing histories and document comments can be fruitful sources of evidence. They may identify the last person to edit a document, explain why a change was made, or provide critical information needed to authenticate the document.

§ 2.09 Audit Trails and Computer Logs

Computer logs and audit trails are seldom considered in creating a discovery plan, but they can provide a wealth of important information. Almost all network operating software automatically records and maintains information about the use of the system. These logs or audit trails record information about when, where, and who accesses the system. The level of detail can include the exact workstation at which a user was working on a specified date and time. Logs and audit trails may also contain information about who modified a file last and when the modification was made. Audit trails may also contain security-related information such as a history of unauthorized attempts to gain access to the system or a restricted area of the system (for example, a protected directory or file) and attempts to create, access, or delete files.

§ 2.10   Access Control Lists

Another important area for discovery is access control records or access control lists (ACL). Each user, and in many instances each file and directory, on a network has certain "rights," which are recorded in the ACL. These rights determine which directories and files a user may access and whether the user can merely view those directories and files or actually edit and/or delete them. The rights granted a user often depend on which group or department the user is working in within a business. For example, the ACL for the accounting files may be limited to persons working in the accounting department and upper management. All other employees will be unable to access or even view the files. The ACL for critical research and development files may be limited to only a handful workers.

▶ COMMENT

If a particular file is in issue in a litigation, reviewing the ACL for the file will reveal the users who had access to it. These persons can then be identified for deposition.

---

§ 2.11   Electronic Data Interchange

Electronic Data Interchange (EDI) is the electronic transfer, from one computer to another, of commercial and administrative data using an agreed upon standard to structure the EDI message. (See, e.g., *The Commercial Use of Electronic Data Interchange: A Report and Model Trading Partner Agreement*, The Business Lawyer, Vol. 45 (1990).) Put another way, EDI is a method of electronically communicating standard business documents (for example, purchase orders, invoices, and shipping receipts) between the computer systems of businesses, government organizations, and banks. EDI was developed in the 1960's as a means of reducing paperwork and accelerating the movement of standard documents related to the shipment and transportation of goods.

By way of example, the series of EDI transactions for a purchase, shipment, and payment are as follows:

Step 1. Company A's computer inventory system detects that it is time to replenish the supply of widgets. Company A's computer automatically sends an electronic purchase order to Supplier's computer.

Step 2. The Supplier's computer sends a confirmation of receipt of the purchase order to Company A's computer.

Step 3. The Supplier's computer sends a booking request to the Shipper's computer.

Step 4. The Shipper's computer sends a booking confirmation to the Supplier's computer.

Step 5. The Supplier's computer sends an invoice to Company A's computer.

Step 6. Company A's computer sends payment to the Supplier's computer.

Step 7. The Supplier's computer sends a delivery notification to the Shipper's computer.

Although EDI can be accomplished by directly connecting one business's computer to another by a physical link or modem connection, most companies transmit their EDI documents through value added networks (VANS) owned by third parties. These networks provide a wide variety of communications services, including the ability to permit normally incompatible computer systems to exchange information. As part of their services, VANS also record audit trails for each transaction. These audit trails generally confirm when a document was sent and by whom and when a document was retrieved by the intended recipient. In addition, VANS may as a matter of course retain copies of each EDI document that passes through the system.

If a dispute arises concerning a particular transaction, the audit trails and other records maintained by the VAN may provide critical evidence of how the transaction occurred and whether it was consummated. And because the electronic records are maintained by a neutral or "trusted" record keeper, they are inherently reliable. (See, e.g., *Wright, Authenticating EDI: The Location of a Trusted Recordkeeper*, Software Law Journal, Vol. IV (1991).)

▶ **COMMENT**

The use of VANS, while still popular, is declining as many businesses turn to the World Wide Web to transmit their EDI documents.

---

§ 2.12   Internet-Related Information

[A]   General Benefits

The vast store of information maintained on the Internet should not be neglected in planning discovery. In many instances, this information cannot be obtained from other sources. The Internet can provide general information about a business's products and services and specific information concerning comments made by employees and customers online. An additional benefit of conducting discovery on the Internet is that it is extremely cost effective: Users are generally granted unlimited access for a nominal, fixed monthly fee.

[B]   Visiting Relevant Web Sites

Every discovery plan should include a visit to the Web sites, if any, of all parties, key witnesses, and experts. These sites will contain a wide range of information that may be of interest in discovery. They are particularly useful in developing background information for use in drafting formal discovery requests and in preparing for depositions.

Business sites may contain detailed information concerning the business's goods and services; products under development; known product problems, defects, and recalls; marketing plans; recent press releases; biographies and photographs of key employees, officers, and directors; SEC filings; links to the Web sites of business partners; example contracts; white papers on various subjects; and reprints of employee published articles. Other areas of interest include customer discussion groups and databases of product support information.

Individuals who maintain Web sites may post their resumes, job histories, articles they have written, opinions on various subjects, personal photographs, links to their favorite sites on the Web, and other information. Experts may also identify significant cases in which they have been involved and even the specific law firms and attorneys who have retained them.

[C]   General Searches on the Internet

Until the development of the Web, locating and retrieving information on the Internet was complicated, time-consuming, and required a working knowledge of the arcane commands of the Unix operating system. Today, however, searching for information online is relatively easy and can be conducted by users with very little training. The primary reason for the ease with which information can be searched and retrieved is the availability of a wide range of Internet "search engines." Search engines catalogue the information contained on Web sites and provide a ready means of quickly searching them for a particular word or phrase. Many search engines even allow complex searches using Boolean logic (that is, using connectors such as *and*, *or*, and *but*).

Search engines acquire new information in two ways. First, the owner of a Web site may register the site with the search engine. As part of the registration, the search engine will catalogue the information on the site. The second method of acquiring information is for the search engine to use automated programs called spiders or robots. These programs automatically traverse the Web looking for new information and sites. Through these methods, search engines collect and index a voluminous amount of information from all over the world. Most popular search engines index between 50 and 100 million Web pages. Because sites can come and go quickly on the Internet, search engines must constantly update their indexes and look for new information.

Each search engine catalogues information differently. Submitting a query to five different search engines will likely yield five very different responses. For this reason, it is always good practice to submit queries to a wide range of search engines and to compare their results to identify the most complete and relevant responses. This can be done either by manually submitting a particular query to several different search engines or by submitting a single query to a "meta-search engine," which will automatically and simultaneously submit the query to a specified list of search engines. A list of the more popular search engines is included in Appendix A.

Searches performed on the Web are an excellent source of background information concerning businesses, products, and, in many instances, individuals. Consider a dispute involving a defective automobile. A search on the Web under the name of the automobile and its manufacturer may reveal comments by other purchasers who experienced or were harmed by the same defect. Indeed, the number of "lemon" sites—Web sites created by disgruntled customers to publicize problems with a product—on the Internet is growing at a dramatic rate. The search may also reveal a discussion by automotive engineers or a journal article concerning the origins of the problem, other models of automobiles with the same or similar defect, and potential fixes.

Information contained on the Internet may also be useful in evaluating jurors. Their names can be searched or, if the names are not provided, group affiliations can be evaluated to provide insight into a particular juror's views and identify potential bias. This type of research formed the basis for a motion to exclude a juror in a suit brought by the State of Minnesota against several tobacco companies. (*Internet Research and Voir Dire*, J. Elect. Discovery and Internet Lit. (Jan. 1998).) During initial screening, a juror admitted belonging to a group named INFACT and that he was good friends with a member of the group's board of directors. Attorneys for the tobacco industry researched INFACT on the Internet, determined the group was "staunchly anti-tobacco," and brought a motion to exclude the juror for cause. Although the trial judge denied the motion, the lesson is clear: The Internet can play a valuable role in evaluating potential jurors.

[D] Public Databases on the Internet

In addition to performing general searches on the Internet using search engines, attorneys should not overlook the vast amount of information contained in free online databases. For example, the Securities Exchange Commission has made all recent corporate filing available on its Web site (*www.sec.gov*). This database includes annual and quarterly reports and other required public filings. Databases are also available for locating individuals and businesses (see, e.g., *www.infoseek.com*; *www.hotbot.com*).

[E] Internet Newsgroups

One of the most popular features of the Internet is the Usenet newsgroups. These newsgroups are basically bulletin boards on which anyone can "post" a message or comment using e-mail. The posting is often called an "article" and can be read by anyone who views the newsgroup. Newsgroups can be viewed using stand-alone news reader programs or any of the popular Web browsers.

There are literally thousands of newsgroups on the Internet, each devoted to a specific topic. Discussions range from particle physics (*sci.phys-ics.particle*) and computer security (*comp.security*) to TV game shows (*alt.tv.game-shows*) and cooking (*alt.creative-cook*). Although there are a number of variations, most newsgroups fall into one of eight general categories, which are incorporated into the name of the newsgroup:

Category	Meaning
alt.	Alternative topics
comp.	Topics relating to computers and software
misc.	General discussion groups
news.	Discussions relating to newsgroups
rec.	Recreation
sci.	Science
soc.	Social topics
talk.	Debates on various subjects

Newsgroups can be used for a number of purposes in discovery:

Sources for Potential Experts. Newsgroups are an excellent source for locating potential experts. For example, an attorney might post queries to mechanical engineering and metallurgy newsgroups for assistance in identifying the leading expert on the stability of solder joints. Postings can be made anonymously (see § 2.14[C]) or through a pseudonym to preserve confidentiality.

Background Information on Products or Companies. In addition to being able to read and post messages to newsgroups, users can also employ search engines to simultaneously search all of the thousands of newsgroups for particular words or phrases. This search capability can be a valuable tool in discovery. Newsgroups can be quickly searched for discussions involving a particular product or business that may be at issue in a litigation. Discussions involving disgruntled employees, customers, or users that may have experienced similar problems with a particular product may all be of interest.

▶**COMMENT**

The search engine at *www.dejanews.com* is particularly useful because it maintains an archive of several years worth of Usenet postings. The search engine at *www.altavista.digital.com* can also be used to search Usenet postings.

Tracking a Particular Individual's Postings. The most controversial aspect of newsgroup searches is that they can be used to track the postings of a specified user. This can be done in one of two ways. First, if a particular posting to a newsgroup is of interest, a search can be done for all other postings by that particular user—whether they are posted on the same newsgroup or one of the thousands of other newsgroups. Second, searches can be done to locate postings from a particular e-mail address. Among other things, these types of searches can be used to identify employees who use company time to visit sexually oriented newsgroups, who are disclosing or attempting to sell corporate proprietary information online, or who are libeling a competitor's goods and services.

[F]　Cookies

A growing number of Web sites on the Internet now issue "cookies" to track their visitors. When the visitor views the Web site, it installs a small data file known as a cookie on the visitor's hard disk. The cookie is read by the site when it is revisited to track the areas of the site the user is most interested in and to collect other marketing information. As they are collected, cookies are automatically stored in a common directory on the user's hard disk. The directory containing the various cookie files may be a source of very revealing information concerning the user's activities on the Internet. Parties seeking discovery of this information, however, should be aware that most Web browsers provide an option (called a "cookie filtering tool") for users to block cookie information from being stored on their hard disks. There are also programs that users can download from the Internet that automatically erase cookie information after it is stored.

[G] Web Site Log Files

In addition to cookies, the operators of Web sites usually record information about each visitor to their sites in a "log file." The log file is stored on the server on which the Web site is located. The most common type of log file is the "access log." Access logs record the Internet address of each visitor, the date and time of the visit to the Web site, the particular pages viewed, prior Web sites visited, and whether the visit was successful or whether a failure resulted (that is, an error occurred on the Web site). Log files can also record critical information about host down time and referrals (sites containing hyperlinks that transfer a visitor to the subject site). Log files are typically backed-up at least once every 24 hours. Consequently, log information will exist on both the Web server and on backup tapes.

Web site operators use the information gained from cookies and log files to refine their marketing efforts. Because the volume of information contained in a log file can be voluminous for even mildly popular sites, most operators use specialized software to automatically analyze the log files to provide summaries of activity and to identify usage trends. If it is relevant to determine the activity on a particular Web site, the log files are a natural starting place for discovery.

[H] Cache Files

With regard to the Internet, caching refers to the process of storing popular or frequently visited Web sites on a hard disk or in RAM so that the next time the site is accessed it is retrieved from memory rather than from the Internet. Caching is used to reduce traffic on the Internet and to vastly decrease the time it takes to access a Web site. There are two general types of caching: local and proxy.

The Web browsers on most personal computers "locally" cache recently visited Web sites in the computer's RAM or on its hard disk. During the course of a particular Internet session, if the user decides to return to a previously visited site, the site will usually be retrieved from local memory instead of actually being downloaded from the Internet. Local caches can range from a few megabytes of RAM to tens of megabytes of hard disk storage. If the computer is connected to a network, local caching is sometimes referred to as "client level caching."

Caching can also occur at the server level—called "proxy" caching. Large online service providers and some businesses have such significant Internet traffic that they cache popular sites on their own servers. These caches are frequently updated to track recent changes to the sites that are cached. When a user connected to one of these servers sends a request for a particular Web site, the server will check the cache for the site before downloading it from the Internet. If the site is in the cache, the server will automatically retrieve it from the computer's memory instead of the Internet.

When cache files are stored on the hard disk of a computer or server, the stored Web sites will generally not be erased until they are overwritten by new information. This means that evidence of a particular user's or, in the case of a business, group of users' Internet activity may be contained in cache files long after the Web sites were visited.

[I]   History Files

An area related to cookies is the history file. Cookies are automatically issued by sites visited on the Internet—in most cases without the user's knowledge. In contrast, a history file is created by the user's Web browser to record the online address of each of the locations visited on the Internet. A typical entry would appear as follows:

Internet Address	Title	Last Visited
http://www.westgroup.com	West Group	12/1/98 10:43 a.m.

Some of the newer Web browsers store the addresses for the sites visited in directories labeled according to the dates on which the sites were visited (for example, "Week of 12/9/98," "Wednesday," or "Today").

The purpose of the history file is to assist users in easily returning to sites they previously visited. Web browsers typically give users the option of setting the period of time for which a history file will track the sites visited (for example, one month, one week, or never). Users can also manually clear their history files by deleting the contents of the files. If they have not been deleted, the history file can be used in combination with cookies and cache files to provide a fairly complete record of a user's Internet usage.

The discovery of information relating to Internet use has already been the subject of several cases. (See, e.g., *In the Matter of Quad/Graphics Inc. v. Southern Adirondack Library System* (N.Y. Sup. 1997) 174 Misc.2d 291 [664 N.Y.S.2d 225]; *The Putnam Pit Inc. v. City of Cookeville* (M.D. Tenn. 1998) 23 F. Supp.2d 822 [98 WL 732925].) In *Quad/Graphics*, employees used their employer's computers to access the Internet through a local library. The employer sought access to the library's Internet log files in connection with an investigation of misappropriation of the company's computer resources by its employees. Citing the important public policy of preserving the confidentiality of library records, the trial court held that the library cannot be compelled to disclose the Internet information.

In *Putnam Pit*, a newspaper cited a state public records act as the basis for its request for access to the cookie, browser history, and cache files on municipal computers. The newspaper contended the files would show that public employees were using their computers to visit Web sites with sports, entertainment, and sexually explicit content on government time. The city claimed the files were not public records and refused the request. The newspaper brought suit to compel production.

[J] Employee Monitoring Software

In certain instances, the responding party itself may have willingly prepared the ultimate audit trail. Although still in the minority, a growing number of employers are installing specialized software to monitor various actions their employees take while using their computers. These programs also include features that allow the employer to limit or "filter" employee access to inappropriate, non–business-related information on the Internet. Businesses install these programs to limit employee access to inappropriate or even illegal content on the Internet, increase employee productivity, address security concerns, and reduce potential exposure to employment related litigation. (See *Managing Employee Internet Access: A guide for Creating and Administering Corporate Access Policy with Monitoring and Filtering Software*, Secure Internet Filtering Technology Consortium (Sept. 1997), found at *www.icsa.net.*)

Although monitoring software is generally configured to focus on employee activity on the Internet (for example, Web sites visited, computer bulletin boards and newsgroups contacted, files downloaded, and e-mail sent and received), it can also track general use of the computer system, including programs used, files accessed, and information created or deleted. If an employer has installed monitoring software, the records maintained by the program may prove invaluable in establishing the history of a particular document and the employees who had access to it.

[K] Mirror Sites

Just as mirroring is used to protect network hard disks, mirroring is also used to provide redundant Web sites on the Internet. It is very common for businesses to operate a primary Web site and a mirror site. If the primary site suffers a failure or becomes unavailable because of a communications problem, visitors will automatically be routed to the mirror site without any interruption in service. For added protection, the mirror site typically resides on a computer at a different physical location than the primary site. The greater the physical separation, the less likely a problem effecting the primary server will also impact the mirror site. When conducting discovery concerning the activity on a Web site, it is important to identify whether any mirror sites exist so that the information maintained on those sites can also be examined.

§ 2.13 Corporate Intranets

Many businesses now operate internal versions of the Internet, known as "intranets." These networks use the same protocol used to transmit information over the Internet. Web browsers, e-mail, newsgroups, HTML documents, and Web sites are all found on intranets. Each of the departments within the business, and many individual users, will have their own Web sites on the intranet. The human relations department, for example, might post various corporate policies and employee manuals and provide a place for making suggestions. A research group might post information about a new product under development and solicit comments from other groups and employees about the technology.

The amount of information stored on a corporate intranet can be voluminous, even for a relatively small business, and may contain a wealth of information that would ordinarily be overlooked by the responding party. Discovery requests should be carefully worded to include the information stored on these networks. The propounding party should consider requesting that static copies of relevant Web sites be produced in electronic form. The sites will be produced in HTML format and will provide a snap-shot of the Web site at the time of the production. Once produced, the site can be viewed using any Internet browser. The advantage of having an electronic copy of the site produced is that it can be explored as if the requesting party had actual access to the intranet.

§ 2.14 E-mail

[A] Overview

E-mail has taken its place as one of the primary means by which businesses and individuals communicate. Whether sent over a private LAN or intranet or over a public network such as the Internet, the volume of e-mail is increasing exponentially every day. Over the Internet alone, over one million messages are sent every hour. By the year 2000, the volume of e-mail is expected to reach seven trillion messages a year.

E-mail is a unique medium that is very unlike its traditional counterpart. One of the greatest distinctions, and dangers, of e-mail is that it is treated far more informally than other forms of business communication. Users often express thoughts, emotions, and opinions in e-mail that they would never memorialize in a traditional written document. In large part, this may be because e-mail does not look like a traditional letter or memorandum. Ordinarily, there is no formal letterhead or signature line on e-mail.

Another reason e-mail is treated so informally is that a message can be prepared and sent in seconds. This ease of transmission results in many messages being sent in the heat of the moment, without careful consideration of the consequences.

The most likely reason e-mail is treated so informally is the problem of perceived impermanence. Users incorrectly believe that e-mail is very transitory in nature: When a message is deleted it is gone forever. In fact, using widely available software, deleted messages can be recovered days, weeks, or even months after they were thought deleted.

Even if a message cannot be undeleted, backup copies of the e-mail may exist on the sender's or recipient's personal computers or on their employers' networks or on network backup tapes. If the e-mail was sent through a commercial online service, value added network, or the Internet, the e-mail may have passed through several computers before being delivered. Each computer in the chain between the sender and the recipient may, and normally does, retain a copy of the e-mail for archival purposes.

E-mail has already been the focus of numerous claims for sexual and racial harassment and discrimination. (See, e.g., *Knox v. State of Indiana* (7th Cir. 1996) 93 F.3d 1327 (e-mail from supervisor repeatedly asking employee for sex); *Harley v. McCoach* (E.D. Pa. 1996) 928 F. Supp. 533 (gender and race discrimination action based, in part, on e-mail).)

[B] E-mail Anatomy

Each piece of e-mail has at least one, and as many as three, parts: the header, the message body, and any attachments. While every message must have a header, the message body and attachments are optional. For example, a message can be sent with just a header, a header and message body, or a header, an empty message body, and an attachment.

The header contains information about the sender and the recipient of the message and how the message was sent. The message body holds the particular message to be delivered. Attachments are used to append files to messages. For example, a word-processing file or spreadsheet can be sent as an attachment to a piece of e-mail. At its destination, the recipient can edit the file directly using the same program that created it. Many businesses send documents as attachments because they are more economical than facsimiles and allow the recipient to edit the document directly.

Attachments to e-mail should always be reviewed for copies of files that may not be available from any other source. When a file is attached and sent by e-mail, the e-mail program generally stores a copy of the message and the attachment in a "sent" folder or directory. This copy of the document is separate from the original. If the original is deleted and cannot be recovered by an undelete program or from a backup tape, the copy may still exist in the "sent" folder or directory.

Headers are particularly important in discovery because they contain information about the characteristics of the message, including the following: the date and time the message was sent, the names of intervening computers that relayed the message, the date and times the message was received by each intervening computer, the type of mail transfer software used by the intervening computer, and routing information. In addition, most headers contain several fields that contain repetitive information concerning the sender of the message (for example, sender, from, and message-ID fields). Computer forensics experts can use the information in these fields to detect forged messages and to potentially identify the true sender, or at least the computer that originated the message.

▶ **COMMENT**

Although headers can provide a wealth of important information about a message, complete header information may not be available in all instances. Many popular e-mail programs automatically strip-off all but the

---

most basic header information when a message is received. Once removed, this vital information usually cannot be recovered. It is therefore important to determine the type of e-mail software (both server and client) used by a responding party.

[C] Spoofing and Anonymous Remailers

Two issues complicate the discovery of e-mail: spoofing and anonymous remailers. These practices make it difficult, if not impossible, to determine who sent a particular message. Since authentication will be a central issue at trial (see Evid. Code, § 1401), it is important to understand how these practices are used.

Spoofing is the practice of sending a message so that it appears to have been transmitted by someone else. Spoofing sender information on e-mail, particularly Internet e-mail, is very easy. There are virtually no safeguards in the current Internet e-mail protocols to confirm that a message was really sent by the person indicated in the sender information. In most instances, the only way to determine whether an e-mail has been spoofed is for a forensic computer expert to carefully examine the computer from which the message was purportedly sent and to review the header information for the message, if such information is available.

Spoofing figured prominently in one of the first perjury convictions involving forged e-mail. (*People v. Lee* (San Mateo County Sup. Ct. 1/30/97).) That prosecution arose out of a prior civil litigation for wrongful termination brought by Adelyn Lee against her former employer, Oracle Corp. Lee contended that she had been terminated because she broke off a relationship with Oracle's CEO. The cornerstone of Lee's case was an e-mail allegedly written by her supervisor to the CEO, stating, "I have terminated Adelyn per your request." Oracle settled the suit for $100,000. Further investigation after the settlement revealed that at the time the e-mail was purportedly sent the supervisor was in his car talking on his cellular telephone. It took a jury less than a day to find Lee guilty of two counts of perjury, one count of preparing a false document, and one count of offering a false document into evidence. Lee had apparently gained access to Oracle's computer system and sent the message herself.

An anonymous remailer is a mail server, usually on the Internet, that receives incoming messages, removes the header information that identifies the original sender, and then sends the message to the intended recipient. The sole purpose of anonymous remailers is to hide the identities of senders of e-mail messages. Most remailers fall into one of three categories:

One-way. A one-way remailer removes all sender information from the header and then resends the message as though it originated from the remailer. The recipient of the e-mail has no way to respond to the original sender.

Two-way. The remailer assigns the sender an anonymous identity, usually a random number. The sender information in the message is replaced by the anonymous identity and forwarded to the recipient. The remailer keeps a database of the anonymous identities and their owners. The recipient of the message can respond by sending a message to the anonymous identity care of the remailer. The remailer will forward the response to the original sender.

Encrypted Header. Either a one-way or two-way remailer that allows for the use of encryption in receiving and forwarding messages. The use of encryption in combination with an anonymous remailer affords a very high level of security to the communications.

Because it may be possible to forensically examine an anonymous remailer to construct a list connecting senders to recipients, most users of remailers employ "chaining" for greater security. Chaining refers to the practice of sending messages through several layers of anonymous remailers before delivery to the intended recipient. Careful senders generally chain three or four remailers together, with each remailer located in a different country. Given the number of jurisdictions involved, it is usually difficult and prohibitively expensive to trace an anonymous message back to its source when chaining is employed.

▶ **COMMENT**

For more information on anonymous remailers, see the following web sites: *www.skypoint.com/ members/gimona/anonmail.html* or *www.cs.berkely.edu/~raph/ remailer-faq.html.*

The most prominent case thus far involving anonymous remailers involved the most popular and widely used remailer, *anon.penet.fi*, located in Finland and run by a computer scientist named Johan Helsingius. On February 18, 1995, Finnish police, accompanied by agents from Interpol (the international European law enforcement agency), raided the headquarters of *anon.penet.fi*. The Finnish police were acting on a request from U.S. law enforcement regarding the use of the remailer to disseminate copyrighted and trade secret information belonging to the Church of Scientology. Faced with the possibility that his entire system would be confiscated, Helsingius revealed the identity of the person who had used the system to anonymously transmit the proprietary material. (Greenberg, *Threats, Harassment, and Hate On-line: Recent Developments*, 6 B.U.Int.L.J. 673 (Spring 1997).)

§ 2.15 Laptops and Home Computers

Laptop computers owned by a business and the home computers of its employees should not be overlooked during discovery. These computers may contain long forgotten files that are not available from any other source. These files may include early versions of technical drawings, preliminary drafts of documents, spreadsheet analyses of projects, comments regarding proposals, and e-mail.

§ 2.16 Personal Digital Assistants

Personal digital assistants (PDAs) range from compact personal electronic organizers (for example, calendars and phone lists) to the new breed of palm-sized computers that are capable of running full-featured word processing programs and spreadsheets and of browsing the Internet and sending and receiving e-mail. These devices can hold hundreds, and will soon be able to store thousands, of pages of information. The information stored in a PDA can be printed out either directly from the device (most PDAs can send their information to printers using a wireless, infrared connection) or by first transferring the information to a desktop computer and then printing it out.

PDAs are particularly popular with users who travel frequently or work outside the office. In many instances, these users maintain their entire schedules with their PDAs, choosing to forego a traditional print calendar.

§ 2.17 PCMCIA Memory Cards

In addition to internal memory such as RAM, ROM, and hard disks, Laptop computers and PDAs have another source of internal data storage. Both types of computers usually have one or more PCMCIA slots. Among other things, these slots can accept solid state memory cards (similar to RAM, approximately the size of a credit card) that are capable of storing 4, 8, 16, or more megabytes of information. The information stored on these cards is "non-volatile," meaning the information is maintained by miniature batteries so that it is not lost even if the memory card is removed from the laptop or PDA. The existence of these memory cards should be explored in discovery and the wording of discovery requests expanded to include relevant evidence stored on them.

§ 2.18 Archival Data: Backups and Other Removable Media

To protect against a catastrophic loss when a hard disk fails, almost every business uses backup software to copy the information stored on its system to magnetic tape or some other removable mass storage device. Once created, the backup copy is normally stored at an offsite facility for added security. These storage facilities specialize in handling electronic information. The backup is usually kept in a climate-controlled, physically secure area that is free from any magnetic fields or other radiation that might corrupt the electronic information.

Backups are usually created according to a fixed schedule. Most businesses create nightly backup tapes of their systems, using a different tape for each day of the week. The daily backup tapes are recycled and overwritten each week (that is, Monday's tape is kept for a week and then overwritten with the next Monday's data). Weekly and monthly backup tapes are typically stored offsite for a specified period of time—ranging from a few months to several years.

Backups may prove useful when a business has an electronic document retention plan and claims that evidence has been automatically deleted. In many cases, businesses diligently enforce their document retention plans, but forget that copies of the deleted documents may exist on their backup tapes.

The system operator or manager should be questioned to determine the backup schedule, the location in which the backup tapes are stored, and the length of time backups are typically kept. Discovery of the backup tapes can provide a snapshot of the files on a particular computer system on a specified date. These files can be compared with existing files to detect modifications, tampering, or intentional deletion. It should be kept in mind, however, that most backup software will generally not copy any recoverable data (that is, recently deleted files). (See § 2.19.)

Discovery of backups has recently become more complicated by the advent of Internet backup software. Several vendors now offer software for individual users and small businesses to backup their computer systems over the Internet. Files are sent by modem to the software company's computer where they are stored. The software company may be located in another state or, conceivably, in another country. Since a party can be compelled to produce records located in another state or country if they are under the party's control, this type of Internet storage should not impose a significant burden on discovery. (See, e.g., *Boal v. Price Waterhouse & Co.* (1985) 165 Cal.App.3d 806, 810–811 [212 Cal.Rptr. 42].).

▶ **COMMENT**

When examining backup tapes, do not neglect "off end" data. Off end data refers to information previously stored on a tape that is not overwritten by the next backup when the tape is reused. Recovery of this information is straightforward because the information has never been overwritten and exists in the same form as when it was originally stored on the tape.

---

§ 2.19 Recoverable Data

[A] In General

Recoverable data is information that appears to be gone from a computer system, but is capable of being recovered. The primary sources of recoverable data are recently deleted computer files and information stored in the memory of peripherals (for example, printers, fax machines, and digital copiers).

[B] Deleted Files

To understand how deleted files can be recovered, it is first necessary to understand how computers store and keep track of information. Among other things, computer operating systems manage how files are stored and retrieved from disk. In the DOS and Windows environment, a special file called the "file allocation table" (FAT) is stored at the beginning of every hard or floppy disk. The FAT contains information concerning where each file is stored on the disk. Files are generally not stored in a contiguous fashion. Rather, parts of a file may be located in a number of areas on the disk. The FAT tracks where these areas are and links them together so that the file can be located. As new files are created, the operating system consults the FAT to determine which areas of the disk are available for storage.

When a file is deleted, the operating system does not erase all of the parts of the file from the disk. Instead, the FAT entry for the file is modified by replacing the first letter of the file name with a special character. This change in the file name instructs the FAT that the area of the disk previously occupied by the file is now available to store new data. The various portions of the deleted file remain on the disk until they are eventually overwritten by new data. To the user, the file appears to have been deleted. In reality, remnants of the file may remain on the disk, and be recoverable, for days, weeks, even months after the file was thought deleted.

The time in which a file or portions thereof can be recovered depends on the use of the disk. If the disk is used constantly, the portions of the file may be overwritten quickly, sometimes within hours. In instances where the disk is seldom used (for example, a floppy disk), remnants of the file may persist for months.

Deleted files can be easily recovered using commercially available programs. These programs display a list of the files whose names have been changed to "deleted" in the FAT. To recover a file, the user merely selects the name of the relevant file from the list. In addition to commercial programs, many operating systems, particularly network operating systems, have undelete utility programs built into them. If portions of the file have already been overwritten, a computer forensics expert can use specialized software to recover the remaining remnants.

▶ COMMENT

Recent advances in technology, most notably the development of Magnetic Force Microscopy (MFM), has significantly expanded the ability of computer forensics experts to recover previously deleted data. (Gutman, *Secure Deletion of Data from Magnetic and Solid-State Memory*, Proceedings Sixth USENIX, San Jose, CA (Jul. 1996).) Indeed, until recently it was commonly held in the computer security industry that overwriting the area on a hard disk on which a file was stored a total of nine times would ensure the data could not be recovered. Techniques such as MFM now make recovery possible even if the area of the hard disk has been overwritten a dozen or more times. In simple terms, a hard disk will retain an image of everything ever written to it. While the ability to detect each "layer" becomes progressively harder the further back in time it was made, modern forensic techniques are capable of exposing and retrieving many of these layers.

Even if a particular area of a hard disk has been overwritten a sufficient number of times to make the data irretrievable even with the recent advances in technology, the data may still be available on the hard disk on a defective sector. When a disk drive is manufactured, the surface is carefully scanned for defects. Any defects detected are placed in a list maintained on the hard drive. Before writing data to the disk, the software and hardware operating the drive checks the list to make sure data is not written to a defective area. During the life of the hard disk, additional defective areas may be detected from time-to-time by drive management software. These areas are added to the list of defective sectors and the data copied to good sectors. If the data is later deleted from the good sectors, a copy of the data may still exist and be recoverable from its original location on the defective sector.

The ability to detect and potentially recover previously deleted files depends on having access to the original disk. A copy of a disk will not include "deleted" data. In addition, most commercial backup programs do not capture deleted files. If this information is to be preserved and the original disk cannot be isolated from further use, a mirror or "image" copy of the disk must be made. This is accomplished by making a sector-by-sector copy of the disk. The image disk will contain all active and recoverable data on the original disk. In general, it is good practice to make two image disks: one to be used for expert review and the other to be write-protected and stored in a safe place as a control copy so that a chain of custody can later be established.

The mere fact that certain files have been deleted may prove to be more valuable information than the content of the actual files recovered, especially if the attempted deletion evidences bad faith or some other improper motive. The deletion of large numbers of files, when such activity is not the norm, can be detected using forensic computer software and may provide circumstantial evidence of a party's guilty knowledge.

▶ **COMMENT**

Given the importance of recoverable data, the failure to identify and preserve such evidence may constitute malpractice. (*Gates Rubber Co. v. Bando Chemicals Industries, Ltd.* (D. Colo. 1996) 167 F.R.D. 90 (court criticized party's expert for failing to create an image copy of a relevant hard disk, concluding that a party has a duty "to utilize the method which would yield the most complete and accurate results").)

[C]　Information Stored in Peripherals

Another source of recoverable data is the memory installed in printers, fax machines, and digital copiers. For example, commercial printers, such as those used in most offices, typically have two to five megabytes of RAM. This is enough memory to store several hundred pages of text. A computer expert can search this memory for recent documents sent to the printer. Discovery of the memory in printers, fax machines, and other devices is limited, however, because the information is lost when the device is turned off.

[D]　Source Code Escrows

Software developers generally license their programs instead of selling them outright. Under the terms of the license agreement, the licensee is entitled to a copy of the object code for the software, but not the source code. Source code is jealously guarded by the developer as one of its most important trade secrets.

To protect themselves in the event the developer goes out of business or ceases to support the software, licensees frequently require the developer to deposit a copy of the source code with a source code escrow service. The escrow service will have instructions to release the software to the licensee only on the occurrence of certain events (for example, the developer files bankruptcy, goes out of business, ceases to support the software, or fails to update the software on a regular basis). Under the terms of the license agreement or, alternatively, the escrow agreement, the developer will be required to deposit with the escrow service copies of all enhancements, updates, and new releases of the software. The escrow service will generally not be under an affirmative obligation to delete or discard old versions of the software. As such, the escrow may have a complete record of the evaluation of the software over the term of the escrow, which could range for many years. The existence of these copies of the software may be important evidence in copyright infringement, misappropriation, and patent disputes.

▶ **COMMENT**

In addition to using source code escrows for the benefit of their licensees, a growing number of software developers are using escrow services to track the development of their software. At each significant stage in the development of a new program, the developer will deposit the existing source code with the escrow service. The deposit can be used to establish copyright ownership in the program and trade secret rights during the development process. These deposits may be of evidentiary interest in disputes involving competing claims to the program. It may be extremely important to determine when a particular segment of the program was completed. The deposits may provide that information.

---

§ 2.20 Implications of the Year 2000 Problem on Electronic Evidence

[A] The Year 2000 Problem

As the year 2000 approaches, many computer systems may malfunction or produce incorrect results because they cannot process date-related information properly. The Year 2000 (also known as "Y2K") problem is rooted in the way dates are stored and processed in many computers. The origin of the problem can be traced to decisions made twenty or more years ago when computers were first finding widespread use in business. Those decisions led to industry standards for processing date information that were incorporated into computers and software up to the present day. This means that even recently purchased systems may not be "Year 2000 compliant"—defined broadly as the ability of a system to accurately process date information before, during, and after midnight, December 31, 1999, including leap year calculations.

[B] Causes of the Year 2000 Problem

The Year 2000 problem has three facets: (1) the processing of year information using only two digits; (2) the year 2000 is a leap year; and (3) the use of the number "99" or "9999" by computer programmers to indicate the end of a data file or other special logic.

Two-Digit Date Fields. The most widespread problem posed by the Year 2000 is that of two-digit date processing. In an effort to conserve storage space and speed calculations, early programmers decided to reduce storage of dates from eight digits to six digits (for example, 12/16/1967 was stored as 12/16/67). The two digits representing the century were dropped. The programmers and the software they created assumed the first two digits of the year were "19." This method of processing dates quickly became an industry standard and has persisted until the present day.

Although this decision proved efficient and economical at the time it was made, its long-term consequences were not understood or anticipated. Dates occurring after December 31, 1999, may be processed incorrectly. Non-compliant computers will store the year 2000 as "00" and assume it refers to the year 1900. Consequently, calculations based on dates in 2000 and beyond will lead to erroneous results.

Programs that sort data by date may incorrectly organize information. The sorting logic focuses on the numerical value of the date field. A higher numerical value is interpreted as though it occurs after a year field with a lower value (for example, 96 follows 95, 95 follows 94, and so on). But dates occurring after December 31, 1999, will not be represented by numbers that reflect their true chronological order. That is, the year 2005 will be stored by non-compliant computers as "05," which would appear to come before 1998, not after. The computer would likely sort the data incorrectly because it could not recognize the true chronological order of the dates.

Non-compliant spreadsheets and other software that perform calculations based on dates will likely yield incorrect results. For example, a non-compliant bank spreadsheet used to calculate the interest on a 10-year loan made in 1998 and due in 2007 might instead calculate the interest for the period from 1907 to 1998—for a 92-year period instead of a 10-year period. Because the calculation will produce a negative loan period (for example, 1907–1998 = –92 years), the spreadsheet might also generate an error message and provide no result at all.

Leap Year. Another complication in computing dates at the change in century is that 2000 is a leap year. Leap year calculations can be complex and require careful programming. Non-compliant systems may not perform the calculations correctly.

Special Logic. Many early programmers and designers viewed their systems as having relatively short life spans. Because they did not anticipate their programs would still be in use toward the end of the century, programmers sometimes specified that when the characters "99" or "9999" appeared in a date field special logic would apply. These characters were frequently used to identify the end of a data file or to indicate that a particular item of information had no date. For example, someone entering the dates of documents into a database would enter the number "99" in the date field for undated documents.

The use of the number "99" to indicate something other than a date will result in processing errors when dates occurring after December 31, 1998, are entered. Non-compliant systems will store dates in 1999 as "99," which may activate the special logic, resulting in incorrect processing of the date.

[C]   Impact on Electronic Evidence

If discovery is directed at evidence that is date related, the issue of whether the system that created the evidence is Year 2000 compliant should be addressed. As discussed above, non-compliant systems may organize date-related information incorrectly or make errors in performing calculations based on dates. The reliability and accuracy of the evidence will depend on whether the system is compliant. Discovery requests should solicit information relating to the respondent's efforts to achieve Year 2000 compliance and any date-related errors that have been documented.

§ 2.21 Discovery of Non-Textual Material

Much of the foregoing discussion relates to the discovery of text-based electronic evidence—evidence consisting of words and numbers. This type of evidence can be discovered in a relatively straightforward manner using a text-searching program to scan a disk for particular words or phrases. Unfortunately, many important documents are stored in formats that are not susceptible to this type of searching. Text stored in compressed or encrypted files, graphics files (for example, schematic diagrams, charts, blue prints, and design drawings), and digitized audio files require sophisticated forensic computer software for detection. This software is capable of recognizing common file formats and translating the content of the file so that it can be viewed and evaluated as potential evidence.

Reviewing non-textual information can be extremely time consuming. Text search programs can scan thousands of pages of information per second for key words or phrases. In contrast, each non-textual file must be reviewed manually to determine its relevance to the litigation. For example, in an action against a computer bulletin board operator for storing and disseminating copyrighted photographs, hundreds of thousands of graphics files may have to be reviewed one-at-a-time to identify infringing material.

At least with regard to actions for copyright infringement, review of non-textual information may become easier as the use of "digital watermarks" becomes widespread. A digital watermark consists of indelible, invisible information embedded in graphics files that identifies the copyright owner and other important information relating to the authorized uses of the material. Automated programs can quickly scan for files with digital watermarks on hard disks, computer networks, and on the Internet. At present, digital watermarks are used primarily by businesses that place photographic and musical content on the Internet.

§ 2.22 Federal Guidelines for Searching and Seizing Computers

The Federal Guidelines for Searching and Seizing Computers provide additional information regarding potential sources of electronic evidence. (See Appendix G.)

B. Forms

§ 2.23 Checklist for Handling Electronic Evidence

❑ Avoid inadvertently destroying evidence. Running programs on a computer or even turning the computer on may alter or destroy potentially relevant evidence. An image or mirror copy of the hard disk should be made before the computer is operated.

❑ Document the system configuration. The type of computer hardware, operating system, and software used to create the evidence should be recorded.

❑ Keep a control copy of the evidence. Electronic evidence can easily be altered, usually without leaving a trace. To prevent a claim that produced evidence has been altered, a control copy of the evidence should be maintained in a sealed container or, possibly, deposited with an escrow company that specializes in handling electronic media. In addition, mathematical software can be used to generate a unique number (sometimes called a "hash function") to represent the information stored on the disk. If the information is modified in any way, the number will be different. The hash function can, therefore, be used to authenticate the information on the disk.

❑ Beware of viruses. The presence of computer viruses in the produced evidence or on the requesting party's computer system may corrupt or destroy the evidence. Both should be checked with appropriate virus detection software.

❑ Transport and store electronic evidence with care. Electronic evidence is extremely sensitive to environmental and physical conditions. Heat, electromagnetic fields, smoke, and humidity may all damage electronic evidence. Even placing a floppy disk near a telephone or stereo will subject the disk to potentially damaging electromagnetic fields. The disk holders used in three ring binders may cause enough physical pressure to deform a floppy disk and render it useless.

❑ Use an experienced expert. The advice and assistance of a trained computer professional can be invaluable in identifying potential sources of electronic evidence, in forensically examining that evidence, and in preserving the evidence for trial.

§ 2.24 Checklist of Sources of Electronic Evidence

❑ Computer configuration. Are computers connected in a network? If so, is the network topology peer-to-peer or client-server? What type of operating system or network operating system is used on each computer and server?

❑ Computers, workstations, and file servers. Identify all hard disks on stand-alone computers, workstations, and file servers. Beware of computers that have multiple internal hard disks. Do not neglect "broken" hard disks or hard disks in out of use computers.

❑ Mirror disks. Check for servers with mirror disks.

❑ Floppy disks and removable media. Locate all floppy disks and other removable media that may contain relevant evidence. Some disks may be located with laptops and at the homes of employees and other users.

❑ Temporary files and fragments. Search for undeleted temporary files and fragments of relevant information in swap files.

❑ Software. Identify the types of software used to create relevant documents. At minimum, this information should include the name of the program, the developer of the program, the version or release number of the program, what operating system the program was written to run on, and whether the program has any custom modifications.

❑ Histories and embedded comments. Do any of the relevant documents have editing histories or embedded comments that may not appear in printed copies?

❑ Audit trails and log files. Does the responding party's computer system track user activities and transactions? What type of audit trails and/or log files are created? What type of information is collected?

❑ Access control list. Is there an access control list for relevant users or files?

❑ EDI and VAN. Does the business use EDI? If so, who are its trading partners? What type of VAN is used? What type of transaction records does the VAN maintain?

❑ Source code escrows. If the development of software is at issue, are there any source code escrows? What information has been deposited into the escrow?

❑ Internet information. Which individuals, entities, and key words should be searched?

    ❑ View relevant Web sites.

    ❑ Perform general Internet searches.

    ❑ Search public databases.

    ❑ Identify relevant newsgroups.

    ❑ Check the cookie files of relevant users.

    ❑ Identify Web site log files.

    ❑ Locate browser history files.

❏ Does the business use employee monitoring software? If so, what type of software is used? What type of information is collected?

❏ Are there mirror Web sites? Where are they located?

❏ Corporate intranets. Include corporate intranets, if any, in discovery requests.

❏ E-mail. Identify potential sources of e-mail. Does the relevant user access e-mail from other locations (for example, home, laptop, or PDA)? Does the user have multiple e-mail accounts? Does the user use a pseudonym? Were relevant documents sent as attachments to e-mail? Does the responding party's e-mail system remove header information?

❏ Home computers. Review the hard disks in laptops and relevant home computers.

❏ PDAs. Request copies of files stored in personal digital assistants.

❏ PCMCIA cards. Locate PCMCIA memory cards with potential evidence.

❏ Backup tapes. Does the responding party use backup tapes or other removable media? What schedule is used for backups? Where are the tapes stored? How long are tapes kept before being overwritten?

❏ Deleted files. Is there a possibility that the responding party has deleted relevant files?

❏ Peripherals. Do any potential sources of data exist in peripherals?

❏ Non-textual electronic evidence. Does any non-textual electronic evidence exist?

3 OBTAINING ELECTRONIC EVIDENCE

B. FORMS

A. Text

§ 3.01 Making a Discovery Plan

Computerized data has become commonplace in litigation. Such data includes not only conventional information (for example, documents, spreadsheets, and databases) but also such things as operating systems (programs that control a computer's basic functions), applications (programs used directly by the operator, such as word processing or spreadsheet programs), computer-generated models, and other sets of instructions residing in computer memory. Any discovery plan must address the relevant issues, such as the search for, location, retrieval, form of production and inspection, preservation, and use at trial of information stored in mainframe or personal computers or accessible online. For the most part, such data will reflect information generated and maintained in the ordinary course of business. Some computerized data, however, may have been compiled in anticipation of or for use in the litigation (and may therefore be entitled to protection as trial preparation materials under the work product doctrine). Discovery requests may themselves be transmitted in computer-accessible form; interrogatories served on computer disks, for example, could then be answered using the same disk, avoiding the need to retype them. Finally, computerized data may form the contents for a common document depository. (Manual of Complex Litigation, Third; see Appendix F.)

This chapter provides an introduction to the various methods of discovery available to a party in litigation and the potential for use of such methods in obtaining electronic evidence.

§ 3.02 Discovery Mechanisms

Under the Discovery Act of 1986 (Code Civ. Proc., § 2016 et seq.), a party to a litigation has six methods of conducting discovery from another party: (1) inspection of documents, things, and places; (2) interrogatories; (3) requests for admissions; (4) physical and mental examinations; (5) oral and written depositions; and (6) simultaneous exchange of expert witness information. (Code Civ. Proc., § 2019, subd. (a).) Conducting discovery from a non-party is essentially limited to oral and written depositions and depositions for the production of business records. (Code Civ. Proc., § 2020, subd. (a).)

> ▶ **COMMENT**
>
> In addition to the discovery methods provided under the Discovery Act of 1986, and regardless of whether an action is pending, a party may also inspect most records maintained by a governmental entity under the applicable open records statute. (See Chapter 4.)

§ 3.03 Limitations on Discovery

There are two general types of limitations on a party's ability to conduct discovery: substantive and procedural. Substantive limitations include requirements that the information sought must be non-privileged, relevant to the subject mater of the litigation, and either itself admissible or reasonably calculated to lead to the discovery of admissible evidence. (Code Civ. Proc., § 2017, subd. (a).) Procedural limitations relate primarily to the discovery hold at the outset of litigation and the discovery cutoff before trial. (Code Civ. Proc., §§ 2025, subd. (b)(2), 2030, subd. (b), 2031, subd. (b), 2033, subd. (b), 2024, subd. (a).)

The procedural limitation prohibiting discovery at the outset of the litigation is a particular concern for actions in which important evidence may reside in electronic form. The ability to move quickly in discovering this evidence before it is corrupted, deleted, or changed may be essential. One approach to preserve this evidence is to seek a protective order. (See § 3.12.) Another approach is to seek relief from the discovery holding period. The plaintiff may move the court, *with or without notice*, on a showing of good cause, to propound discovery during the hold period. (See, e.g., Code Civ. Proc., § 2030, subd. (b).) Any such motion should highlight the transitory nature of electronic evidence and the ease with which such evidence may be destroyed or altered, either intentionally or unintentionally.

> ▶ **COMMENT**
>
> In certain instances, depositions and inspection demands may be served prior to the filing of a lawsuit. Such discovery is usually conducted by a party to preserve potentially favorable evidence. The party seeking to conduct pre-lawsuit discovery must obtain a court order by filing a verified petition in accordance with Code of Civil Procedure section 2035.

§ 3.04 Demands for Inspection of Documents and Other Physical Evidence: An Overview

A party to an action may be compelled to produce documents and other physical evidence in its possession, custody, or control in response to a demand for inspection. (Code Civ. Proc., § 2031.) An inspection demand may be served at any time after the initial hold on discovery at the inception of the action and before the discovery cutoff at trial. (See § 3.03.) Each category of evidence to be produced pursuant to the demand must be described with "reasonable particularity." (Code Civ. Proc., § 2031, subd. (c).) Absent a court order, there is no limit on the number of inspection demands that may be served by a party.

▶ Comment

There has been some confusion regarding the relationship, if any, between a party's right to conduct discovery and the Electronic Communications Privacy Act (ECPA). (See § 7.04; see also Appendix C.) Such confusion is unfounded. The ECPA, at least with regard to actions between individuals, concerns the unauthorized interception of or access to electronic communications. (18 U.S.C.A. §§ 2511, 2701.) The act does not, and is not intended to, preclude production of electronic communications in response to a valid subpoena or document demand.

---

§ 3.05 Document Demands

[A] Defining a "Writing"

As used in the Discovery Act of 1986, the terms "document" and "writing" have the definitions provided in section 250 of the Evidence Code. (Code Civ. Proc., § 2016, subd. (b)(3).) The Evidence Code defines "writing" as "handwriting, typewriting, printing, photostating, photographing, and every other means of recording upon any tangible thing any form of communication or representation, including letters, word, pictures, sounds, or symbols, or combinations thereof." (Evid. Code, § 250.) Courts have interpreted this definition of "writing" as including information stored in electronic form, including the memories of computers and on magnetic media. (*Aguimatang v. California State Lottery* (1991) 234 Cal.App.3d 769 [286 Cal.Rptr. 57].)

In drafting document demands, the common definition of "writing" provided in the Evidence Code should be elucidated by examples to ensure the responding party understands the true scope of the writings requested. For example, the definition of "writing" in a document demand may be expanded as follows (see sample form in § 3.16):

> The term **"WRITING"** is defined as in California Evidence Code section 250 and includes, but is not limited to, all **ORIGINALS** and **DUPLICATES** of correspondence, memoranda, records, data sheets, purchase orders, tabulations, reports, work papers, summaries, opinions, journals, calendars, diaries, statistical records, notes, transcriptions, telegrams, teletypes, telex messages, telefaxes, recordings of telephone calls, and other communications, including but not limited to notes, notations, memoranda and other writings of or relating to telephone conversations and conferences, minutes, and notes of transcriptions of all meetings and other communications of any type, microfiche, microfilms, dictobelts, tapes or other records, logs, and any other information that is stored or carried electronically, by means of computer equipment or otherwise, and that can be retrieved in printed, graphic, or audio form, including, but not limited to, information stored in the memory of a computer, data stored on removable magnetic or optical media (for example, magnetic tape, floppy disks, removable cartridge disks, and optical disks), e-mail, data used for electronic data interchange, audit trails, digitized pictures and audio (for example, data stored in MPEG, JPEG, and GIF), digitized audio, and voice mail.

[B] Medium of Production

Although the recipient of a document demand is under a duty, at the reasonable expense of the demanding party, to translate data stored electronically into a "reasonably usable form" (Code Civ. Proc., § 2031, subd. (f)(1)), this may not be the most advantageous form for the demanding party. Requesting documents in "computer readable form," where available, will result in the production of the material on disk or magnetic tape. Production in this form may greatly speed review of the material produced because the disk or tape can be quickly searched electronically for key terms using readily available software. For example, thousands of page of documents could be searched in seconds for every occurrence of the term "Blackacre" within five words of "lease." Performed by hand, this same search could take days.

In arranging for production in electronic form, the software used to create the documents must be identified. In most instances the responding party will volunteer this information as part of the production or the information may be determined from the name and structure of the files produced. If the type of software cannot be ascertained through these means, a special interrogatory can be used to identify the software.

§ 3.06 Documents Stored on Remote Computers

Businesses frequently store documents or backups of documents on computer systems located in other jurisdictions. For example, a growing number of small and medium size businesses backup their computer systems over the Internet. Files are sent by modem to a company that specializes in data storage. The storage company may be located in another state or, conceivably, in another country. Since a party is under an obligation to produce records in its possession, custody, or control (Code Civ. Proc., § 2031, subd. (a)), courts have compelled production of records located in distant jurisdictions if the records are under the party's control. (See, e.g., *Boal v. Price Waterhouse & Co.* (1985) 165 Cal.App.3d 806, 810–811 [212 Cal.Rptr. 42].) As such, storage of electronic evidence on remote computers over which a party has control should not pose a significant obstacle to discovery.

§ 3.07 Demands for Inspection of Other Physical Evidence

[A] In General

In addition to documents, a demand under section 2031 of the Code of Civil Procedure can require a party to permit tangible things in its possession, custody, or control to be inspected, photographed, and subjected to test or sampling. (Code Civ. Proc., § 2031, subd. (a)(2).) In the context of electronic evidence, storage devices, file servers, stand-alone computers, and PDAs, among other things, may all be the subject of an inspection under section 2031.

[B] Inspection of Computer Systems

If significant electronic evidence is suspected to exist, careful consideration should be given to the possibility of demanding an inspection of the opposing party's computer system. Merely serving a document demand may not result in the production of all relevant evidence. Indeed, because most responding parties will conduct a cursory search of their computers, at best, the documents produced will likely represent only a small fraction of the electronic evidence that may exist. Whether intentionally or unintentionally, there is a substantial probability that critical documents will be overlooked. As such, the requesting party should always consider serving a demand for the physical inspection of the responding party's computer system. (Code Civ. Proc., § 2031, subd. (a)(2).) The decision whether to conduct such an examination will ultimately be an economic one—balancing the cost of the examination against the possibility of discovering important evidence that might not otherwise come to light.

Since a physical inspection of a party's computer system will almost certainly raise issues concerning the protection of trade secrets and proprietary and confidential information, the responding party may seek a protective order. (Code Civ. Proc., § 2031, subd. (e); see § 3.12.) In response to a motion for a protective order, the requesting party may argue that a physical inspection is necessary to identify and preserve evidence. As discussed in Chapter 2, there are many areas in a computer system that may contain valuable evidence that can only be discovered by a trained computer expert. Exigent circumstances may also exist if there is an indication that files may be deleted or have recently been deleted. Deleted files can be recovered, but only within a limited time after their deletion. (See § 2.19.) As such, an immediate inspection of the computer may be necessary. Finally, the requesting party may consider offering to enter into a strict confidentiality agreement to protect the information from public disclosure and to limit its use to the pending litigation.

▶ COMMENT

Given the intrusiveness of an inspection of a party's computer system by an opponent in litigation, many courts may be inclined to issue a protective order barring the examination. As a reasonable alternative, the party seeking the inspection can request the court appoint a neutral expert to perform the inspection. The cost of the inspection can be split between the parties. Each party's experts can also be present at the inspection to monitor the areas on the computer examined and the methods employed by the appointed expert. The parties should also agree on methods to be used to establish a chain-of-custody for the evidence (for example, depositing a copy of all electronic evidence with an escrow agent or the court).

---

§ 3.08 Special Interrogatories

Interrogatories are written questions served by one party on another. The responding party must provide written answers to the questions under oath. (Code Civ. Proc., § 2030, subd. (a).) Interrogatories may be served at any time after the initial hold on discovery at the inception of the action and before the discovery cutoff at trial. (See § 3.03.) A party may propound a total of 35 special interrogatories on another party. (Code Civ. Proc., § 2030, subd. (c)(1).) Additional interrogatories may be served if the greater number is warranted because of any of the following circumstances: (1) the complexity or the quantity of issues involved; (2) the financial burden on the requesting party if it must conduct the discovery by oral deposition; and (3) expediency. (Code Civ. Proc., § 2030, subd. (c)(2).)

In conducting electronic discovery, interrogatories may be useful in establishing the following types of information:

- The names, addresses, and e-mail addresses of relevant witnesses.

- The types of software used to create relevant files.

- Descriptions of a party's backup and security procedures.

- Instances of security breaches.

- Persons responsible for maintaining the responding party's computer system.

- Persons who were authorized to access a particular file or directory.

- Descriptions of relevant computer systems and related hardware, including topographical and network descriptions.

§ 3.09 Requests for Admissions

Requests for admissions are used to require a party to admit or deny the truth of a relevant fact or the genuineness of a relevant document. (Code Civ. Proc., § 2033, subd. (a).) Requests for admissions may be served at any time after the initial hold on discovery at the inception of the action and before the discovery cutoff at trial. (See § 3.03.) A party may propound a total of 35 requests on another party. (Code Civ. Proc., § 2033, subd. (c)(1).) Additional requests may be served if accompanied by a declaration of need. (Code Civ. Proc., § 2033, subd. (c)(3).) There is no limit, except as justice requires, on the number of requests that may be served regarding the genuineness of documents.

Unlike the other methods of discovery discussed in this chapter, requests for admissions are not used to identify information, but to provide the requesting party with an admission by the responding party regarding a particular fact. Such admissions may be used as support for a dispositive motion or for cross-examination at trial. They may also be used to obviate the need for authenticating a document at trial. Being able to authenticate electronic documents in this manner is particularly useful. Because of their nature, it is frequently difficult to authenticate electronic documents. (See Chapter 8.) As such, to the extent possible, they should be authenticated in this manner.

Requests for admissions may be useful in establishing the following types of facts:

- The creator of a particular document.

- The owner of an e-mail address or domain name.

- The date a specified file was created or deleted.

§ 3.10 Depositions

Depositions are used to orally examine a witness under oath. Defendants may serve notice of deposition at any time after they are served or appear in the action. Plaintiffs, on the other hand, may not serve a notice of deposition until 20 days after the defendant appears in the action or is served with the summons. (Code Civ. Proc., § 2025, subd. (b)(2).) Depositions are also subject to a cutoff before trial. (Code Civ. Proc., §§ 2024, subd. (a), 2034.) In the absence of a court order or certain other conditions, each natural person may only be deposed once during the course of an action. (Code Civ. Proc., § 2025, subd. (t).) Written depositions are also provided for under the Discovery Act of 1986, but are not considered here. They may be treated in much the same way as interrogatories.

A computer forensics expert can be invaluable in preparing for depositions of computer-related witnesses. Attorneys should also consider having the forensics expert attend the deposition to render advice on the fly. In many cases, one of the first witnesses to be deposed should be a member of the opposing party's information technology (IT) department. Such a witness can provide valuable insight into the topology and operation of the party's computer system and network, the methods used to insure security of data, sources of potential physical evidence, access limitations, and potential security breaches. The information obtained can then be used to develop document demands that are focused on specific evidence in specific locations. (For a sample deposition notice directed toward a member of an IT department, see § 3.21.)

§ 3.11 Exchange of Expert Witness Information

Any party to an action may compel disclosure of expert witness information by serving a demand for exchange of expert witness lists. (Code Civ. Proc., § 2034, subd. (a).) The demand requires all parties to the action to simultaneously exchange information regarding the experts they intend to use as witnesses at trial. The demand may be made no later than the 10th day after the initial trial date has been set, or 70 days before trial, whichever is later. (Code Civ. Proc., § 2034, subd. (b).) The date for the exchange of information can be set 50 days before the initial trial date, or 20 days after service of the demand, whichever is later. (Code Civ. Proc., § 2034, subd. (c).)

For experts who are parties to the action, an employee of a party, or retained by a party for the purpose of rendering opinions at trial, the following information must be disclosed (Code Civ. Proc., § 2034, subd. (f)):

1. The expert's name and address;

2. A brief statement of the expert's qualifications to testify;

3. The general substance of the expert's intended testimony;

4. A statement that the expert is ready to testify; and

5. The expert's fees for testimony.

For all other experts, only their name and address must be disclosed.

The information obtained from the exchange of expert witness information can be used to craft search requests on the Internet to obtain background material regarding the expert for use at deposition and trial. The expert's name should be searched on the Internet using a variety of search engines and directories. Searches should also be performed to identify any postings the expert may have made to newsgroups. The expert may have a personalized Web site that contains information about his or her publications, affiliations, educational history, past testimony, and other information. If the expert belongs to one of the services that provides experts to attorneys, the service's Web site may be another source of potential information about the expert. (For additional information on conducting informal discovery online, see § 2.12.)

§ 3.12 Protective Orders

A party to whom discovery has been propounded may seek a protective order to limit or excuse entirely its obligation to respond. (See, e.g., Code Civ. Proc., §§ 2030, subd. (e), 2031, subd. (e), 2033, subd. (e).) For "good cause shown," a court may make any order that justice requires to protect the responding party from "unwarranted annoyance, embarrassment, or oppression, or undue burden and expense." Code Civ. Proc., §§ 2030, subd. (e), 2031, subd. (e), 2033, subd. (e).) In particular, a court may order any of the following: that the party not need not respond to all or a portion of the discovery request, that the time for responding be extended, that the place for production be changed, that certain matters be placed under seal with the court, that matters be provided for *in camera* review before production or a response is ordered, and that the dissemination of confidential information be limited. (Code Civ. Proc., §§ 2030, subd. (e), 2031, subd. (e), 2033, subd. (e).)

In responding to a request for the production of electronic evidence, the responding party may argue that searching its various computer systems may impose an undue burden, both in time and expense. It may further argue that paper records should suffice or that the requesting party should bear the entire expense, which may be substantial, in searching for and retrieving the requested records. Avoiding an obligation to search electronic records in their entirety seems unlikely. Courts now recognize that businesses routinely store most, if not all, of their records in computers and that it "would be a dangerous development in the law if new techniques for easing the use of information became a hindrance to discovery or disclosure in litigation." (*In re Brand Name Prescription Drug Antitrust Litigation* (N.D. Ill. 1995) 1995 WL 360526 [Case Nos. 94-C-897, MDL 997].)

With regard to who should bear the cost of searching and retrieving electronic records, there is no clear guidance in California. But it appears likely courts will require the responding party to bear the cost of searching for the records—because, after all, it chose to store the records electronically. Nevertheless, the requesting party will bear the cost of translating data compilations into "reasonably usable form" (that is, generating printouts of the material or translating the material into an acceptable file format). (Code Civ. Proc., § 2031, subd. (f)(1); see also *O'Meara v. Internal Revenue Service* (N.D. Ill. 1997) 1997 WL 312054 (IRS could charge plaintiff actual costs of retrieving data in response to request for information contained in an online database).)

§ 3.13　Preservation Requests and Orders

When it appears likely that important evidence may exist in electronic form, consideration should be given to methods to ensure that such evidence is not lost, destroyed, or altered. One approach is to send a "preservation letter" to opposing counsel cautioning them that relevant evidence exists in electronic form and that parties to the action are under a duty to preserve that evidence. (See Chapter 16.)

Another approach to preserving evidence is to seek a preservation order from the court. Such an order can be obtained by moving the court for an injunction (Code Civ. Proc., § 525 et seq.) requiring the parties to the action to preserve and retain documents, files, and records that may be relevant to the litigation. (An example preservation order is provided in § 3.23.) Because such an order may interfere with the normal operations of the parties and impose perhaps unforeseen burdens, the parties and the judge should discuss the need for a preservation order and, if one is required, what terms will best serve the purposes of preserving relevant matter without imposing undue burdens. A preservation order may be difficult to implement perfectly and cause hardship when records are stored in data-processing systems that automatically control the period of retention. Revision of existing computer programs to provide for longer retention, even if possible, may be prohibitively expensive (though print-out and retention of hard copies, or duplication of databases at periodic intervals before deletions occur, may be feasible). Such an order should ordinarily permit destruction after reasonable notice to opposing counsel; if opposing counsel objects, the party seeking destruction should be required to show good cause before destruction is permitted. The order may also exclude specified categories of documents whose cost of preservation is shown to outweigh substantially their relevance in the litigation, particularly if copies of the documents are filed in a document depository or if there are alternative sources for the information. If relevance cannot be fairly evaluated until the litigation progresses, destruction should be deferred. As issues in the case are narrowed, the court may reduce the scope of the order. (See *Manual of Complex Litigation*, Third, § 21.442; *Gates Rubber Co. v. Bando Chemical Indus., Ltd.* (D. Co. 1996) 167 F.R.D. 90, 112 (preservation order that no records be destroyed and permitting expedited discovery of electronic evidence).)

§ 3.14 Federal Guidelines for Searching and Seizing Computers

The Federal Guidelines for Searching and Seizing Computers provides information for drafting descriptions of computer-related information for inclusion in search warrants. Although this language is directed at discovery in criminal matters, the material is also relevant for civil actions. In particular, the example descriptions of where electronic evidence may reside are applicable to any type of action. (See Appendix G.)

§ 3.15 References

📖 **WITKIN** For general discussion of discovery methods, see the following:

- Depositions (2 Witkin, Cal. Evidence (3d ed. 1986) Discovery and Production of Evidence, § 1436 et seq.).

- Interrogatories (2 Witkin, Cal. Evidence (3d ed. 1986) Discovery and Production of Evidence, § 1480 et seq.).

- Inspection of records (2 Witkin, Cal. Evidence (3d ed. 1986) Discovery and Production of Evidence, § 1507 et seq.).

- Exchange of expert witnesses (2 Witkin, Cal. Evidence (3d ed. 1986) Discovery and Production of Evidence, § 1531 et seq.).

- Requests for admissions (2 Witkin, Cal. Evidence (3d ed. 1986) Discovery and Production of Evidence, § 1553 et seq.).

- Protective orders (2 Witkin, Cal. Evidence (3d ed. 1986) Discovery and Production of Evidence, § 1507 et seq.).

THE RUTTER GROUP For a practical guide to discovery procedures, see California Practice Guide: Civil Procedure Before Trial, ch. 8.

WEST'S KEY NUMBER SYSTEM See the following key numbers in West's Cal. Digest 2d, Pretrial Procedure (Topic 307A):

- Discovery in general (Pretrial Procedure ☞ 11 et seq.).

- Depositions (Pretrial Procedure ☞ 91 et seq.).

- Interrogatories (Pretrial Procedure ☞ 241 et seq.).

- Inspection demands (Pretrial Procedure ☞ 331 et seq.).

- Requests for admission (Pretrial Procedure ☞ 471 et seq.).

💻 **WESTLAW** See the WESTLAW Electronic Research Guide at the beginning of this volume.

B. Forms

§ 3.16 Sample Document Demands

_____

State Bar No. _____

_____

_____

_____

Attorneys for _____

_____ COURT OF THE STATE OF CALIFORNIA
COUNTY OF _____

_____ _____ Plaintiff(s), v. _____ Defendant(s). _____	) Case No. _____) BEFORE HON. _____)) **PLAINTIFF'S REQUEST FOR**) **PRODUCTION OF**) **DOCUMENTS, FIRST SET**)) [Civ. Proc. Code, § 2031])) Date: _____) Time: _____) Place: _____) Date action filed: _____) Trial date: _____

REQUESTING PARTY: _____

RESPONDING PARTY: _____

SET NUMBER:_____

NOTICE

Pursuant to Code of Civil Procedure section 2031, the Responding Party is requested to identify the documents set forth below in its possession, custody, or control or in the possession, custody, or control of the Responding Party's agents, attorneys, employees, and/or representatives.

The documents are to be produced for inspection on the date and time and at the location specified above. The Responding Party may satisfy this Demand for Production of Documents by mailing copies of the documents requested to the Requesting Party's attorney and making the originals available on reasonable notice.

INSTRUCTIONS

A. Copies of writings.

If there are several copies of a writing, and if any of the copies are not identical or are no longer identical because they have been written on or modified in any way, front or back, then each of the nonidentical copies is considered a separate writing and must be produced.

B. Withholding documents under a claim of privilege.

If any document is withheld under a claim of privilege, please identify the writing by providing the following information: the basis for the claim of privilege, the date of the document, the subject of the document, the author, the addressee(s) and all other persons who received the writing or copies of the document, as well as all those to whom the document or copies became available at any time, together with each person's job title and address. **AS REQUIRED BY CODE OF CIVIL PROCEDURE SECTION 2031(f)(3), A PRIVILEGE LOG MUST BE INCLUDED WITH YOUR WRITTEN RESPONSE.**

C. Documents no longer in the Responding Party's possession or control.

If any writing to be produced is no longer in the Responding Party's possession or control or is no longer in existence, please state whether the writing is missing or lost, destroyed, transferred voluntarily or involuntarily to others (and if so, to whom), or otherwise disposed of. In each instance, explain the circumstances surrounding the authorization for the disposition and the date of the disposition.

D. Documents stored electronically.

Pursuant to Code of Civil Procedure section 2031(f)(1), documents stored electronically (for example, in the memory of a computer or on a hard disk, floppy, memory card, magnetic tape, etc.) shall be reduced to hardcopy form.

DEFINITIONS

For purposes of this Demand certain terms are defined as follows:

__. The term **"WRITING"** is defined as in California Evidence Code section 250 and includes, but is not limited to, all **ORIGINALS** and **DUPLICATES** of correspondence, memoranda, records, data sheets, purchase orders, tabulations, reports, evaluations, work papers, summaries, opinions, journals, calendars, diaries, statistical records, checks, notes, transcriptions, telegrams, teletypes, telex messages, telefaxes, recordings of telephone calls, and other communications, including but not limited to notes, notations, memoranda, and other writings of or relating to telephone conversations and conferences, minutes and notes of transcriptions of all meetings and other communications of any type, microfiche, microfilms, dictobelts, tapes or other records, logs and any other information that is stored or carried electronically, by means of computer equipment or otherwise, and that can be retrieved in printed, graphic, or audio form, including, but not limited to, information stored in the memory of a computer, data stored on removable magnetic or optical media (for example, magnetic tape, floppy disks, removable cartridge disks, and optical disks), e-mail, data used for electronic data interchange, audit trails, digitized pictures and audio (for example, data stored in MPEG, JPEG, and GIF), digitized audio, and voice mail.

__. The term **"ORIGINAL"** is defined as in Evidence Code section 255 and includes the writing itself or any counterpart intended to have the same effect by a person executing or issuing it. An **ORIGINAL** of a photograph includes the negative or any print therefrom. If data are stored in a computer or similar device, any printout or other output readable by sight, shown to reflect the data accurately, is an **ORIGINAL**.

__. The term **"DUPLICATE"** is defined as in Evidence Code section 260 and includes a counterpart produced by the same impression as the original, or from the same matrix, or by means of photography, including enlargements and miniatures, or by mechanical or electronic rerecording, or by chemical reproduction, or by equivalent technique that accurately reproduces the original.

__. The term **"PERSON"** is defined as in Evidence Code section 175 and includes a natural person, firm, association, organization, partnership, business trust, corporation, limited liability company, or public entity.

__. The term **"RELATING TO"** includes referring to, embodying, in connection with, referencing, evidencing, commenting on, corresponding to, sharing, describing, concerning, analyzing, reflecting, or constituting.

__. The terms **"YOU"** or **"YOUR"** refer to _____ [Defendant XYZ Corporation] and its agents, employees, representatives, and attorneys.

__. The term **"COMPUTER"** includes, but is not limited to, personal computers, microcomputers, laptop computers, portable computers, note-book computers, palmtop computers, personal digital assistants, file servers, application servers, workstations, network computers (sometimes called "thin clients"), minicomputers, and mainframes.

__. The term **"COMPUTER SYSTEM"** refers to all file servers, stand-alone computers, workstations, laptops, and personal digital assistants owned or leased by _____ [Defendant XYZ Corporation] [or physically located at _____].

__. The term **"NETWORK"** refers to the local area network located at _____, including, but not limited to, all files servers, client computers, workstations, firewalls, routers, proxy servers, Internet servers, mail servers, and application servers.

__. The term **"LOG FILE"** refers to the information automatically col-lected by Web sites on the Internet. Such information includes, but is not lim-ited to, the Internet address of each visitor, the date and time of the visit to the Web site, the particular pages of the site viewed, prior Web sites visited, and whether the visit was successful or whether a failure resulted (that is, an error occurred on the Web site).

__. The term **"WEB SITE"** refers to the World Wide Web site located at _____ [www.xyzcorp.com], the Hypertext Markup Language (HTML) pages making up the site, and all information collected and stored by the site, including all **LOG FILES** relating to the usage of the site.

__. The term **"E-MAIL"** refers to the exchange of text messages and computer files over a communications network, such as a local area network, intranet, extranet, or public network such as the Internet or other online ser-vice provider.

DOCUMENTS REQUESTED

The documents or writings to be identified and produced pursuant to this Demand are as follows:

Requests Relating to Corporate Policies and Guidelines

__. All **WRITINGS RELATING TO** guidelines and policies govern-ing employee use of the **COMPUTER SYSTEM** prepared or adopted within the last five years, including, but not limited to, drafts of all such guide-lines and policies.

__. All **WRITINGS RELATING TO** guidelines and policies govern-ing maintenance of hard disks on the **COMPUTER SYSTEM**, including, but not limited to, guidelines and policies regarding the use of utility software to scan the disks for errors, to optimize disks, and to conduct low and high level formatting of disks.

___. All **WRITINGS RELATING TO** guidelines and policies governing employee use of **E-MAIL** prepared or adopted within the last five years, including, but not limited to, drafts of all such guidelines and policies.

___. All **WRITINGS RELATING TO** guidelines and policies governing employee use of the Internet prepared or adopted within the last five years, including, but not limited to, drafts of all such guidelines and policies.

___. All **WRITINGS RELATING TO** guidelines and policies governing when files are deleted from the **COMPUTER SYSTEM**.

Requests Relating to Use of the Computer System

___. All **WRITINGS RELATING TO** instances in which an employee has been disciplined in any way for misusing or abusing the **COMPUTER SYSTEM**.

___. All **WRITINGS RELATING TO** instances in which an employee has been disciplined in any way during the past five years for sending harassing, offensive, or sexually explicit **E-MAIL** to another employee.

___. Copies of all **E-MAIL** sent or received by [*specify individual*] **RE-LATING TO** _____ [Blackacre].

___. Copies of all **E-MAIL** during [*specify period*] sent or received by [*specify first individual*] in which [*specify second individual*] was also a recipient, including **E-MAIL** in which [*specify second individual*] was copied or blind-copied.

___. Copies of all **E-MAIL** sent or received by account name [*specify account name, e.g.,* j_smith@xyzcorp.com].

Requests Relating to Security

___. All **WRITINGS RELATING TO** procedures and policies **YOU** followed during [*specify period*] for backing up files and other data from **YOUR** computer.

___. All **WRITINGS RELATING TO** procedures and policies **YOU** followed during [*specify period*] concerning the security of the **COMPUTER SYSTEM**, including, but not limited to, all training materials for employees.

___. All **WRITINGS RELATING TO** any security reviews or analyses of the **COMPUTER SYSTEM** prepared within the last five years, including, but not limited to, reports, memoranda, and correspondence prepared by or sent to third party security consultants.

__. All **WRITINGS RELATING TO** any instances in the last five years in which an unauthorized party gained access to the **COMPUTER SYSTEM.**

__. All **WRITINGS RELATING TO** any instances in the last five years in which a virus or other destructive program caused any data loss on the **COMPUTER SYSTEM.**

__. All **WRITINGS RELATING TO** any instances in the last five years in which an equipment or software malfunction caused data loss on the **COMPUTER SYSTEM.**

__. All **WRITINGS RELATING TO** any instances in the last five years in which a hard disk has been replaced in any computer on the **NET-WORK.**

__. All **WRITINGS RELATING TO** any disaster recovery plans established during [*specify period*] for the **NETWORK.**

__. All **WRITINGS RELATING TO** methods of accessing the **NET-WORK** from outside **YOUR** company (that is, remote access procedures).

Employee Monitoring

__. All **WRITINGS RELATING TO YOUR** efforts to monitor employee use of the **NETWORK.**

__. All **WRITINGS RELATING TO YOUR** efforts to monitor employee use of the Internet.

__. All **WRITINGS RELATING TO YOUR** efforts to monitor employee use of **E-MAIL.**

Requests Relating to the Web Site

__. All **WRITINGS RELATING TO** the design and development of the **WEB SITE,** including, but not limited to, copies of the executed development agreement and all drafts of the agreement with [*specify developer*].

__. All **WRITINGS RELATING TO** orders for merchandise made through the **WEB SITE** during [*specify period*].

__. All **WRITINGS RELATING TO** instances in which an unauthorized party attempted to gain access to the **WEB SITE** during [*specify period*].

__. All **WRITINGS RELATING TO** any instances in the last five years in which an equipment or software malfunction caused data loss on the **WEB SITE.**

__. Copies of all **LOG FILES** generated by the **WEB SITE** from [*specify beginning date*] to [*specify ending date*], including, but not limited to, **LOG FILES** generated by duplicate or mirror Web sites.

__. All **E-MAIL RELATING TO** _____ [the acquisition of Blackacre], including, but not limited to, **E-MAIL** stored on desktop computer hard disks, floppy disks and other removable electronic storage media, file servers, workstations, laptops, handheld organizers, backup tapes, and Internet e-mail servers.

Requests Relating to Trading Partner Agreements

__. A copy of the trading partner agreement between **YOU** and [specify trading partner], dated [specify date].

__. All **WRITINGS RELATING TO** the negotiation of the trading partner agreement between **YOU** and [specify trading partner], including, but not limited to, drafts of the agreement, negotiation notes, and correspondence.

__. All **WRITINGS RELATING TO** the trading partner agreement between [specify trading partner] and **YOU**, dated [specify contract date], including, but not limited to, confirmations of orders, acknowledgements of receipt, and tracking information.

__. All **WRITINGS RELATING TO** communications with [specify value added network] regarding electronic data interchange transactions with [specify trading partner].

Miscellaneous Requests

__. An organizational chart for **YOUR** Information Systems Department.

__. A list of all authorized users of the **COMPUTER SYSTEM**.

__. A copy of the **NETWORK** map.

__. All **WRITINGS RELATING TO** source code escrow agreements for [specify software].

__. Copies of any and all source code escrow agreements for [specify software], including, but not limited to, copies of all drafts of such agreements.

DATED: _____   _____

_____

_____

By _____

Attorneys for _____

§ 3.17 Sample Points and Authorities Supporting Application to Compel Production of Documents and Computers

1   JACKSON, DeMARCO & PECKENPAUGH
     4 Park Plaza, 16ᵗʰ Floor
     Post Office Box 19704
     Irvine, California 92713-9704

2   JOHN W. COCHRANE, ESQ., STATE BAR #97135
     ATTORNEYS FOR PLAINTIFF GARRETH E. SHAW

3

4

5

6

7

8   SUPERIOR COURT OF THE STATE OF CALIFORNIA

9   FOR THE COUNTY OF ORANGE

10

11 GARRETH E. SHAW, AN INDIVIDUAL,)   CASE NO. 74-33-68

)

12   PLAINTIFF,   )   **ASSIGNED FOR ALL PURPOSES**
)   **TO: JUDGE FREDERICK HORN**
    V.   )   DEPARTMENT 21

13   )

14 PAUL BOGENREIF, AN INDIVIDUAL;)   **PLAINTIFF'S MEMORANDUM**
   HUGHES ARICRAFT COMPANY, A   )   **OF POINTS AND AUTHORITIES**
   DELAWARE CORPORATION; JOHN   )   **IN SUPPORT OF APPLICATION**

15 HIGGINS, AN INDIVIDUAL; DONALD   )   **FOR ORDER COMPELLING**
   SCHROCK, AN IDIVIDUAL; AND DOES   )   **PRODUCTION OF DOCUMENTS**

16 1 THROUGH 100,   )   **AND COMPUTERS**
)

17   DEFENDANTS.   )   DATE: _____
)   TIME: _____

18   )   DEP'T: _____

19 _____)   TRIAL DATE: _____

20

21

22

23

24

25

26

27

28
                            PLAINTIFF'S MEMORANDUM OF POINTS AND
                            AUTHORITIES IN SUPPORT OF APPLICATION
                            FOR ORDER COMPELLING PRODUCTION OF
                            DOCUMENTS AND COMPUTERS

I.

INTRODUCTION

Hughes Aircraft Company is an enterprise of monumental proportions. If Hughes want to make things difficult and expensive, it can. This motion is necessary because of the way Hughes, and the lawyers which Hughes instructs, have consciously sought to delay, obfuscate, sandbag and evade their discovery obligations with respect to the obviously relevant issue of "e-mail discovery" in connection with this wrongiul discharge case. This application is made on the first day of trial because the defendants asked for, and received, numerous extensions to respond to very particularized e-mail discovery requests — to which they only provided partial responses on July 1 and then, after this Court continued the trial for a week to permit plaintiff to explore those improper responses, they continued to stonewall.

There is more at stake here than some discovery just not completed. Plaintiff and his counsel respectfully request the indulgence of this Court in considering what the discovery is, how courteous and up-front plaintiffs counsel have been from minute one in trying to facilitate and streamline that discovery, and the incredible job of deception and avoidance and "cost enhancement" that Hughes has consciously and intentionally foisted upon not only the adversary but upon the courts throughout this process. Plaintiff respectfully requests the entirely appropriate relief of a court order compelling Hughes to allow plaintiffs experts appropriate access to Hughes' computer system(s), at Hughes' expense, to properly undertake the discovery that Hughes refuses to do.

II.

HUGHES' ABJECT REFUSAL TO RESPOND IN GOOD FAITH TO ANY EFFORT TO ENGAGE IN LEGITIMATE "ELECTRONIC DISCOVERY"

-1-

PLAINTIFF'S MEMORANDUM OF POINTS AND
AUTHORITIES IN SUPPORT OF APPLICATION
FOR ORDER COMPELLING PRODUCTION OF
DOCUMENTS AND COMPUTERS

1   **HAS BEEN A CALCULATED SCHEME TO DELAY AND DENY**

2   **LEGITIMATE DISCOVERY**

3   A chronology of what has gone on with respect to the e-mail

4   discovery issue is very material to an understanding of why this matter is in its

5   present posture and why the requested relief is justified and appropriate.

6   A.   Preliminary Communications Seeking Retention of E-Mail.

7   Gary Shaw was fired on September 3, 1993. On that date, Gary

8   Shaw's then-counsel, Carla Feldman, Esq., faxed to Hughes' General Counsel,

9   defendant John Higgins, a letter demanding that Hughes preserve "all documents

10   which in any manner pertain to Gary Shaw, as appropriate legal action is

11   contemplated. . . . These materials should include . . . tapes, computer files,

12   e-mail. . . ."[1] Hughes immediately responded to this fax, stating "Hughes'

13   practice is to preserve all documents relating to personnel actions, and we will do

14   so in this matter."[2]

15   At the same time, Hughes commenced a straightforward policy

16   somewhat reminiscent of Nikita Kruschev's "we will bury you." Carla Feldman,

17   Mr. Shaw's initial counsel, was flatly told by Hughes Associate General Counsel

18   T. Warren Jackson that either Mr. Shaw must give up and go away or Hughes

19   would spend unlimited amounts on his case; John Cochrane, Mr. Shaw's present

20   counsel, was told exactly the same thing.[3] That is how this matter has proceeded.

21   Before the Complaint was filed in this action on August 9, 1994,

22   Mr. Shaw's counsel wrote to Hughes' General Counsel, Mr. Higgins, and

23

24   _____

     [1]   Letter from Carla Feldman to John Higgins, September 3, 1993 [Copy attached as
25   Exhibit 1 to Declaration of John W. Cochrane, submitted herewith].

26   [2]   Letter, T. Warren Jackson to Carla Feldman, September 3, 1993 [Cochrane Dec.
     Ex. 2].

27   [3]   *See* Excerpts of Deposition of Carla Feldman, June 28, 1996 [Cochrane Dec. Ex. 3].

28
                                           PLAINTIFF'S MEMORANDUM OF POINTS AND
                              -2-   AUTHORITIES IN SUPPORT OF APPLICATION
                                           FOR ORDER COMPELLING PRODUCTION OF
                                           DOCUMENTS AND COMPUTERS

1   specifically reiterated and even elaborated upon Ms. Feldman's prior demand for
2   preservation of electronic media. By letter dated August 3, 1994, Mr. Cochrane
3   wrote that "this is to confirm and reiterate the demand previously made on
4   Mr. Shaw's behalf regarding the Company's retention of documents and
5   records — particularly electronically-stored information —pertaining to
6   Mr. Shaw. . . ."[4] That letter then continued to identify the specific individuals at
7   Hughes whose e-mail should be retained because discovery would be pursued
8   with respect to that issue. When Hughes' T. Warren Jackson responded to
9   Mr. Cochrane's letter on August 11 [Cochrane Dec. Ex. 5], he said "we stand by
10 our September 3, 1993 letter to Carla J. Feldman, Esq. and you are not entitled
11 to further assurances." Mr. Cochrane replied that notice having been duly given,
12 "[a]ll rights respectfully are reserved in the event that it subsequently is
13 determined that Hughes Aircraft Company or its agents have caused or permitted
14 the deletion, destruction or spoliation of potentially relevant and admissible
15 evidence."[5]
16   Hughes' in-house lawyer, Mr. Jackson, next faxed off a letter on
17 August 16, 1994, complaining that plaintiff was making "extremely burdensome
18 demands" in seeking confirmation that electronic data be retained.[6] Frankly
19 wondering how it could be burdensome to simply not destroy what already
20 existed, counsel for plaintiff wrote to seek an explanation about that concern;
21 Mr. Jackson responded that Hughes "can agree do to no more than what it has
22 already agreed to do."[7]

23

24 [4]   Letter, John Cochrane to John Higgins, August 3, 1994 [Cochrane Dec. Ex. 4].

25 [5]   Letter, Cochrane to Jackson, August 15, 1994 [Cochrane Dec. Ex. 6].

26 [6]   Letter, Jackson to Cochrane, August 16, 1994 [Cochrane Dec. Ex. 7].

27 [7]   Letter, Cochrane to Jackson, Aug. 19, 1994 [Cochrane Dec. Ex. 8]; Letter, Jackson to
        Cochrane, Aug. 23, 1994 [Cochrane Dec. Ex. 9].

28

-3-   PLAINTIFF'S MEMORANDUM OF POINTS AND
             AUTHORITIES IN SUPPORT OF APPLICATION
             FOR ORDER COMPELLING PRODUCTION OF
             DOCUMENTS AND COMPUTERS

B.   Initial Efforts by Plaintiffs Counsel to Focus Electronic Discovery Issues
      are Stonewalled.

            Hughes identified the Quinn Emanuel Urquhart & Oliver ("QEUO")
law firm as defendants' counsel. Interestingly, several members of that law firm
are former colleagues of plaintiffs counsel from prior positions with Jones Day
Reavis & Pogue.[8] By letter of September 19, 1994, on the first day of
communication with QEUO, it was reiterated that electronic media must be
preserved:

> "Now that outside counsel is involved on behalf of
> Hughes and the individual defendants, we again state
> and renew plaintiffs demand that documents and
> materials relating to the persons and issues previously
> described be retained by Hughes Aircraft Company and
> that, specifically, no electronic media be overwritten,
> destroyed or altered pending further proceedings in this
> litigation. This could not really be considered an extra-
> ordinary demand, but Hughes' elliptical responses from
> the office of its inside counsel have not provided any
> assurances of this basic level of evidence preservation.
> An unequivocal response on behalf of Hughes is,
> therefore, respectfully demanded so that we may
> proceed in this case without being concerned that the
> Company is allowing the destruction of evidence while
> the action is pending. We are particularly concerned
> the information generated or derived from the
> Company's "Proffs" system be retained; that
> information generated or retained by or within the
> Company's CC-Mail system(s) or other e-mail systems
> be retained; that information including backups and files
> managed by Hughes Mainframe Computing Services in
> El Segundo be retained; and that information backed up
> at the local network levels in Newport Beach, Torrance
> and El Segundo be retained. It is my belief that most if
> not all such information would likely be preserved by
> Hughes in any event, given Hughes' reporting and

---

[8]   Indeed, defendants' present lead trial counsel (Mr. Feess) was a partner of
Mr. Cochrane and also of plaintiffs co-counsel, Joanne M. Frasca of Frasca & Associates,
when all three were partners in Jones, Day's Los Angeles office several years ago. Quinn
Emanuel associate (now partner) Douglas Kuber, who initially was assigned to this action by
that firm, was formerly an associate at the Jones Day Los Angeles office. These facts are
related so that the Court more readily may appreciate why repeated requests for extensions of
time from these former colleagues were accommodated, not only as a matter of professional
courtesy, but of personal respect.

-4-

PLAINTIFF'S MEMORANDUM OF POINTS AND
AUTHORITIES IN SUPPORT OF APPLICATION
FOR ORDER COMPELLING PRODUCTION OF
DOCUMENTS AND COMPUTERS

1 accountability obligations to others. What we are
seeking to confirm is that things are not being and will
2 not be deleted, overwritten or destroyed."[9]

3 The only response received to this was a September 21 letter which

4 simply "refer[s] you to Warren Jackson's letters dated August 16 and August 23,

5 1994."[10]

6 Plaintiff retained the "electronic discovery" firm of Electronic

7 Evidence Discovery, Inc., one of the leading experts in this field.[11] On

8 October 4, 1994, plaintiff then served a Notice of Deposition of Hughes' Person

9 Most Knowledgeable Concerning Electronic Media [Cochrane Dec. Ex. 13],

10 which was specifically designed to allow preliminary inquiry into precisely how

11 Hughes' electronic media is stored in order to facilitate more focused requests for

12 specific categories of information. Plaintiff also served a First Request for

13 Identification of Documents — but even here sought to minimize inconvenience

14 and burden by specifically including an instruction that electronic information be

15 generally identified but need not be actually printed out and produced at that

16 stage.[12]

17 The purpose of this proposed discovery was spelled out in

18 correspondence dated October 10, 1994:

19

20 [9] Letter, Cochrane to Adisa-Mari Abudu, Esq., Sept. 19, 1994 [Cochrane Dec. Ex. 10].

21 [10] Letter, Abudu to Cochrane, Sept. 21, 1994 [Cochrane Dec. Ex. 11].

22 [11] In October of 1994, Mr. Cochrane and John Jessen (President of EED) appeared as
speakers at a seminar sponsored by the Orange County Business Journal entitled "What Every
23 Business Should Consider About Electronic Evidence and Discovery", see Kenneth Shear
Declaration. Mr. Jessen is one of the leading experts in this area, and was featured on Sixty
24 Minutes on such topics just this past June 30, 1996. A copy of Mr. Jessen's May, 1994
article, "The Impact of Electronic Data Discovery on the Corporation," are attached as
25 Exhibit 12 to the Cochrane Declaration herein. This article was supplied to Hughes' counsel
as an exhibit to Mr. Cochrane's October 10, 1994 letter.

26 [12] See Plaintiffs First Request For Identification and Production of Documents, served
27 October 4, 1994 [Copy attached to Cochrane Dec. as Ex. 14], specifically at Page 4, Para. G
(instruction concerning CCP 203 1(f)).

28

-5-   PLAINTIFF'S MEMORANDUM OF POINTS AND
AUTHORITIES IN SUPPORT OF APPLICATION
FOR ORDER COMPELLING PRODUCTION OF
DOCUMENTS AND COMPUTERS

1
2
3
4
5
6
7
8
9
10
11
12
13

"[Y]our cooperation is requested in facilitating the proper and economical completion of this discovery rather than engaging in costly and dilatory battles concerning its permissibility, as I think I was hearing suggested when I provided you and your client with a courtesy copy of the deposition notice. The deposition notice and its attached document request specifically are designed to permit the plaintiff to identify the location and accessibility of electronically stored evidence pertaining to this case. The purpose in providing you with specific statutory and published citations is to minimize the need for having to incur the time and expense of having to cite them in court filings. I already am on record as agreeing to appropriate protective orders in this action and requesting your cooperation in identifying areas which Hughes wishes to shield, and in considering protective order language which you may wish to propose; that offer stands with respect to the instant deposition notice and electronic media discovery, as well. Should you and Hughes decline this request to cooperate in these regards, I believe and would argue that Hughes could not prevail — or argue in good faith — against the present discovery requests and my specific offer to work with you to address whatever specific concerns you may have."[13]

14
15
16
17
18
19
20
21
22
23
24
25

Hughes never did produce *any* witness, or identify or produce any category of electronic information, in response to this effort to do this in the least intrusive way possible. The defendants served written objections to the Deposition Notice [Cochrane Dec. Ex. 16] and interposed written objections — including "national security" — to document requests seeking general identification of e-mail categories [See Cochrane Dec. Ex. 17]. Plaintiff tried to elicit any good faith narrowing of issues while, on other fronts, the case went through the motions of Hughes changing venue from Los Angeles[14] to Orange County, which took several months. Plaintiff first agreed to continue the "person most knowledgeable" deposition to November 15, 1994 [Cochrane Dec. Ex. 18] and

26
27
28

[13]   Letter Cochrane to John Quinn, Oct. 10, 1994 [Cochrane Dec. Ex. 15].

[14]   In October of 1994, a Los Angeles jury handed down a $94 million verdict against Hughes in an employment discrimination case.

-6-

PLAINTIFF'S MEMORANDUM OF POINTS AND
AUTHORITIES IN SUPPORT OF APPLICATION
FOR ORDER COMPELLING PRODUCTION OF
DOCUMENTS AND COMPUTERS

1   then agreed to take it "off calendar" to try to reach an accommodation.[15]

2   A review of correspondence confirms that plaintiffs counsel sought

3   for months to engage in any kind of meaningful dialogue about the review of

4   Hughes' electronic media. Plaintiffs counsel's letters of November 14 and

5   December 1, 1994 reflect early efforts; a letter of QEUO attorney Kuber dated

6   December 28 1994 reflects "we will get back to you on your proposal sometime

7   in January" and, in February, plaintiffs counsel is still trying to elicit that

8   promised response, stating "[a]s I have discussed with you, I am willing to have

9   a meeting with Hughes' experts and lawyers at which we can discuss Hughes'

10 media and programs with my experts, Electronic Evidence Discovery, Inc., and

11 can determine how to most effectively and economically complete this

12 discovery."[16] No response received, on March 7 yet another letter goes out[17] —

13 and on April 21 Hughes simply wrote "[o]ur position is unchanged"[18] and refuses

14 to do anything at all.

15   In short, following eight months of one-sided but thoroughly

16 encouraged efforts to cooperate, minimize potential dislocation to Hughes and

17 engage in economical attention to this area of discovery, counsel for Hughes

18 simply slammed the door shut on this discussion.

19 C.   The Instant Specific Discovery Requests are Ignored While Extensions are

20   Given as a Courtesy to Counsel, then Improperly, Incompletely and

21

22 [15]   *See* Cochrane Declaration.

23 [16]   Letter, Cochrane to Kuber, February 21, 1995 at p. 2; that letter and the November 14,
    December 1 and December 28, 1994 letters described in the text are collectively attached to the
24 Cochrane Declaration as Ex. 19.

25 [17]   Letter, Cochrane to Kuber, March 7, 1995 at p. 3 [Cochrane Dec. Ex. 20].

26 [18]   Letter, Robert Juman [QEUO] to Cochrane, Apr. 21, 1995 [Cochrane Dec. Ex. 21].
    This leads to two more letters — one on April 27 indicating that the "person most
27 knowledgeable" deposition would be put back on calendar, and a response telling us not to
    bother because Hughes would not produce anyone. [Cochrane Dec. Ex. 22 and 23].

28

-7-   PLAINTIFF'S MEMORANDUM OF POINTS AND
       AUTHORITIES IN SUPPORT OF APPLICATION
       FOR ORDER COMPELLING PRODUCTION OF
       DOCUMENTS AND COMPUTERS

Falsely are "Answered".

Hughes' calculated recalcitrance sufficed to prevent plaintiff from obtaining utterly appropriate information concerning the particulars of Hughes' retention practices and, had plaintiff moved to compel, Hughes would have had to supply that information. But the fact that Hughes has not provided preliminary information in good faith responses to discovery does not mean that the information cannot be obtained otherwise or that any particular item is shielded from ultimate production; it just means that Hughes has succeeded in making the discovery process more costly.

As the trial date approached, then, plaintiff propounded very precise discovery requests pursuant to Section 2031 of the Code of Civil Procedure. **PLAINTIFF'S SECOND REQUEST FOR PRODUCTION OF DOCU-MENTS AND FOR THE INSPECTION OF TANGIBLE THINGS TO DEFENDANT HUGHES AIRCRAFT COMPANY**, served on April 2, 1996, sought two separate categories of things: First, Hughes was directed to *produce, for physical inspection,* such computers and electronic media storage facilities as are sufficient to locate defined e-mail information. Second, Hughes was directed to produce "All electronic mail messages which were either authored by or received by *[eight specifically named individuals]*, which in any manner whatsoever RELATE to PLAINTIFF" and certain other limited information.[19]

Hughes only served generic objections to this Second Request [Cochrane Dec. Ex. 25]. When confronted with the inadequacy of these boilerplate objections, Hughes' counsel did ask for, and was afforded, extensions of time to supplement Hughes' responses to these requests. Counsel for plaintiff

---

[19]   A true and correct copy of **plaintiffs SECOND REQUEST FOR PRODUCTION OF DOCUMENTS AND FOR THE INSPECTION OF TANGIBLE THINGS TO DEFENDANT HUGHES AIRCRAFT COMPANY** is attached as Exhibit 24 to the Cochrane Declaration.

PLAINTIFF'S MEMORANDUM OF POINTS AND AUTHORITIES IN SUPPORT OF APPLICATION FOR ORDER COMPELLING PRODUCTION OF DOCUMENTS AND COMPUTERS

1   was seeking to accommodate Hughes' counsel, just as counsel for Hughes

2   appeared to be accommodating counsel for plaintiff in several discovery areas

3   (particularly in the designation of expert witnesses). At all times, counsel for

4   Hughes represented that the reason additional time was needed to further respond

5   to the Second Request for Production and Inspection was to permit the client to

6   locate and produce responsive information. At no time was it represented that

7   Hughes was going to respond to anything less than the whole set of Requests, or

8   that nothing would be produced. Although plaintiffs counsel expressed concern

9   over the amount of time the process was taking, we essentially "bought"

10 counsel's representation that they were in good faith seeking to respond

11 meaningfully to the discovery requests prior to trial.[20]

12   On July 1, counsel for Hughes finally provided a verified (on

13 information and belief) response" to the Second Request [Cochrane Dec.

14 Ex. 26]. That Response, however, does not even deign to include most of the

15 requests — no response, no objection, not even an acknowledgment that the

16 requests were even made. And as to those items where a response is afforded,

17 Hughes just says that it possess "no responsive documents." There is no

18 identification of the steps taken, if any, to seek to determine whether the answer

19 given is true, which is required by the Code;[21] there is no identification of

20 anything.

21   Immediately upon receiving this inadequate and surprising response,

22 counsel for plaintiff sought Hughes' stipulation to continue the trial to address

23

24 [20]   Cochrane Declaration.

25 [21]   Where a party contends, that it is unable to produce the requested documents, Code of
    Civil Procedure § 2031 requires a certification: (1) that a diligent and reasonable inquiry has
26 been made in an effort to locate the items demanded; and (2) the reason why the party is
    unable to comply with the request, i.e., whether the documents never existed or whether they
27 have been lost or destroyed. Defendants have provided *none* of this information in their
    belated response.

28

                                          -9-   PLAINTIFF'S MEMORANDUM OF POINTS AND
                                                       AUTHORITIES IN SUPPORT OF APPLICATION
                                                       FOR ORDER COMPELLING PRODUCTION OF
                                                       DOCUMENTS AND COMPUTERS

1   this issue. Hughes' counsel ignored three faxes and numerous phone calls on

2   July 1[22] but, when an ex parte appearance was made on the morning of July 3,

3   counsel for Hughes showed up with a half-inch thick written Opposition that had

4   the chutzpa to claim that plaintiffs counsel was somehow at fault for Hughes'

5   failure to provide adequate discovery responses after all this.[23]

6   The Court granted an extension and counsel for plaintiff immediately

7   sought to conduct the deposition of the individual who verified Hughes' discovery

8   responses, in a good faith effort to at least try to understand what Hughes had

9   done to try to determine whether or not it actually possessed any responsive

10   e-mail. Five days later, nothing. All that counsel for Hughes have suggested is

11   that "they have a call in to Hughes, but he hasn't called back."[24] Hughes and its

12   counsel simply have ignored these requests, in the obvious hope that time will

13   allow them to escape having to deal with their incompetent responses.

14   *Is it even remotely credible for Hughes to suggest that it possesses no*

15   *e-mail* responsive to the categories set out above? Of course not. Indeed,

16   Mr. Shaw himself can testify that he sent e-mails to some or all of these

17   identified people during the relevant time period [Shaw Dec., submitted

18   herewith]. Moreover, as confirmed by the Declaration of Gary Hawkins — the

19   man who actually managed all of Hughes' computer facilities for the Group that

20   employed Mr. Shaw in 1993 — e-mails generated by Hughes were and are

21

22

23   [22]   Letters, Cochrane to Stein and Cochrane to Feess, July 1, 1996 [Cochrane Dec. Ex. 27].

24   [23]   Hughes Opp., filed July 3, 1996. Of course, Hughes' counsel's *real* reason for

25   opposing the application, as stated on the record, was that one of Hughes' lawyers had a vacation planned in August. In the hallway after the Court granted the extension, counsel for

26   Hughes acknowledged that the amazing language in their Opposition was "just rhetoric." Great. *See* Cochrane Dec. Para. 8.

27   [24]   *See* Cochrane Dec. at Para. 9 and Letters, Cochrane to Stein, July 7, 8, 9, 1996 [Cochrane Dec. Ex, 28].

28

-10-   PLAINTIFF'S MEMORANDUM OF POINTS AND AUTHORITIES IN SUPPORT OF APPLICATION FOR ORDER COMPELLING PRODUCTION OF DOCUMENTS AND COMPUTERS

1   "saved", "backed-up" and then stored on a regular basis. Mr. Hawkins confirms

2   not only that Hughes does store things, but that Hughes has to store things to

3   comply with government retention rules and that Hughes' systems are specifically

4   configured to avoid carrying "national security" classified information.

5   [Hawkins Dec. at para. 7].

6   Frankly, somebody at Hughes is lying. If they are not lying, then

7   somebody at Hughes has destroyed evidence that Hughes was specifically on

8   notice to preserve, and actually agreed to preserve — and given the existing

9   retention practices, somebody must have gone out of their way to do it.

10

11   III.

12   **THE COURT CAN AND SHOULD ORDER HUGHES TO PROVIDE**

13   **ACCESS TO ELECTRONIC EVIDENCE DISCOVERY, INC., AT HUGHES'**

14   **EXPENSE, TO REVIEW HUGHES' ELECTRONIC MEDIA FOR**

15   **PURPOSES OF RESPONDING TO DISCOVERY IN THIS ACTION**

16   There is absolutely no doubt but that information maintained in

17   electronic form is subject to discovery. Section 2031 of the California Evidence

18   Code expressly identifies electronic media as a proper subject of discovery.

19   There already is a protective order in place with respect to this action and

20   plaintiff will agree to any reasonable protective arrangements that the Court

21   considers appropriate.[25]

22   There is absolutely no doubt but that Hughes' written discovery

23   responses of July 1 are patently inadequate. Failing even to identify, let alone

24   respond to, the majority of the requests alone confirms the propriety of further

25

26   ───────────────
    [25]   As the history reflected above establishes, plaintiff has throughout offered such an
27   agreement. At this juncture, it should be for the Court to dictate — not Hughes to maybe get
    around to discussing — any limitations upon dissemination of accessed or retrieved materials.
28

                                        -11-   PLAINTIFF'S MEMORANDUM OF POINTS AND
                                               AUTHORITIES IN SUPPORT OF APPLICATION
                                               FOR ORDER COMPELLING PRODUCTION OF
                                               DOCUMENTS AND COMPUTERS

1   relief, even as to those items to which Hughes has deigned to respond, Hughes'

2   answer that it possesses "no responsive documents" is on its face incompatible

3   with Section 2031's requirement that the basis be provided for a determination

4   that a reasonable inquiry has been made. And, when the Court allowed an extra

5   week to permit plaintiff to evaluate that precise question, Hughes and its counsel

6   flatly ignored *multiple* requests to be permitted to evaluate exactly that

7   fundamental question. The evidence now before the Court, in the form of

8   Mr. Hawkins' and Mr. Shaw's declarations, establishes beyond reasonable

9   question that what Hughes has told us is just not true.

10   What Hughes has done is deplorable. What is the remedy? "The

11   sanctions the court may impose are such as are suitable and necessary to enable

12   the party seeking discovery to obtain the objects of the discovery he seeks."

13   Motown Record Corp. v. Superior Court (1984)155 Cal.App.3d 482, 489,

14   *quoted in* Laguna Auto Body v. Farmers Ins. Exchange (1991) 231 Cal.App.3d

15   481, 488. In this case, what plaintiff asks is that he be allowed to have

16   recognized, professional experts in the field of electronic data searches — the

17   respected firm of Electronic Evidence Discovery, Inc. — do exactly that.

18   Plaintiff does not seek a punitive order of default, and does not seek any order

19   disproportionate to the gravity of the delict.

20   The only thing Hughes apparently has to say in its behalf is "too

21   bad; too late." If there is nothing else clear from the history set forth above,

22   however, it is that Hughes courted itself into a position where it could then

23   sandbag plaintiff and plaintiffs counsel. Even after this Court granted an

24   extension of time to allow plaintiffs counsel to try to address the problem created

25   by Hughes' July 1 discovery response, Hughes and its counsel *still* consciously

26   compounded the delay and prejudice inherent in their conduct by the patently

27   evasive ploy of not returning phone calls and suggesting no more than the

28

-12-   PLAINTIFF'S MEMORANDUM OF POINTS AND
AUTHORITIES IN SUPPORT OF APPLICATION
FOR ORDER COMPELLING PRODUCTION OF
DOCUMENTS AND COMPUTERS

1　declarant at Hughes "has not returned a phone call." Does the Court doubt for

2　one moment the ability of Hughes and its counsel to produce that individual if

3　they wanted to do so?

4　　　　　In the *Laguna Auto Body* case the Court of Appeal for the Fourth

5　District unequivocally set to rest any thought that it is somehow acceptable to

6　take advantage of professional courtesies extended in discovery. In that case, the

7　court affirmed a trial court order dismissing an action, as a discovery sanction.

8　The responding party there failed to answer interrogatories, sought and obtained

9　stipulations for extensions that were then not met, and filed evasive responses

10　when something finally was provided. The words of the Court of Appeal are

11　appropriate here:

> This court has traditionally encouraged trial attorneys to
> adhere to their professional responsibilities of
> cooperating, stipulating, and working together within
> the law to move cases toward a prompt and fair
> resolution, consistent with the principle "that justice
> delayed is justice denied. . . ." (Laborers' Internat.
> Union of North America v. El Dorado Landscape Co.
> (1989) 208 Cal.App.3d 993, 1007, 256 Cal.Rptr. 632.)
> As former trial judges and as appellate justices, we
> frown on and condemn the lack of cooperation among
> attorneys in complying with discovery. The failure or
> refusal of a party to submit voluntarily to discovery
> which is inevitable can only be viewed as an attempt to
> harass the opposition or as a technique to churn
> attorney's fees. At the same time, we have never
> approved of attorneys who habitually make unnecessary
> motions for sanctions, greedily seeking the unnecessary
> involvement of the court in the discovery process.
> Accordingly, it is our belief that attorneys who extend
> professional courtesies and cooperate with opposing
> counsel should not be punished for their professionalism
> and patience. We believe equally firmly that attorneys
> who fail to extend common courtesies to their opposi-
> tion, who fail to voluntarily comply with proper dis-
> covery requests and instead obstruct discovery, who fail
> to file, where appropriate, written opposition to motion
> to compel discovery, and who act in defiance of the
> courts, must be sanctioned appropriately. Such is the
> case here.

27　231 Cal.App.3d at 486-87.

PLAINTIFF'S MEMORANDUM OF POINTS AND
AUTHORITIES IN SUPPORT OF APPLICATION
FOR ORDER COMPELLING PRODUCTION OF
DOCUMENTS AND COMPUTERS

-13-

1   The relief that is requested here is precisely co-extensive with the
2   legitimate discovery that has wrongfully and evasively been denied to plaintiff
3   The record reflects that plaintiffs counsel tried very hard to approach this area of
4   discovery in as circumspect and economical a manner as could be devised, by
5   seeking first to identify the specifics of Hughes' systems and only second to seek
6   specific information, this approach was dallied with by Hughes for several
7   months and then flatly rejected, without ever engaging in any meaningful
8   discussion. So, plaintiffs counsel constructed relatively circumspect and precise,
9   albeit somewhat generic, electronic media requests delimited by user and time
10   period (both eminently reasonable and readily distinguishable identifying features
11   under CC:Mail and Profs) — and then is at best to be faulted for accepting the
12   representation of Hughes' counsel that additional time was needed to compile
13   responsive materials.
14   Sanctions such as issue preclusion for failure to produce documents
15   in discovery would be permissible in this instance, *e.g.* Do It Urself Moving &
16   Storage, Inc. v. Brown, Leifer, Slatkin & Berns (1992) 7 Cal.App.4th 27, and
17   the Court definitely will be justified in giving BAJI 2.03 regarding willful
18   suppression of evidence at time of trial. *E.g.,* West v. Johnson & Johnson
19   Products, Inc. (1985) 174 Cal.App.3d 831, 872-74 & n.40 (affirming trial
20   court's giving BAJI 2.03 where defendant shielded documents from discovery
21   and, when they were identified in a deposition eleven days before trial, defense
22   counsel refused to produce them because trial was imminent). But that really
23   does not address the question.
24   The *appropriate* "sanction" is to make Hughes do what it is
25   supposed to do: respond to the discovery and produce the items requested.
26   Since Hughes has demonstrated its refusal to do that left to its own devices, the
27   Court should allow this to be done by the best available means: here, the use of
28

-14-   PLAINTIFF'S MEMORANDUM OF POINTS AND
                AUTHORITIES IN SUPPORT OF APPLICATION
                FOR ORDER COMPELLING PRODUCTION OF
                DOCUMENTS AND COMPUTERS

1   the retained experts that plaintiff has had available for this purpose for two years.

2   And because Hughes had the chance to do it right itself but refused, it is fair and

3   appropriate that the Court visit the cost of this process upon Hughes. There is no

4   reason not to do so and, in fact, it would at this juncture be massively unjust to

5   visit upon the plaintiff the cost of assuring Hughes' compliance with an obligation

6   Hughes has refused to abide to date.

7

8   **IV.**

9   **CONCLUSION**

10   This case is set to commence a lengthy trial. It is unfortunate that

11   Hughes has tried so hard to engage in dilatory gamesmanship as part and parcel

12   of Hughes' openly announced strategy of burying the plaintiff in the cost of

13   litigating against Hughes. But it is neither fair to reward Hughes' blatant strategy

14   nor tolerable to punish the plaintiff by any result less than allowing plaintiff to

15   see what it is that Hughes is so intent upon hiding — or has destroyed. Anything

16   less than an order that Hughes permit and pay for a competent evaluation and

17   review works a sanction upon the plaintiff for the unconscionable and intentional

18   misconduct of the defendant corporation.

19   For the reasons set forth herein it is respectfully requested that the

20   Court should order Hughes to permit access to its electronic storage devices and

21   provide the appropriate password access to permit searches of backups to

22   accurately locate and review information responsive to plaintiffs Second Request

23   for Production; that Hughes be ordered to do so immediately in order to permit

24   prompt evaluation and production of relevant materials for use in this trial; and

25   that the cost of the exercise be borne entirely by Hughes.

26

27

28

-15-

PLAINTIFF'S MEMORANDUM OF POINTS AND
AUTHORITIES IN SUPPORT OF APPLICATION
FOR ORDER COMPELLING PRODUCTION OF
DOCUMENTS AND COMPUTERS

1

2

DATE: JULY 12, 1996

JACKSON, DeMARCO &
PECKENPAUGH
JOHN W. COCHRANE, ESQ.

3

4

BY: _____

5

ATTORNEYS FOR PLAINTIFF
GARRETH E. SHAW

6

7

8

9

10

11

12

13

14

15

16

17

18

19

20

21

22

23

24

25

26

27

28

-16-

PLAINTIFF'S MEMORANDUM OF POINTS AND
AUTHORITIES IN SUPPORT OF APPLICATION
FOR ORDER COMPELLING PRODUCTION OF
DOCUMENTS AND COMPUTERS

> **COMMENT**

The foregoing points and authorities are reproduced with permission from the Law Offices of John W. Cochrane in Irvine, California.

§ 3.18 Special Interrogatories

_____

State Bar No. _____

_____

_____

_____

Attorneys for _____

_____ COURT OF THE STATE OF CALIFORNIA
COUNTY OF _____

_____ _____ Plaintiff(s), v. _____ Defendant(s).	) Case No. _____)) **PLAINTIFF'S SPECIAL**) **INTERROGATORIES**) [Civ. Proc. Code, § 2030])) Set No. ____) Interrogatories Nos. ____-____

REQUESTING PARTY: _____

RESPONDING PARTY: _____

SET NUMBER: _____

INTERROGATORIES: _____ THROUGH _____

___. Identify each authorized user of **YOUR COMPUTER SYSTEM**. For purposes of these Special Interrogatories, certain terms have the following definitions: The term **"COMPUTER SYSTEM"** refers to all file servers, stand-alone computers, workstations, and laptops owned or leased by _____ [Defendant XYZ Corporation] [or physically located at _____]; the term **"YOUR"** refers to Defendant XYZ Corporation; the term **"E-MAIL"** refers to the exchange of text messages and computer files over a communications network, such as a local area network, intranet, extranet, or public network such as the Internet or other online service provider.

___. Describe all hardware modifications to the **COMPUTER SYSTEM** in the past twelve months.

Software Applications

___. Describe the software (e.g., version, manufacturer, any custom modifications) used to create _____ [the Blackacre Request For Proposals].

___. Describe each of the software applications (e.g., version, manufacturer, any custom modifications) installed on [*specify computer*].

___. Describe any and all utility programs (e.g., disk maintenance programs, file recovery programs, network maintenance programs) used to maintain the following computer(s): [*identify computer*].

___. Describe the software (e.g., version, manufacturer, any custom modifications) used to remotely access the **COMPUTER SYSTEM**.

___. Describe all upgrades made to any software on the **COMPUTER SYSTEM** during [*specify period*].

___. Describe any software that has been installed on the **COMPUTER SYSTEM** during [*specify period*].

___. Describe any document management software used by XYZ Corporation during [*specify period*].

___. Identify all escrow agents/services who may have copies of the source code for [*specify software*].

___. Identify all customers who self-escrowed the source code for [*specify software*].

___. Describe the file format used to store information created by [*specify software*].

Security

___. Describe each instance during the last five years in which an unauthorized party gained access to the **COMPUTER SYSTEM**.

___. Describe each instance during the last five years in which a virus or other destructive program caused any data loss on the **COMPUTER SYSTEM**.

___. Describe any disaster recovery plans for the **COMPUTER SYSTEM** that were in effect during [*specify time period*].

___. Describe all security measures relating to employee desktop computers.

___. Describe any methods used during [*specify period*] to monitor employee use of the **COMPUTER SYSTEM**.

___. Describe any methods used during [*specify period*] to monitor employee use of the Internet.

___. Describe any methods used during [*specify period*] to monitor employee use of **E-MAIL**.

___. Describe **YOUR** procedures, if any, for deleting files from the **COMPUTER SYSTEM**.

___. Describe all methods of accessing the **COMPUTER SYSTEM** from outside **YOUR** company (that is, remote access procedures).

___. Describe all methods used to restrict access to the [*specify name of database*] database.

Computer Backups

___. Identify each computer in the **COMPUTER SYSTEM** that is backed up.

___. Describe the backup schedule, if any, for each computer in the **COMPUTER SYSTEM**.

___. Describe the backup procedures, if any, for each computer in the **COMPUTER SYSTEM**.

___. Identify the backup software (e.g., version, manufacturer, any custom modifications) used, if any, for each computer in the **COMPUTER SYSTEM**.

___. Identify the storage location for **YOUR** archival backups.

___. Describe the types of files routinely backed up from the **COMPUTER SYSTEM**.

___. Describe the procedures followed by _____ [XYZ Corporation] during [*specify time period*] for backing up information stored on its computer system(s), including, but not limited to, the frequency of backups, the software used to accomplish the backups, the type of media backups are stored on, and the location where backups are stored.

___. Describe any and all changes to **YOUR** backup procedures in the last twelve months.

Miscellaneous

___. Describe the **COMPUTER SYSTEM(S)** used by [*specify individual*].

___. Describe any methods used to verify the accuracy of information input into the [*identify software application*].

___. Identify all **E-MAIL** addresses used by [*specify individual's name or business name*], including the complete address and the dates during which the address was used.

___. Identify any computers on which a disk maintenance program (e.g., de-fragment, optimize, or compression software) has been run in the last six months.

___. Identify the person(s) responsible for the ongoing operation and maintenance of the **COMPUTER SYSTEM**.

___. Identify each employee in **YOUR** Information Systems Department.

DATED: _____   _____

                                 _____

                                 _____

                                 By _____

                                 Attorneys for _____

§ 3.19 Requests for Admissions

_____

State Bar No. _____

_____

_____

_____

Attorneys for _____

_____ COURT OF THE STATE OF CALIFORNIA
COUNTY OF _____

_____)	Case No. _____
_____)	
Plaintiff(s),)	**PLAINTIFF'S REQUESTS FOR**
)	**ADMISSIONS**
v.)	[Civ. Proc. Code, § 2033]
)	
_____)	SET NO. ____
Defendant(s).)	REQUESTS ____ THROUGH ____

REQUESTING PARTY: _____

RESPONDING PARTY: _____

SET NUMBER: _____

REQUESTS: _____ THROUGH _____

TRUTHFULNESS OF FACTS

Please admit the truthfulness of each of the facts set forth below.

REQUEST FOR ADMISSION NO. 1:

Admit that [*specify employee name*] was assigned the following e-mail address: [*specify e-mail address*].

REQUEST FOR ADMISSION NO. 2:

Admit that [*specify company name*] is the registered owner of the following domain name: [*specify domain name*].

REQUEST FOR ADMISSION NO. 3:

Admit that on or about *[specify date]* the following files were deleted from *[specify user name]*'s desktop computer.

REQUEST FOR ADMISSION NO. 4:

Admit that _____ [XYZ Corporation] had no disaster recovery plan in effect for the **NETWORK** as of *[specify date]*. For purposes of these Requests for Admissions, certain terms have the following definitions: The term "**NET-WORK**" refers to the local area network located at _____, including, but not limited to, all file servers, client computers, workstations, firewalls, routers, proxy servers, Internet servers, mail servers, and application servers.

GENUINENESS OF DOCUMENTS

Please admit the genuineness of each of the documents described below; copies of the documents are attached to this Request.

REQUEST FOR ADMISSION RE GENUINENESS OF DOCUMENT NO. 1:

Admit that the e-mail dated *[specify date]* from *[specify sender]* to *[specify recipient]* is genuine. A copy of the e-mail is attached as Exhibit A.

REQUEST FOR ADMISSION RE GENUINENESS OF DOCUMENT NO. 2:

Admit that the audit trail, with a printout date of *[specify date]*, is genuine. A copy of the audit trail is attached as Exhibit B.

REQUEST FOR ADMISSION RE GENUINENESS OF DOCUMENT NO. 3:

Admit that the printout, dated *[specify date]*, of the files and directories residing on the hard disk of *[specify user]*'s computer is genuine. A copy of the file and directory printout is attached as Exhibit C.

REQUEST FOR ADMISSION RE GENUINENESS OF DOCUMENT NO. 4:

Admit that the Employee Computer Use Policy, dated *[specify date]*, is genuine. A copy of the e-mail is attached as Exhibit D.

REQUEST FOR ADMISSION RE GENUINENESS OF DOCUMENT NO. 5:

Admit that the Disaster Recovery Plan, dated *[specify date]*, is genuine. A copy of the Disaster Recovery Plan is attached as Exhibit E.

DATED: _____   _____

                                  _____

                                  _____

                              By _____

                              Attorneys for _____

§ 3.20 Request for Physical Inspection

_____

State Bar No. _____

_____

_____

_____

Attorneys for _____

_____ COURT OF THE STATE OF CALIFORNIA
COUNTY OF _____

_____	)	Case No. _____
_____	)	
Plaintiff(s),	)	**PLAINTIFF'S FIRST REQUESTS**
v.	)	**FOR EXAMINATION OF**
_____	)	**COMPUTER**
Defendant(s).	)	[Civ. Proc. Code, § 2031]

REQUESTING PARTY: _____

RESPONDING PARTY: _____

TO DEFENDANT _____ AND ITS ATTORNEYS OF RECORD:

Pursuant to section 2031 of the Code of Civil Procedure, Plaintiff _____ ("Plaintiff") requests that Defendant _____ ("Defendant") permit Plaintiff, its attorneys, and consultants to enter onto the premises located at [*specify address*] and inspect the computer described as: [*specify computer to be examined, e.g., serial number, type and model*]. Such entry and inspection will include, but will not necessarily be limited to, the following activities: photographing, physical inspection of network topography, preparation of a network map, and creation of a mirror copy of the hard disk(s).

DATED: _____   _____

                                     _____

                                     _____

                              By _____

                              Attorneys for _____

§ 3.21 Sample Notice of Deposition

1 Joanne M. Frasca (State Bar No. 102684)
   John W. Cochrane (State Bar No. 97135)
2 **FRASCA & ASSOCIATES**
   5 Park Plaza, Suite 1500
3 Irvine, California 92614
   Telephone: (714) 553-8193
4
       -and-
5
   Kenneth Y. Choy
6 **BRAND, FARRAR & BUXBAUM, LLP**
   100 Maiden Lane
7 New York, New York 10038
   Telephone: (212) 504-6109
8
   Attorneys for Defendants
9 REAP TECHNOLOGY CORP., NICHE
   INFORMATION CORP., ANNA LIN and
10 GEONG-SHONG TSENG

11
                UNITED STATES DISTRICT COURT
12
                CENTRAL DISTRICT OF CALIFORNIA
13

14
15 PHILIPS ELECTRONICS NV and   ) Civil Action No. 97-8804 MRP (MANx)
   PHILIPS ELECTRONICS NORTH   )
   AMERICA CORPORATION,   )
16   ) DEFENDANT REAP TECHNOLOGY
               Plaintiffs,   ) CORP.'s NOTICE OF **RESCHEDULED**
17   ) DEPOSITION OF PHILIPS ELECTRONICS
               vs.   ) NV's PERSON MOST KNOWLEDGEABLE
18   ) CONCERNING ELECTRONIC DATA
   REAP TECHNOLOGY CORP., ANNA   ) SYSTEMS AND STORAGE
19 LIN, GEONG-SHONG TSENG aka   )
   TSENG YUNG HSIANG aka FRANK   ) Date: April 28, 1998
20 TSENG, and NICHE INFORMATION   ) Time: 10:00 a.m.
   CORP.,   ) Place: Frasca & Associates
21   )   5 Park Plaza, Suite 1500
               Defendants.   )   Irvine, California 92614
22 _____)

23

24 TO ALL PARTIES AND TO THEIR ATTORNEYS OF RECORD:

25 PLEASE TAKE NOTICE that defendant Reap Technology Corp. will take the deposition upon

26 oral examination of plaintiff Philips Electronics NV on April 30, 1998 commencing at 10:00 a.m.

27 at the offices of Frasca & Associates, 5 Park Plaza, 15th Floor, Irvine, California 92614, which

28 deposition shall continue thereafter, Saturdays, Sundays and holidays excepted, until completed.

   The deposition will be taken before a certified shorthand reporter authorized to administer oaths

1 in the State of California, who will be present at the specified time and place for the deposition.

2   Pursuant to Rule 30(b)(6), Philips Electronics NV shall designate

3 and produce at the deposition one or more of its officers, directors, managing agents, employees,

4 and/or agents who are most qualified to testified on its behalf as to the matters described in

5 Exhibit "1" attached hereto.

6   This Notice of Rescheduled Deposition and attached Exhibit is

7 materially identical to that previously served in this action and taken off calendar, without

8 prejudice, to permit exploration of possible settlement.

9

10 DATED: April 9, 1998   FRASCA & ASSOCIATES

11

12   _____
                                            John W. Cochrane
13   Attorneys for Defendants

14

15

16

17

18

19

20

21

22

23

24

25

26

27

28

-2-

1   **EXHIBIT 1**

2

3   **I.**   **GENERAL DEFINITIONS**

4   A. The terms **"DOCUMENT"** and **"DOCUMENTS"** shall mean and

5 refer to a writing and/or recording as defined in Federal Rules of Evidence, Rule 1001(a),

6 including, without limitation, any printed, written, recorded (in any audio, video, digital or any

7 other electronic or electromagnetic medium), graphic, or other tangible matter from whatever

8 source, however produced or reproduced, whether sent, received, or neither, including, without

9 limitation, the original, all drafts, and any non-identical copies (whether different from the

10 original because of notes made on or attached to the copy or otherwise) thereof.

11   B. The terms **"YOU"**, **"YOUR"** and **"PHILIPS NV"** shall mean and

12 refer to plaintiff Philips Electronics NV, and shall include all of its affiliates, subsidiaries, and

13 parents, and any person acting under the control or on behalf of PHILIPS NV and/or its affiliates,

14 subsidiaries, and/or parents, including their directors, officers, partners, employees,

15 representatives, agents, attorneys and investigators.

16   C. The term **"DEFENDANTS"** shall mean and refer to defendants

17 Reap Technology Corp., Niche Information Corp., Frank Tseng and Anna Lin, conjunctively or

18 disjunctively.

19   D. The term **"COMPLAINT"** shall mean and refer to the Complaint

20 filed by Philips NV in this action on or about December 2, 1997.

21   E. The term **"PHILIPS NA"** shall mean plaintiff Philips Electronics

22 North America.

23   F. The term **"SUBJECT MATTERS"** refers to all allegations of

24 YOUR COMPLAINT herein and to all factual and legal assertions or claims made by YOU in

25 that COMPLAINT and in the preliminary injunction proceedings before he above-captioned

26 Court in this matter.

27   **II.**   **TECHNICAL DEFINITIONS**

28   A. The term **"ACTIVE FILE"** shall mean and refer to any file of

-3-

1   ELECTRONIC DATA that can be utilized by a COMPUTER in any manner without

2   modification and/or re-construction. An ACTIVE FILE is any file of ELECTRONIC DATA that

3   has not been erased or otherwise destroyed and/or damaged and which is readily visible to the

4   operating system and/or the software with which it was created.

5   B. The terms **"ARCHIVE"** and/or **"BACKUP"** shall mean and refer

6   to any processes for copying and storage, whether temporary or permanent, of ELECTRONIC

7   DATA in a COMPUTER or a NETWORK, other than ACTIVE FILES in on-line storage. The

8   term **"BACKUP"** shall mean and refer to all processes used with the purpose of maintaining a

9   copy of ELECTRONIC DATA so that such data can be restored if the primary copies thereof are

10   lost or damaged, or with the purpose of keeping a record of ELECTRONIC DATA on a

11   COMPUTER or a NETWORK at a given point or several given points in time. The terms

12   **"ARCHIVE"** and **"ARCHIVING"** shall mean and refer to any process for maintaining

13   ELECTRONIC DATA off-line, whether referred to as an archive, dump, purge or any other

14   terms, and also to any process or procedure for storage of ELECTRONIC MEDIA which is not

15   in current use on a COMPUTER or a NETWORK.

16   C. The term **"COMPUTER"** shall include, but is not limited to,

17   microcomputers (also known as personal computers), laptop computers, portable computers,

18   notebook computers, palmtop computers, personal digital assistants, minicomputers and

19   mainframe computers.

20   D. The term **"CONFIGURATION"** shall mean and refer to the

21   elements and relationships which make up a COMPUTER or a NETWORK, including, but not

22   limited to, the following information:

23   1.   COMPUTER type, brand, model and serial number;

24   2.   Brand, model, capacity, technical specifications and

25   arrangement of all devices capable of storing and/or retrieving ELECTRONIC DATA in

26   magnetic and/or optical form, including, but not limited to, hard disk drives, floppy diskette

27   drives, Bernoulli Box devices, fixed and portable tape and tape cartridge drives, magneto-optical

28   disks, CD-ROM drives, DVD devices and other such drives (rewritable or WORM), flash

-4-

1   memory, and arrays or combination of such devices;

2   3.   Brand and version of all software, including operating

3   system, private and custom developed applications, commercial applications, shareware and/or

4   work-in-progress; and

5   4.   Communications capability, whether asynchronous and/or

6   synchronous, including, but not limited to, terminal to mainframe emulation, data download

7   and/or upload capability to mainframe, and computer to computer connections via network

8   modem and/or direct connect.

9   E. The term **"DATA"** shall be equivalent to the term "ELECTRONIC

10   DATA" as defined herein.

11   F. The term **"DELETED FILE"** shall mean and refer to any file of

12   ELECTRONIC DATA that has been erased or deleted from the ELECTRONIC MEDIA on

13   which it resided. A DELETED FILE includes any file of ELECTRONIC DATA whose File

14   Allocation Table (FAT) entry has been modified to indicate such data as being deleted and/or

15   which is not readily visible to the operating system and/or the software with which it was

16   created.

17   G. The term **"DOCUMENTATION"**, when used in reference to

18   COMPUTERS, operating systems and utilities, application software and/or hardware devices,

19   shall mean and refer to all DOCUMENTS and files of ELECTRONIC DATA containing written

20   and/or on-line information provided by the manufacturer or seller of the item and/or by in-house

21   sources, including all manuals, guides, instructions, programming notes, protocols, policies,

22   procedures and other sources of information about technical specifications, installation, usage

23   and functioning of the COMPUTER, operating systems and utilities, application software and/or

24   hardware devices.

25   H. The term **"ELECTRONIC DATA"** shall mean information of all

26   kinds created, maintained and/or utilized by COMPUTERS and/or NETWORKS, including all

27   non-identical copies of such information. ELECTRONIC DATA includes, but is not limited to,

28   software (whether private, commercial or work-in-progress), programming notes or instructions,

-5-

1   and input and/or output used or produced by any software or utility (including electronic mail

2   messages and all information referencing or relating to such messages anywhere on a

3   COMPUTER or a NETWORK, word processing documents and all information stored in

4   connection with such documents, electronic spreadsheets, databases including all records and

5   fields and structural information, charts, graphs and outlines, arrays of information and all other

6   information used or produced by any software), operating systems, source code of all types,

7   programming languages, linkers and compilers, peripheral drivers, PIF files, batch files, any and

8   all ASCII files, and any and all miscellaneous files and/or FILE FRAGMENTS, regardless of the

9   MEDIA on which they reside and regardless of whether such ELECTRONIC DATA consists of

10   an ACTIVE FILE, DELETED FILE or FILE FRAGMENT. ELECTRONIC DATA includes

11   any and all information stored on computer memories, hard disks, floppy disks, CD-ROM drives,

12   Bernoulli Box drives and their equivalent, magnetic tape of all types, microfiche, punched cards,

13   punched tape, computer chips, including, but not limited to, EPROM, PROM, RAM and ROM,

14   or on or in any other vehicle for digital data storage and/or transmittal. ELECTRONIC DATA

15   also includes the file, folder tabs and/or containers and labels appended to, or associated with,

16   any physical storage device associated with the information described above.

17   I.   The terms **"ELECTRONIC MEDIA"** and **"MEDIA"** shall mean

18   and refer to any magnetic, optical or other storage device used to record ELECTRONIC DATA.

19   ELECTRONIC MEDIA storage devices may include, but are not limited to, computer memories,

20   hard disk drives, floppy diskettes, CD-ROM disks, Bernoulli Box drives and their equivalent,

21   magnetic tape of all types, microfiche, punched cards, punched tape, computer chips, including,

22   but not limited to, EPROM, PROM, RAM and ROM, or on or in any other vehicle for digital

23   data storage and/or transmittal.

24   J.   The terms **"FILE FRAGMENT"** and **"FRAGMENTARY FILE"**

25   shall mean and refer to any file of ELECTRONIC DATA that exists as a subset of an original

26   ACTIVE FILE. A FILE FRAGMENT may be an ACTIVE FILE or DELETED FILE. The

27   cause of fragmentation resulting in the FRAGMENTARY FILE can include, but is not limited

28   to, manual intervention, electronic surges, and/or physical defects on ELECTRONIC MEDIA.

-6-

1   K. **"IDENTIFY"**, when used in reference to any ELECTRONIC

2   DATA, shall mean to provide information specifying the software and/or operating system under

3   which the DATA was created; the type of DATA (example: word processing document,

4   spreadsheet, database, application program, etc.); and all other means of describing it with

5   sufficient particularity to meet the requirements for its inclusion in a request for production of

6   documents pursuant to the Federal Rules of Civil Procedure.

7   L. The term **"LAYOUT"** shall mean and refer to the interconnections

8   and relationships between COMPUTERS and ELECTRONIC MEDIA in a computer system.

9   The term "LAYOUT" includes, but is not limited to:

10   1.   The physical locations and relationships of all

11   COMPUTERS and/or their peripherals, of all sorts, whether physically attached or not to a given

12   COMPUTER;

13   2.   The nature and type of any sort of Local Area, Wide Area or

14   any other type of NETWORK, whether consisting of physical connections between nodes or not,

15   including the functional and physical relationships of servers, workstations and terminals in each

16   such NETWORK and the brand, name and version of all operating systems in use on the

17   NETWORK as well as the brand, name and version of all application software available through

18   the NETWORK; and

19   3.   The nature, type and functions of all software and/or

20   hardware or devices which operate in a capacity to share or exchange DATA and/or information

21   between two or more COMPUTERS, especially any electronic mail, database or executive

22   information system.

23   M. The term **"NETWORK"** shall mean and refer to any hardware

24   and/or software combination that connects two or more COMPUTERS together and which

25   allows such COMPUTERS to share and/or transfer digital signals between them. For the

26   purposes of this definition, the connection between or among the COMPUTERS need not be

27   either physical or direct (i.e., wireless NETWORKS utilizing radio frequencies and data sharing

28   via indirect routes utilizing modems and phone company facilities). In addition, there need not

-7-

1   be a central file or data server nor a central network operating system in place (i.e., peer-to-peer

2   NETWORKS and NETWORKS utilizing a mainframe host to facilitate DATA transfer). The

3   ability to share DATA is the key factor.

4   N. The term **"ROTATION"** shall mean and refer to any plan, policy,

5   or scheme that involves the re-use of ELECTRONIC MEDIA after it has been used for

6   BACKUP, ARCHIVE or other ELECTRONIC DATA storage purposes, particularly if such re-

7   use results in the alternation and/or destruction of the ELECTRONIC DATA residing on such

8   device prior to or in connection with its re-use.

9   O. The term **"SUPPORT"** shall mean and refer to any help or

10   assistance provided to a user of a COMPUTER by another individual, whether as an official job

11   function or not. Such help or assistance may take the form of, but is not limited to, answering

12   questions, whether in person or via mechanical means; direct intervention; training; software

13   troubleshooting; hardware troubleshooting; programming; systems consulting; maintenance;

14   repair and/or user forums. Providers of support may be employees, contractors and/or other third

15   party providers.

16   P. The term **"ENCRYPTION"** shall mean and refer to any system,

17   program or device utilized to obtain, impart or maintain security to electronic data transmitted or

18   stored in or by means of YOUR COMPUTERS.

19

20   **III.**   **MATTERS ON WHICH EXAMINATION IS REQUESTED**

21   A. The CONFIGURATION, DOCUMENTATION and LAYOUT of

22   the COMPUTERS and/or NETWORKS used by PHILIPS NV to create, process and/or store

23   ELECTRONIC DATA referencing or relating to the SUBJECT MATTERS.

24   B. ARCHIVING and BACKUP systems and procedures available on

25   COMPUTERS and/or NETWORKS used by PHILIPS NV to create, process and/or store

26   ELECTRONIC DATA referencing or relating to the SUBJECT MATTERS, including, but not

27   limited to:

28   1.   The name and version number of all software used for

-8-

1　ARCHIVING and/or BACKUP purposes;

2　　　　　　　　　　　　2.　　DOCUMENTATION of the ARCHIVING and/or BACKUP

3　systems and procedures, both on line and in paper form;

4　　　　　　　　　　　　3.　　The criteria used to classify and move sets of ELECTRONIC

5　DATA for ARCHIVING;

6　　　　　　　　　　　　4.　　BACKUP schedules and protocols;

7　　　　　　　　　　　　5.　　The manner in which ARCHIVE and BACKUP sets of

8　ELECTRONIC DATA are organized, and tracking and logging of such DATA;

9　　　　　　　　　　　　6.　　Storage of and access to ARCHIVE and BACKUP sets of

10　ELECTRONIC DATA, including the manner in which such DATA are written and retrieved and

11　use of compression routines;

12　　　　　　　　　　　　7.　　Storage MEDIA used for ARCHIVE and BACKUP

13　purposes, including the manufacturer, model and type of such MEDIA;

14　　　　　　　　　　　　8.　　Records of the existence, location and custodianship of

15　ARCHIVE and BACKUP MEDIA, including inventories, databases, catalogs, logs, lists, and

16　indexes of such MEDIA; and

17　　　　　　　　　　　　9.　　MEDIA labeling conventions and all other codes and

18　abbreviations used for ARCHIVE and BACKUP purposes.

19　　　　　　　　　　C.　Record retention plans, policies and procedures of PHILIPS NV

20　applicable to ELECTRONIC DATA referencing or relating to the SUBJECT MATTERS,

21　including, but not limited to:

22　　　　　　　　　　　　1.　　The contents of YOUR retention plans, policies and

23　procedures;

24　　　　　　　　　　　　2.　　Implementation of YOUR retention plans, policies and

25　procedures;

26　　　　　　　　　　　　3.　　DOCUMENTATION, whether on line or in paper form, of

27　YOUR retention plans, policies and procedures; and

28　　　　　　　　　　　　4.　　Whether any changes have been made in YOUR retention

-9-

1 plans, policies and procedures since January 1, 1992 and, if so, the nature of the changes and who

2 authorized them.

3   D. All steps taken by YOU to preserve ELECTRONIC DATA as

4 evidence in connection with this action, including all steps taken to prevent or stop deletion,

5 overwriting or modification of ELECTRONIC DATA which may be relevant to this action.

6   E. Deletion, erasure and/or destruction of storage MEDIA including

7 BACKUP and/or ARCHIVE sets of ELECTRONIC DATA referencing or relating to the

8 SUBJECT MATTERS; damage to and/or destruction of MEDIA containing such ELECTRONIC

9 DATA; and logs and records of such activity.

10   F. The system utilities and application software programs available on

11 COMPUTERS and NETWORKS used by PHILIPS NV which have the capability of searching,

12 retrieving, copying, writing, offloading and/or exporting ELECTRONIC DATA referencing or

13 relating to the SUBJECT MATTERS.

14   G. The electronic mail and/or messaging systems used by PHILIPS

15 NV to transmit or receive ELECTRONIC DATA or other information referencing or relating to

16 the SUBJECT MATTERS, including, but not limited to, internal electronic mail and external

17 electronic mail communications. (For the purpose of this item, "messaging systems" include

18 paging systems, groupware, and other systems for which one of the primary purposes is

19 transmission of documents or messages among users of YOUR COMPUTERS and/or

20 NETWORK or between users of YOUR COMPUTER and/or NETWORK and other such

21 systems.) The deponent(s) should have knowledge regarding all aspects of YOUR electronic

22 mail system(s), including, but not limited to, the following:

23   1.   Hardware and software used for electronic mail and

24 messaging functions;

25   2.   DOCUMENTATION for the electronic mail and messaging

26 system and its usage;

27   3.   The nature and the location of directories and/or lists of

28 electronic mail or messaging system users, and all systems, codes and numbers identifying users;

-10-

1   4.   Fields, headings and other subdivisions appearing in

2   electronic mail messages, including, but not limited to, message numbers, message trails and/or

3   sequences, message titles and subject matter lines, locations of senders and recipients, dates of

4   sending and receipt of messages;

5   5.   Technical specifications for the creation, transmission and

6   storage of messages, including, but not limited to, specifications as to host systems, gateways

7   and routers, and ELECTRONIC DATA files or sets in which messages are stored and the

8   location of such DATA on the system;

9   6.   Message logging functions;

10   7.   ELECTRONIC DATA storage, BACKUP and ARCHIVING

11   activity specifically relating to electronic mail and other messaging systems, including retention

12   plans, guidelines, rules, standards, protocols, policies and procedures;

13   8.   BACKUP and/or ARCHIVE MEDIA specifically relating to

14   electronic mail and other messaging systems, including inventories, databases, catalogs, logs,

15   lists, indexes, and other DOCUMENTATION;

16   9.   Format and character sets used to write messages, and

17   encoding, ENCRYPTION, decoding and decryption of messages; and

18   10.   Outside services for electronic mail and/or for information

19   transmission and retrieval with which YOUR COMPUTERS and/or NETWORK is

20   interconnected, including the name of the service, the time period during which YOUR

21   COMPUTERS and/or NETWORK has been connected to it, the purposes for which the outside

22   services are used, and which users of YOUR COMPUTERS and/or NETWORK are able to use

23   such services.

24   H. Policies, procedures, guidelines, rules, standards, and protocols

25   relating to the functioning and use of personal COMPUTERS and local area NETWORKS which

26   may have been used to create or process ELECTRONIC DATA referencing or relating to the

27   SUBJECT MATTERS, including, but not limited to:

28   1.   Availability and usage of particular application software to

-11-

1   users;

2   2.   Directory organization access, and naming conventions;

3   3.   Storage of files of ELECTRONIC DATA at local

4   workstations and/or on NETWORK servers;

5   4.   Codes, abbreviations and naming conventions applicable to

6   file and extension names;

7   5.   Diskette storage and labeling; and

8   6.   Logging and recording user and file activity.

9   I.   Systems for storing and retrieving recordings of telephone calls.

10   J.   Any other information needed to identify, access, copy and read

11   ELECTRONIC DATA referenced in the above items.

12   K.   Any other information needed to identify, access, copy and read

13   ELECTRONIC DATA reflecting electronically-facilitated communications (via e-mail or

14   otherwise) among PHILIPS NV personnel concerning DEFENDANTS, or any of them, or the

15   events and transactions encompassed within the allegations of PHILIPS NV's Complaint herein.

16

17

18

19

20

21

22

23

24

25

26

27

28

-12-

▶ **COMMENT**

The foregoing deposition notice is reproduced with permission from the Law Offices of John W. Cochrane in Irvine, California.

§ 3.22 Sample Deposition Outline

- Computer-related experience of deponent
  - Formal training (degrees, certificate programs, continuing education)
  - Positions held
  - Descriptions of job functions
  - Length of employment
  - Reasons for leaving prior employers
- Description of computer system
  - General description of network topology (network operating system, type of file server, client computer operating system)
  - Recent instances of hardware failures
  - Existence of dial-up access to the network
- Security of computer system
  - Physical security measures (access control systems, such as passwords and key cards)
  - Electronic protection (firewalls, virus software, intrusion detection software)
  - Instances of attempted unauthorized access
  - Prior instances of data loss
  - Security policies
- Backup Procedures
  - Identify systems that are backed up
  - Frequency of backups
  - Location of backup tapes
  - Instances of loss of backup data
  - Software used to create backups
  - Internet backups
  - Backup policies
  - Changes in backup procedures in the last twelve months

- Software used to create relevant data
    - Name of vendor and program
    - Version number of program
    - Service/maintenance updates
    - Any custom modifications to the program
    - Procedures for ensuring accurate entry of data
    - Procedures for ensuring accuracy of output
    - File format for data storage

§ 3.23　Preservation Order

_____ COURT OF THE STATE OF CALIFORNIA
COUNTY OF _____

_____)	Case No. _____
_____)	
Plaintiff(s),　　　　　　)	**ORDER FOR PRESERVATION**
v.　　　　　　　)	**OF RECORDS**
_____)	
Defendant(s).　　　　　　)	

IT IS ORDERED:

1. <u>Preservation.</u> During the pendency of this litigation, and for _____ days after entry of a final judgment or order closing all cases, each of the parties herein and its/his/her respective officers, agents, servants, employees, and attorneys, and all persons in active concert or participation with it/him/her/them who receive actual notice of this order by personal service or otherwise, are restrained and enjoined from altering, interlining, destroying, permitting the destruction of, or in any other fashion changing any "Document" in the actual or constructive care, custody, or control of such person, wherever such document is physically located, or irrevocably changing the form or sequence of the files in which the document is located. Such persons are also enjoined from changing the location of any such documents except to facilitate compilation, review, or production (as by filing in a document depository).

2. <u>Scope.</u>

(a) "Document" shall mean any writing, drawing, film, videotape, chart, photograph, phonograph record, tape record, mechanical or electronic sound recording or transcript thereof, retrievable data (whether carded or tape coded, electrostatically or electromagnetically recorded, or otherwise), or other data compilation from which information can be obtained, including (but not limited to) notices, memoranda, diaries, minutes, purchase records, purchase invoices, market data, correspondence, computer storage tapes, computer storage cards or disks, books, journals, ledgers, statements, reports, invoices, bills, vouchers, worksheets, jottings, notes, letters, abstracts, audits, charts, checks, diagrams, drafts, recordings, instructions, lists, logs, orders, recitals, telegram messages, telephone bills and logs, resumes, summaries, compilations, computations, and other formal and informal writings or tangible preservations of information.

(b) This Order pertains only to documents containing information that may be relevant to, or may lead to the discovery of information relevant to [*describe general subject matter of litigation*] [which have been written or generated after _____ (*date*), and before _____ (*date*)]. Any document described or referred to in any discovery request or response made during this litigation shall, from the time of the request or response, be treated for purposes of this order as containing such information unless and until the court rules such information to be irrelevant.

(c) Counsel are directed to confer to resolve questions as to what documents are outside the scope of this order or otherwise need not be preserved and as to an earlier date for permissible destruction of particular categories of documents. If counsel are unable to agree, any party may apply to the court for clarification or relief from this order upon reasonable notice. A party failing, within sixty (60) days after receiving written notice from another party that specified documents will be destroyed, lost, or otherwise altered pursuant to routine policies and programs, to indicate in writing its objection shall be deemed to have agreed to such destruction.

3. Implementation. Each party will, within ten (10) days after receiving this Order, designate an individual who shall be responsible for ensuring that the party carries out the requirements of this order.

Dated:_____   _____
                              JUDGE OF THE SUPERIOR COURT

▶ **COMMENT**

This example preservation order is based in large part on the Order for Preservation of Records provided in the *Manual of Complex Litigation, Third,* by the Federal Judicial Center.

---

4 OPEN RECORDS STATUTES

A. Text

§ 4.01 Access to Government Records

Many states, including California, and the federal government have enacted open records statutes to provide citizens with access to information created and collected by the government. The basic purpose of these statutes is to "ensure an informed citizenry, vital to the functioning of a democratic society, needed to check against corruption and to hold governors accountable to the governed." (*NLRB v. Robbins Tire & Co.* (1978) 437 U.S. 214, 242 [98 S.Ct. 2311, 57 L.Ed.2d 159].)

This chapter provides an overview of the California and federal open records statutes and their potential application to the discovery of electronic evidence. These statutes provide an additional means beyond the subpoena for conducting discovery from a third party, namely the government. Moreover, these open records statutes authorize inspection requests even when no action is pending.

§ 4.02 Public Records Act

[A] In General

Under the California Public Records Act (CPRA) (Gov. Code, § 6250 et seq.), any member of the public may, on request and subject to certain limitations, inspect and obtain copies of "any writing containing information relating to the conduct of the public's business prepared, owned, used, or retained by any state or local agency regardless of physical form or characteristics." (Gov. Code, § 6252, subd. (d).) Each agency, upon any request for a copy of records, must determine within 10 days of receipt of the request whether it will comply with the request and must immediately notify the person making the request of the agency's determination and the reasons therefor. (Gov. Code, § 6256.)

Certain state and local bodies must establish written guidelines for accessibility of records. (Gov. Code, § 6253.) A copy of these guidelines must be posted in a conspicuous public place at the offices of these bodies, and a copy of the guidelines made available upon request free of charge to any person requesting that body's records. (See Appendix D for a list of California state and local bodies required to have such guidelines.)

The CPRA is analogous to the federal Freedom of Information Act (FOIA), discussed in Section 4.03.

[B] What May Be Inspected?

The CPRA defines the types of writings that may be inspected and copied in broad terms as "handwriting, typewriting, printing, photostating, photographing, and every other means of recording upon any form of communication or representation, including letters, words, pictures, sounds, or symbols, or combination thereof, and all papers, maps, magnetic or paper tapes, photographic films and prints, magnetic or punched cards, discs, drums, and other documents." (Gov. Code, § 6252, subd. (e).) The CPRA was intended to encompass records stored on computers; this is confirmed by the references to magnetic media in the definition of "writing" and the reference to computer data in Government Code section 6256, which provides that each agency has discretion in determining the form in which computer data will be produced.

Although there is little California law regarding the application of the CPRA to electronic records, similar statutes in other states have been used to gain production of purely electronic records. For example, a newspaper cited a state public records act as the basis for its request for access to a city to produce cookie, browser history, and cache files for certain employees. The newspaper contended the files would show that public employees were using their computers to visit Web sites with sports, entertainment, and sexually explicit content on government time. The city claimed the files were not public records and refused the request. The newspaper brought suit to compel production. (See *The Putnam Pit Inc. v. City of Cookeville* (M.D. Tenn. 1998) 23 F. Supp.2d 822.)

▶ COMMENT

While most information stored on computers is subject to inspection under the CPRA, one notable exception is software developed by a state or local agency. Such software is not considered a "public record" under the CPRA. The agency developing the software is free to sell, lease, or license its work for commercial or noncommercial use. (Gov. Code, § 6254.9.)

[C] Records Exempt from Disclosure

The inspection rights conferred by the CPRA are not absolute. Certain categories of documents may be withheld by the agency (Gov. Code, § 6254), including, but not limited to, the following:

- Preliminary drafts, notes, or interagency or intra-agency memoranda that are not retained by the public agency in the ordinary course of business, provided that the public interest in withholding those records clearly outweighs the public interest in disclosure. (Gov. Code, § 6254, subd. (a).)

* Records relating to pending litigation in which the public agency is a party. (Gov. Code, § 6254, subd. (b).)

* Personnel, medical, or similar files, the disclosure of which would constitute an unwarranted invasion of personal privacy. (Gov. Code, § 6254, subd. (c).)

* The attorney-client privilege and work product doctrine. (Gov. Code, §§ 6254, subd. (k), 6254.25.)

* Information required from any taxpayer in connection with the collection of local taxes that is received in confidence and the disclosure of the information to other persons would result in unfair competitive disadvantage to the person supplying the information. (Gov. Code § 6254, subd. (i).)

* Library circulation records. (Gov. Code § 6254, subd. (j).)

* Any other document that "on the facts of the particular case the public interest served by not making the record public clearly outweighs the public interest served by disclosure of the record." (Gov. Code, § 6255.)

If only a portion of a document is exempt from production, the public agency must redact the exempt portion and produce the remainder of the document. (Gov. Code, § 6257.)

[D] Enforcing Inspection Right

Any person may institute proceedings for injunctive or declarative relief or writ of mandate to enforce his or her right to inspect or to receive a copy of any public record or class of public records available under the CPRA. The times for responsive pleadings and for hearings in such proceedings will be set by the judge assigned to the matter with a view to obtaining a decision at the earliest possible time. (Gov. Code, § 6258.) The venue for such a proceeding will be in the county where the records or some portion of them are located. (Gov. Code, § 6259, subd. (a).) If the plaintiff is successful in enforcing its inspection right, the court must award reasonable attorney fees and costs. If the plaintiff's action is deemed frivolous, the court must award attorney fees and costs to the public agency. (Gov. Code, § 6259, subd. (d).)

[E] Review of Trial Court's Decision

If the trial court finds that the public official's decision to refuse disclosure is not justified, the judge will order the public official to make the record public. If the judge determines that the public official was justified in refusing to make the record public, the judge will return the document to the public official without disclosing its contents with an order supporting the decision refusing disclosure. (Gov. Code, § 6259, subd. (c).)

An order of the trial court, either directing disclosure by a public official or supporting the decision of the public official refusing disclosure, is not a final judgment or order within the meaning of Code of Civil Procedure section 904.1, from which an appeal may be taken. Instead, the order is immediately reviewable by petition to the appellate court for the issuance of an extraordinary writ. To obtain review of the order, a party must file a petition within 20 days after service upon him or her of a written notice of entry of the order, or within such further time not exceeding an additional 20 days as the trial court may for good cause allow. If the notice is served by mail, the period within which to file the petition will be increased by 5 days. A stay of an order or judgment will not be granted unless the petitioning party demonstrates it will otherwise sustain irreparable damage and probable success on the merits. Any person who fails to obey the order of the court will be cited to show cause why he or she is not in contempt of court. (Gov. Code, § 6259, subd. (c).)

§ 4.03 Freedom of Information Act

[A] In General

Like the CPRA, the federal Freedom of Information Act ("FOIA") (5 U.S.C.A. § 552) requires the mandatory disclosure of public information, subject to certain exemptions. Among other things, executive branch agencies are required to publish their final opinions, statements of policy and interpretations, and administrative staff materials. (5 U.S.C.A. § 552, subd. (a)(2).) Other records require the requesting party to submit a written request in conformance with rules published by the agency in the Federal Register. (5 U.S.C.A. § 552, subd. (a)(1).) A copy of the FOIA, including the recent amendments known as the Electronic Freedom of Information Act, is included in Appendix B.

On receipt of an inspection request, an agency has 20 business days to decide whether it will comply with the request and to notify the requesting party of its decision and the reasoning therefor. In unusual circumstances, the foregoing time limit may be extended by the agency on written notice to the requesting party. But no such extension may be greater than 10 business days. (5 U.S.C.A. § 552, subd. (a)(6)(A)–(B).) "Unusual circumstances" means the following, but only to the extent reasonably necessary to the proper processing of the request (5 U.S.C.A. § 552, subd. (a)(6)(B)(iii)):

- The need to search for and collect the requested records from facilities separate from the office processing the request;

- The need to search for, collect, and examine voluminous material; or

- The need to consult with another agency having an interest in the request.

If the records are sought for commercial use, the requesting party must pay "reasonable standard charges" for document search, duplication, and review. If the records are to be used for educational or noncommercial scientific purposes, the requesting party will only be charged for the cost of duplicating the documents. The fees for all other requests will be the reasonable standard charges for document search and duplication. (5 U.S.C.A. § 552, subd. (a)(4)(A)(ii).)

💣 WARNING

In preparing a request under the FOIA, the documents or information to be produced should be described with as much particularity as possible. The scope of the request defines the scope of the search to be made by the agency. Agencies are generally not obligated to search alternate spellings, secondary references, or other potential sources of information to find responsive documents. (*Maynard v. CIA* (1st Cir. 1993) 986 F.2d 547, 560.) Indeed, agencies are "not obliged to look beyond the four corners of the request for leads to the location of responsive documents." (*Kowalczyk v. Department of Justice* (DC Cir. 1996) 73 F.3d 386, 389.)

[B] Access to Electronic Records

The original version of the FOIA enacted in 1966 was silent on the issue of information stored electronically. As computerization of government records became commonplace, there was substantial confusion as to whether such records were subject to production under the FOIA. There was a concern that agencies might hide information in their computers and refuse disclosure requests. (L. Sorokin, *The Computerization of Government Information: Does It*

Circumvent Public Access Under the Freedom of Information Act and the Depository Library Program? 24 Colum. J.L. & Soc. Probs. 267, 277 (1991).) However, a number of courts required agencies to provide electronic records in response to FOIA requests in the same way as paper-based documents. (*Long v. Internal Revenue Service* (9th Cir. 1979) 596 F.2d 362, 365; *Yeager v. Drug Enforcement Administration* (D.C. Cir. 1982) 678 F.2d 315, 321 (there is no difference whether an agency stores its records in paper form or electronically; both are subject to the FOIA).)

Many of the unresolved issues regarding the application of the FOIA to electronic records were resolved by the enactment in 1996 of the Electronic Freedom of Information Act (EFOIA), which constituted various amendments to the existing FOIA. With regard to electronic records, the EFOIA accomplished three important goals. First, it made clear that electronic records are accessible under the FOIA: " 'record' and any other term used . . . in reference to information includes information that would be an agency record . . . maintained by an agency in any format, including an electronic format." (5 U.S.C.A. § 552, subd. (f)(2).) Second, it requires agencies to provide information in electronic format when technically feasible: "[A]n agency shall provide the record in any form or format requested by the person if the record is readily reproducible by the agency in that form or format." (5 U.S.C.A. § 552, subd. (a)(3)(B)–(C).) This second goal reversed a presumption that agencies had the discretion to determine the format of the records provided under the FOIA. (*Dismukes v. Department of Interior* (D.D.C. 1984) 603 F.Supp. 760.) Agencies frequently relied upon this presumption to deny access to electronic records. Finally, the EFOIA encourages agencies to place their records online when possible. (5 U.S.C.A. § 552, subd. (a)(2).) Being able to request the production of information in electronic form will be of significant benefit when voluminous records or large databases of information are to be produced.

▶ **COMMENT**

In the event information is produced in electronic form, it is essential to determine the format of the information (for example, the word processing, database, e-mail ,or spreadsheet program that created the records). In many instances the format can be determined by examining the file name or viewing the contents of the file. In other cases, the requesting party may have to consult with the producing agency to ascertain the proper format. In certain cases, the software that created the records will be proprietary and not generally available or available only at a significant cost. In such cases, the requesting party should inquire whether the software can export records to a known format (for example, ASCII). If exporting to a known format is not possible, the requesting party may have to settle for production in hardcopy form.

[C] Records Exempt from Disclosure

Nine categories of information are exempt from mandatory disclosure under the FOIA, however an agency has discretionary power to produce information for eight of the categories. The range of material subject to the exemptions is substantial. The general categories of exempt material are as follows (5 U.S.C.A. § 552, subd. (b)(1)–(9)):

- National security or foreign policy.
- Internal personnel rules and practices of an agency.
- Material exempted from disclosure by statute.
- Trade secrets and commercial or financial information obtained from a person and privileged or confidential.
- Agency memoranda and correspondence that would not otherwise be available for review.
- Personnel and medical files, the disclosure of which would constitute an unwarranted invasion of privacy.
- Certain law enforcement records.
- Certain reports prepared in connection with the regulation or supervision of financial institutions.
- Geological and geophysical information.

If only a portion of a document is exempt from production, the agency must redact the exempt portion and produce the remainder of the document. The amount of information deleted must be indicated on the released portion of the document, unless doing so would jeopardize an interest protected by the redaction. (5 U.S.C.A. § 552, subd. (b).)

[D] Enforcing Inspection Right

If the request for inspection is denied in whole or in part, the requesting party may appeal to the head of the agency processing the request. (5 U.S.C.A. § 552, subd. (a)(6)(A)(i).) If the denial of the inspection request is upheld by the head of the agency, the agency is obligated to inform the requesting party that it may seek judicial review of the denial by filing a complaint in the federal district court in the district in which the requesting party resides, or where the records are located, or the District of Columbia. (5 U.S.C.A. § 552, subds. (a)(4)(B), (a)(6)(A)(ii).) The district court may determine the matter *de novo* and, if appropriate, issue an order compelling the agency to produce the records. (5 U.S.C.A. § 552, subd. (a)(4)(B).) The court may also award a successful plaintiff its reasonable attorney fees and costs. (5 U.S.C.A. § 552, subd. (a)(4)(E).)

B. Forms

§ 4.04 Public Records Act Request

[*Date*]

_____

_____

_____

Re: <u>Public Records Act Request</u>

Dear _____:

  Pursuant to the California Public Records Act (Gov. Code, § 6250 et seq.), we request that the documents described below be made available for inspection and copying at 10:00 a.m. on _____ [*date*], at your office located at _____:

  [*Provide reasonable description of the documents to be produced*, *e.g.*, printouts of the current history files for each employee having access to the Internet in _____ (*specify name of agency*). For purposes of this request, a "history" file contains a listing of each site on the Internet visited by a particular user during a defined period of time (usually 1 to 4 weeks). Such files are usually, but not always, stored on the employee's individual hard disk.]

  In furtherance of your obligations under Government Code section 6256, we request that you provide a written response to this request within ten (10) days of receipt. In your written response, please identify any fees or costs that will be incurred in complying with this request. In particular, please notify us immediately if the total charges for responding to this request will exceed _____ ($____).

  If you have any questions regarding the foregoing, please do not hesitate to call me. Thank you for your assistance in this matter.

Sincerely,

_____

§ 4.05 Freedom of Information Request

[*Date*]

_____

_____

_____

Attn: Freedom of Information Act Officer

Re: Freedom of Information Act Request

Dear _____:

This request is made pursuant to the Freedom of Information Act (5 U.S.C.A. § 552).

We request that a copy of the following documents:

[*Provide reasonable description of the documents to be produced, e.g.*, all agency related e-mail sent by or addressed to _____ (*specify individual*) from _____ (*specify start date*) to _____ (*specify end date*).]

In furtherance of your obligations under section 552 of Title 5 of the United States Code, we request that you provide a written response to this request within twenty (20) business days of receipt. For purposes of assessing any applicable fees, please be advised that this request is made by a [*provide description of requesting entity, e.g.*, a private corporation for its business purposes, a non-profit educational institution, or news organization as part of its news gathering efforts and not for commercial use]. Please notify us immediately if the total fees for responding to this request will exceed _____ ($____).

If you have any questions regarding the foregoing, please do not hesitate to call me. Thank you for your assistance in this matter.

Sincerely,

_____

[*If required by the agency's applicable rules, include the following declaration*]
I declare under penalty of perjury under the laws of the State of California that the foregoing is true and correct.

_____

[*Signature of declarant*]

5 LIMITS ON DISCOVERABILITY

A. Text

§ 5.01 Overview

Although other privileges and exclusions may apply (see, e.g., Evid. Code, §§ 990 (physician-patient privilege), 1010 (psychotherapist-patient privilege), 1030 (clergyman-penitent privilege)), there are three primary limitations on the discoverability of electronic evidence: the attorney-client privilege, the work product doctrine, and the protection of trade secrets and other proprietary information. This chapter provides an overview of each of these protections and discusses circumstances under which otherwise protected communications or information may be discovered.

§ 5.02 Attorney-Client Privilege

[A] In General

To encourage open and frank communication between attorneys and their clients, the law has long recognized the need to protect such communications from disclosure. The attorney-client privilege protects confidential communications between clients and their lawyers, provided the communications are not disclosed to third persons other than those who are present to further the interest of the client or those who are necessary to the transmission of the communication or those who are present to assist the attorney. (Evid. Code, § 952.) The client is the holder of the privilege and is the only one that can waive it. (Evid. Code, §§ 912, 953.) Waiver of the privilege occurs when a significant part of the communication is voluntarily disclosed. (Evid. Code, § 912; see, e.g., *Southern California Gas. Co. v. Public Utilities Comm'n* (1990) 50 Cal.3d 31, 49 [265 Cal.Rptr. 801].) Such disclosure vitiates one of the essential elements of the privilege: confidentiality.

[B] E-mail Communications

A relatively recent amendment to the Evidence Code makes clear that use of electronic communications methods by attorneys and their clients will not, in and of themselves, prevent application of the privilege: "A communication between a client and his or her lawyer is not deemed lacking in confidentiality solely because the communication is transmitted by facsimile, cellular telephone, or other electronic means between client and his or her lawyer." (Evid. Code, § 952.) This does not mean, however, that if the client or attorney is careless in the use of these new methods of communication that the privilege will still be available.

As discussed above, one of the key requirements for the attorney-client privilege to attach is that the communication be "confidential." If the communication is not confidential, if it is revealed to unnecessary third parties, the privilege may be deemed waived. (Evid. Code, § 912.) Communications between client and attorney using e-mail raises a number of questions regarding the "confidentiality" requirement that are not answered by Evidence Code section 952. For example:

- Are messages sent over an inherently insecure public network like the Internet "confidential"?

- Should attorney-client communications sent over a public network be encrypted?

- Is the privilege lost if an attorney-client e-mail is misaddressed and delivered to an unrelated third party? What if the message is properly delivered, but the authorized recipient shares the message with persons unnecessary to the communication?

- Is the privilege lost if a business stores its attorney-client e-mail in the same computer directory as all other e-mail and such directory may be accessed by all employees and the business's independent contractors?

- Is the privilege lost if a system error causes a message to be misdelivered to an unrelated third party or is read by a system operator for purposes of troubleshooting the e-mail system?

Even with the guidance provided by the amendment to section 952, the answers to these questions remains unclear. Because the use of e-mail for attorney-client communications is still a relatively new phenomenon, few courts have had an opportunity to consider these issues. However, we can expect courts to resolve such issues by focusing on whether the client, the holder of the privilege, evinced an intent to keep the communications confidential, as required by Evidence Code section 952. One aspect of a court's analysis will likely be whether the client took or failed to take precautions to protect the confidentiality of the electronic communications. (See, e.g., *Hartman v. El Paso Natural Gas Co.* (1988) 107 N.M. 679 [763 P.2d 1144] (identifying the reasonableness of precautions taken to prevent inadvertent disclosure as a factor in determining whether the attorney-client privilege has been lost).)

If a communication was disclosed by a genuine mistake and there is little evidence the client was negligent in revealing the message, the privilege will probably be upheld. (See, e.g., *American Mutual Liability Ins. Co. v. Superior Court* (1974) 38 Cal.App.3d 579, 595 [113 Cal.Rptr. 561].) But the result is by no means certain. (See, e.g., *Aerojet-Gen. Corp. v. Transport Indemnity Insurance* (1993) 18 Cal.App.4th 996, 1006 [22 Cal.Rptr.2d 862] (opposing party allowed to use otherwise privileged documents received through inadvertence).) If there is evidence the client failed to act reasonably to protect the confidentiality of the communication, a court may be more inclined to rule the privilege has been waived.

Based on the foregoing discussion, attorney-client e-mail may be subject to discovery under any of the following circumstances:

1. Messages are accidentally delivered to unintended parties.

2. Messages are received by the intended parties, but later forwarded to third parties.

3. Messages are stored where they are accessible by unnecessary third parties (for example, in publicly accessible computer directories; such practices are common in most organizations).

4. Messages are transmitted in such a way that it would be unreasonable for the client to believe the communications would be confidential.

§ 5.03 Work Product Doctrine

[A] In General

The work product doctrine was created to further the state policy to (1) preserve the rights of attorneys to prepare cases for trial with the degree of privacy necessary to encourage them to prepare their cases thoroughly and to investigate not only the favorable but the unfavorable aspects of those cases and (2) to prevent attorneys from taking undue advantage of their adversary's industry and efforts. (Code Civ. Proc., § 2018, subd. (a).) Unlike the attorney-client privilege, the work product doctrine is a qualified privilege. In certain circumstances a court may order disclosure. Whether work product may be subject to disclosure will depend on the type of material involved. Any writing that reflects an attorney's impressions, conclusions, opinions, or legal research or theories is absolutely privileged and, therefore, not subject to discovery "under any circumstances." (Code Civ. Proc., § 2018, subd. (c).) Any other work product is entitled to only a qualified privilege. A court may order disclosure if it determines "that denial of discovery will unfairly prejudice the party seeking discovery in preparing that party's claim or defense or will result in an injustice." (Code Civ. Proc., § 2018, subd. (b); see, e.g., *People v. Superior Court* (1995) 44 Cal.App.4th 1757 [44 Cal.Rptr.2d 734] (work product is discoverable to extent that denial of disclosure will prejudice the party seeking discovery or work an injustice, and the burden is on the party asserting the privilege to prove the material in question is work product and therefore privileged).)

[B] Discovery of Computerized Litigation Support Databases

Businesses and their attorneys have embraced computer technology as an invaluable aid in organizing and managing document intensive litigation. Litigation support systems, which are essentially database programs, provide a means for instantly searching large quantities of documents for key words and quickly retrieving matching documents. The benefits provided by these systems do not come without a price. Litigation support databases are becoming a frequent target in discovery. Whether these databases must be produced will depend on the level of involvement the attorney has in their creation.

Most litigation support systems fall into one of two categories: (1) full text retrieval and (2) index or summary format.

Full text retrieval systems require each document to be electronically scanned into the database. The scanning process is accomplished using optical character recognition (OCR) software that converts the document into computer readable text. Each word, phrase, and number in the document is then indexed for later searching. The foregoing process is extremely labor intensive and costly. Under ideal conditions, most OCR software is 95-99% accurate. While these numbers may appear impressive, the results are not: every paragraph of text scanned will likely contain a dozen or more errors. Reviewing the scanned text for these errors and correcting them can be very time consuming.

Index or summary systems require a paralegal, attorney, or, in some instances, an employee of the client, to provide a summary description of each document. The summary and other information about each document are usually entered into a number of fields in the database, which may later be searched for key words. Typical fields include the following: "from," "to," "cc," "date," "type of document" (for example, letter, memo, e-mail, agreement), and "summary." In addition, a field is usually included to tie each document to a particular issue or witness in the case. Some of the information entered into these fields will be "objective" (for example, the creator or recipient of a document or the type of document). Other information will be subjective (for example, comments concerning relevancy or the importance of the document to the case).

Index or summary systems are frequently augmented by including a scanned picture of each document with its summary. In such cases, the document is not translated by the computer into text and cannot be searched for key words. Instead, the document is essentially stored as a photograph.

Although it may appear that litigation support databases will be protected by the work product doctrine, it should be recalled that the work product doctrine generally is only a qualified protection. A court may order disclosure if it determines that denial of the discovery "will unfairly prejudice the party seeking discovery in preparing that party's claims or defenses or will result in an injustice." (Code Civ. Proc., § 2018, subd. (b).) The requesting party may argue it will suffer extreme financial hardship and prejudice if it is denied access to the database. This argument is usually raised in cases involving voluminous data and documents that have already been organized in an opponent's computer system. (See, e.g., *Minnesota v. Phillip Morris Inc.* (1995 Dist. Ct. Minn.) No. C1-94-8465; *Hoffman v. United Telecommunications, Inc.* (D. Kan. 1987) 117 F.R.D. 436; *Fauteck v. Montgomery Ward* (N.D. Ill. 1980) 91 F.RD. 393.) If the information is merely printed out, the requesting party would be forced to spend an inordinate amount of time and money analyzing it. This would arguably deprive the party of an adequate opportunity to investigate the facts and prepare for trial.

Whether a court will order the production of a litigation support database will likely turn on the answers to several questions:

- Was the database constructed by the attorney or the client?

- Was the database constructed by merely scanning the documents so that it reflects only the content and type of documents catalogued? Or does the database contain comments that reflect the attorney's opinions as in an index or summary database?

- Can any such opinions be easily redacted?

- How much time and effort was spent in creating the database?

- How many documents are in the database?

- How much would it cost for the requesting party to construct a similar database?

- Were any of the documents in the database created by an attorney?

- Was the information relied upon by the responding party's experts in forming their opinions?

§ 5.04 Trade Secrets and Other Proprietary Information

A trade secret is information, including formulas, patterns, compilations, programs, devices, techniques, and processes, that has independent economic value because it is not generally known and is the subject of reasonable efforts under the circumstances to maintain its secrecy. (Civ. Code, § 3426.1, subd. (d).) Because of their nature, most trade secrets are stored, to one extent or another, on electronic media. Since businesses generally do not segregate their trade secrets from other information stored on their computer systems, conducting electronic discovery will frequently involve such secrets—even if they are not the specific target of the discovery request. Under the Uniform Trade Secrets Act (Civ. Code, § 3426 et seq.), a court must use "reasonable means" to protect alleged trade secrets. Such means include, but are not limited to, issuing protective orders in connection with discovery proceedings, holding *in camera* hearings, sealing court records, and ordering any person involved in the litigation not to disclose an alleged trade secret without prior authorization from the court. (Civ. Code, § 3426.5.)

Under the Evidence Code, the owner of a trade secret has a qualified privilege to refuse to disclose the secret, and to prevent another from disclosing it, "if the allowance of the privilege will not tend to conceal fraud or otherwise work injustice." (Evid. Code, § 1060.) Thus, unlike the attorney-client privilege, which is absolute, a court may order the production of trade secret information if necessary to prevent fraud or injustice. In determining whether to order production, the court must consider whether a protective order, or some other less intrusive alternative, will protect the parties' interests. (*Bridgestone/Firestone, Inc. v. Superior Court* (1992) 7 Cal.App.4th 1384, 1393 [9 Cal.Rptr.2d 709].)

Discovery problems relating to the production of trade secrets and other proprietary information can usually be addressed through an appropriate confidentiality agreement or protective order. (See the example of a confidentiality agreement in § 5.07.)

§ 5.05 Copyright and License Restrictions on the Discoverability of Electronic Evidence

[A] Copyright

Another potential limitation on the discoverability of documentary evidence is the law of copyright. Under the Copyright Act of 1976, original works of authorship are subject to copyright protection the moment they are memorialized in any tangible medium of expression. [18 U.S.C.A., § 102.] Almost every document, in hard copy or electronic form, is protected under federal copyright law. E-mail, software, software documentation, word processing documents, spreadsheets, and other electronic evidence may all be subject to third party copyrights. This means that if such documents are produced during discovery, the party who requests and later copies the documents may, at least theoretically, be subject to a claim of direct copyright infringement. The party producing the documents may, arguably, be held liable for contributory copyright infringement. (*Religious Technology Center v. Netcom* (N.D. Cal. 1995) 907 F. Supp. 1361 (contributory infringement arises when a party knowingly contributes to another's infringing activities).) To date, no court has directly addressed the issue of the interplay between the law of copyright and discovery. This does not mean, however, that this potential liability can or should be ignored. Counsel must be aware of the implications copyright may have on the production of certain documents and, where appropriate, take action to minimize potential liability.

Actions to minimize potential liability for copyright infringement include the following:

Produce, But Do Not Copy. The Discovery Act does not require the responding to reproduce documents, but only to "permit the party making the demand, or someone acting on that party's behalf, to inspect and to copy a document." (Code Civ. Proc., § 2031.) As such, the responding party should consider merely producing the documents and permitting the requesting party to perform the copying. While this procedure will greatly reduce the potential for a claim of direct copyright infringement, the responding party may still be subject to a claim of contributory infringement.

Provide Notice to the Requesting Party. Provide notice to the requesting party that certain responsive documents are subject to the intellectual property rights of third parties, that copying such documents may infringe those rights, and that the requesting party acts at its own peril in making such copies.

Produce Under a Confidentiality Agreement. Offer to produce the copyrighted material under a confidentiality agreement that will ensure use of the material is limited to the pending litigation. If the requesting party refuses, a motion for a confidentiality/protective order will almost certainly be granted.

Provide Notice to the Copyright Owner. Provide notice to the copyright owner that the material has been requested as part of a litigation and that if the owner has an objection to the production it should file a motion in the appropriate court. (See the sample notice letter to copyright owner in § 5.09)

Seek Court Intervention. If the threat of an infringement suit is significant, the responding party should consider seeking an order from the court compelling it to make the production. The motion should identify the nature of the copyrighted material and detail the responding party's concerns regarding potential liability for copyright infringement.

[B]　License Restrictions

In addition to potential copyright infringement, the producing party may also be subject to a claim of breach of contract. Most intellectual property, particularly software, is licensed, not purchased. (See § 2.19.) Thus, use of the intellectual property is subject to the terms and conditions of the license agreement. Common restrictions include, but are not limited to, limitations on the type of individuals who may access and use the intellectual property (for example, only employees of the licensee or third party consultants who have been approved in writing by the licensor) and covenants by the licensee to maintain the confidentiality of the intellectual property. Producing such intellectual property during discovery—indeed, even making such information available to the producing party's own attorneys—may constitute a breach of the license agreement. Although many license agreements have specific provisions that permit disclosure by the licensee in response to lawful process, such provisions are not present in every agreement. As such, the producing party and its counsel should carefully review all applicable license agreements before producing any licensed material.

§ 5.06　References

    📖 **WITKIN** For general discussion of limits on discovery, see the following:

        ▦ Attorney-client privilege (2 Witkin, Cal. Evidence (3d ed. 1986) Witnesses, § 1107 et seq.).

        ▦ Attorney's work product (2 Witkin, Cal. Evidence (3d ed. 1986) Witnesses, § 1142 et seq.).

        ▦ Trade secret (2 Witkin, Cal. Evidence (3d ed. 1986) Witnesses, § 1299).

    ▦ **THE RUTTER GROUP** See the following sections regarding limits on discovery:

        ▦ Attorney-client privilege (Cal. Practice Guide: Civ. Trials & Evidence, ¶ 8:1985 et seq.).

        ▦ Trade secrets (Cal. Practice Guide: Civ. Trials & Evidence, ¶ 8:2550 et seq.).

        ▦ Attorney work product doctrine (Cal. Practice Guide: Civ. Trials & Evidence, ¶ 8:2670 et seq.).

☞ **WEST'S KEY NUMBER SYSTEM** See the following key numbers in West's Cal. Digest 2d, Witnesses (Topic 410) and Federal Civil Procedure (Topic 170A):

   ▧ Attorney-client privilege (Witnesses ☞ 197 et seq.).

   ▧ Attorney work product (Federal Civil Procedure ☞ 1600.2 et seq.).

💻 **WESTLAW** See the WESTLAW Electronic Research Guide at the beginning of this volume.

B. Forms

§ 5.07 Confidentiality Agreement

_____

State Bar No. _____

_____

_____

_____

Attorneys for _____

_____ COURT OF THE STATE OF CALIFORNIA
COUNTY OF _____

_____)	Case No. _____	
_____)		
Plaintiff(s),)	**STIPULATION FOR ENTRY**	
v.)	**OF PROTECTIVE ORDER**	
_____)	**REGARDING CONFIDENTIAL**	
Defendant(s).)	**MATERIAL**	
_____)		

    IT IS HEREBY STIPULATED by and among the parties, through their respective counsel of record, that on approval of this Court the following Protective Order may be entered:

    1. <u>Defined Terms:</u> The word "document" shall have the full meaning ascribed to it in California Code of Civil Procedure section 2031, and shall include any "writing," as that term is defined in California Evidence Code section 250.

    2. <u>Scope of Order:</u> This Order shall govern the handling of all documents produced and testimony given in this action designated as "Confidential."

    3. <u>Labeling of Confidential Material:</u> Any party producing or filing a document in this action may obtain confidential treatment, as defined in Paragraph 6, for such document, or its contents, by typing or stamping on the document, or on its cover, or on the portion of the document for which confidential treatment is desired, the word "Confidential."

    4. <u>Designating Confidential Testimony:</u> Any party or person giving testimony in this action may obtain confidential treatment, as described in Paragraph 6, for such testimony or any portion thereof by so advising the court reporter during the course of any testimony for which confidential treatment is desired. The reporter shall then transcribe and/or bind the testimony so

designated and shall mark the face of the transcript so bound with the words "Confidential" or "Confidential Pursuant to Court Order." Any portion of any transcript so marked shall be lodged under seal with the Clerk of the Court if it is required to be lodged.

5. <u>Use of Confidential Material at Deposition:</u> Whenever any documents or transcripts afforded confidential treatment pursuant to this Order are introduced as exhibits in connection with a deposition given in this action, counsel introducing such exhibits shall advise the court reporter that the portions of the testimony that refer to such exhibits and the exhibits themselves shall be afforded confidential treatment pursuant to this Order. The reporter shall transcribe the testimony so designated, attach the confidential exhibits to which the testimony refers, and mark the face of the bound transcript with the words "Confidential" or "Confidential Pursuant to Court Order." Any portion of any transcript or any exhibit so marked shall be lodged under seal with the Clerk of the Court if it is required to be lodged.

6. <u>Persons to Whom Confidential Material May Be Disclosed:</u> Except by prior Court order or the prior written consent of the party or person designating the document or transcript as "Confidential," no document or transcript so designated, and no information contained or derived from any such document or transcript, shall be disclosed to any person other than:

(a) Counsel of record for the respective parties to this litigation;

(b) Employees of such counsel, including secretaries, legal assistants, and consultants or experts retained to assist such counsel in this litigation; and

(c) The respective parties to this litigation and any employees or officers of a party receiving "Confidential" materials that such party chooses to designate.

Before disclosure of any Confidential information is made to any of the persons identified above, that person shall be shown a copy of this Order, shall agree to be bound by its terms, and shall consent to the jurisdiction of this Court. Counsel shall require each such person to sign and date a copy of this Order. Counsel shall maintain a list of all persons to whom disclosure is made and, for good cause shown, make the list available for inspection by counsel for other parties on order of this Court.

7. <u>Use of Confidential Information:</u> Any document or transcript designated "Confidential," or any information therein, shall be used solely for the purpose of preparing for and conducting pretrial and/or trial proceedings in this action, and shall not be utilized for any other purpose whatsoever. No

person receiving Confidential information shall disclose it to any person other than those described in Paragraph 6 above and then solely for the express purposes set forth in this paragraph.

8. Written Authorization Required for Disclosure to Others: Counsel desiring to disclose confidential information to persons other than those specifically identified in Paragraph 6 shall make a written request on each of the other counsel (the "Request"). If the other counsel do not object in writing within five (5) days of receipt of the Request, counsel seeking such disclosure may reveal confidential information to the persons identified in the Request only after such persons have been fully advised as to the contents of this Order and have signed and dated a copy of it. If any of the other counsel object in writing within five (5) days of receiving the Request to the disclosure of confidential information to the persons identified in the Request, then disclosure to such persons shall only be made by order of this Court after a properly noticed motion.

9. Labeling of Confidential Material Provided to the Court: If any counsel lodges, files with, or submits to the Court any (a) documents or transcripts afforded confidential treatment pursuant to this Order, (b) any information derived from such documents, transcript, or information, or (c) papers containing or summarizing such documents, transcripts, or information, then such documents shall be lodged or filed in sealed envelopes on which shall be endorsed the caption of this action and a statement substantially in the following form:

CONFIDENTIAL

> This envelope contains documents that are subject to an Order governing the use of confidential material entered by the Court in this action. This envelope shall not be opened nor the contents thereof displayed or revealed except by Order of this Court. Violation of this Order may be regarded as contempt of the Court.

10. Documents to Be Maintained Under Seal: Any document or transcript designated "Confidential Pursuant to Court Order" or "Confidential" that is lodged or filed with the Court shall be maintained under seal by the Clerk and shall be made available only to the Court and to counsel for the parties until further order of this Court.

11. Objections to Confidential Designation: If a party objects to the designation of a document or transcript as "Confidential," it shall notify the party seeking confidential treatment in writing. Within a reasonable time after receiving such written notice, but not to exceed ten (10) days, the party seeking confidential treatment may apply to the Court by noticed motion for a ruling that the

document or transcript shall be treated as Confidential pursuant to the terms of this Order. Pending the outcome of the application, the document or testimony shall be afforded the confidential treatment described in Paragraph 6.

12. Disposal of Confidential Material at Conclusion of Litigation: Within ninety (90) days of the conclusion of this litigation (that is, upon its final dismissal or judgment), all copies of all documents or transcripts designated "Confidential" or "Confidential Pursuant to Court Order" shall either be destroyed or returned to the party or person furnishing them. In addition, all copies of all summaries or other materials containing or disclosing information contained in "Confidential" documents or transcripts shall be either destroyed or returned to the party or person furnishing them. This Order shall continue to be binding after the conclusion of this litigation, except that, unless otherwise ordered by this Court, there shall be no restriction on documents or transcripts that are (a) used as exhibits and/or offered into evidence in the trial of this action and (b) not covered by any subsequent and inclusive confidentiality order.

DATED: _____   _____

                                    By: _____
                                    Attorneys for Plaintiff

DATED: _____   _____

                                    By: _____
                                    Attorneys for Defendant

ORDER

IT IS SO ORDERED.

DATED: _____.

                                    _____
                                    Judge of the Superior Court

§ 5.08 Sample Notice Letter to Requesting Party

[*Date*]

_____
_____
_____

Re: Smith v. ABC Corporation

Dear _____:

We are in receipt of Plaintiff's First Request for Production of Documents and write to advise you that certain of the documents requested for production may be subject to the copyright interests of third parties. Such documents are described in Attachment A to this letter. We will produce such documents for your inspection, but caution you that any reproduction may, and likely will, constitute copyright infringement. ABC Corporation will not be responsible for any such activities. Mr. Smith shall be solely liable for any infringement claims that may arise from such reproduction.

If you have any questions regarding the foregoing, please do not hesitate to call me.

Sincerely,

_____

§ 5.09 Sample Notice Letter to Copyright Owner

[Date]

_____

_____

_____

Re: <u>Smith v. ABC Corporation, Case No. ######## (LA Sup. Ct.)</u>

Dear _____:

    In connection with the above-referenced action, we write to advise you that certain materials produced by your company have been requested for production during discovery. Such materials are described in Attachment A to this letter. Production of the materials is set for _____ [*specify date*] at _____ [*specify location*]. The requesting party's attorney is _____ [*specify name and address of requesting attorney*]. If you intend to object to the production, such objection must be made by filing an appropriate motion prior to the date specified above.

    If you have any questions regarding the foregoing, please do not hesitate to call me.

Sincerely,

_____

6   SPOLIATION OF EVIDENCE

A. Text

§ 6.01 Electronic Document Retention

[A] Introduction

Most businesses have retention policies governing how long documents are to be retained before being destroyed or discarded. A growing number of businesses are extending their existing retention policies to include electronic documents, particularly e-mail. For example, a common retention policy for e-mail would require deletion after 60 days. In many instances, the deletion is accomplished automatically by programming the business's computers to review the dates on e-mail and to delete those messages having dates beyond the allowed limit. If an employee desires to keep a message past the automatic dele-tion date, she or he must take affirmative action to preserve the e-mail (for exam-ple, contact the MIS department or copy the e-mail to a special directory).

In the absence of a law specifically requiring certain documents to be retained, document retention policies in the electronic context accomplish three goals:

- Document retention policies conserve valuable computer storage space.

- Reducing the volume of stored electronic documents improves the efficiency of the computer system.

- Provided there is no legal obligation to preserve evidence, deleting electronic documents when they are no longer necessary reduces the likelihood that such documents may be exploited in future litigation.

▶ **COMMENT**

Examples of laws specifically requiring document retention include the Occupational Safety and Health Act (OSHA), which requires retention of testing and medical records for decades, and the Employee Retirement Income Security Act of 1974 (ERISA), which requires businesses to retain employee information.

Because of the informality with which e-mail is treated by employees, it is a frequent target of discovery in litigation. As illustrated in the following example, failing to implement an effective retention policy for e-mail can sub-stantially increase litigation costs and lead to greater liability.

Example: XYZ corporation is sued by one of its employees for wrongful termination. During the course of discovery, the plaintiff serves a document request seeking all relevant e-mail. If the business does not have a practice of periodically deleting e-mail, which were of no reasonable value after some relevant period, it would be under an obligation to search through all of the e-mail on its systems. This could mean reviewing an enormous volume of e-mail accumulated over many years. If XYZ is like most companies, it not only does not have an established retention policy for electronic documents, it also has no policy requiring where e-mail messages are to be stored on its systems. This means that instead of requiring that all e-mail be stored in a specific place, messages may be found in a variety of locations. As such, the search for relevant messages will likely require a review of the local area network's hard disks, network backup tapes, the hard disks installed in relevant employee's desktop computers, company laptop computers, handheld PDAs, and the home computers of certain employees. A search of the foregoing nature can cost thousands of dollars and take substantial time to complete. If the company had a retention policy in effect and had required e-mail to be stored in a central location, the expense and time required to respond to the discovery request would be significantly reduced.

[B]   Basic Requirements for a Retention Policy

Developing a records retention policy requires careful consideration of the way in which a client conducts business and the potential laws applicable to its business that may require records to be retained. While a review of the broad range of applicable laws is beyond the scope of this book, there are certain general guidelines for the establishment and implementation of a retention program that should be considered in developing a policy:

- The policy should clearly define the types of documents to which it will apply. In particular, electronic documents such as e-mail should be specifically identified. If certain electronic documents are to be stored in designated locations, those locations should be clearly identified.

- The retention period for each type of document should be listed.

- Procedures should be provided for excepting certain documents from the program (for example, copying files to a specified directory on the LAN used to store important "permanent" files).

- The policy should describe how the retention program will be implemented (for example, the network will be programmed to automatically delete e-mail more than 60 days old).

- An individual or group of individuals should be specified as being responsible for maintaining the program and responding to questions about its implementation.

- An audit procedure should be developed to ensure the retention policy is properly implemented.

[C] Legal Implications of Document Destruction

The implementation of a document retention policy will, of necessity, require the destruction or deletion of certain documents. Such destruction or deletion may have certain legal implications. Destroying documents relevant to a threatened or ongoing litigation may result in liability for spoliation of evidence or subject the business to sanctions for abuse of the discovery process. (See § 6.02.) Destroying documents needed for a criminal investigation and prosecution may subject the business to white-collar criminal liability (for example, perjury, aiding and abetting, and conspiracy). Such destruction may also violate federal obstruction of justice laws. (18 U.S.C.A. §§ 1503 (obstruction of judicial proceedings), 1505 (obstruction of an administrative proceeding), 1510 (obstruction of criminal investigation).)

§ 6.02 Duty to Preserve Evidence in Litigation

A party to a litigation is under a duty to preserve evidence. Such duty arises by reason of the pendency of the litigation itself, not by reason of any potential court intervention (*Coca-Cola Bottling Co. v. Superior Court* (1991) 233 Cal.App.3d 1273, 1293 fn.10 [286 Cal.Rptr. 855]):

> Coca-Cola also urged, at oral argument, that as the owner of the truck it had an unfettered right to dispose of the truck without notice to anyone else and with total immunity from any liability for such disposal. This argument ignores the fact that Coca-Cola, as a complainant in intervention, was a party litigant, with a duty not to lose or destroy evidence relevant to the lawsuit.

Fulfilling the duty to preserve evidence may be particularly difficult when information is stored electronically and can be easily deleted or altered. For example, the normal operation of a computer may result in the inadvertent destruction of relevant evidence. The simple act of turning a computer on may cause certain system files to be overwritten or deleted. Those files may have contained important information about prior activity on the computer (for example, the identity of the last person to use the computer, the last file printed on the computer, and temporary backup files containing the most recent documents accessed by word processing or spreadsheet programs).

The following example illustrates another way in which important evidence may be inadvertently destroyed.

Example: A business is sued for copyright infringement regarding a new computer game program. During discovery, the plaintiff requests all e-mail relating to the development of the software. Like most businesses, the defendant creates monthly backup tapes of the files, including e-mail, on its system. The monthly backup files are typically recycled and overwritten each month. (See § 2.18.) By the time the discovery request makes its way from the business's outside counsel to its in-house attorneys and then, ultimately, to its MIS department, a monthly backup tape containing relevant evidence has been deleted.

> ▶ **COMMENT**
>
> When it appears likely important evidence may exist in electronic form, consideration should be given to methods to ensure that such evidence is not lost, destroyed, or altered. One approach is to seek a preservation order from the court. (See § 3.23.) Another approach is to send a "preservation letter" to opposing counsel cautioning them that relevant evidence exists in electronic form and that parties to the action are under a duty to preserve that evidence. (See § 6.06.)

§ 6.03 Spoliation of Evidence and Discovery Sanctions

"Spoliation is the destruction or significant alteration of evidence, or the failure to preserve property for another's use as evidence." (*Willard v. Caterpillar* (1995) 40 Cal.App.4th 892, 907 [48 Cal.Rptr.2d 607].) The tort is considered an infringement of personal property rights in the evidence. The interest interfered with by the tort of spoliation of evidence is the possibility of winning a lawsuit. (*Smith v. Superior Court* (1984) 151 Cal.App.3d 491, 502–503 [198 Cal.Rptr. 829].)

The California Supreme Court recently substantially narrowed the availability of the tort of spoliation of evidence, holding that there is no tort remedy for the intentional spoliation of evidence by a party to an underlying cause of action if the spoliation victim knew of or should have known of the spoliation before the decision on the merits of the underlying action. (*Cedars-Sinai Medical Center v. Superior Court* (1998) 18 Cal.4th 1 [74 Cal.Rptr.2d 248].) In reaching its decision, the court acknowledged the substantial harm and prejudice a litigant may incur as a result of the destruction of evidence, but voiced concern over using tort law to correct misconduct arising during litigation. In the past, the court has favored remedying litigation-related misconduct by sanctions imposed within the underlying lawsuit rather than by creating derivative torts. (*Cedars-Sinai Medical Center v. Superior Court* (1998) 18 Cal.4th 1, 8–9 [74 Cal.Rptr.2d 248].) Potential non-tort remedies available to punish and deter intentional spoliation include adverse evidentiary inferences and discovery sanctions. (*Cedars-Sinai Medical Center v. Superior Court* (1998) 18 Cal.4th 1, 11–12 [74 Cal.Rptr.2d 248].)

Evidence Code section 413 provides an evidentiary inference that evidence that one party has destroyed or rendered unavailable was unfavorable to that party. A similar inference is included in the standard California jury instructions: "If you find that a party willfully suppressed evidence in order to prevent its being presented at trial, you may consider that fact in determining what inferences to draw from the evidence." (BAJI No. 2.03 (8th ed. 1994).)

In addition to an adverse evidentiary inference, the Discovery Act provides a broad range of sanctions for "misuse of the discovery process." (Code Civ. Proc., § 2023.) The California Supreme Court has indicated that destroying evidence in response to a discovery request after litigation has commenced would "surely be a misuse of discovery within the meaning of section 2023, as would such destruction in anticipation of a discovery request." (*Cedars-Sinai Medical Center v. Superior Court* (1998) 18 Cal.4th 1, 12 [74 Cal.Rptr.2d 248].) The sanctions available under section 2023 are potent. They include monetary sanctions, contempt sanctions, issue sanctions ordering that designated facts be taken as established or precluding the offending party from supporting or opposing designated claims or defenses, evidence sanctions prohibiting the offending party from introducing designated matters into evidence, and terminating sanctions that include striking part or all of the pleadings, dismissing part or all of the action, or granting a default judgment against the offending party. (Code Civ. Proc., § 2023; *Cedars-Sinai Medical Center v. Superior Court* (1998) 18 Cal.4th 1, 12 [74 Cal.Rptr.2d 248].)

Finally, Penal Code section 135 creates criminal penalties for spoliation:

> Every person who knowing that any book, paper, record, instrument in writing, or other matter or thing, is about to be produced in evidence upon any trial, inquiry, or investigation whatever, authorized by law, willfully destroys or conceals the same, with intent thereby to prevent it from being produced, is guilty of a misdemeanor.

The use of adverse evidentiary inferences and discovery sanctions to redress instances of intentional spoliation has found favor in other jurisdictions. For example, the court of appeal in *The Lauren Corp. v. Century Geophysical Corp.* (Co. Ct. App. 1998) 953 P.2d 200 used this approach to remedy a party's intentional destruction of electronic evidence. *Century Geophysical* involved an action for breach of software license agreements. During discovery, plaintiff sought to inspect defendant's computers for evidence supporting its claim that defendant had used the software on unauthorized computers, in violation of the applicable license agreement. While a dispute regarding defendant's discovery responses was ongoing, defendant destroyed certain items of computer hardware. Employees and senior management involved in the destruction later testified that they were aware of the significance of the computers as evidence in the pending litigation at the time the hardware was destroyed.

The trial court found defendant's actions to be a clear case of bad faith destruction of evidence and imposed the following sanctions: (1) a presumption at trial that defendant had used the software on machines other than those permitted under the licensed agreements and (2) an award to plaintiff of its attorneys' fees and costs incurred in its attempts to conduct discovery of the computer hardware. The court of appeal affirmed the imposition of sanctions, holding that the trial court had not abused its discretion in sanctioning defendant for intentional spoliation of evidence.

§ 6.04 Continuing Viability of the Tort of Spoliation of Evidence

The Supreme Court's decision in *Cedars-Sinai* did not signal the death of the tort of spoliation of evidence in California. Rather, the court specifically noted that it was not deciding whether a tort cause of action for spoliation should be recognized in cases of "third party" spoliation (that is, spoliation by a nonparty to any cause of action to which the evidence is relevant) or in cases of first party spoliation in which the spoliation victim neither knows nor should have know of the spoliation until after a decision on the merits of the underlying action. (*Cedars-Sinai Medical Center v. Superior Court* (1998) 18 Cal.4th 1, 18 fn. 4 [74 Cal.Rptr.2d 248].) Thus, it remains unclear whether the tort is available as a remedy against, for example, (a) an Internet service provider who intentionally overwrites e-mail backup tapes to prevent the messages from being used as evidence in a litigation or (b) a party to a litigation who does not learn until after the litigation has concluded that the opposing party erased evidence on a hard disk shortly before its was produced for inspection and testing.

§ 6.05 References

　　📖 **WITKIN** For general discussion of suppression or spoliation of evidence, see 3 Witkin, Cal. Evidence (3d ed. 1986) Introduction of Evidence at Trial, § 1775 et seq.).

　　💻 **WESTLAW** See the WESTLAW Electronic Research Guide at the beginning of this volume.

B. Forms

§ 6.06 Preservation Letter

[Date]

_____
_____
_____

Re: <u>Smith v. ABC Corporation</u>

Dear _____:

　　As evidenced by the attached discovery requests, much of the evidence in this matter resides on ABC Corporation's ("ABC") computer system. This "electronic evidence" includes, but is not limited to, word processing documents, spreadsheets, calendar information, e-mail, Internet history and favorites files, Graphic Interchange Format ("GIF") files, and computer access control data. In particular, e-mail and GIF files exchanged between John Smith and Mary Doe and e-mail relating to ABC's decision to terminate Ms. Doe will be directly relevant to this action. Such evidence may not be available from any other source.

　　Because electronic evidence can be easily modified, corrupted, or deleted, we are writing this letter to insure that ABC takes reasonable steps to preserve this important source of relevant evidence. In particular, ABC must refrain from overwriting backup tapes and other mass storage media that may contain such evidence.

　　If you have any questions regarding the foregoing, please do not hesitate to call me.

Sincerely,

_____

7 PRIVACY ISSUES

A. Text

§ 7.01   Employee Privacy Rights in Electronic Documents

In addition to business-related documents, the computers and networks of a company may also contain personal files and e-mail of its employees. If the employees are not parties to the litigation and the contents of the files are not at issue, reviewing or producing them during discovery may theoretically give rise to claims by the employees of, among other things, invasion of privacy, violation of state and federal constitutional protections, and violation of the Electronic Communications Privacy Act of 1986 (18 U.S.C.A. § 2510 et seq.). To date, California courts have not specifically addressed this issue. They have, however, addressed a related problem: employers who review and monitor employee e-mail for purposes of investigating potential employee misconduct and use as evidence in litigation between the employer and employee. For example, an employer may monitor a particular employee's e-mail because the employee has previously been caught sending sexually explicit material through the business's e-mail system. (See, e.g., *Bourke v. Nissan Motor Corp.*, No. B068705 (Cal. Ct. of Appeal, July 26, 1993).) Or, an employer might monitor the e-mail of an employee who is thought to be smuggling trade secrets out of the company to a competitor. In such cases, the employee may have a privacy-related claim against the employer. To reduce the potential for such claims and to clarify their right to access employee computer files and communications, employers are adopting written policies regarding employee use of computers, e-mail, and the Internet. These policies can substantially reduce or eliminated potential liability for privacy claims.

▶ COMMENT

As used above, "monitoring" refers to the practice of using human or automated means to examine the content of e-mail for inappropriate or unauthorized material. Commercially available programs can be used to review each piece of e-mail for sexually explicit material, excessive use of profanity, or trade secret or other proprietary information. When the program detects such content in a message, the message will be forwarded to a designated person within the business for review. If the message is authorized, the reviewer simply forwards the e-mail on to its intended recipient. If the message contains unauthorized content, appropriate action can be taken against the sender. The software provides the means of preventing potentially damaging messages from ever being delivered.

---

§ 7.02 Common Law Invasion of Privacy

As in most states, California courts recognize a common law right of privacy. (See, e.g., *Miller v. National Broadcasting Co.* (1986) 187 Cal.App.3d 1463, 1482–1484 [232 Cal.Rptr. 668].) A frequently cited definition of the tort of invasion of privacy is provided in the Restatement Second of Torts as follows: "One who intentionally intrudes, physically or otherwise, upon the solitude or seclusion of another or his private affairs or concerns, is subject to liability to the other for invasion of privacy, if the intrusion would be highly offensive to a reasonable person." (Rest. 2d, Torts § 625B.) Thus, for an employee to successfully maintain a claim for invasion of privacy against his or her employer for reviewing computer files or communications, the employee must generally establish two elements. First, that the employee had a reasonable expectation of privacy in the files. Second, the employer's review of the files would be highly offensive to a reasonable person.

Most decisions that have addressed the issue of employee privacy claims in the context of electronic documents have focused on e-mail. Employees who have brought such claims against their employers for invasion of privacy for monitoring e-mail have generally been unsuccessful. (See, e.g., *Bourke v. Nissan Motor Corp.*, No. B068705 (Cal. Ct. of Appeal, July 26, 1993); *Flanagan v. Epson America*, No. BC007036 (Cal. Super. Ct., Jan. 4, 1991) (denying motion for class certification on the ground that plaintiffs did not have a reasonable expectation of privacy in e-mail related to their employer's business); *Smyth v. Pillsbury Co.* (E.D. Pa. 1996) 914 F. Supp. 97).)

In *Bourke*, a system manager at Nissan Motor Accidentally discovered a sexually explicit e-mail message while conducting a training seminar for new employees. The incident was reported to a supervisor, who ordered a review of the sending employee's e-mail, as well as the e-mail of the employee's fellow workgroup members. Despite several warnings, the employees continued sending inappropriate messages. The employees were ultimately terminated. They sued Nissan for wrongful termination and invasion of privacy. The court of appeal upheld the trial court's summary judgment in favor of Nissan, holding that the plaintiffs had no expectation of privacy in the e-mail, since they had signed written e-mail policies limiting use of the e-mail system to business purposes only and were aware that messages were, from time-to-time, read by persons other than the intended recipient. The court of appeal also rejected the plaintiffs' argument that the fact that the employees had been issued personal passwords for the computer system created a reasonable expectation of privacy in their online communications.

Similarly, in *Smyth*, plaintiff, who was terminated for sending inappropriate and threatening e-mail, argued that his termination was wrongful because it was based on information obtained from his messages in violation of his right of privacy. The District Court rejected this argument, stating: "[W]e do not find a reasonable expectation of privacy in e-mail communications voluntarily made by an employee to his supervisor over the company e-mail system notwithstanding any assurances that such communications would not be intercepted by management. Once plaintiff communicated the alleged unprofessional comments to a second person (his supervisor) over an e-mail system which was apparently utilized by the entire company, any reasonable expectation of privacy was lost." (*Smyth v. Pillsbury Co.* (E.D. Pa. 1996) 914 F. Supp. 97).) Indeed, even if the employee had been able to establish the elements of a claim for invasion of privacy, the court indicated that the employee's privacy interest may be outweighed by the employer's legitimate business interest in intercepting and monitoring the communications: "[T]he company's interest in preventing inappropriate and unprofessional comments or even illegal activity over its e-mail system outweighs any privacy interest the employee may have in those comments." (*Smyth v. Pillsbury Co.* (E.D. Pa. 1996) 914 F. Supp. 97).)

§ 7.03 Constitutional Privacy Rights

In addition to the common law right of privacy, federal, state, and local government employees may also raise the Fourth Amendment's prohibition against unreasonable searches and seizures in response to employer review and monitoring of online activities. While several state constitutions also include a right of privacy for public employees, California is the only state that has extended its constitutional privacy protection to private employees. (Cal. Const., art. I, § 1; *Flanagan v. Epson America*, No. BC007036 (Cal. Super. Ct., Jan. 4, 1991); *Porten v. University of San Francisco* (1976) 64 Cal.App.3d 825, 829–830 [134 Cal.Rptr. 839] (state constitutional privacy rights extend to both public and private employees).)

State and federal constitutional privacy rights generally turn on the same considerations as those of the common law right of privacy. In both, the primary issue is whether the employee had a reasonable expectation of privacy. Employees who have raised constitutional claims in response to employer review of employee computer files and communications have generally met with little success, particularly when the employer has an established computer and e-mail policy that restricts use of the system to business purposes and grants the employer the right to monitor. (See, e.g., *Bourke v. Nissan Motor*

Corp., No. B068705 (Cal. Ct. of Appeal, July 26, 1993); *Flanagan v. Epson America*, No. BC007036 (Cal. Super. Ct., Jan. 4, 1991).)

In *Flanagan*, an employee of Epson brought a class action for invasion of privacy against Epson, alleging that Epson bypassed their passwords and routinely read their e-mail. The court rejected the employees' constitutional claim, holding that an extension of state constitutional privacy rights to protect employee e-mail from employer monitoring was an issue for the Legislature, not the judiciary.

§ 7.04 Electronic Communication Privacy Act of 1986

When it became clear that claims for invasion of privacy or violation of state and federal constitutional protections were generally unsuccessful, employees turned to the Electronic Communications Privacy Act of 1986 (ECPA), which was an amendment to the Omnibus Crime Control and Safe Streets Act of 1968 (frequently referred to as the Federal Wiretap Act). (18 U.S.C.A. § 2510 et seq.) One of the motivating factors for enactment of the amendment was a 1985 Congressional study that graphically described potential threats that new technology posed to citizen's civil liberties. Congress passed the ECPA, in part, to address perceived deficiencies in individual privacy protections.

For purposes of this overview, the ECPA is essentially directed at preventing two types of conduct: (1) unauthorized interception of an electronic communication and (2) unauthorized disclosure of communications stored electronically. (18 U.S.C.A. §§ 2511, subd. (1), 2702, subd. (a).) Violations of the ECPA will enable employees to bring a civil action against their employers for damages. (18 U.S.C.A. § 2707.)

Although the ECPA has been in existence for over 10 years, few courts have interpreted its provisions with regard to employer monitoring of e-mail. For example, it remains unclear how the ECPA will apply, if at all, to e-mail systems maintained by private businesses (for example, local area networks and wide area networks). One of the few decisions to address this issue was the District Court for the Northern District of Illinois's decision in *Andersen Consulting LLP v. UOP* (N.D. Ill. 1998) 991 F. Supp. 1041. In *Andersen*, Andersen Consulting was granted access to UOP's internal e-mail system in connection with consulting activities it was conducting for UOP. UOP allegedly disclosed certain of Andersen's e-mail communications to a newspaper during an earlier lawsuit. Andersen filed an ECPA-based claim against UOP for the disclosure.

The District Court dismissed the claim, finding that to be liable under the ECPA, UOP must provide electronic communication services to the community at large. Section 2702(a)(1) of the ECPA provides that "a person or entity providing an electronic communication service to the public shall not knowingly divulge to any person or entity the contents of a communication while in electronic storage of that service." Whether other courts will follow the interpretation adopted by the *Andersen* court is unclear. Other courts may focus on whether the defendant's computer is connected to the Internet or allows third parties to access from outside the company. These factors may be construed as making the network "public" for purposes of the ECPA.

§ 7.05 Computer/E-mail Use Policies

One of the exceptions to liability under the ECPA is if one of the parties to a communication consents to the interception or disclosure of a message. (18 U.S.C.A. §§ 2511, subd. (2)(d), 2702, subd. (b)(3).) Thus, if the ECPA applies to a business's computer network, an employer can avoid potential liability by ensuring it has a written e-mail policy that includes a specific provision regarding the employer's right to monitor e-mail. (For an example, see § 7.06.) Such language will also substantially reduce or eliminate potential liability to employees for claims of invasion of privacy or violation of state or federal constitutional protections. (See, e.g., *Bourke v. Nissan Motor Corp.*, No. B068705 (Cal. Ct. of Appeal, July 26, 1993).)

B. Forms

§ 7.06 Employee Computer Use Policy

EMPLOYEE COMPUTER USE POLICY

I. PURPOSE

XYZ Corporation relies on its computer network to conduct its business. To ensure its computer resources are used properly by its employees, independent contractors, agents, and other computer users, XYZ Corporation has created this Computer Use Policy (the "Policy").

The rules and obligations described in this Policy apply to all users of XYZ Corporation's computer network, wherever they may be located. Violations will be taken very seriously and may result in disciplinary action, including possible termination, and civil and criminal liability.

It is every employee's duty to use XYZ Corporation's computer resources responsibly and in a professional, ethical, and lawful manner.

II. DEFINITIONS

From time-to-time in this Policy, we will refer to several terms that have the following definitions:

"Computer Resources" refers to XYZ Corporation's entire computer network. Specifically, Computer Resources includes, but is not limited to, the following: host computers, file servers, application servers, communication servers, mail servers, fax servers, Web servers, workstations, stand-alone computers, laptops, software, data files, and all internal and external computer and communications networks (e.g., Internet, commercial online services, value added networks, e-mail systems) that may be accessed directly or indirectly from our computer network.

"Users" refers to all employees, independent contractors, consultants, temporary workers, and other persons or entities who use our Computer Resources.

III. POLICY

The Computer Resources are the property of XYZ Corporation and may be used only for legitimate business purposes. Users are permitted access to the Computer Resources to assist them in the performance of their jobs. Use of the computer system is a privilege that may be revoked at any time.

In using or accessing our Computer Resources, Users must comply with the following provisions:

A. No Expectation of Privacy

No Expectation of Privacy. The computers and computer accounts given to Users are to assist them in the performance of their jobs. Users should not have an expectation of privacy in anything they create, store, send, or receive on the computer system. The computer system belongs to the company and may only be used for business purposes.

Waiver of Privacy Rights. Users expressly waive any right of privacy in anything they create, store, send, or receive on the computer or through the Internet or any other computer network. Users consent to personnel of the company accessing and reviewing all materials Users create, store, send, or receive on the computer or through the Internet or any other computer network. Users understand that XYZ Corporation may use human or automated means to monitor the use of its Computer Resources.

B. Passwords

Responsibility for Passwords. Users are responsible for safeguarding their passwords for access to the computer system. Individual passwords should not be printed, stored online, or given to others. Users are responsible for all transactions made using their passwords. No User may access the computer system using another User's password or account.

Passwords Do Not Imply Privacy. Use of passwords to gain access to the computer system or to encode particular files or messages does not imply that Users have an expectation of privacy in the material they create or receive on the computer system. XYZ Corporation has global passwords that permit it access to all material stored on its computer system—regardless of whether that material may have been encoded with a particular User's password.

I have read and agree to comply with the terms of this Policy governing the use of XYZ Corporation's Computer Resources. I understand that a violation of this Policy may result in disciplinary action, including possible termination, as well as civil and/or criminal liability.

Date: _____

_____
Signature

_____
Printed Name

§ 7.07 Computer Use Memo

Guidelines for Employee Use of E-mail

E-mail is quickly becoming one of our most important methods of communicating with each other and with our clients, customers, vendors, and consultants. To maximize the benefits of this new medium and minimize potential liability, XYZ Corporation has created the following guidelines. Please keep in mind that these guidelines are not intended to discourage your use of e-mail in the performance of your job. Rather, they are intended to ensure e-mail is used responsibly and with discretion.

You should never consider your electronic communications to be either private or secure. E-mail may be stored indefinitely on any number of computers, including that of the recipient. Copies of your messages may be forwarded to others either electronically or on paper. In addition, e-mail sent to nonexistent or incorrect usernames may be delivered to persons that you never intended.

In using the e-mail system every employee must comply with the following guidelines:

- THINK before sending a message. It is very important that you use the same care and discretion in drafting e-mail as you would for any other written communication. Anything created or stored on the computer may, and likely will, be reviewed by others. Before sending a message, ask yourself the following question: Would I want a judge or jury to see this message?

- Material that is fraudulent, harassing, embarrassing, sexually explicit, profane, obscene, intimidating, defamatory, or otherwise unlawful or inappropriate may not be sent by e-mail. If you encounter this kind of material, you are obligated to report it to your supervisor.

- Do not forward e-mail to any person or entity without the express permission of the sender.

- Never alter the "From" line or other attribution of origin information on your e-mail. Anonymous or pseudonymous messages are forbidden.

Employees who fail to comply with these guidelines may be subject to disciplinary action, including revocation of e-mail privileges. Repeated violations of this policy may result in termination.

PART II

ADMISSIBILITY OF ELECTRONIC EVIDENCE

OVERVIEW

As with traditional writings, electronic writings constitute evidence that may be used to prove the existence or nonexistence of a fact in issue. (Evid. Code, § 140.) Such writings may be used as direct or circumstantial evidence. In addition, they may also be used as demonstrative evidence. The admissibility of an electronic document depends on the same questions that must be answered for traditional writings:

1. Can the document be properly authenticated? (See Chapter 8.)
2. Does the Secondary Evidence Rule (formerly known as the Best Evidence Rule) require the original of the document to be produced? (See Chapter 9.)
3. Is the document hearsay and not subject to an exception? (See Chapter 10.)

Responding to these questions in the context of an electronic document requires the proponent of the evidence to be able to establish who created the document, the contents of the document, how the document was created, and that the document has not been altered, either intentionally or unintentionally. (McKeon, *Electronic Date Interchange: Uses and Legal Aspects in the Commercial Arena*, 12 J. Marshall J. Computer & Info. L. 511 (1994).)

The use of computer-generated visual evidence (CGVE) at trial is rapidly increasing. The admissibility of CGVE involves similar issues as listed above. (See Chapter 11.)

8   AUTHENTICATION

A. Text

§ 8.01 In General

Writings must be authenticated before they can be introduced into evidence. (Evid. Code, § 1401, subd. (a).) The proponent of the writing bears the burden of offering sufficient evidence to authentic the writing. (Evid. Code, § 403, subd. (a)(3).) California Evidence Code section 250 defines a "writing" as any "means of recording upon any tangible thing any form of communication or representation." This broad definition includes information stored on magnetic media, such as hard disks, floppy disks, and tapes, or on optical disks or in semiconductor memory chips. (See, e.g., *Aguimatang v. California State Lottery* (1988) 234 Cal.App.3d 769, 798 [286 Cal.Rptr. 57]; *People v. Lugashi* (1988) 205 Cal.App.3d 632, 638 [252 Cal.Rptr. 434].)

Authentication is a particular problem for electronic documents because they can be edited or altered without leaving a trace. There is a danger that if the identity of the originator or the contents of an electronic document is disputed, it may be difficult, if not impossible, to authenticate.

Absent a stipulation or an admission of authenticity by the party against whom a document is offered, a writing is authenticated by introducing sufficient evidence to sustain a finding that "it is the writing that the proponent of the evidence claims it is." (Evid. Code, § 1400, subd. (a).) In other words, a connection must be made between the document and the person, place, or thing to which it relates. Authentication can be accomplished through direct evidence, such as testimony by the creator of the document, or through circumstantial evidence, by demonstrating that the document contains information only the creator would know. (Evid. Code, § 1421.)

Direct evidence of the authenticity of an electronic document may be given by the person who wrote it or a person who witnessed its creation or execution. (Evid. Code, §§ 1411–1413.) Absent such a witness, authenticity must be established indirectly through evidence showing that only the purported author could have created the document, that the document was received in response to a communication sent to the purported author of the writing, or that the writing was acted upon as authentic by the party against whom it is offered. (Evid. Code, § 1414.)

Writings are frequently authenticated by introducing evidence of the handwriting of the author. (Evid. Code, §§ 1415–1419.) In certain instances, analogous procedures can be used for electronic documents. Three such procedures are audit trails, encryption authentication (that is, digital signatures), and transmission via an intermediary. (See Kurzban, *Authentication of*

Computer-Generated Evidence in the United States Federal Courts, 35 J.L. & Tech. 437 (1995); Reed, *Authenticating Electronic Mail Messages—Some Evidential Problems*, IV Software L.J. 161 (1991); Wright, *Authenticating EDI: The Location of a Trusted Recordkeeper*, IV Software L.J. 173 (1991).)

▶ COMMENT

The burden of authenticating electronic documents can be eased substantially by soliciting a pre-trial stipulation from opposing counsel regarding the authenticity of all documents that are not disputed or by seeking admissions during discovery regarding the genuineness of the documents.

---

§ 8.02 In General Audit Trails

The National Computer Security Center, which establishes standards for computer security, defines an "audit trail" as follows: "A chronological record of system activities that is sufficient to enable the reconstruction, reviewing, and examination of the sequence of environments and activities surrounding or leading to an operation, a procedure, or an event in a transaction from its inception to final results." (Cooper, *Implementing Internet Security*, at 129 (New Riders 1995).) In less abstract terms, audit trails are simply computer files that record system usage, such as when a user logs in, the location of the user at the time of login, and what activities the user engages in while using the computer. (See § 2.09.) At its most basic level, an audit trail can be analogized to the way fax machines identify the sender at the top or bottom of each page of a transmitted document.

Audit trails are most likely to be found on large computer systems or networks, particularly those running the Unix or Windows NT operating systems. In the case of e-mail, an audit trail would be created for billing purposes if it is sent through an online provider such as America Online, CompuServe, or Prodigy.

The system manager or operator of the computer or network is normally the only person who has access to audit trail information. Since the audit trail provides a link between a particular person's or entity's computer and a document, it can be used for authentication purposes under Evidence Code section 1400.

Like the identification provided by a fax machine, however, an audit trail has certain inherent limitations for purposes of authentication:

▪ The audit trail only identifies the *computer* that sent the message or document, not the *sender*.

- It is possible to program a computer to produce a false audit trail.

- The audit trail does not provide any evidence as to whether the contents of the document have been altered.

§ 8.03 Encryption Authentication

[A] Overview

Encryption is a means of coding messages and other documents so they appear to be random characters. For example, the message "meet me Monday" may look like "#*%Mn yUj78#" when encrypted. The original message, "meet me Monday," is called the "plaintext" version of the message. The encoded message, "#*%Mn yUj78#," is called the "ciphertext" version of the message. Without an appropriate password, the message cannot be read once it is encrypted.

The plaintext version of a message is related to the ciphertext version by a mathematical algorithm. But it is "computationally infeasible" to derive one from the other. In other words, it would take so many years of round-the-clock computer time to discover the relationship between the plaintext and ciphertext that the message would no longer be relevant or useful.

There are essentially two types of encryption in general use today: private key encryption and public key encryption. The primary difference between the two methods is the number of passwords or "keys" that are used. Public key encryption is clearly the encryption method of choice for most e-mail users. On the other hand, private key encryption is very popular for securing documents and other information on private computer networks.

The keys used to encrypt and decrypt information are unique random numbers of a specified length. The numbers are expressed in binary form (that is, either a "1" or a "0"). Popular key lengths are 40, 56, and 128 binary digits or "bits." For example, a simple 8-bit key might appear as 10001001. While a person attempting to guess an 8-bit key has only to try 2^8 or 256 combinations to find the correct number, a 128-bit key has 2^{128} or 3.4×10^{38} (that is a 3 followed by 38 zeros) combinations and would take years of computer time to break.

[B] Private Key Encryption

Private key (symmetric) encryption uses only one secret password. The same secret password is used to encode and decode the document. An example of private key encryption would be the passwords used to encode word-processing or spreadsheet files. A popular form of private key encryption used on the Internet, particularly in newsgroups, is the ROT13 cipher. Basically, this code substitutes each letter of a message with the letter 13 places away from it in the alphabet. For example, the message "hi" would encode to "uv." Because of its prevalence, most Internet browser software can automatically decode ROT13 ciphers.

Private key encryption can be made as simple or as complex as desired, but the documents encoded can be no more secure than the security of the password. If the password falls into the wrong hands, the security of all documents encrypted with that password is compromised. This is why private key encryption is normally only appropriate for the protection of computer files, such as word processing files, that are used on a single machine and require one or, at most, a few users to have access to them.

Private key systems for e-mail are difficult to implement unless there is a secure means of exchanging the password between the sender and recipient of the message. This apparent weak-link in security is overcome by the use of "public key encryption."

[C] Public Key Encryption

In public key (asymmetric) encryption every user has two passwords: one private, the other public. The public passwords are exchanged freely and are frequently listed in public directories on the Internet. In contrast, the private password is known only to its owner and is never shared with anyone else. The public and private passwords are related by a complex mathematical formula, which prevents one password from being deduced from the other. The public password can be widely disseminated without compromising security.

As illustrated by the following examples, public key encryption can be used to encode messages to achieve various purposes:

Sending Confidential E-Mail. If a business wants to send a confidential message to a client, the business would use the client's public key to encode the message. On receipt of the e-mail, the client would decode the message using its private key. If the message is intercepted by an unauthorized party, the message will be unreadable and cannot be decoded with the client's public key. Only the client's private key can be used to read the message.

Ensuring the Authenticity of a Message. Public key encryption can also be used to ensure a message is authentic (that is, that the message was actually sent by the sender and that the message has not been altered or modified in anyway). This is accomplished when the sender encrypts the message using its private key. On receipt of the e-mail, the recipient can decode the message using the sender's public key. The sender's public key will only decode the message if (1) the message was encrypted with the sender's private key and (2) the message has not been modified or altered in any way. If even a single character of the message has been changed, it will not decode properly. This method of encrypting messages is frequently used by the publishers of electronic newsletters to prevent unauthorized modifications of the information they provide. Subscribers merely use the publisher's public key to decode the newsletter when it is received.

Confidential Messages with Electronic Signatures. If both authenticity and confidentiality are required, the sender must encrypt the message twice—first with the public key of the recipient and then with the sender's own private key. The recipient can decode the message by reversing the process using the sender's public key and the recipient's private key. Provided the public keys of the sender and recipient have not been compromised, this method of sending a message ensures the message was sent by the sender, the message has not been altered, and only the intended recipient can read the message.

The usefulness of public key encryption for purposes of authentication under Evidence Code 1400 should be obvious. As long as the sender's private password has not been compromised, the message must have come from the sender and cannot have been altered. Use of encryption authentication is limited, however, because relatively few computer users employ encryption to protect their documents and communications.

§ 8.04 Intermediary Transmission

The final method of authenticating electronic documents is transmission via an intermediary. In some instances the parties themselves have intentionally built into their communications a means of ensuring authentication. Specifically, the parties agree to send each of their electronic messages through a trusted intermediary who retains a copy of each transmission. Such agreements are common in electronic banking and certain shipping transactions. (Reed, *Authenticating Electronic Mail Messages—Some Evidential Problems*, IV Software L.J. 161, 168 (1991);. see *Model Electronic Data Interchange Trading Partner Agreement and Commentary*, IV Software L.J. 179 (1991).) If a question arises as to the contents or originator of a particular communication, the intermediary can easily resolve the dispute by consulting its copy of the message. The copy retained by the intermediary can also be used to authenticate the document. The downside of this method is that the use of an intermediary, like encryption, is not commonplace.

§ 8.05 References

    WITKIN For general discussion of authentication of evidence, see 2 Witkin, Cal. Evidence (3d ed. 1986) Documentary Evidence, § 903 et seq.).

    THE RUTTER GROUP For a practical guide to authentication issues at trial, see Cal. Practice Guide: Civ. Trials & Evidence, ¶ 8:310 et seq.

    WEST'S KEY NUMBER SYSTEM See the following key numbers in West's Cal. Digest 2d, Evidence (Topic 157):

        Preliminary evidence for authentication (Evidence ☞ 369 et seq.).

    WESTLAW® See the WESTLAW Electronic Research Guide at the beginning of this volume.

B. Forms

§ 8.06 Example Direct Examination

[A] Authenticating an E-mail Message by Its Author

Q: Mr. Black, I am handing you a copy of a piece of e-mail, which has been marked as Defense Exhibit A for identification. Do you recognize this document?

A: Yes.

Q: How do you recognize the document?

A: I wrote this e-mail to Mr. Jones on January 5, 1998.

Q: Does this Exhibit accurately reflect the message you sent?

A: Yes it does.

Q: Your Honor, I offer the e-mail as Defense Exhibit next in order.

[B] Authenticating an Electronic Record

Q: Mr. Black, does your employer record information about employee activity on the Internet?

A: Yes it does.

Q: How is that activity recorded?

A: We use a computer program to monitor Internet activity. It automatically logs or records each Web site an employee visits.

Q: And how is this information stored?

A: The computer stores the date, time, employee name, and Web sites visited in a special file on the hard disk of our network.

Q: Who has access to that file?

A: Only the system manager has access to the file. The file is password protected and may not be accessed by any other user on the system.

Q: And who is the system manager?

A: I am.

Q: Are you familiar with the operation and use of the monitoring software?

A: Yes I am. I personally installed and configured the software. I am responsible for ensuring the logging information is properly recorded.

Q: Mr. Black, I am handing you a computer printout, which has been marked as Defense Exhibit A for identification. Do you recognize this document?

A: Yes I do.

Q: How do you recognize the document?

A: I prepared it.

Q: What does the exhibit represent?

A: This is a printout of a portion of the log file created by our Internet monitoring software.

Q: How was this printout prepared?

A: I directed our monitoring software to printout the Internet activity of employee Jim Smith on March 3, 1998.

Q: And is this exhibit a copy of the printout generated by the monitoring software?

A: Yes it is.

Q: Your Honor, I offer the printout as Defense Exhibit next in order.

9   THE SECONDARY EVIDENCE RULE

A. Text

§ 9.01 Secondary Evidence Rule Replaces Best Evidence Rule

In the absence of an exception, the former Best Evidence Rule provided that no evidence other than the original of a writing was admissible to prove the content of the writing. (Former Evid. Code, § 1500 et seq. (repealed Jan. 1, 1999, by Stats. 1998, ch. 100, § 1).) The rule was designed to minimize the possibility of misinterpreting or misrepresenting the contents of a writing. (*People v. Bizieff* (1991) 226 Cal.App.3d 1689 [277 Cal.Rptr. 678].) In essence, the Best Evidence Rule maintains that it is preferable for the trier of fact to review the complete original document rather than a copy that may have been tampered with or that may only represent some portion of the original.

To adapt to changes in technology, the California Legislature made several substantive revisions to the Best Evidence Rule over the years, ultimately culminating in the recent repeal of the entire rule. In 1983, an exception to the rule was enacted for hardcopy printouts of information stored on computers. (Former Evid. Code, § 1500.5.) At the urging of law enforcement agencies, the Legislature acted again in 1996 to add an exception for images stored on video tape and digital media. (Former Evid. Code, 1500.6.) In 1998, the Legislature took the dramatic step of repealing (as of January 1, 1999) the entire Best Evidence Rule article in the Evidence Code and replacing it with an entirely new article, entitled "Proof of the Content of a Writing." As a result, California no longer has a "Best Evidence Rule."

Under the new rule, the "content of a writing may be proved by an otherwise admissible original." (Evid. Code, § 1520.) In particular, the content of a writing may be proved by otherwise admissible secondary evidence, unless (1) a genuine dispute exists concerning material terms of the writing and justice requires its exclusion or (2) admission of the secondary evidence would be unfair. (Evid. Code, § 1521, subd. (a).) This new rule is known as the "Secondary Evidence Rule." (Evid. Code, § 1521, subd. (d).) Evidentiary determinations made prior to the operative date of the Secondary Evidence Rule are not invalidated, but proponents of evidence excluded under the former Best Evidence Rule may, before entry of judgment, make a new request for admission of the evidence based on the new rule. (Stats. 1998, ch. 100, § 9(c).)

§ 9.02 When Is an Electronic Copy Best?

If the contents of a writing are in dispute, both the traditional Best Evidence Rule and the new Secondary Evidence Rule ordinarily require the original (or an acceptable copy) to be introduced. (Evid. Code, §§ 1520, 1521; former Evid. Code, § 1500.) For electronic documents, the concept of an "original" is difficult to define. The Evidence Code, however, provides a simple answer: if "data are stored in a computer or similar device, any printout or other output readable by sight, shown to reflect the data accurately," constitutes an "original" of the electronic information. (Evid. Code, § 255.) The approach adopted in Evidence Code section 255 allows for the possibility that multiple or, even, an infinite number of originals may exist. Each time an electronic document is printed, a new "original" is created. (See, e.g., *Aguimatang v. California State Lottery* (1991) 234 Cal.App.3d 769, 797 [286 Cal.Rptr. 57] (interpreting former Evid. Code, § 1500).)

Because Evidence Code section 255 does not require printouts of an electronic document to be made from any particular copy of the document, anomalous results may occur. Consider the following example:

> A flower store sends an e-mail order to its supplier requesting the delivery of 1,000 roses. The supplier delivers 10,000 roses. A dispute arises regarding the amount of the order. The flower store prints out a copy of the e-mail it sent, which states that 1,000 roses were ordered. A hardcopy of the e-mail received by the supplier shows that the flower store ordered 10,000 roses. Under Evidence Code section 255, both messages are "originals" of the same electronic document.

In the foregoing example, the trier of fact will have to weigh the evidence offered in support of each "original" and make a determination as to which e-mail accurately reflects the flower store's order. In such a case, the deciding factor may be the existence of a copy of the message in the possession of an independent third party. If the message was sent over the Internet or through a commercial online service, the service provider may have a copy of the message on a backup tape. Such records can be subpoenaed to confirm which copy of the e-mail is the true message. It should be noted that a printout of the e-mail in the service provider's possession will also constitute an "original" of the message. (Evid. Code, § 255.)

§ 9.03 Printed Representations of Electronic Documents

Printed representations of computer information and computer programs are "presumed to be accurate representations of the computer information or computer program that it purports to represent." (Evid. Code, § 1552, subd. (a).) This presumption, however, only affects the burden of producing evidence. If another party to the litigation introduces evidence showing the printed representation is unreliable or inaccurate, the proponent of the computer information has the burden of showing, by a preponderance of the evidence, that the printed representation is an accurate representation of the existence and content of the computer information or computer programs that it purports to represent. (Evid. Code, § 1552, subd. (a).)

▶ **COMMENT**

It appears that computer-generated summaries and graphs (for example, monthly sales information or graphs of utility usage) may be introduced under the new Secondary Evidence Rule. Under the former rules, such materials could be admitted under the voluminous writings exception to the Best Evidence Rule. (Former Evid. Code, § 1509.)

---

§ 9.04 Images on Video or Digital Media

A printed representation of images stored on video or digital media is "presumed to be an accurate representation of the images it purports to represent." (Evid. Code, § 1553; see former Evid. Code § 1500.6, subd. (a).) This presumption, however, only affects the burden of producing evidence. If another party to the litigation introduces evidence showing the printed representation is unreliable or inaccurate, the proponent of the image will have the burden of showing, by a preponderance of the evidence, that the printed representation is "an accurate representation of the existence and content of the images that it purports to represent." (Evid. Code, § 1553; see former Evid. Code § 1500.6, subd. (a).)

§ 9.05 References

📖 **WITKIN** For general discussion of secondary evidence and the former best evidence rule, see 2 Witkin, Cal. Evidence (3d ed. 1986) Documentary Evidence, § 922 et seq.).

▦ **THE RUTTER GROUP** For a practical guide to proving contents of writings, see Cal. Practice Guide: Civ. Trials & Evidence, ¶ 8:375 et seq.

⚷ **WEST'S KEY NUMBER SYSTEM** See the following key numbers in West's Cal. Digest 2d, Evidence (Topic 157):

▪ Best and secondary evidence (Evidence ⚷ 157 et seq.).

▭ **WESTLAW®** See the WESTLAW Electronic Research Guide at the beginning of this volume.

B. Forms

§ 9.06 Example Direct Examination

Q: Mr. Black, I am handing you a copy of a piece of e-mail, which has been marked as Defense Exhibit A for identification. Do you recognize this document?

A: Yes.

Q: How do you recognize the document?

A: I received this e-mail in response to an e-mail that I had sent to Mr. Green.

Q: How do you know that this e-mail was in response to the message you had sent to Mr. Green?

A: On June 2, 1998, I sent an e-mail to Mr. Green inquiring about the status of our purchase order. I was concerned that our order had not been filled. The day after I sent my message, I received an e-mail from Mr. Green stating that our purchase order would be filled within five business days.

Q: Does this exhibit accurately reflect the message you received?

A: Yes. This is the printout of the message I made at your request using my company's e-mail software.

Q: Your Honor, I offer the printout as Defense Exhibit next in order.

Opposing Counsel: Objection. Counsel has failed to authenticate the exhibit.

Counsel: Your Honor, we have laid a proper foundation for the exhibit under Evidence Code section 1414. The message was received in response to a communication sent to Mr. Green.

Court: Objection overruled.

Opposing Counsel: Your Honor, we further object to the exhibit on the ground that it does not satisfy the requirements of Section 1520 of the Evidence Code.

Counsel: Your honor, the document constitutes an accurate printed representation of computer information and as such constitutes an otherwise admissible original.

Court: Objection overruled.

10 THE HEARSAY RULE

A. Text

§ 10.01 Introduction

Hearsay is a "statement that was made other than by a witness while testifying at the hearing and that is offered to prove the truth of the matter stated." (Evid. Code, § 1200, subd. (a).) The word "statement" is defined broadly in Evidence Code section 225 as an (a) oral or written verbal expression or (b) nonverbal conduct of a person intended by him as a substitute for oral or written verbal expression.

If an electronic document is offered for the truth of its contents, it would be hearsay and inadmissible in the absence of an applicable exception. The three most frequently used exceptions to the hearsay rule for electronic documents are those for admissions, business records, and official records. (Evid. Code, §§ 1270–1284; *Aguimatang v. California State Lottery* (1991) 234 Cal.App.3d 769, 797 [286 Cal.Rptr. 57] (computerized lottery records as official records); *People v. Lugashi* (1988) 205 Cal.App.3d 632, 638 [252 Cal.Rptr. 434] (computerized bank records as business records); Zupanec, Annotation, *Admissibility of Computerized Private Business Records*, 7 A.L.R.4th 8; Goger, Annotation, *Proof of Public Records Kept or Stored on Electronic Computing Equipment*, 71 A.L.R.3d 232, 236–240.) These exceptions are discussed in Sections 10.03–10.05.

Electronic documents may also be relevant for purposes other than to prove the facts stated in them. In such cases, the documents do not constitute hearsay. (*Smith v. Whittier* (1892) 95 Cal. 279 [30 P. 529].) The operative fact doctrine is one such nonhearsay use of an electronic document.

§ 10.02 Operative Fact Doctrine

As with any other document, electronic documents are not hearsay if they are merely used to establish an operative fact, such as documents having legal consequences in and of themselves. As originally articulated, the operative fact doctrine was as follows: "There is a well established exception or departure from the hearsay rule applying to cases in which the fact in controversy is whether certain things were said or done and not as to whether these things were true or false, and in these cases the words or acts are admissible not as hearsay, but as original evidence." (*People v. Fields* (1998) 61 Cal.App.4th 1063, 1069 [72 Cal.Rptr.2d 255], quoting *People v. Henry* (1948) 86 Cal.App.2d 785, 789 [195 P.2d 478].)

Two examples will illustrate the application of the operative fact doctrine to electronic evidence:

- An e-mail sent by a manufacturer to a supplier accepting the terms of a contract are not hearsay. The message "I accept" can be used not to prove the truth of any facts asserted but just that the words were transmitted, because the transmission of the words creates an agreement under substantive contract law.

- Invoices sent from independent contractor to a software developer may be admissible as operative facts to establish the nature of their relationship (employer/independent contractor versus employer/employee) and not as proof for the truth of the matters stated in the invoices. (See *Rogers v. Whitson* (1964) 228 Cal.App.2d 662, 675 [39 Cal.Rptr. 849] (addressing introduction of hardcopy invoices).)

§ 10.03 Admissions

Evidence of an out of court statement is not made inadmissible by the hearsay rule when offered against the declarant in an action to which the declarant is a party. (Evid. Code, § 1220.) Thus, when information obtained from a party's own computer is offered against that party, the evidence will generally be admissible as an admission. Similarly, if an electronic document, such as an e-mail, is properly authenticated as having been created by a party, the document is admissible against that party as an admission.

§ 10.04 Business and Official Records

Offering an electronic document under either the business records or official records exceptions to the hearsay rule is similar to authentication. (See Chapter 8.) In both instances, the proponent of the evidence has the burden of laying a foundation that shows the records are trustworthy. (Evid. Code, §§ 1271, subd. (d), 1280, subd. (c).) Such a showing requires the proponent to establish each of the following elements:

1. The writing was made in the regular course of business or, if an official record, was made by and within the scope of duty of a public employee;

2. The writing was made at or near the time of the act, condition, or event;

3. The custodian or other qualified witness testifies to its identity and the mode of its preparation (proof of this element is not required for official records [Evid. Code, § 1280]); and

4. The sources of information and method and time of preparation were such as to indicate its truthfulness.

The decision in *People v. Lugashi* (1988) 205 Cal.App.3d 632 [252 Cal.Rptr. 434] provided one of the first substantive discussions of the use of the business records exception in the context of electronic documents. *Lugashi* involved the conviction of a rug merchant for grand theft and receiving stolen property. The charges were based in large part on computer records of credit card transactions. The defendant appealed the conviction, arguing the prosecution had failed to lay a sufficient foundation for the introduction of the computer records. The computer records were authenticated at trial by a bank employee who worked in the credit card fraud and loss control department. Although the employee was not a computer expert, she was familiar with the system, had supervised the preparation of the records, and knew how to interpret the records. The prosecution did not offer any authority regarding the computer hardware or software, its maintenance or reliability, or any system of internal checks to ensure the accuracy of the data collected.

Relying on authority from other states, the defendant urged the court of appeal to adopt a test requiring the proponent of computer evidence to introduce testimony on the acceptability and reliability of the particular hardware and software involved, as well as internal maintenance and accuracy checks, as a prerequisite to admissibility under the business records exception to the hearsay rule. (*People v. Lugashi* (1988) 205 Cal.App.3d 632, 638 [252 Cal.Rptr. 434].) The court of appeal rejected the proposed test, finding that it "incorrectly presumes computer data to be unreliable, and, unlike any other business record, requires its proponent to disprove the possibility of error, not to convince the trier of fact to accept it, but merely to meet the minimal showing required for admission." (*People v. Lugashi* (1988) 205 Cal.App.3d 632, 640 [252 Cal.Rptr. 434].) If such a standard was applied to conventional hand-entered accounting records, the court reasoned, the defendant's argument would require not only the testimony of the bookkeeper records custodian, but that of an expert in accounting theory that the particular system of accounting employed, if properly applied, would yield accurate and relevant information.

The appellate court also rejected the argument that only a computer expert, who could personally perform the programming and inspect and maintain the software and hardware, is competent to testify as to the preparation and interpretation of the computer records. Instead, the court found that any "person who generally understands the system's operation and possesses sufficient knowledge and skill to properly use the system and explain the resultant data, even if unable to perform every task from initial design and programming to final printout is a 'qualified witness' for purposes of Evidence Code section 1271." (*People v. Lugashi* (1988) 205 Cal.App.3d 632, 640 [252 Cal.Rptr. 434]; see *Aguimatang v. California State Lottery* (1991) 234 Cal.App.3d 769, 797 [286 Cal.Rptr. 57].)

Finally, the court of appeal reasoned that requiring testimony regarding the accuracy and reliability of the computer system "could require production of a horde of witnesses representing each department of a company's data processing system, not to rebut an actual attack on the reliability of their data, but merely to meet the minimal requirement for admissibility." (*People v. Lugashi* (1988) 205 Cal.App.3d 632, 640 [252 Cal.Rptr. 434].) The time required to produce this additional testimony would unduly burden the already crowded trial courts to no real benefit. Even if some businesses can produce such a phalanx of witnesses, most cannot afford to do so. This is particularly so when the business producing the records is neither a party to the litigation nor interested in the outcome. "Common sense compels rejection of such a requirement." (*People v. Lugashi* (1988) 205 Cal.App.3d 632, 640 [252 Cal.Rptr. 434].)

▶ **COMMENT**

Not every electronic record created in the ordinary course of business constitutes a "business record" for purposes of the exception to the hearsay rule. Entering hearsay into a computer in the normal course of business does not render such evidence nonhearsay when it is retrieved from the computer, even when most of the requirements of the business records exception to the hearsay rule are met. (*People v. Hernandez* (1997) 55 Cal.App.4th 225, 241 [63 Cal.Rptr.2d 769].) For example, even though there may be a duty on the part of a police officer to create and file certain reports, such a requirement does not transform the report of an accident into competent, reliable, trustworthy evidence merely because the information contained in the report is transferred to a computer. (*People v. Hernandez* (1997) 55 Cal.App.4th 225, 240–241 [63 Cal.Rptr.2d 769]; *Carlton v. Department of Motor Vehicles* (1988) 203 Cal.App.3d 1428, 1433 [250 Cal.Rptr. 809].) If hearsay is contained within a business record, a separate exclusion must exist for the evidence (for example, admission or excited utterance).

---

§ 10.05   Qualifying the Authenticating Witness

Even though California has adopted a somewhat relaxed standard for qualified witnesses under Evidence Code section 1271, to withstand cross-examination such witnesses should be capable of testifying, at minimum, to all of the following:

- The type and reliability of the computer equipment used to store and produce the records.

- The manner in which the data was entered into the computer system and that the entry was made in the ordinary course of business.

- The data was entered at or near the time the events occurred and by persons who had personal knowledge of the events.

- Measures taken to ensure the accuracy of the data as it was entered, sometimes referred to as error detection or "trapping." Many computer programs have built-in error trapping to prevent incorrect information from being entered, such as calendaring programs that warn when events are scheduled on weekends and holidays.

- The method of storing the data, such as disk, tape, and optical drives, and the precautions taken to prevent its loss or modification. Questions may arise as to whether the data was corrupted or altered. Data loss may occur from temperature changes, power surges, and mishandling of the storage device. For example, the data stored on magnetic media, such as floppy disks or tapes, can be corrupted by coming in contact with a magnetic field or x-ray.

- If a computer program manipulates data, the reliability of the program to perform such manipulations or calculations accurately must be established. For example, if information is entered into a spreadsheet, the calculations performed by the spreadsheet must be shown to be accurate. The creator of the computer program will normally provide, on request, audit information demonstrating the accuracy of the software.

- The employees or other persons who had access to the data. Many data entry programs record the date, time, and identity of each person entering or modifying information on the computer.

- Whether passwords or other security measures were used to limit access to the data. If a system requires a password, the computer probably maintains a "password log" containing the date, time, and identity of each person who accessed the system.

- The time and method of preparing the hardcopy/printout of the data. Questions may arise as to whether the data is "raw" (printed directly from the computer's memory) or has been formatted or modified for purposes of the printout.

● WARNING

A distinction should be made between cases like *Lugashi* (see § 10.04) involving computers that merely *store* data and cases in which the computer performs calculations or otherwise manipulates the data. In the latter cases, the system will generally receive greater scrutiny to ensure the calculations or manipulations are performed accurately (that is, the information is trustworthy): "Systems . . . which perform calculations must be scrutinized more thoroughly than those systems which merely retrieve information." (*People v. Bovio* (1983) 118 Ill.App.3d 836, 833 [455 N.E.2d 829].) As such, the authenticating witness should be prepared, at least in a general way, to address these more technical issues.

▶ COMMENT

Care should be exercised in situations where the authenticating witness goes beyond merely authenticating the electronic record, and is essentially rendering expert opinion testimony. This problem may arise when the electronic evidence is statistical in nature or represents a compilation of information and there is a danger that the witness's testimony may give a "false aura of computer infallibility." (*People v. Hernandez* (1997) 55 Cal.App.4th 225, 241 [63 Cal.Rptr.2d 769].) In *Hernandez*, the prosecution introduced the testimony of a police officer regarding the results of searches she performed in a sex crimes database for crimes similar to those committed by the defendant. The testimony was introduced to link the defendant to additional crimes. In ruling the testimony was not admissible under the business records exception to the hearsay rule, the court of appeal focused on the following facts: the various sources of information that were input into the database may not have been trustworthy, the information input into the database was itself hearsay, and the testifying police officer was portrayed, without appropriate qualification, as an expert.

---

§ 10.06 References

📖 **WITKIN** For general discussion of the hearsay rule, see 1 Witkin, Cal. Evidence (3d ed. 1986) The Hearsay Rule, § 558 et seq.

▦ **THE RUTTER GROUP** For a practical guide to hearsay evidence and hearsay exceptions, see Cal. Practice Guide: Civ. Trials & Evidence, ¶ 8:1000 et seq.

🔑 **WEST'S KEY NUMBER SYSTEM** See the following key numbers in West's Cal. Digest 2d, Evidence (Topic 157):

▪ Hearsay (Evidence 🔑 314 et seq.).

💻 **WESTLAW®** See the WESTLAW Electronic Research Guide at the beginning of this volume.

B. Forms

§ 10.07 Checklist of Authentication Issues for the Business Records Exception

❑ The business uses a computer in the normal course of its operations.

❑ The computer and related software are reliable (e.g., the business stores its critical data on the system, the hardware and software are from leading vendors, other businesses use the same hardware and software).

❑ The business has developed procedures for entering data into the computer to ensure that entry errors are minimized (the software itself may be written to detect and flag potential errors).

❑ The data entry procedures were followed in this case.

❑ The computer and software were in good working order at the time of the entry of the data.

❑ The computer and software were in good working order at the time the information was printed out for purposes of trial.

❑ The authenticating witness testifies that he/she recognizes the printout.

❑ The authenticating witness testifies how he or she recognizes the printout.

§ 10.08 Example Direct Examination

[A] Admission of Party

Q: Mr. Black, I am handing you a copy of a piece of e-mail, which has been marked as Defense Exhibit A for identification. Do you recognize this document?

A: Yes.

Q: How do you recognize the document?

A: I received this e-mail in response to an e-mail that I had sent to Mr. Green.

Q: How do you know that this e-mail was in response to the message you had sent to Mr. Green?

A: On June 2, 1998, I sent an e-mail to Mr. Green inquiring about the status of our purchase order. I was concerned that our order had not been filled. The day after I sent my message, I received an e-mail from Mr. Green stating that our purchase order would be filled within five business days.

Q: Does this exhibit accurately reflect the message you received?

A: Yes. This is the printout of the message I made at your request using my company's e-mail software.

Q: Your Honor, I offer the printout as Defense Exhibit next in order.

Opposing Counsel: Objection. The e-mail is hearsay, not within any recognized exception.

Counsel: Your Honor, the e-mail is admissible as an admission of a party opponent.

Court: Objection overruled.

[B] Business Records

Q: Ms. Green, are you employed?

A: Yes.

Q: Where do you work?

A: At Stagecoach Bank.

Q: Does your job have a title?

A: I am chief investigator in the credit card fraud department.

Q: How long have you held that position?

A: Approximately five years.

Q: Would you briefly describe your duties as chief investigator?

A: I am responsible for overseeing the bank's investigations of potential credit card fraud. In most instances our investigations focus on the analysis of credit card transactions to identify unusual activity or other indicia of fraudulent use. Our work is conducted using the bank's computer system.

Q: Do you use the computer system yourself?

A: Yes. I have used the computer system on a daily basis since I was first employed by the bank.

Q: Are you familiar with how reports of credit card activity are generated?

A: Yes. I personally prepare and print those types of reports several times each day.

Q: I am handing you a document, which has been marked as Defense Exhibit A for identification. Do you recognize this document?

A: Yes.

Q: How do you recognize the document?

A: This is a report of the purchasing activity for credit card number xxxx-xxxxx-xxxx. I printed this report at your request.

Q: Can you describe in more detail what this report shows us?

A: This report shows the date, amount, and location of each purchase made with this particular credit card from April through June of this year.

Q: Where does this information come from?

A: Each time the credit card is used at a merchant's location, information concerning the merchant, the date of the purchase, and the amount of the purchase is transmitted to the bank's central computer over the telephone. The information can be phoned in orally by the merchant, in which case the information is entered into the computer by one of our employees trained to record such transactions. The information can also be transmitted by a point of sale terminal directly into our computer. Once the information is stored in our computer, it is available to be printed out in the form shown in this exhibit.

Q: Are any calculations performed on the information?

A: No. None of the information is changed once it is stored on our computer. The printout merely arranges the transactions in chronological order.

Q: How soon after the transaction occurs is the information recorded in the bank's computer?

A: Seconds. Before the merchant will allow the purchase it waits for an authorization from the bank. The authorization is transmitted to the merchant at the same time as the transaction information is stored in the computer. For all practical purposes the information is stored contemporaneously with the purchase.

Q: Your Honor, I offer the printout as Defense Exhibit next in order.

11   ELECTRONIC PRESENTATIONS

A. Text

§ 11.01 Computer-Generated Visual Evidence

Computer-generated visual evidence (CGVE) is evidence created by a computer for use at trial, generally as demonstrative evidence. CGVE can be as simple as a pie chart printed out from a popular spreadsheet program or as complex as a simulation of a plane crash costing tens of thousands of dollars to create. CGVE is generally used to assist the trier of fact in understanding complex facts and in visualizing abstract scientific principles. A few examples will serve to illustrate the use of CGVE in litigation:

- A criminal forensics expert uses an off-the-shelf computer-aided design/drafting program to generate printouts of a crime scene. The printouts are used to illustrate the expert's opinions at trial.

- In an environmental cleanup action, a complex mathematical simulation is used to demonstrate how a toxic plume seeping from an underground storage tank spread to a nearby river.

- In a patent infringement suit, a computer animation is used to illustrate the basic operation of an invention used to synthesize various chemicals.

Although it is difficult to pinpoint the first use of CGVE in California, the first substantial use of such evidence in federal court appears to have occurred during the trial following the crash of Delta Airlines flight 191 at the Dallas/Fort Worth Airport on August 2, 1985. (See *In re Air Crash at Dallas/Fort Worth Airport* (N.D. Tex. 1989) 720 F. Supp. 1258.) The crash killed 128 passengers, 8 crew, and 1 person on the ground. Both sides in the litigation used CGVE simulations to support their versions of the cause of the crash. Both sides objected to the introduction of the other's simulation. The trial court allowed both simulations to be admitted into evidence.

Because of the tremendous persuasive capability of CGVE, courts have been justifiably concerned about potential of such evidence to mislead juries. (*People v. Hernandez* (1997) 55 Cal.App.4th 225, 241 [63 Cal.Rptr.2d 769] (computers may give a "false aura of . . . infallibility"); 2 McCormick on Evidence 19 (4th ed. 1992) (With respect to one party's staged reproduction of facts "not only is the danger that the jury may confuse art with reality particularly great, but the impressions generated by the evidence may prove particularly difficult to limit . . . .").) Consequently, courts generally focus on two issues in considering the admissibility of CGVE:

[February 1999]

- Whether the evidence is more prejudicial than probative.

- Whether the evidence is sufficiently "trustworthy"; that is, whether the underlying scientific principles are sound; whether the evidence is based on accurate data; and whether the evidence accurately portrays that which it purports to represent.

▶ **COMMENT**

Because only a handful of California decisions have addressed the admissibility of CGVE, seminal decisions from other jurisdictions are included in this chapter to illustrate approaches used by other courts in analyzing this type of evidence.

---

§ 11.02   Types of CGVE

In general, CGVE can be grouped into three general categories: (1) diagrams, charts, and graphs; (2) animations; and (3) simulations.

[A]   Diagrams, Charts, and Graphs

Diagrams, charts, and graphs are by far the most common, least controversial, and least expensive form of CGVE. Such evidence is typically generated by off-the-shelf word processing, spreadsheet, and presentation graphics programs. For example, a spreadsheet program could be used to take a list of monthly sales figures and generate a summary graph showing how sales declined after a particular date or event. A spreadsheet could be used to create damage calculation charts. Commercially available electronic drafting software (sometimes called computer-aided design or CAD software) could be used to draw the layout of a factory floor and the location of relevant pieces of machinery. CAD software is also frequently used in criminal actions to depict the relative location of bodies and the direction in which bullets were fired.

The hallmark of this type of CGVE is that it is a static two or three dimensional representation of data or some physical device or location. Given sufficient time, such evidence could be created by an individual using pen and paper (for example, manually plotting each sales figure on a piece of graph paper). The computer is merely used to automate the process. (See *Department of Environmental Resources v. Al Hamilton Contracting Company* (Pa.Cmwlth. 1995) 665 A.2d 849.)

[B] Animations

A computer animation is essentially a video or movie of an expert's theory of a particular event or occurrence. A computer is used to create a series of still images, just as a cartoonist would draw by hand the movements of a figure. The images are recorded, one image at a time, in the computer's memory or transferred to videotape. Like the cartoonist's drawings, the computer images can be played back in succession, resulting in a moving picture or graphic. Courts generally view animations as demonstrative, rather than substantive, evidence. They are used to visually demonstrate some aspect of an expert's opinion or a scientific principle. Animations are not intended to represent precise recreations of an event.

For example, in a case of first impression in Florida, a trial court was found to have properly admitted a three-minute computer animation of an automobile accident as demonstrative evidence to illustrate an expert's view of how the fatal crash occurred. (*Pierce v. State* (Fla.App. 4th Dist. 1996) 671 So.2d 186 [1996 WL 106372].) Similarly, a district court in New York admitted an animation that illustrated the plaintiff's expert's theory of how a fire started in the engine compartment of a plane. (*Datskow v. Teledyne Continental Motors* (W.D.N.Y. 1993) 826 F. Supp. 677, 685.) The defendants attempted to exclude the evidence, arguing the animation was "less an illustration of [the expert's theory] than a purported recreation of the accident." The court rejected defendants' argument on the grounds that the jury had been instructed that the tape was only being shown "to help the jury understand the expert's opinion as to what happened and that it's not a recreation" and that the court had ordered potentially prejudicial radio communications between the airport and the control tower be turned off so that the jury could not hear them. (*Datskow v. Teledyne Continental Motors* (W.D.N.Y. 1993) 826 F. Supp. 677, 685.)

[C] Simulations

In contrast to a computer-generated animation, which is intended to merely illustrate an expert's conception of an event or process, a simulation combines the ability of the computer to create animations with its ability to perform complex calculations and projections to present a purported recreation of an actual event. For example, computers are frequently used to apply the laws of physics based on known data from the scene of an accident, such as the weight of the cars, road surface conditions, lighting conditions, skid mark measurements, and other data. This data is processed by the computer to generate a recreation of the accident.

§ 11.03 When to Consider Using CGVE

Because of its cost and potential hurdles to admissibility, CGVE may not be appropriate in every action. In general, CGVE should be considered if one or more of the following circumstances exist:

- The event, process, or condition at issue is difficult to explain verbally.
- The relevant event is complex or includes many interrelated or simultaneously operating factors (for example, the operation of a complex piece of machinery).
- A traditional recreation or re-enactment is impractical or impossible.
- The timing of the event is relevant (for example, the timing of the progress of a fire or explosion).
- Large volumes of data must be manipulated or presented.

☀ WARNING

To avoid a claim of unfair surprise and to increase the likelihood that a judge will permit the introduction of CGVE, the proponent of the evidence should consider providing notice to both the court and opposing counsel of its intent to introduce CGVE. Such notice should be gauged to provide adequate time for the opposing party to conduct discovery regarding the evidence and, possibly, to prepare its own responsive evidence. (See, e.g., *Lopez v. Foremost Paving, Inc.* (TX 1990) 796 S.W.2d 473 (admission of videotape simulating defendant's version of an automobile accident that was not timely produced in response to plaintiff's discovery request constituted reversible error).)

---

§ 11.04 Admissibility of CGVE—In General

[A] Foundational Requirements

CGVE is generally viewed as demonstrative, not substantive, evidence. Demonstrative evidence is admissible to the same extent as the underlying testimony to which it relates. As discussed in [C] below, Evidence Code section 352 provides courts with broad discretion to exclude demonstrative evidence when its probative value is substantially outweighed by the risks of undue consumption of time, undue prejudice, or potentially confusing the jury.

The foundational requirements imposed on the proponent of demonstrative evidence depend on the nature of the evidence. With regard to graphics, charts, diagrams, and models, such demonstrative evidence is generally admissible if it constitutes a "fair representation" of the evidence it purports to represent. (See, e.g., *People v. De La Plane* (1979) 88 Cal.App.3d 223 [151 Cal.Rptr. 843] (trial judge exercised sound discretion in admitting material objects for illustrative purposes, notwithstanding that such material objects were not established to be the specific objects involved in the crime charged); *People v. Slocum* (1975) 52 Cal.App.3d 867 [125 Cal.Rptr. 442] (admission of substantially similar physical objects to illustrate testimony not error).) In contrast, experiments and simulations that purport to represent actual events or occurrences are usually subject to a requirement that they were created or conducted under "substantially similar" circumstances. (*People v. Bonin* (1989) 47 Cal.3d 808, 846–848 [254 Cal.Rptr. 298].)

While there is little guidance as yet from California courts regarding the specific foundational requirements for the various types of CGVE discussed above, it appears likely that diagrams, charts, and graphs and most animations will be governed by the "fair representation" standard (that is, that the offered evidence provides a fair representation of the matter to which it relates), while simulations will require a showing that they are based on substantially similar conditions and facts. This is the approach used in several other jurisdictions. (See, e.g., *Robinson v. Missouri Pacific Railroad Company* (10th Cir. 1994) 16 F.3d 1083; *Loevsky v. Carter* (1989) 70 Haw. 419 [773 P.2d 1120, 1124–1126].) For example, the Hawaii Supreme Court distinguished between videotapes whose purpose is the demonstration of a scientific principle from those that attempt to reenact an occurrence. (*Loevsky v. Carter* (1989) 70 Haw. 419 [773 P.2d 1120, 1124–1126].) The Hawaii court held that video used to illustrate a principle does not require strict adherence to the facts of the event being depicted if the jury is carefully instructed as to the extent to which they are to use and consider the videotape. However, where the video purports to recreate an incident, it must depict all the material facts surrounding the incident.

The Tenth Circuit used a similar approach in affirming the admission of an animation in *Robinson v. Missouri Pacific Railroad Company*. *Robinson* involved a wrongful death suit brought on behalf of a motorist and her child against a railroad for fatal injuries sustained in an intersection collision. The plaintiffs contended that the failure of the crossing gates to close at the proper time allowed them to enter the crossing despite the oncoming train and to become trapped. (*Robinson v. Missouri Pacific Railroad Company* (10th Cir. 1994) 16 F.3d 1083, 1085.) The defendant contended the accident was caused because the plaintiffs attempted to circumvent the crossing gates by driving around them. In support of their claim, plaintiffs offered a computer animation that purportedly showed both versions of the collision. Plaintiffs' expert argued that the final positions of the car and train, as demonstrated in the computer animations, supported his conclusion that the crossing gates had not operated properly. Among other things, the defendant appealed the introduction of the animation, arguing the trial court had abused its discretion. (*Robinson v. Missouri Pacific Railroad Company* (10th Cir. 1994) 16 F.3d 1083, 1086.)

Plaintiffs' expert created his animation by making a scale model of the accident scene, examining the physical evidence and photographs of the wreckage, and observing the scene of the accident. Based on his investigation, the expert created a two-minute silent color video that depicted first his theory of the collision—the car enters the crossing with the gates up and is trapped and hit broadside by the train, then defendant's theory—the car weaves around the lowered gates and is hit by the train. The trial court admitted the animation with the following instruction to the jury (*Robinson v. Missouri Pacific Railroad Company* (10th Cir. 1994) 16 F.3d 1083, 1086):

> Again, I want to emphasize to you that you're not to take this as a recreation of the accident because there's no way that a year or two years after the fact that an accident can be recreated. The only reason this is shown is that . . . [plaintiffs' expert] will testify about certain principles that he feels that this video would show to the jury and perhaps it would be helpful to you. So just bear in mind that you cannot recreate an accident.

The court in *Robinson* followed much the same approach as that outlined in the Hawaii Supreme Court's decision in *Loevsky*: The court determined that the animation was merely intended to illustrate a principle on which the plaintiffs' expert based his theory of the accident and was not intended to represent a recreation of the actual accident. Because the animation was not required to depict all material facts surrounding the incident, the trial court overruled defense objections to certain missing or inaccurate details (for example, lighting at the crossing gates, sound, and unproven vehicle speeds). "Given the limited, solely illustrative purpose for introducing the exhibit, the cautionary instruction to the jury, and the opportunity for vigorous cross-examination," the court of appeal affirmed the trial court's exercise of discretion in admitting the animation. (*Robinson v. Missouri Pacific Railroad Company* (10th Cir. 1994) 16 F.3d 1083, 1088.)

💣 WARNING

As discussed in Section 11.05, CGVE, like all other scientific evidence, is subject to the foundational requirements of *People v. Kelly* (1976) 17 Cal.3d

24 [130 Cal.Rptr. 144]. The scientific principles, tests, and theories on which the evidence is based must have gained general acceptance in the particular field in which they belong. Else, a proper foundation for the evidence cannot be established.

[B]　Hearsay

If the CGVE is offered purely as demonstrative evidence—evidence that is not itself at issue in the case, but merely used to illustrate or clarify a witness's testimony—the CGVE should not be subject to the hearsay rule because it is not offered for the truth of the matter asserted, but only for illustrative purposes. (Evid. Code, § 1200.) If, on the other hand, the CGVE is offered as substantive evidence, it will be subject to potential objections based on the hearsay rule.

With regard to the hearsay rule, there are essentially two types of CGVE: computer-generated evidence that is based on or reiterates human declarations, and computer-generated evidence that is not based on extrajudicial assertions. Examples of the former include invoices, reports, accounting records, and databases of comments made by others. (See, e.g., *People v. Hernandez* (1997) 55 Cal.App.4th 225, 241 [63 Cal.Rptr.2d 769] (underlying data contained in a database was itself hearsay comments of police officers and witnesses).) Examples of the latter, less common, form of CGVE include automated test results and measurements, automated telephone records, and any other information that is recorded or processed by a computer that is not based on or derived from human declarations. Because the former form of CGVE is based on extrajudicial assertions, such evidence is subject to the hearsay rule and will only be admissible if it comes within a recognized exception (for example, business record, official record, or admission). The latter form of CGVE would not be subject to a hearsay objection because it does not constitute an out of court statement by a witness. (Evid. Code, § 1200.)

One of the problems with many forms of CGVE is that it may represent several levels of hearsay, each of which must come within a recognized exception for the evidence as a whole to be admissible. (Evid. Code, § 1201 (admissibility of multiple hearsay).) For example, a police officer may take a statement from a witness at the scene of a crime. The officer then incorporates the statement into her written report. The information contained in the report is reviewed and analyzed by a detective who inputs the information into a database of sex crimes. The original witness statement is one level of hearsay, the officer's report another level, and the detective's interpretation and entry of the information into the database may possibly be a third level of hearsay. (See, e.g., *People v. Hernandez* (1997) 55 Cal.App.4th 225, 241 [63 Cal.Rptr.2d 769].)

▶ **COMMENT**

Another approach to the issue of hearsay and CGVE is Evidence Code section 801, subdivision (b). Section 801, subdivision (b) expressly permits expert witnesses to base their opinions on inadmissible evidence if the evidence "is of a type that reasonably may be relied upon by an expert in forming an opinion upon the subject to which [the] testimony relates . . . ." Thus, experts may be allowed to not only base their opinions on hearsay evidence, but also, arguably, to illustrate those opinions using CGVE in court.

[C]　Discretionary Exclusion

Section 352 of the Evidence Code provides trial courts with broad discretion to exclude evidence if its probative value is substantially outweighed by the probability that is admission will (a) necessitate undue consumption of time or (b) create substantial danger of undue prejudice, of confusing the issues, or of misleading the jury. Each of these concerns may arise when CGVE is offered. Setting up the necessary equipment and presenting CGVE can be time consuming. And, because of the undue weight jurors tend to give CGVE, the threat that such evidence may cause prejudice, confuse the issues, or mislead the jury can be substantial. As a result, the possibility that a motion to exclude proffered CGVE on the basis of section 352 will be found meritorious can be substantial. To blunt the impact of such a motion, the following actions should be considered:

- Provide early notice to the court and opposing counsel regarding your intent to use CGVE.

- Where possible, avoid animations or simulations with accompanying audio. Instead, have the witness with whom the exhibit is used testify regarding the content of the animation or simulation.

- Ensure the CGVE will be useful to the jury (that is, the evidence demonstrates a scientific principle that is difficult to explain verbally), instead of merely highlighting or repeating a witness's testimony.

- Avoid presentations that can be construed as "argumentative" (that is, the evidence reflects counsel's theories as opposed to that of the testifying witness).

- Avoid CGVE that presents unnecessarily graphic detail.

- Consider using an animation that "illustrates" a witness's theory of a particular event, rather than attempting to use computer evidence to "recreate" the event itself.

- Offer an appropriate limiting instruction to reduce the potential for juror confusion. (See § 11.06.)

§ 11.05   Admissibility of Computer Animations

[A]   *People v. Hood*

The recent decision in *People v. Hood* (1997) 53 Cal.App.4th 965 [62 Cal.Rptr.2d 137] provides the first significant discussion of the admissibility of computer animations. *Hood* is important for three reasons. It finds that the computer animation at issue was demonstrative, not substantive, evidence. It discusses the potential impact of *People v. Kelly* (1976) 17 Cal.3d 24 [130 Cal.Rptr. 144] on CGVE, and includes illustrative limiting instructions to the jury.

[B]   Procedural History

Following a hung jury in his first trial, the defendant in *Hood* was retried and convicted of first degree murder with a handgun. The defendant appealed arguing, among other things, that certain CGVE was improperly admitted. The court of appeal rejected defendant's arguments and affirmed the conviction.

Before the first trial, the prosecution moved to introduce a computer animation depicting the shooting. The animation was based on the testimony of several witnesses and a detective who performed various measurements at the scene, on the reports and opinions of the pathologist who performed the autopsy on the victim, on prosecution ballistics, and on information obtained from gunshot residue experts. Defendant opposed the admission of the animation, claiming, among other things, that under the parameters established by the California Supreme Court in *People v. Kelly* (1976) 17 Cal.3d 24 [130 Cal.Rptr. 144] (a scientific principle must be "sufficiently established to have gained general acceptance in the particular field in which it belongs"), computer animations had not gained the scientific acceptance necessary for admissibility. The trial court ruled that the animation was illustrative, similar to an expert who draws on a board, and was not being introduced as evidence in and of itself, but only to illustrate the testimony of various prosecution experts. (*People v. Hood* (1997) 53 Cal.App.4th 965, 968 [62 Cal.Rptr.2d 137].)

Both the prosecution and the defense introduced computer animations of the shooting during the first trial. However, the defense later concluded that its animation was not as accurate as it could have been and, therefore, prepared a revised animation for the second trial. Prior to the commencement of the second trial, the defense renewed its objection to the prosecution's CGVE on the basis of lack of foundation. The trial court overruled the objection, finding that both the prosecution's and the defense's animations had adequate foundations. (*People v. Hood* (1997) 53 Cal.App.4th 965, 968 [62 Cal.Rptr.2d 137].)

[C] Limiting Instructions to the *Hood* Jury

Before the prosecution's computer animation was presented to the jury, the trial court instructed the jury as follows (*People v. Hood* (1997) 53 Cal.App.4th 965, 968 [62 Cal.Rptr.2d 137]):

> [Y]ou're reminded that . . . this is an animation based on a compilation of a lot of different experts' opinions. And there are what we call crime scene reconstruction experts who could, without using a computer, get on the stand and testify that based on this piece of evidence and this piece of evidence and this piece of evidence that they've concluded that the crime occurred in a certain manner. And then they can describe to you the manner in which it occurred. And they can sometimes use charts or diagrams or re-create photographs to demonstrate that. And the computer animation that we have here is nothing more than that kind of an expert opinion being demonstrated or illustrated by the computer animation, as opposed to charts and diagrams.

In addition to the foregoing instruction, during the defendant's testimony the trial court reminded the jury regarding the nature of the animation (*People v. Hood* (1997) 53 Cal.App.4th 965, 969 [62 Cal.Rptr.2d 137]):

> I . . . again remind you that all of the animated video reenactments or recreations are only designed to be an aid to testimony or reconstruction, the same as if an expert testified and drew certain diagrams on the board. They are not intended to be a film of what actually occurred or an exact re-creation. And, therefore, there may be things in each of the videos—in fact, you've heard from some of the witnesses [that] in each of the videos[,] . . . there are things that are not exactly accurate or not exactly as they occurred, but reasonably close, and it's important to keep that in mind with regard to all of the animated videos, that they are not actual films of what occurred nor are they intended to be exact, detailed replications of every detail or every event or every movement. They are only an aid to giving an overall

view of a particular version of the events, based on particular view-points or particular interpretations of the evidence.

[D] Appellate Review

On appeal, defendant renewed his argument made before the first trial that admission of the prosecution's computer animation did not meet the requirements of the *Kelly* formulation. The court of appeal agreed with the trial court's conclusion that the CGVE did not need to satisfy *Kelly*.

The *Kelly* formulation applies to "new scientific procedures" (*People v. Bury* (1996) 41 Cal.App.4th 1194, 1202 [49 Cal.Rptr.2d 107]) or a "new scientific technique . . . [or] novel proof." (*People v. Kelly* (1976) 17 Cal.3d 24, 30 [130 Cal.Rptr. 144].) The *Kelly* formula was created to prevent jurors from tending to give considerable weight to scientific evidence when presented by "experts" with impressive credentials and to acknowledge the existence of a "misleading aura of certainty which often envelopes a new scientific process, obscuring its currently experimental nature." Indeed, "scientific proof may in some instances assume a posture of mystic infallibility in the eyes of a jury . . . ." (*People v. Kelly* (1976) 17 Cal.3d 24, 31–32 [130 Cal.Rptr. 144].)

The court in *Hood* concluded the scientific procedures and techniques envisioned in *Kelly* and the potential dangers associated therewith were not present in the CGVE offered at the first and second trials. The animations presented by both the prosecution and defense were "tantamount to drawings by the experts from both sides to illustrate their testimony." (*People v. Hood* (1997) 53 Cal.App.4th 965, 969 [62 Cal.Rptr.2d 137].) They are nothing more than a mechanized version of what a human animator does when he or she draws each frame of activity, based on information supplied by experts, then fans the frames, making the drawings appear to move. If the animations were drawn by hand, rather than by computer, there would have been no *Kelly* issue as to the work done by the animators. By the same token, there was no *Kelly* issue as to the functioning of the computer in creating the animations. Given the nature of the testimony at trial as to how the prosecution's animation had been prepared, the testimony of the experts who supplied the information on which the animation was based, the introduction of the defense's contradictory animation, and the instructions given the jury concerning both animations, "there was no danger that the jury was swept away by the presentation of a new scientific technique which it could not understand and, therefore, would not challenge." Finally, the court emphasized that the defense was unable to cite any authority applying the *Kelly* formulation to computer animation. (*People v. Hood* (1997) 53 Cal.App.4th 965, 969 [62 Cal.Rptr.2d 137].)

▶**COMMENT**

The approach used in *Hood* has proven popular in other jurisdictions. For example, in *Department of Environmental Resources v. Al Hamilton Contracting Company* (Penn. 1995) 665 A.2d 849, the court considered the admissibility of a computer-generated structure contour map that purported to illustrate the inclination and elevation of the geologic strata of an underground coal seam. The map was based on drilling data taken from the site and created using a computer and plotter (a form of printer used to plot points on a graph, generally on oversized paper). An expert testified at trial that the computer-generated contour lines could have been drawn without the use of the computer, but that the computer was used for the simple reason that it was quicker. The map was later excluded because the expert did not have sufficient knowledge to testify that the map accurately represented the data taken from the site. (*Department of Environmental Resources v. Al Hamilton Contracting Company* (Penn. 1995) 665 A.2d 849, 853.)

§ 11.06 Limiting Instructions to the Jury

Objections or concerns regarding the potential of CGVE to mislead or confuse the jury can frequently be addressed through use of appropriate limiting instructions. In developing limiting instructions, the following questions should be considered:

- What is the purpose for which the CGVE is offered?

  - To illustrate a scientific principle that would not be otherwise easily visualized or understood?

  - To show in graphic form the results of some calculation or compilation of data?

  - To demonstrate or recreate a party's version of an event or occurrence?

- Are there any underlying assumptions on which the CGVE is based that should be considered by the jury in weighing the evidence?

- Are there any material differences between the CGVE and the event, condition, or circumstances that it purports to represent?

The California decision in *Hood* (see § 11.05) and the Tenth Circuit's decision in *Robinson* (see § 11.04[A]) provide specific examples of limiting instructions used by trial courts at the time of admission of CGVE.

§ 11.07 References

📖 **WITKIN** For discussion of the presentation of evidence, see the following:

▣ Exclusion of evidence involving undue prejudice (1 Witkin, Cal. Evidence (3d ed. 1986) Circumstantial Evidence, § 298 et seq.).

▣ Demonstrative, experimental, and scientific evidence (2 Witkin, Cal. Evidence (3d ed. 1986) Demonstrative, Experimental and Scientific Evidence, § 822 et seq.).

▣ **THE RUTTER GROUP** For a practical guide to the introduction of audio or visual recordings, see Cal. Practice Guide: Civ. Trials & Evidence, ¶ 8:524 et seq.

💻 **WESTLAW®** See the WESTLAW Electronic Research Guide at the beginning of this volume.

B. Forms

§ 11.08 Checklist of Potential Objections to CGVE

- ❑ The evidence is not relevant to the proceedings.

- ❑ The evidence lacks a sufficient foundation.

- ❑ The evidence is more prejudicial than probative and is likely to mislead the jury.

- ❑ The evidence is argumentative in that it reflects counsel's theories as opposed to that of the testifying witness.

- ❑ The evidence constitutes inadmissible hearsay not within any recognized exception.

- ❑ The evidence is based on a scientific principle that does not satisfy the requirements of *People v. Kelly* (1976) 17 Cal.3d 24 [130 Cal.Rptr. 144].

§ 11.09 Checklist of Key Authentication Issues

❑ Data Collection and Completeness

    ❑ Are the data on which the CGVE is based complete?

    ❑ Are critical data missing?

    ❑ Is the integrity of the data certain? Could the data have been corrupted or either intentionally or unintentionally modified?

    ❑ Were invalid assumptions made?

    ❑ Were all known facts incorporated into the creation of the CGVE?

❑ Manipulation of the Data

    ❑ Have the data been manipulated in any way?

    ❑ Were calculations performed on the date?

    ❑ How complex were the calculations?

    ❑ What are the underlying mathematical principles?

    ❑ Is the underlying science generally accepted?

❑ Confirmation of Results

    ❑ Are the results verifiable and repeatable?

PART III

APPENDICES

APPENDIX A

INTERNET DISCOVERY RESOURCES

This appendix provides an outline of some of the resources available on the Internet for conducting discovery and background research. Given the accessibility of these resources and their low cost, they should be a part of almost every discovery plan.

1. Internet Search Engines

General Search Engines:

www.yahoo.com

www.infoseek.com

www.nothernlight.com

www.excite.com

www.hotbot.com

www.lycos.com

www.webcrawler.com

www.altavista.digital.com

Meta-Search Engines:

www.stpt.com

www.dogpile.com

www.metafind.com

www.searchthe.net

www.1blink.com

www.2q.to

www.flycatcher.com

www.isleuth.com

www.mamma.com

www.surfy.com

www.webtaxi.com

guaraldi.cs.colostate.edu:2000

search5.metacrawler.com

Newsgroup Search Engines:

www.dejanews.com

www.infoseek.com

Multimedia Search Engines:

www.scour.net

2. **Business Trackers/Locators**

BellSouth yellow pages: *www.yellowpages.bellsouth.com*

Companies online by Dun & Bradstreet and Lycos: *www.companiesonline.com*

Europages, the European Business Directory: *www.europages.com/home-en.html*

GTE SuperPages Yellow Pages: *www.yp.gte.net*

Thomas Register: *www. Thomasregister.com*

3. **Mailing Lists/Listserv Lists/Online Newsletters**

The Official Catalog of Listserv Lists: *www.lsoft.com/lists/listref.html*

Publicly Accessible Mailing Lists: *www.neosoft.com/internet/paml/*

Internet Scout New-List tracks mailing lists as they are created: *scout.cs.wisc.edu/scout/new-list*

WWW Virtual Library Electronic Journals List: *www.edoc.com/ejournal*

4. **Periodicals and Journals Online**

Ecola Newstand offers links to more than 6,500 newspapers and magazines around the world: *www.ecola.com*

Excite Trade Press Listing:
www.excite.com/news/business/trade_press/

Newspapers Online: *www.newspapers.com*

Colorado Alliance of Research Libraries provides electronic journal database of links to thousands of Web-based publications: *www.coalliance.org/ejournal*

Database of top online journals: *www.dominis.com/zines*

5. **Business and People Information**

AT&T's AnyWho provides information about whether an address is a business or residence and who or what occupies adjacent addresses; also provides a reverse telephone number lookup: *www.anywho.com/bgq.html*

MCI Web Investigative Resources: *ird.security.mci.net/search.html*

Whois provides information regarding ownership of Web sites: *rs.internic.net/cgi-bin/whois*

Information regarding individuals who have moved or changed their names, e-mail addresses, or Web sites: *www.semaphorecorp.com/wdtg/jump.html*

Ancestry.com provides a Social Security Death Index. The SSDI allows visitors to look up by name the birth and death dates and Social Security numbers of the deceased: *www.ancestry.com*

6. **Translation of Foreign Language Web Pages**

www.babelfish.altavista.digital.com/cgi-bin/translate?

7. **Miscellaneous Information**

MapQuest provides maps of any United States address and driving instructions to get there from any other location: *www.mapquest.com*

Medical information, including drug interaction database: *www.drkoop.com*

Information Please database of facts: *www.infoplease.com*

Weather reports: *www.internetweather.com*

APPENDIX B

FREEDOM OF INFORMATION ACT AND ELECTRONIC FREEDOM OF INFORMATION ACT

5 U.S.C. § 552.   Public information; agency rules, opinions, orders, records, and proceedings

(a) Each agency shall make available to the public information as follows:

(1) Each agency shall separately state and currently publish in the Federal Register for the guidance of the public—

(A) descriptions of its central and field organization and the established places at which, the employees (and in the case of a uniformed service, the members) from whom, and the methods whereby, the public may obtain information, make submittals or requests, or obtain decisions;

(B) statements of the general course and method by which its functions are channeled and determined, including the nature and requirements of all formal and informal procedures available;

(C) rules of procedure, descriptions of forms available or the places at which forms may be obtained, and instructions as to the scope and contents of all papers, reports, or examinations;

(D) substantive rules of general applicability adopted as authorized by law, and statements of general policy or interpretations of general applicability formulated and adopted by the agency; and

(E) each amendment, revision, or repeal of the foregoing.

Except to the extent that a person has actual and timely notice of the terms thereof, a person may not in any manner be required to resort to, or be adversely affected by, a matter required to be published in the Federal Register and not so published. For the purpose of this paragraph, matter reasonably available to the class of persons affected thereby is deemed published in the Federal Register when incorporated by reference therein with the approval of the Director of the Federal Register.

(2) Each agency, in accordance with published rules, shall make available for public inspection and copying—

(A) final opinions, including concurring and dissenting opinions, as well as orders, made in the adjudication of cases;

(B) those statements of policy and interpretations which have been adopted by the agency and are not published in the Federal Register;

(C) administrative staff manuals and instructions to staff that affect a member of the public;

(D) copies of all records, regardless of form or format, which have been released to any person under paragraph (3) and which, because of the nature of their subject matter, the agency determines have become or are likely to become the subject of subsequent requests for substantially the same records; and

(E) a general index of the records referred to under subparagraph (D); unless the materials are promptly published and copies offered for sale. For records created on or after November 1, 1996, within one year after such date, each agency shall make such records available, including by computer telecommunications or, if computer telecommunications means have not been established by the agency, by other electronic means. To the extent required to prevent a clearly unwarranted invasion of personal privacy, an agency may delete identifying details when it makes available or publishes an opinion, statement of policy, interpretation, staff manual, instruction, or copies of records referred to in subparagraph (D). However, in each case the justification for the deletion shall be explained fully in writing, and the extent of such deletion shall be indicated on the portion of the record which is made available or published, unless including that indication would harm an interest protected by the exemption in subsection (b) under which the deletion is made. If technically feasible, the extent of the deletion shall be indicated at the place in the record where the deletion was made. Each agency shall also maintain and make available for public inspection and copying current indexes providing identifying information for the public as to any matter issued, adopted, or promulgated after July 4, 1967, and required by this paragraph to be made available or published. Each agency shall promptly publish, quarterly or more frequently, and distribute (by sale or otherwise) copies of each index or supplements thereto unless it determines by order published in the Federal Register that the publication would be unnecessary and impracticable, in which case the agency shall nonetheless provide copies of such index on request at a cost not to exceed the direct cost of duplication. Each agency shall make the index referred to in subparagraph (E) available by computer telecommunications by December 31, 1999. A final order, opinion, statement of policy, interpretation, or staff manual or instruction that affects a member of the public may be relied on, used, or cited as precedent by an agency against a party other than an agency only if—

    (i) it has been indexed and either made available or published as provided by this paragraph; or

    (ii) the party has actual and timely notice of the terms thereof.

(3) (A) Except with respect to the records made available under paragraphs (1) and (2) of this subsection, each agency, upon any request for records which (i) reasonably describes such records and (ii) is made in accordance with published rules stating the time, place, fees (if any), and procedures to be followed, shall make the records promptly available to any person.

    (B) In making any record available to a person under this paragraph, an agency shall provide the record in any form or format requested by the person if the record is readily reproducible by the agency in that form or format. Each agency shall make reasonable efforts to maintain its records in forms or formats that are reproducible for purposes of this section.

    (C) In responding under this paragraph to a request for records, an agency shall make reasonable efforts to search for the records in electronic form or format, except when such efforts would significantly interfere with the operation of the agency's automated information system.

    (D) For purposes of this paragraph, the term "search" means to review, manually or by automated means, agency records for the purpose of locating those records which are responsive to a request.

(4) (A) (i) In order to carry out the provisions of this section, each agency shall promulgate regulations, pursuant to notice and receipt of public comment, specifying the schedule of fees applicable to the processing of requests under this section and establishing procedures and guidelines for determining when such fees should be waived or reduced. Such schedule shall conform to the guidelines which shall be promulgated,

pursuant to notice and receipt of public comment, by the Director of the Office of Management and Budget and which shall provide for a uniform schedule of fees for all agencies.

(ii) Such agency regulations shall provide that—

(I) fees shall be limited to reasonable standard charges for document search, duplication, and review, when records are requested for commercial use;

(II) fees shall be limited to reasonable standard charges for document duplication when records are not sought for commercial use and the request is made by an educational or noncommercial scientific institution, whose purpose is scholarly or scientific research; or a representative of the news media; and

(III) for any request not described in (I) or (II), fees shall be limited to reasonable standard charges for document search and duplication.

(iii) Documents shall be furnished without any charge or at a charge reduced below the fees established under clause (ii) if disclosure of the information is in the public interest because it is likely to contribute significantly to public understanding of the operations or activities of the government and is not primarily in the commercial interest of the requester.

(iv) Fee schedules shall provide for the recovery of only the direct costs of search, duplication, or review. Review costs shall include only the direct costs incurred during the initial examination of a document for the purposes of determining whether the documents must be disclosed under this section and for the purposes of withholding any portions exempt from disclosure under this section. Review costs may not include any costs incurred in resolving issues of law or policy that may be raised in the course of processing a request under this section. No fee may be charged by any agency under this section—

(I) if the costs of routine collection and processing of the fee are likely to equal or exceed the amount of the fee; or

(II) for any request described in clause (ii)(II) or (III) of this subparagraph for the first two hours of search time or for the first one hundred pages of duplication.

(v) No agency may require advance payment of any fee unless the requester has previously failed to pay fees in a timely fashion, or the agency has determined that the fee will exceed $250.

(vi) Nothing in this subparagraph shall supersede fees chargeable under a statute specifically providing for setting the level of fees for particular types of records.

(vii) In any action by a requester regarding the waiver of fees under this section, the court shall determine the matter de novo: Provided, That the court's review of the matter shall be limited to the record before the agency.

(B) On complaint, the district court of the United States in the district in which the complainant resides, or has his principal place of business, or in which the agency records are situated, or in the District of Columbia, has jurisdiction to enjoin the agency from withholding agency records and to order the production of any agency records improperly withheld from the complainant. In such a case the court shall determine the matter de novo, and may examine the contents of such agency records in camera to determine whether such records or any part thereof shall be withheld under any of the exemptions set forth in subsection (b) of this section, and the burden is on the agency to sustain its action. In addition to any other matters to which a court accords substantial weight, a court shall accord substantial weight to an affidavit of an agency concerning the agency's determination as to technical feasibility under paragraph (2)(C) and subsection (b) and reproducibility under paragraph (3)(B).

(C) Notwithstanding any other provision of law, the defendant shall serve an answer or otherwise plead to any complaint made under this subsection within thirty days after service upon the defendant of the pleading in which such complaint is made, unless the court otherwise directs for good cause shown.

[(D) Repealed. Pub.L. 98-620, Title IV, S 402(2), Nov. 8, 1984, 98 Stat. 3357]

(E) The court may assess against the United States reasonable attorney fees and other litigation costs reasonably incurred in any case under this section in which the complainant has substantially prevailed.

(F) Whenever the court orders the production of any agency records improperly withheld from the complainant and assesses against the United States reasonable attorney fees and other litigation costs, and the court additionally issues a written finding that the circumstances surrounding the withholding raise questions whether agency personnel acted arbitrarily or capriciously with respect to the withholding, the Special Counsel shall promptly initiate a proceeding to determine whether disciplinary action is warranted against the officer or employee who was primarily responsible for the withholding. The Special Counsel, after investigation and consideration of the evidence submitted, shall submit his findings and recommendations to the administrative authority of the agency concerned and shall send copies of the findings and recommendations to the officer or employee or his representative. The administrative authority shall take the corrective action that the Special Counsel recommends.

(G) In the event of noncompliance with the order of the court, the district court may punish for contempt the responsible employee, and in the case of a uniformed service, the responsible member.

(5) Each agency having more than one member shall maintain and make available for public inspection a record of the final votes of each member in every agency proceeding.

(6) (A) Each agency, upon any request for records made under paragraph (1), (2), or (3) of this subsection, shall—

(i) determine within 20 days (excepting Saturdays, Sundays, and legal public holidays) after the receipt of any such request whether to comply with such request and shall immediately notify the person making such request of such determination and the reasons therefor, and of the right of such person to appeal to the head of the agency any adverse determination; and

(ii) make a determination with respect to any appeal within twenty days (excepting Saturdays, Sundays, and legal public holidays) after the receipt of such appeal. If on appeal the denial of the request for records is in whole or in part upheld, the agency shall notify the person making such request of the provisions for judicial review of that determination under paragraph (4) of this subsection.

(B) (i) In unusual circumstances as specified in this subparagraph, the time limits prescribed in either clause (i) or clause (ii) of subparagraph (A) may be extended by written notice to the person making such request setting forth the unusual circumstances for such extension and the date on which a determination is expected to be dispatched. No such notice shall specify a date that would result in an extension for more than ten working days, except as provided in clause (ii) of this subparagraph.

(ii) With respect to a request for which a written notice under clause (i) extends the time limits prescribed under clause (i) of subparagraph (A), the agency shall notify the person making the request if the request cannot be processed within the time limit specified in that clause and shall provide the person an opportunity to limit the scope of the request so that it may be processed within that time limit or an opportunity to arrange with the agency an alternative time frame for processing the request or a modified request. Refusal by the person to reasonably modify the request or arrange such an alternative time frame shall be considered as a factor in determining whether exceptional circumstances exist for purposes of subparagraph (C).

(iii) As used in this subparagraph, "unusual circumstances" means, but only to the extent reasonably necessary to the proper processing of the particular requests—

(I) the need to search for and collect the requested records from field facilities or other establishments that are separate from the office processing the request;

(II) the need to search for, collect, and appropriately examine a voluminous amount of separate and distinct records which are demanded in a single request; or

(III) the need for consultation, which shall be conducted with all practicable speed, with another agency having a substantial interest in the determination of the request or among two or more components of the agency having substantial subject-matter interest therein.

(iv) Each agency may promulgate regulations, pursuant to notice and receipt of public comment, providing for the aggregation of certain requests by the same requestor, or by a group of requestors acting in concert, if the agency reasonably believes that such requests actually constitute a single request, which would otherwise satisfy the unusual circumstances specified in this subparagraph, and the requests involve clearly related matters. Multiple requests involving unrelated matters shall not be aggregated.

(C) (i) Any person making a request to any agency for records under paragraph (1), (2), or (3) of this subsection shall be deemed to have exhausted his administrative remedies with respect to such request if the agency fails to comply with the applicable time limit provisions of this paragraph. If the Government can show exceptional circumstances exist and that the agency is exercising due diligence in responding to the request, the court may retain jurisdiction and allow the agency additional time to complete its review of the records. Upon any determination by an agency to comply with a request for records, the records shall be made promptly available to such person making such request. Any notification of denial of any request for records under this subsection shall set forth the names and titles or positions of each person responsible for the denial of such request.

(ii) For purposes of this subparagraph, the term "exceptional circumstances" does not include a delay that results from a predictable agency workload of requests under this section, unless the agency demonstrates reasonable progress in reducing its backlog of pending requests.

(iii) Refusal by a person to reasonably modify the scope of a request or arrange an alternative time frame for processing a request (or a modified request) under clause (ii) after being given an opportunity to do so by the agency to whom the person made the request shall be considered as a factor in determining whether exceptional circumstances exist for purposes of this subparagraph.

(D) (i) Each agency may promulgate regulations, pursuant to notice and receipt of public comment, providing for multitrack processing of requests for records based on the amount of work or time (or both) involved in processing requests.

(ii) Regulations under this subparagraph may provide a person making a request that does not qualify for the fastest multitrack processing an opportunity to limit the scope of the request in order to qualify for faster processing.

(iii) This subparagraph shall not be considered to affect the requirement under subparagraph (C) to exercise due diligence.

(E) (i) Each agency shall promulgate regulations, pursuant to notice and receipt of public comment, providing for expedited processing of requests for records—

(I) in cases in which the person requesting the records demonstrates a compelling need; and

(II) in other cases determined by the agency.

(ii) Notwithstanding clause (i), regulations under this subparagraph must ensure—

(I) that a determination of whether to provide expedited processing shall be made, and notice of the determination shall be provided to the person making the request, within 10 days after the date of the request; and

(II) expeditious consideration of administrative appeals of such determinations of whether to provide expedited processing.

(iii) An agency shall process as soon as practicable any request for records to which the agency has granted expedited processing under this subparagraph. Agency action to deny or affirm denial of a request for expedited processing pursuant to this subparagraph, and failure by an agency to respond in a timely manner to such a request shall be subject to judicial review under paragraph (4), except that the judicial review shall be based on the record before the agency at the time of the determination.

(iv) A district court of the United States shall not have jurisdiction to review an agency denial of expedited processing of a request for records after the agency has provided a complete response to the request.

(v) For purposes of this subparagraph, the term "compelling need" means—

(I) that a failure to obtain requested records on an expedited basis under this paragraph could reasonably be expected to pose an imminent threat to the life or physical safety of an individual; or

(II) with respect to a request made by a person primarily engaged in disseminating information, urgency to inform the public concerning actual or alleged Federal Government activity.

(vi) A demonstration of a compelling need by a person making a request for expedited processing shall be made by a statement certified by such person to be true and correct to the best of such person's knowledge and belief.

(F) In denying a request for records, in whole or in part, an agency shall make a reasonable effort to estimate the volume of any requested matter the provision of which is denied, and shall provide any such estimate to the person making the request, unless providing such estimate would harm an interest protected by the exemption in subsection (b) pursuant to which the denial is made.

(b) This section does not apply to matters that are—

(1) (A) specifically authorized under criteria established by an Executive order to be kept secret in the interest of national defense or foreign policy and (B) are in fact properly classified pursuant to such Executive order;

(2) related solely to the internal personnel rules and practices of an agency;

(3) specifically exempted from disclosure by statute (other than section 552b of this title), provided that such statute (A) requires that the matters be withheld from the public in such a manner as to leave no discretion on the issue, or (B) establishes particular criteria for withholding or refers to particular types of matters to be withheld;

(4) trade secrets and commercial or financial information obtained from a person and privileged or confidential;

(5) inter-agency or intra-agency memorandums or letters which would not be available by law to a party other than an agency in litigation with the agency;

(6) personnel and medical files and similar files the disclosure of which would constitute a clearly unwarranted invasion of personal privacy;

(7) records or information compiled for law enforcement purposes, but only to the extent that the production of such law enforcement records or information (A) could reasonably be expected to interfere with enforcement proceedings, (B) would deprive a person of a right to a fair trial or an impartial adjudication, (C) could reasonably be expected to constitute an unwarranted invasion of personal privacy, (D) could reasonably be expected to disclose the identity of a confidential source, including a State, local, or foreign agency or authority or any private institution which furnished information on a confidential basis, and, in the case of a record or information compiled by criminal law enforcement authority in the course of a criminal investigation or by an agency conducting a lawful national security intelligence investigation, information furnished by a confidential source, (E) would disclose techniques and procedures for law enforcement investigations or prosecutions, or would disclose guidelines for law enforcement investigations or prosecutions if such disclosure could reasonably be expected to risk circumvention of the law, or (F) could reasonably be expected to endanger the life or physical safety of any individual;

(8) contained in or related to examination, operating, or condition reports prepared by, on behalf of, or for the use of an agency responsible for the regulation or supervision of financial institutions; or

(9) geological and geophysical information and data, including maps, concerning wells.

Any reasonably segregable portion of a record shall be provided to any person requesting such record after deletion of the portions which are exempt under this subsection. The amount of information deleted shall be indicated on the released portion of the record, unless including that indication would harm an interest protected by the exemption in this subsection under which the deletion is made. If technically feasible, the amount of the information shall be indicated at the place in the record where such deletion is made.

(c) (1) Whenever a request is made which involves access to records described in subsection (b)(7)(A) and—

(A) the investigation or proceeding involves a possible violation of criminal law; and

(B) there is reason to believe that (i) the subject of the investigation or proceeding is not aware of its pendency, and (ii) disclosure of the existence of the records could reasonably be expected to interfere with enforcement proceedings, the agency may, during only such time as that circumstance continues, treat the records as not subject to the requirements of this section.

(2) Whenever informant records maintained by a criminal law enforcement agency under an informant's name or personal identifier are requested by a third party according to the informant's name or personal identifier, the agency may treat the records as not subject to the requirements of this section unless the informant's status as an informant has been officially confirmed.

(3) Whenever a request is made which involves access to records maintained by the Federal Bureau of Investigation pertaining to foreign intelligence or counterintelligence, or international terrorism, and the existence of the records is classified information as provided in subsection (b)(1), the Bureau may, as long as the existence of the records remains classified information, treat the records as not subject to the requirements of this section.

(d) This section does not authorize withholding of information or limit the availability of records to the public, except as specifically stated in this section. This section is not authority to withhold information from Congress.

(e) (1) On or before February 1 of each year, each agency shall submit to the Attorney General of the United States a report which shall cover the preceding fiscal year and which shall include—

(A) the number of determinations made by the agency not to comply with requests for records made to such agency under subsection (a) and the reasons for each such determination;

(B) (i) the number of appeals made by persons under subsection (a)(6), the result of such appeals, and the reason for the action upon each appeal that results in a denial of information; and

(ii) a complete list of all statutes that the agency relies upon to authorize the agency to withhold information under subsection (b)(3), a description of whether a court has upheld the decision of the agency to withhold information under each such statute, and a concise description of the scope of any information withheld;

(C) the number of requests for records pending before the agency as of September 30 of the preceding year, and the median number of days that such requests had been pending before the agency as of that date;

(D) the number of requests for records received by the agency and the number of requests which the agency processed;

(E) the median number of days taken by the agency to process different types of requests;

(F) the total amount of fees collected by the agency for processing requests; and

(G) the number of full-time staff of the agency devoted to processing requests for records under this section, and the total amount expended by the agency for processing such requests.

(2) Each agency shall make each such report available to the public including by computer telecommunications, or if computer telecommunications means have not been established by the agency, by other electronic means.

(3) The Attorney General of the United States shall make each report which has been made available by electronic means available at a single electronic access point. The Attorney General of the United States shall notify the Chairman and ranking minority member of the Committee on Government Reform and Oversight of the House of Representatives and the Chairman and ranking minority member of the Committees on Governmental Affairs and the Judiciary of the Senate, no later than April 1 of

the year in which each such report is issued, that such reports are available by electronic means.

(4) The Attorney General of the United States, in consultation with the Director of the Office of Management and Budget, shall develop reporting and performance guidelines in connection with reports required by this subsection by October 1, 1997, and may establish additional requirements for such reports as the Attorney General determines may be useful.

(5) The Attorney General of the United States shall submit an annual report on or before April 1 of each calendar year which shall include for the prior calendar year a listing of the number of cases arising under this section, the exemption involved in each case, the disposition of such case, and the cost, fees, and penalties assessed under subparagraphs (E), (F), and (G) of subsection (a)(4). Such report shall also include a description of the efforts undertaken by the Department of Justice to encourage agency compliance with this section.

(f) For purposes of this section, the term—

(1) "agency" as defined in section 551(1) of this title includes any executive department, military department, Government corporation, Government controlled corporation, or other establishment in the executive branch of the Government (including the Executive Office of the President), or any independent regulatory agency; and

(2) "record" and any other term used in this section in reference to information includes any information that would be an agency record subject to the requirements of this section when maintained by an agency in any format, including an electronic format.

(g) The head of each agency shall prepare and make publicly available upon request, reference material or a guide for requesting records or information from the agency, subject to the exemptions in subsection (b), including—

(1) an index of all major information systems of the agency;

(2) a description of major information and record locator systems maintained by the agency; and

(3) a handbook for obtaining various types and categories of public information from the agency pursuant to chapter 35 of title 44, and under this section.

APPENDIX C

ELECTRONIC COMMUNICATIONS PRIVACY ACT OF 1986

UNITED STATES CODE

TITLE 18. CRIMES AND CRIMINAL PROCEDURE

PART I. CRIMES

CHAPTER 119. WIRE AND ELECTRONIC COMMUNICATIONS INTERCEPTION AND INTERCEPTION OF ORAL COMMUNICATIONS

Sec. 2510. Definitions

As used in this chapter—

(1) "wire communication" means any aural transfer made in whole or in part through the use of facilities for the transmission of communications by the aid of wire, cable, or other like connection between the point of origin and the point of reception (including the use of such connection in a switching station) furnished or operated by any person engaged in providing or operating such facilities for the transmission of interstate or foreign communications or communications affecting interstate or foreign commerce and such term includes any electronic storage of such communication, but such term does not include the radio portion of a cordless telephone communication that is transmitted between the cordless telephone handset and the base unit;

(2) "oral communication" means any oral communication uttered by a person exhibiting an expectation that such communication is not subject to interception under circumstances justifying such expectation, but such term does not include any electronic communication;

(3) "State" means any State of the United States, the District of Columbia, the Commonwealth of Puerto Rico, and any territory or possession of the United States;

(4) "intercept" means the aural or other acquisition of the contents of any wire, electronic, or oral communication through the use of any electronic, mechanical, or other device.

(5) "electronic, mechanical, or other device" means any device or apparatus which can be used to intercept a wire, oral, or electronic communication other than—

(a) any telephone or telegraph instrument, equipment or facility, or any component thereof, (i) furnished to the subscriber or user by a provider of wire or electronic communication service in the ordinary course of its business and being used by the subscriber or user in the ordinary course of its business or furnished by such subscriber or user for connection to the facilities of such service and used in the ordinary course of its business; or (ii) being used by a provider of wire or electronic communication service in the ordinary course of its business, or by an investigative or law enforcement officer in the ordinary course of his duties;

(b) a hearing aid or similar device being used to correct subnormal hearing to not better than normal;

(6) "person" means any employee, or agent of the United States or any State or political subdivision thereof, and any individual, partnership, association, joint stock company, trust, or corporation;

(7) "Investigative or law enforcement officer" means any officer of the United States or of a State or political subdivision thereof, who is empowered by law to conduct investigations of or to make arrests for offenses enumerated in this chapter, and any attorney authorized by law to prosecute or participate in the prosecution of such offenses;

(8) "contents," when used with respect to any wire, oral, or electronic communication, includes any information concerning the substance, purport, or meaning of that communication;

(9) "Judge of competent jurisdiction" means—

(a) a judge of a United States district court or a United States court of appeals; and

(b) a judge of any court of general criminal jurisdiction of a State who is authorized by a statute of that State to enter orders authorizing interceptions of wire, oral, or electronic communications;

(10) "communication common carrier" shall have the same meaning which is given the term "common carrier" by section 153(h) of title 47 of the United States Code;

(11) "aggrieved person" means a person who was a party to any intercepted wire, oral, or electronic communication or a person against whom the interception was directed;

(12) "electronic communication" means any transfer of signs, signals, writing, images, sounds, data, or intelligence of any nature transmitted in whole or in part by a wire, radio, electromagnetic, photoelectronic or photooptical system that affects interstate or foreign commerce, but does not include—

    (A) the radio portion of a cordless telephone communication that is transmitted between the cordless telephone handset and the base unit;

    (B) any wire or oral communication;

    (C) any communication made through a tone-only paging device; or

    (D) any communication from a tracking device (as defined in section 3117 of this title);

(13) "user" means any person or entity who—

    (A) uses an electronic communication service; and

    (B) is duly authorized by the provider of such service to engage in such use;

(14) "electronic communications system" means any wire, radio, electromagnetic, photooptical or photoelectronic facilities for the transmission of electronic communications, and any computer facilities or related electronic equipment for the electronic storage of such communications;

(15) "electronic communication service" means any service which provides to users thereof the ability to send or receive wire or electronic communications;

(16) "readily accessible to the general public" means, with respect to a radio communication, that such communication is not—

    (A) scrambled or encrypted;

    (B) transmitted using modulation techniques whose essential parameters have been withheld from the public with the intention of preserving the privacy of such communication;

    (C) carried on a subcarrier or other signal subsidiary to a radio transmission;

    (D) transmitted over a communication system provided by a common carrier, unless the communication is a tone only paging system communication; or

(E) transmitted on frequencies allocated under part 25, subpart D, E, or F of part 74, or part 94 of the Rules of the Federal Communications Commission, unless, in the case of a communication transmitted on a frequency allocated under part 74 that is not exclusively allocated to broadcast auxiliary services, the communication is a two-way voice communication by radio;

(17) "electronic storage" means—

(A) any temporary, intermediate storage of a wire or electronic communication incidental to the electronic transmission thereof; and

(B) any storage of such communication by an electronic communication service for purposes of backup protection of such communication; and

(18) "aural transfer" means a transfer containing the human voice at any point between and including the point of origin and the point of reception.

Sec. 2511. Interception and disclosure of wire, oral, or electronic communications prohibited

(1) Except as otherwise specifically provided in this chapter any person who—

(a) intentionally intercepts, endeavors to intercept, or procures any other person to intercept or endeavor to intercept, any wire, oral, or electronic communication;

(b) intentionally uses, endeavors to use, or procures any other person to use or endeavor to use any electronic, mechanical, or other device to intercept any oral communication when—

(i) such device is affixed to, or otherwise transmits a signal through, a wire, cable, or other like connection used in wire communication; or

(ii) such device transmits communications by radio, or interferes with the transmission of such communication; or

(iii) such person knows, or has reason to know, that such device or any component thereof has been sent through the mail or transported in interstate or foreign commerce; or

(iv) such use or endeavor to use (A) takes place on the premises of any business or other commercial establishment the operations of which affect interstate or foreign commerce; or (B) obtains or is for the purpose of obtaining information relating to the operations of any business or other commercial establishment the operations of which affect interstate or foreign commerce; or

(v) such person acts in the District of Columbia, the Commonwealth of Puerto Rico, or any territory or possession of the United States;

(c) intentionally discloses, or endeavors to disclose, to any other person the contents of any wire, oral, or electronic communication, knowing or having reason to know that the information was obtained through the interception of a wire, oral, or electronic communication in violation of this subsection; or

(d) intentionally uses, or endeavors to use, the contents of any wire, oral, or electronic communication, knowing or having reason to know that the information was obtained through the interception of a wire, oral, or electronic communication in violation of this subsection; shall be punished as provided in subsection (4) or shall be subject to suit as provided in subsection (5).

(2) (a) (i) It shall not be unlawful under this chapter for an operator of a switchboard, or an officer, employee, or agent of a provider of wire or electronic communication service, whose facilities are used in the transmission of a wire communication, to intercept, disclose, or use that communication in the normal course of his employment while engaged in any activity which is a necessary incident to the rendition of his service or to the protection of the rights or property of the provider of that service, except that a provider of wire communication service to the public shall not utilize service observing or random monitoring except for mechanical or service quality control checks.

(ii) Notwithstanding any other law, providers of wire or electronic communication service, their officers, employees, and agents, landlords, custodians, or other persons, are authorized to provide information, facilities, or technical assistance to persons authorized by law to intercept wire, oral, or electronic communications or to conduct electronic surveillance, as defined in section 101 of the Foreign Intelligence Surveillance Act of 1978 if such provider, its officers, employees, or agents, landlord, custodian, or other specified person, has been provided with—

(A) a court order directing such assistance signed by the authorizing judge, or

(B) a certification in writing by a person specified in section 2518(7) of this title or the Attorney General of the United States that no warrant or court order is required by law, that all statutory requirements have been met, and that the specified assistance is required, setting forth the period of time during which the provision of the information, facilities, or technical assistance is authorized and specifying the information, facilities, or technical assistance required. No provider of wire or electronic communication service, officer, employee, or agent thereof, or landlord, custodian, or other specified person shall disclose the existence of any interception or surveillance or the device used to accomplish the interception or surveillance with respect to which the person has been furnished an order or certification under this subparagraph, except as may otherwise be required by legal process and then only after prior notification to the Attorney General or to the principal prosecuting attorney of a State or any political subdivision of a State, as may be appropriate. Any such disclosure, shall render such person liable for the civil damages provided for in section 2520. No cause of action shall lie in any court against any provider of wire or electronic communication service, its officers, employees, or agents, landlord, custodian, or other specified person for providing information, facilities, or assistance in accordance with the terms of a court order or certification under this chapter.

(b) It shall not be unlawful under this chapter for an officer, employee, or agent of the Federal Communications Commission, in the normal course of his employment and in discharge of the monitoring responsibilities exercised by the Commission in the enforcement of chapter 5 of title 47 of the United States Code, to intercept a wire or electronic communication, or oral communication transmitted by radio, or to disclose or use the information thereby obtained.

(c) It shall not be unlawful under this chapter for a person acting under color of law to intercept a wire, oral, or electronic communication, where such person is a party to the communication or one of the parties to the communication has given prior consent to such interception.

(d) It shall not be unlawful under this chapter for a person not acting under color of law to intercept a wire or oral communication where such person is a party to the communication or where one of the parties to the communication has given prior consent to such interception unless such communication is intercepted for the purpose of committing any criminal or tortious act in violation of the Constitution or laws of the United States or of any State.

(e) Notwithstanding any other provision of this title or section 705 or 706 of the Communications Act of 1934, it shall not be unlawful for an officer, employee, or agent of the United States in the normal course of his official duty to conduct electronic surveillance, as defined in section 101 of the Foreign Intelligence Surveillance Act of 1978, as authorized by that Act.

(f) Nothing contained in this chapter or chapter 121, or section 705 of the Communications Act of 1934, shall be deemed to affect the acquisition by the United States Government of foreign intelligence information from international or foreign communications, or foreign intelligence activities conducted in accordance with otherwise applicable Federal law involving a foreign electronic communications system, utilizing a means other than electronic surveillance as defined in section 101 of the Foreign Intelligence Surveillance Act of 1978, and procedures in this chapter and the Foreign Intelligence Surveillance Act of 1978 shall be the exclusive means by which electronic surveillance, as defined in section 101 of such Act, and the interception of domestic wire, oral, or electronic communications may be conducted.

(g) It shall not be unlawful under this chapter or chapter 121 of this title for any person—

(i) to intercept or access an electronic communication made through an electronic communication system that is configured so that such electronic communication is readily accessible to the general public;

(ii) to intercept any radio communication which is transmitted—

(I) by any station for the use of the general public, or that relates to ships, aircraft, vehicles, or persons in distress;

(II) by any governmental, law enforcement, civil defense, private land mobile, or public safety communications system, including police and fire, readily accessible to the general public;

(III) by a station operating on an authorized frequency within the bands allocated to the amateur, citizens band, or general mobile radio services; or

(IV) by any marine or aeronautical communications system;

(iii) to engage in any conduct which—

(I) is prohibited by section 633 of the Communications Act of 1934; or

(II) is excepted from the application of section 705(a) of the Communications Act of 1934 by section 705(b) of that Act;

(iv) to intercept any wire or electronic communication the transmission of which is causing harmful interference to any lawfully operating station or consumer electronic equipment, to the extent necessary to identify the source of such interference; or

(v) for other users of the same frequency to intercept any radio communication made through a system that utilizes frequencies monitored by individuals engaged in the provision or the use of such system, if such communication is not scrambled or encrypted.

(h) It shall not be unlawful under this chapter—

(i) to use a pen register or a trap and trace device (as those terms are defined for the purposes of chapter 206 (relating to pen registers and trap and trace devices) of this title); or

(ii) for a provider of electronic communication service to record the fact that a wire or electronic communication was initiated or completed in order to protect such provider, another provider furnishing service toward the completion of the wire or electronic communication, or a user of that service, from fraudulent, unlawful or abusive use of such service.

(3) (a) Except as provided in paragraph (b) of this subsection, a person or entity providing an electronic communication service to the public shall not intentionally divulge the contents of any communication (other than one to such person or entity, or an agent thereof) while in transmission on that service to any person or entity other than an addressee or intended recipient of such communication or an agent of such addressee or intended recipient.

(b) A person or entity providing electronic communication service to the public may divulge the contents of any such communication—

(i) as otherwise authorized in section 2511(2)(a) or 2517 of this title;

(ii) with the lawful consent of the originator or any addressee or intended recipient of such communication;

(iii) to a person employed or authorized, or whose facilities are used, to forward such communication to its destination; or

(iv) which were inadvertently obtained by the service provider and which appear to pertain to the commission of a crime, if such divulgence is made to a law enforcement agency.

(4) (a) Except as provided in paragraph (b) of this subsection or in subsection (5), whoever violates subsection (1) of this section shall be fined under this title or imprisoned not more than five years, or both.

(b) If the offense is a first offense under paragraph (a) of this subsection and is not for a tortious or illegal purpose or for purposes of direct or indirect commercial advantage or private commercial gain, and the wire or electronic communication with respect to which the offense under paragraph (a) is a radio communication that is not scrambled or encrypted, then—

(i) if the communication is not the radio portion of a cellular telephone communication, a public land mobile radio service communication or a paging service communication, and the conduct is not that described in subsection (5), the offender shall be fined under this title or imprisoned not more than one year, or both; and

(ii) if the communication is the radio portion of a cellular telephone communication, a public land mobile radio service communication or a paging service communication, the offender shall be fined not more than $ 500.

(c) Conduct otherwise an offense under this subsection that consists of or relates to the interception of a satellite transmission that is not encrypted or scrambled and that is transmitted—

(i) to a broadcasting station for purposes of retransmission to the general public; or

(ii) as an audio subcarrier intended for redistribution to facilities open to the public, but not including data transmissions or telephone calls, is not an offense under this subsection unless the conduct is for the purposes of direct or indirect commercial advantage or private financial gain.

(5) (a) (i) If the communication is—

(A) a private satellite video communication that is not scrambled or encrypted and the conduct in violation of this chapter is the private viewing of that communication and is not for a tortious or illegal purpose or for purposes of direct or indirect commercial advantage or private commercial gain; or

(B) a radio communication that is transmitted on frequencies allocated under subpart D of part 74 of the rules of the Federal Communications Commission that is not scrambled or encrypted and the conduct in violation of this chapter is not for a tortious or illegal purpose or for purposes of direct or indirect commercial advantage or private commercial gain, then the person who engages in such conduct shall be subject to suit by the Federal Government in a court of competent jurisdiction.

(ii) In an action under this subsection—

(A) if the violation of this chapter is a first offense for the person under paragraph (a) of subsection (4) and such person has not been found liable in a civil action under section 2520 of this title, the Federal Government shall be entitled to appropriate injunctive relief; and

(B) if the violation of this chapter is a second or subsequent offense under paragraph (a) of subsection (4) or such person has been found liable in any prior civil action under section 2520, the person shall be subject to a mandatory $ 500 civil fine.

(b) The court may use any means within its authority to enforce an injunction issued under paragraph (ii)(A), and shall impose a civil fine of not less than $ 500 for each violation of such an injunction.

Sec. 2515. Prohibition of use as evidence of intercepted wire or oral communications

Whenever any wire or oral communication has been intercepted, no part of the contents of such communication and no evidence derived therefrom may be received in evidence in any trial, hearing, or other proceeding in or before any court, grand jury, department, officer, agency, regulatory body, legislative committee, or other authority of the United States, a State, or a political subdivision thereof if the disclosure of that information would be in violation of this chapter.

Sec. 2520. Recovery of civil damages authorized

(a) In general. Except as provided in section 2511(2)(a)(ii), any person whose wire, oral, or electronic communication is intercepted, disclosed, or intentionally used in violation of this chapter may in a civil action recover from the person or entity which engaged in that violation such relief as may be appropriate.

(b) Relief. In an action under this section, appropriate relief includes—

(1) such preliminary and other equitable or declaratory relief as may be appropriate;

(2) damages under subsection (c) and punitive damages in appropriate cases; and

(3) a reasonable attorney's fee and other litigation costs reasonably incurred.

(c) Computation of damages.

(1) In an action under this section, if the conduct in violation of this chapter, is the private viewing of a private satellite video communication that is not scrambled or encrypted or if the communication is a radio communication that is transmitted on frequencies allocated under subpart D of part 74 of the rules of the Federal Communications Commission that is not scrambled or encrypted and the conduct is not for a tortious or illegal purpose or for purposes of direct or indirect commercial advantage or private commercial gain, then the court shall assess damages as follows:

(A) If the person who engaged in that conduct has not previously been enjoined under section 2511(5) and has not been found liable in a prior civil action under this section, the court shall assess the greater of the sum of actual damages suffered by the plaintiff, or statutory damages of not less than $ 50 and not more than $ 500.

(B) If, on one prior occasion, the person who engaged in that conduct has been enjoined under section 2511(5) or has been found liable in a civil action under this section, the court shall assess the greater of the sum of actual damages suffered by the plaintiff, or statutory damages of not less than $ 100 and not more than $ 1000.

(2) In any other action under this section, the court may assess as damages whichever is the greater of—

(A) the sum of the actual damages suffered by the plaintiff and any profits made by the violator as a result of the violation; or

(B) statutory damages of whichever is the greater of $ 100 a day for each day of violation or $ 10,000.

(d) Defense. A good faith reliance on—

(1) a court warrant or order, a grand jury subpoena, a legislative authorization, or a statutory authorization;

  (2) a request of an investigative or law enforcement officer under section 2518(7) of this title; or

  (3) a good faith determination that section 2511(3) of this title permitted the conduct complained of; is a complete defense against any civil or criminal action brought under this chapter or any other law.

  (e) Limitation. A civil action under this section may not be commenced later than two years after the date upon which the claimant first has a reasonable opportunity to discover the violation.

Sec. 2521. Injunction against illegal interception

  Whenever it shall appear that any person is engaged or is about to engage in any act which constitutes or will constitute a felony violation of this chapter, the Attorney General may initiate a civil action in a district court of the United States to enjoin such violation. The court shall proceed as soon as practicable to the hearing and determination of such an action, and may, at any time before final determination, enter such a restraining order or prohibition, or take such other action, as is warranted to prevent a continuing and substantial injury to the United States or to any person or class of persons for whose protection the action is brought. A proceeding under this section is governed by the Federal Rules of Civil Procedure, except that, if an indictment has been returned against the respondent, discovery is governed by the Federal Rules of Criminal Procedure.

CHAPTER 121. STORED WIRE AND ELECTRONIC COMMUNICATIONS AND TRANSACTIONAL RECORDS ACCESS

Sec. 2701. Unlawful access to stored communications

  (a) Offense. Except as provided in subsection (c) of this section whoever—

   (1) intentionally accesses without authorization a facility through which an electronic communication service is provided; or

   (2) intentionally exceeds an authorization to access that facility; and thereby obtains, alters, or prevents authorized access to a wire or electronic communication while it is in electronic storage in such system shall be punished as provided in subsection (b) of this section.

  (b) Punishment. The punishment for an offense under subsection (a) of this section is—

   (1) if the offense is committed for purposes of commercial advantage, malicious destruction or damage, or private commercial gain—

(A) a fine of not more than $ 250,000 or imprisonment for not more than one year, or both, in the case of a first offense under this subparagraph; and

(B) a fine under this title or imprisonment for not more than two years, or both, for any subsequent offense under this subparagraph; and

(2) a fine of not more than $ 5,000 or imprisonment for not more than six months, or both, in any other case.

(c) Exceptions. Subsection (a) of this section does not apply with respect to conduct authorized—

(1) by the person or entity providing a wire or electronic communications service;

(2) by a user of that service with respect to a communication of or intended for that user; or

(3) in section 2703, 2704 or 2518 of this title.

Sec. 2702. Disclosure of contents

(a) Prohibitions. Except as provided in subsection (b)—

(1) a person or entity providing an electronic communication service to the public shall not knowingly divulge to any person or entity the contents of a communication while in electronic storage by that service; and

(2) a person or entity providing remote computing service to the public shall not knowingly divulge to any person or entity the contents of any communication which is carried or maintained on that service—

(A) on behalf of, and received by means of electronic transmission from (or created by means of computer processing of communications received by means of electronic transmission from), a subscriber or customer of such service; and

(B) solely for the purpose of providing storage or computer processing services to such subscriber or customer, if the provider is not authorized to access the contents of any such communications for purposes of providing any services other than storage or computer processing.

(b) Exceptions. A person or entity may divulge the contents of a communication—

(1) to an addressee or intended recipient of such communication or an agent of such addressee or intended recipient;

(2) as otherwise authorized in section 2517, 2511(2)(a), or 2703 of this title;

(3) with the lawful consent of the originator or an addressee or intended recipient of such communication, or the subscriber in the case of remote computing service;

(4) to a person employed or authorized or whose facilities are used to forward such communication to its destination;

(5) as may be necessarily incident to the rendition of the service or to the protection of the rights or property of the provider of that service; or

(6) to a law enforcement agency, if such contents—

(A) were inadvertently obtained by the service provider; and

(B) appear to pertain to the commission of a crime.

Sec. 2704. Backup preservation

(a) Backup preservation.

(1) A governmental entity acting under section 2703(b)(2) may include in its subpoena or court order a requirement that the service provider to whom the request is directed create a backup copy of the contents of the electronic communications sought in order to pre-serve those communications. Without notifying the subscriber or customer of such subpoena or court order, such service provider shall create such backup copy as soon as practicable consistent with its reg-ular business practices and shall confirm to the governmental entity that such backup copy has been made. Such backup copy shall be cre-ated within two business days after receipt by the service provider of the subpoena or court order.

(2) Notice to the subscriber or customer shall be made by the governmental entity within three days after receipt of such confirma-tion, unless such notice is delayed pursuant to section 2705(a).

(3) The service provider shall not destroy such backup copy until the later of—

(A) the delivery of the information; or

(B) the resolution of any proceedings (including appeals of any proceeding) concerning the government's subpoena or court order.

(4) The service provider shall release such backup copy to the requesting governmental entity no sooner than fourteen days after the governmental entity's notice to the subscriber or customer if such service provider—

(A) has not received notice from the subscriber or customer that the subscriber or customer has challenged the governmental entity's request; and

(B) has not initiated proceedings to challenge the request of the governmental entity.

(5) A governmental entity may seek to require the creation of a backup copy under subsection (a)(1) of this section if in its sole discretion such entity determines that there is reason to believe that notification under section 2703 of this title of the existence of the subpoena or court order may result in destruction of or tampering with evidence. This determination is not subject to challenge by the subscriber or customer or service provider.

(b) Customer challenges.

(1) Within fourteen days after notice by the governmental entity to the subscriber or customer under subsection (a)(2) of this section, such subscriber or customer may file a motion to quash such subpoena or vacate such court order, with copies served upon the governmental entity and with written notice of such challenge to the service provider. A motion to vacate a court order shall be filed in the court which issued such order. A motion to quash a subpoena shall be filed in the appropriate United States district court or State court. Such motion or application shall contain an affidavit or sworn statement—

(A) stating that the applicant is a customer or subscriber to the service from which the contents of electronic communications maintained for him have been sought; and

(B) stating the applicant's reasons for believing that the records sought are not relevant to a legitimate law enforcement inquiry or that there has not been substantial compliance with the provisions of this chapter in some other respect.

(2) Service shall be made under this section upon a governmental entity by delivering or mailing by registered or certified mail a copy of the papers to the person, office, or department specified in the notice which the customer has received pursuant to this chapter. For the purposes of this section, the term "delivery" has the meaning given that term in the Federal Rules of Civil Procedure.

(3) If the court finds that the customer has complied with paragraphs (1) and (2) of this subsection, the court shall order the governmental entity to file a sworn response, which may be filed in camera if the governmental entity includes in its response the reasons which

make in camera review appropriate. If the court is unable to determine the motion or application on the basis of the parties' initial allegations and response, the court may conduct such additional proceedings as it deems appropriate. All such proceedings shall be completed and the motion or application decided as soon as practicable after the filing of the governmental entity's response.

(4) If the court finds that the applicant is not the subscriber or customer for whom the communications sought by the governmental entity are maintained, or that there is a reason to believe that the law enforcement inquiry is legitimate and that the communications sought are relevant to that inquiry, it shall deny the motion or application and order such process enforced. If the court finds that the applicant is the subscriber or customer for whom the communications sought by the governmental entity are maintained, and that there is not a reason to believe that the communications sought are relevant to a legitimate law enforcement inquiry, or that there has not been substantial compliance with the provisions of this chapter, it shall order the process quashed.

(5) A court order denying a motion or application under this section shall not be deemed a final order and no interlocutory appeal may be taken therefrom by the customer.

Sec. 2707. Civil action

(a) Cause of action. Except as provided in section 2703(e), any provider of electronic communication service, subscriber, or customer aggrieved by any violation of this chapter in which the conduct constituting the violation is engaged in with a knowing or intentional state of mind may, in a civil action, recover from the person or entity which engaged in that violation such relief as may be appropriate.

(b) Relief. In a civil action under this section, appropriate relief includes—

(1) such preliminary and other equitable or declaratory relief as may be appropriate;

(2) damages under subsection (c); and

(3) a reasonable attorney's fee and other litigation costs reasonably incurred.

(c) Damages. The court may assess as damages in a civil action under this section the sum of the actual damages suffered by the plaintiff and any profits made by the violator as a result of the violation, but in no case shall a person entitled to recover receive less than the sum of $ 1,000.

(d) Defense. A good faith reliance on—

(1) a court warrant or order, a grand jury subpoena, a legislative authorization, or a statutory authorization;

(2) a request of an investigative or law enforcement officer under section 2518(7) of this title; or

(3) a good faith determination that section 2511(3) of this title permitted the conduct complained of; is a complete defense to any civil or criminal action brought under this chapter or any other law.

(e) Limitation. A civil action under this section may not be commenced later than two years after the date upon which the claimant first discovered or had a reasonable opportunity to discover the violation.

Sec. 2708. Exclusivity of remedies

The remedies and sanctions described in this chapter are the only judicial remedies and sanctions for nonconstitutional violations of this chapter.

APPENDIX D

CALIFORNIA STATE AND LOCAL BODIES REQUIRED TO HAVE PUBLIC RECORDS ACT GUIDELINES

Under the Public Records Act, the following state and local bodies must establish written guidelines for accessibility of records. (Gov. Code, § 6253.) A copy of these guidelines shall be posted in a conspicuous public place at the offices of these bodies, and a copy of the guidelines must be available upon request free of charge to any person requesting that body's records:

All regional water quality control boards

Bay Area Air Quality Management District

California Coastal Commission

Department of Parks and Recreation

Department of Consumer Affairs

Department of Corporations

Department of Corrections

Department of General Services

Department of Industrial Relations

Department of Insurance

Department of Justice

Department of Motor Vehicles

Department of Real Estate

Department of the Youth Authority

Department of Toxic Substances Control

Department of Transportation

Department of Veterans Affairs

Department of Water Resources

Employment Development Department
Golden Gate Bridge, Highway and Transportation District
Los Angeles County Air Pollution Control District
Office of Environmental Health Hazard Assessment
Office of Statewide Health Planning and Development
Public Employees' Retirement System
Public Utilities Commission
San Francisco Bay Area Rapid Transit District
San Francisco Bay Conservation and Development Commission
Secretary of State
State Air Resources Board
State Board of Equalization
State Department of Alcohol and Drug Abuse
State Department of Developmental Services
State Department of Health Services
State Department of Mental Health
State Department of Social Services
State Water Quality Control Board
Teachers' Retirement Board

APPENDIX E

FEDERAL EXPERTS FOR COMPUTER CRIME INVESTIGATIONS

The following is a list of various federal resources for computer crime investigations:

Bureau of Alcohol, Tobacco, and Firearms
Forensic Science Laboratory
1401 Research Boulevard
Rockville, MD 20850
301-217-5717

Drug Enforcement Administration
Chief, Technical Operations Section
8199 Backlick Road
Lorton, VA 20079
703-557-8250

Federal Bureau of Investigation
Computer Crime Squad
Washington Metropolitan Field Office
7799 Leesburg Pike
Suite 200, South Tower
Falls Church, VA 22043
202-324-9164

Internal Revenue Service
SCER Program Coordinator
Criminal Investigation Division
CI:R:I Room 2246
1111 Constitution Avenue, N.W.
Washington, DC 20224
202-535-9130

United States Air Force
Computer Crime Division
Office of Special Investigations
HQ AFOSI/IVSC
Bolling Air Force Base
Washington, DC 20332-6001
202-767-5847

United States Department of Justice
Computer Crime & Intellectual Property Section
Criminal Division
1001 G Street, N.W.
Suite 200
Washington, DC 20001
202-514-1026

United States Secret Service
Electronic Crimes Branch
1310 L Street, N.W.
Washington, DC 20005
202-435-7700

APPENDIX F

DISCOVERY OF COMPUTERIZED DATA, MANUAL FOR COMPLEX LITIGATION

DISCOVERY OF COMPUTERIZED DATA
[See *Manual of Complex Litigation*, Third (Federal Judicial Center) § 21.446]

Computerized data have become commonplace in litigation. Such data include not only conventional information but also such things as operating systems (programs that control a computer's basic functions), applications (programs used directly by the operator, such as word processing or spreadsheet programs), computer-generated models, and other sets of instructions residing in computer memory. Any discovery plan must address the relevant issues, such as the search for, location, retrieval, form of production and inspection, preservation, and use at trial of information stored in mainframe or personal computers or accessible "online." For the most part, such data will reflect information generated and maintained in the ordinary course of business. Some computerized data, however, may have been compiled in anticipation of or for use in the litigation (and may therefore be entitled to protection as trial preparation materials). Discovery requests may themselves be transmitted in computer-accessible form; interrogatories served on computer disks, for example, could then be answered using the same disk, avoiding the need to retype them. Finally, computerized data may form the contents for a common document depository.

Some of the relevant issues to be considered follow:

Form of production. Rule 34 provides for the production, inspection, and copying of computerized data (i.e., "data compilations from which information can be obtained, translated, if necessary, by the respondent through detection devices into reasonably usable form"); Rule 33(d) permits parties to answer interrogatories by making available for inspection and copying business records, including "compilations," where "the burden of deriving or ascertaining the answer is substantially the same for the party serving the interrogatory as for the party served." The court will need to consider, among other things, whether production and inspection should be in computer-readable form (such as by translation onto CD-ROM disks) or of printouts (hard copies); what information the producing party must be required to provide (such as manuals and similar materials) to facilitate the requesting party's access to and inspection of the producing party's data; whether to require the parties to agree on a standard format for production of computerized data; and how to minimize and allocate the costs of production (such as the cost of computer runs or of special programming to facilitate production) and equalize the burdens on the parties. The cost of production may be an issue, for example, where production is to be made of E-mail (electronic mail) or voice- mail messages erased from hard disks but capable of being retrieved.

Search and retrieval. Computer-stored data and other information responsive to a request will not necessarily be found in an appropriately labeled file. Broad database searches may be necessary, and this may expose confidential or irrelevant data to the opponent's scrutiny unless appropriate safeguards are installed. Similarly, some data may be maintained in the form of compilations that may themselves be entitled to trade secret protection or that reflect attorney work product, having been prepared by attorneys in contemplation of litigation. Data may have been compiled, for example, to produce studies and tabulations for use at trial or as a basis for expert opinions.

Use at trial. In general, the Federal Rules of Evidence apply to computerized data as they do to other types of evidence. Computerized data may, however, raise unique issues concerning the accuracy and authenticity of the database. Accuracy may be impaired as a result of incorrect or incomplete entry of data, mistakes in output instructions, programming errors, damage and contamination of storage media, power outages, and equipment malfunctions. The proponent of computerized evidence has the burden of laying a proper foundation by establishing its accuracy. Issues concerning accuracy and reliability of computerized evidence, including any necessary discovery, should be addressed during pretrial proceedings and not raised for the first time at trial.

When the data are voluminous, verification and correction of all items may not be feasible. In such cases, verification may be made of a sample of the data. Instead of correcting the errors detected in the sample—which might lead to the erroneous representation that the compilation is free from error—evidence may be offered (or stipulations made) by way of extrapolation from the sample of the effect of the observed errors on the entire compilation. Alternatively, it may be feasible to use statistical methods to determine the probability and range of error.

The complexity, general unfamiliarity, and rapidly changing character of the technology involved in the management of computerized materials may at times make it appropriate for the court to seek the assistance of a special master or neutral expert. Alternatively, the parties may be called on to provide the court with expert assistance, in the form of briefings on the relevant technological issues.

APPENDIX G

FEDERAL GUIDELINES FOR SEARCHING AND SEIZING COMPUTERS

NOTE: The July 1994 edition of the Federal Guidelines for Searching and Seizing Computers and its October 1997 Supplement are merged together in the following appendix for your convenience. The text is reformatted and Appendices B–F (primarily reference aids) of the Guidelines are removed to conserve space. Although written for federal agents and attorneys involved with searches and seizures of computers, the Guidelines provide a good background on potential sources of electronic evidence and admissibility issues.

UNITED STATES DEPARTMENT OF JUSTICE

FEDERAL GUIDELINES

FOR

SEARCHING AND SEIZING COMPUTERS

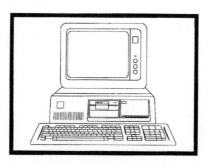

PREFACE

These Guidelines are the product of an interagency group, informally called the Computer Search and Seizure Working Group. Its members were lawyers, agents, and technical experts from the Federal Bureau of Investigation; the United States Secret Service; the Internal Revenue Service; the Drug Enforcement Administration; the United States Customs Service; the Bureau of Alcohol, Tobacco, and Firearms; the United States Air Force; the Department of Justice; and United States Attorneys' offices. Most of us have consulted widely within our own agencies to find the diversity of opinion on these topics. Our object was to offer some systematic guidance to all federal agents and attorneys as they wrestle with cases in this emerging area of the law. These Guidelines have not been officially adopted by any of the agencies, and are intended only as assistance, not as authority. They have no regulatory effect, and confer no right or remedy on anyone. Moreover, the facts of any particular case may require you to deviate from the methods we generally recommend, or may even demand that you try a completely new approach.

Many of our recommendations must be tentative, because there is often so little law directly on point. As the law develops and as technology changes (thereby altering or even transforming our assumptions), the Working Group may well find itself a Standing Committee with open membership.

If you have any comments, corrections, or contributions, please contact Marty Stansell-Gamm at the Computer Crime Unit, General Litigation Section, Department of Justice (202-514-1026). As you confront these issues in your practice, we will be eager to hear about your experience and to assist in any way we can.

Scott C. Charney,
Chief, Computer Crime Unit

Martha J. Stansell-Gamm
Computer Crime Unit
Chair, Computer Search and Seizure
Working Group

General Litigation and Legal
Advice Section
Criminal Division
Department of Justice

PREFACE [TO OCTOBER 1997 SUPPLEMENT]

This Supplement is intended to update the Federal Guidelines for Searching and Seizing Computers that was published in July 1994. The Supplement describes relevant federal and state cases decided since July 1994 as well as a number of additional earlier decisions.[1] The cases in this Supplement are organized according to the sections in the Guidelines. Where a case relates to more than one section, it is discussed in more than one place.

In order for us to stay abreast of the current developments in this fast changing area of the law, we invite you to contact us about your experiences. Please also contact us with any comments, corrections or contributions regarding the Guidelines or this Supplement at (202) 514-1026. This Supplement was prepared by David Movius, who was a student intern for the Computer Crime and Intellectual Property Section, under the supervision of David Goldstone and Peter Toren.

Scott Charney, Chief
Martha Stansell-Gamm, Deputy Chief
Computer Crime & Intellectual Property Section
Criminal Division
U.S. Department of Justice

---

[1] This text is not intended to create or confer any rights, privileges or benefits to anyone. It is also not intended to have the force of law or a United States Department of Justice directive. See United States v. Caceres, 440 U.S. 741 (1979).

TABLE OF CONTENTS

V. NETWORKS AND BULLETIN BOARDS

[February 1999]

5. Approval of Deputy Assistant Attorney General Required
6. Liability Under the Privacy Protection Act
C. STORED ELECTRONIC COMMUNICATIONS

VI. DRAFTING THE WARRANT

A. DRAFTING A WARRANT TO SEIZE HARDWARE
B. DRAFTING A WARRANT TO SEIZE INFORMATION
    1. Describing the Place to be Searched
        a. General Rule: Obtain a Second Warrant
        b. Handling Multiple Sites Within the Same District
        c. Handling Multiple Sites in Different Districts
        d. Information at an Unknown Site
        e. Information/Devices Which Have Been Moved
    2. Describing the Items to be Seized
    3. Removing Hardware to Search Off-Site: Ask the Magistrate for Explicit Permission
    4. Seeking Authority for a No-Knock Warrant
        a. In General
        b. In Computer-Related Cases

VII. POST-SEARCH PROCEDURES

A. INTRODUCTION
B. PROCEDURES FOR PRESERVING EVIDENCE
    1. Chain of Custody
    2. Organization
    3. Keeping Records
    4. Returning Seized Computers and Materials
        a. Federal Rules of Criminal Procedure: Rule 41(e)
        b. Hardware
        c. Documentation
        d. Notes and Papers
        e. Third-Party Owners

VIII. EVIDENCE

A. INTRODUCTION
B. THE BEST EVIDENCE RULE
C. AUTHENTICATING ELECTRONIC DOCUMENTS
    1. "Distinctive" Evidence
    2. Chain of Custody
    3. Electronic Processing of Evidence
D. THE HEARSAY RULE

IX. APPENDICES

APPENDIX A: SAMPLE COMPUTER LANGUAGE FOR SEARCH WARRANTS
    1. Tangible Objects
        a. Justify Seizing the Objects
        b. List and Describe the Objects
    2. Information: Records, Documents, Data
        a. Describe the Content of Records, Documents, or other Information
        b. Describe the Form which the Relevant Information May Take
        c. Electronic Mail: Searching and Seizing Data from a BBS Server under 18 U.S.C. § 2703

   d. Ask Permission to Seize Storage Devices when an Off-Site Search Is Necessary
   e. Ask Permission to Seize, Use, and Return Auxiliary Items, as Necessary
   f. Data Analysis Techniques
  3. Stipulation for Returning Original Electronic Data
APPENDICES B-F [not included]

INTRODUCTION

As computers and telecommunications explode into the next century, prosecutors and agents have begun to confront new kinds of problems. These Guidelines illustrate some of the ways in which searching a computer is different from searching a desk, a file cabinet, or an automobile. For example, when prosecutors must interpret Rule 41 (which requires that the government obtain a search warrant in the district where the property to be searched is "located"), applying it to searches of physical items is usually uncomplicated. But when they must try to "locate" electronic data, the discussion can quickly become more metaphysical than physical.

Even so, it is important to remember throughout the process that as dazzling and confounding as these new-age searches and seizures may be, they are in many essential ways just like all other searches. The cause must be just as probable; the description of items, just as particular. The standard investigative techniques that work in other cases (like finding witnesses and informants) are just as valuable in computer cases. The evidence that seals a case may not be on the hardware or software, but in an old-fashioned form: phone bills, notes in the margins of manuals, or letters in a drawer.

The sections that follow are an integration of many legal sources, practical experiences, and philosophical points of view. We have often had to extrapolate from existing law or policies to try to strike old balances in new areas. We have done our best to anticipate the questions ahead from the data available today. Even so, we recognize that rapid advances in computer and telecommunications technologies may require that we revisit these Guidelines, perhaps in the near future. In the meantime, as law struggles to catch up to technology, it is important to remember that computer cases are just like all others in one respect at least: under all the "facts and circumstances," there is no substitute for reasonable judgment.

I. KEY TERMS AND CONCEPTS

Searching and seizing computers raises unique issues for law enforcement personnel. Before addressing these issues, however, it is important to have a basic understanding of key terms and fundamental concepts that will influence the government's search and seizure decisions. This section describes these central terms and concepts. A more complete glossary can be found at APPENDIX B [not included].

A. DEFINITIONS

When people speak of searching or seizing computers, they usually are not referring only to the CPU (Central Processing Unit). After all, a computer is useless without the devices that allow for input (e.g., a keyboard or mouse) and output (e.g., a monitor or printer) of information. These devices, known as "peripherals,"[1] are an integral part of any "computer system."

Failure to more specifically define the term "computer" may cause misunderstandings. Having probable cause to seize a "computer" does not necessarily mean there is probable cause to seize the attached printer. Therefore, we need to be clear about our terms.

1. Hardware -- "The physical components or equipment that make up a computer system. . . ." Webster's Dictionary of Computer Terms 170 (3d ed. 1988). Examples include keyboards, monitors, and printers.

2. Software -- "The programs or instructions that tell a computer what to do." Id. at 350. This includes system programs which control the internal operation of the computer system (such as Microsoft's Disk Operating System, "MS-DOS," that controls IBM-compatible PCs) and applications programs which enable the computer to produce useful work (e.g., a word processing program such as WordPerfect).

3. Data -- "A formalized representation of facts or concepts suitable for communication, interpretation, or processing by people or by automatic means." Id. at 84. Data is often used to refer to the information stored in the computer.

4. Documentation -- Documents that describe technical specifications of hardware components and/or software applications and how to use them.

5. Input/Output (I/O) Device -- A piece of equipment which sends data to, or receives data from, a computer. Keyboards, monitors, and printers are all common I/O devices.

6. Network -- "A system of interconnected computer systems and terminals." Id. at 253.

7. System Administrator (or System Operator, "sysop") -- The individual responsible for assuring that the computer system is functioning properly. He is often responsible for computer security as well.

---

[1] Peripheral equipment means "[t]he input/output units and auxiliary storage units of a computer system, attached by cables to the central processing unit." Webster's Dictionary of Computer Terms 279 (3d ed. 1988).

8.   Internet --
"(a) Generally, (not capitalized) any collection of distinct networks working together as one.
(b) Specifically (capitalized), the world-wide 'network of networks' that are connected to each other, using the IP protocol and other similar protocols. The Internet provides file transfer, remote login, electronic mail, news, and other services."

Ed Krol, The Whole Internet 509 (2d ed. 1994).

9.   IP -- "The Internet Protocol; the most important of the protocols on which the Internet is based. It allows a packet to traverse multiple networks on the way to its final destination."

Ed Krol, The Whole Internet 509 (2d ed. 1994).

For search and seizure purposes, unless the text specifically indicates otherwise, the term "computer" refers to the box that houses the CPU, along with any internal storage devices (such as internal hard drives) and internal communications devices (such as an internal modem or fax card). Thus, "computer" refers to the hardware, software, and data contained in the main unit. Printers, external modems (attached by cable to the main unit), monitors, and other external attachments will be referred to collectively as "peripherals" and discussed individually where appropriate. When we are referring to both the computer and all attached peripherals as one huge package, we will use the term "computer system." "Information" refers to all the information on a computer system, including both software applications and data.

It is important to remember that computer systems can be configured in an unlimited number of ways with assorted input and output devices. In some cases, a specific device may have particular evidentiary value (e.g., if the case involves a bookie who prints betting slips, the printer may constitute valuable evidence); in others, it may be the information stored in the computer that may be important. In either event, the warrant must describe, with particularity, what agents should search for and seize.

B. LIST OF COMPUTER SYSTEM COMPONENTS

The following is an abridged list of hardware components which may play a role in a criminal offense and, therefore, be subject to search and seizure under warrant. For a more extensive list, see the "GLOSSARY" at APPENDIX B [not included]. It is important to remember that electronic components are constantly changing, both in nature and in number, and no list can be comprehensive.

Device Name	Description
CPU:	The central processing unit.
Hard Disk Drive:	A storage device based on a fixed, permanently-mounted disk drive. It may be either internal or external. Both applications and data may be stored on the disk.
Floppy Disk Drive:	A drive that reads from or writes to floppy diskettes. Information is stored on the diskettes themselves, not on the drive.
Mouse:	A pointing device that controls input. Normally, the user points to an object on the screen and then presses a button on the mouse to indicate her selection.

Modem: A device allowing the computer to communicate with another computer, normally over standard telephone lines. Modems may be either external or internal.

Fax Peripheral: A device, normally inserted as an internal card, that allows the computer to function as a fax machine.

CD ROM: CD ROM stands for Compact Disk Read-Only Memory. CD ROMs store and read massive amounts of information on a removable disk platter. Unlike hard drives and diskettes, CD ROMs are read-only and data cannot be written to the platter.

Laser Disk: Similar to a CD ROM drive but uses lasers to read and write information.

Scanner: Any optical device which can recognize characters on paper and, using specialized software, convert them into digital form.

Printer: A number of technologies exist, using various techniques. The most common types of computer printers are:

1.   Dot matrix - characters and graphics are created by pins hitting the ribbon and paper;

2.   Laser - electrostatically charges the printed page and applies toner;

3.   Ink jet - injects (sprays) ink onto the paper;

4.   Thermal - a hot printer head contacts special paper that reacts to heat;

5.   Band - a rotating metal band is impacted as it spins;

6.   Daisy wheel - a small print wheel containing the form of each character rotates and hits the paper, character by character;

7.   Plotter - moves ink pens over the paper surface, typically used for large engineering and architectural drawings.

C. DETERMINING THE COMPUTER'S ROLE IN THE OFFENSE

Before preparing a warrant to seize all or part of a computer system and the information it contains, it is critical to determine the computer's role in the offense. First, the computer system may be a tool of the offense. This occurs when the computer system is actively used by a defendant to commit the offense. For example, a counterfeiter might use his computer, scanner, and color printer to scan U.S. currency and then print money. Second, the computer system may be incidental to the offense, but a repository of evidence. For example, a drug dealer may store records pertaining to customers, prices, and quantities delivered on a personal computer, or a blackmailer may type and store threatening letters in his computer.

In each case, the role of the computer differs. It may constitute "the smoking gun" (i.e., be an instrumentality of the offense), or it may be nothing more than an electronic filing cabinet (i.e., a storage device). In some cases, the computer may serve both functions at once. Hackers, for example, often use their computers both to attack other computer systems and to store stolen files. In this case, the hacker's computer is both a tool and storage device. Whatever the computer's role in each case, prosecutors must consider this and tailor warrants accordingly.

By understanding the role that the computer has played in the offense, it is possible to focus on certain key questions:

Is there probable cause to seize hardware?

Is there probable cause to seize software?

Is there probable cause to seize data?

Where will this search be conducted? Is it practical to search the computer system on site, or must the examination be conducted at a field office or laboratory?

If agents remove the system from the premises to conduct the search, must they return the computer system, or copies of the seized data, to its owner/user before trial?

Considering the incredible storage capacities of computers, how will agents search this data in an efficient, timely manner?

Before addressing these questions, it is important to recognize that general Fourth Amendment principles apply to computer searches, and traditional law enforcement techniques may provide significant evidence of criminal activity, even in computer crime cases. Therefore, we begin with a brief overview of the Fourth Amendment.

II. GENERAL PRINCIPLES

A. SEARCH WARRANTS

There is, of course, "a strong preference for warrants," and courts will scrutinize a warrantless search. Indeed, as the Supreme Court indicated in United States v. Leon, 468 U.S. 897, 914 (1984), a warrant can save a search where probable cause is doubtful or marginal. Most searches of computer systems will be pursuant to warrant, but the recognized exceptions to the warrant requirement apply equally to the search and seizure of computers.

B. PLAIN VIEW

Evidence of a crime may be seized without a warrant under the plain view exception to the warrant requirement. To rely on this exception, the officer must be in a lawful position to observe the evidence, and its incriminating character must be immediately apparent. See Horton v. California, 496 U.S. 128 (1990). For example, if agents with a warrant to search a computer for evidence of narcotics trafficking find a long list of access codes taped to the computer monitor, the list should also be seized.

In Ivatury v. Texas, 792 S.W.2d 845 (Ct. App. 1990), the appellant contended that the trial court should have suppressed evidence in the form of computer tape obtained by the search of a safety deposit box. Officers executing the search had procured a valid warrant for the deposit box to search for a photograph, but failed to specifically describe the computer tape. The court upheld the seizure pursuant to the plain view exception to the warrant requirement. Id. at 850-51. First, according to the court, the officer was lawfully searching the safety deposit box where the tape was found pursuant to the warrant. Second, the agent inadvertently discovered the computer tape. Third, the agent, who first had become aware of the appellant as part of an espionage investigation, had immediately recognized the tape as a kind used by the defense industry and as the kind of tape on which the appellant had previously offered to sell him stolen defense information. The court emphasized that the immediacy with which an agent should recognize the evidence requires only a "reasonable belief." Id. at 851.

See also City of Akron v. Patrick, C.A. No. 10428, 1982 WL 5049, at *4 (Ohio Ct. App. 1982) (unpublished decision) (approving seizure of computers pursuant to search warrant authorizing seizure of gambling paraphernalia because police officer "immediately deduced" from words on computer screen that computers were being used in gambling operation); Oklahoma v. One Pioneer CD-ROM Changer, et. al., 891 P.2d 600, 605 (Okla. App. 1994) (approving seizure of computer system in search for obscene material and equipment used in violation of state obscenity laws where computer screen display indicated that computer was being used to view or copy files named "lesbian sex" or "oral sex").

C. EXIGENT CIRCUMSTANCES

"When destruction of evidence is imminent, a warrantless seizure of that evidence is justified if there is probable cause to believe that the item seized constitutes evidence of criminal activity." United States v. David, 756 F. Supp. 1385, 1392 (D. Nev. 1991).[2] If a target's screen is displaying evidence which agents reasonably believe to be in danger, the "exigent circumstances" doctrine would justify downloading the information before obtaining a warrant. For example, agents may know that the incriminating data is not actually stored on the suspect's machine, but is only temporarily on line from a second network storage site in another building, city, or district. Thus, even if the agents could secure the target's computer in front of them, someone could still electronically damage or destroy the data--either from the second computer where it is stored or from a third, unknown site. Of course, when agents know they must search and seize data from two or more computers on a wide-area network, they should, if possible, simultaneously execute separate search warrants. (See "Describing the Place to be Searched," infra [].) But sometimes that is not possible, and agents must then analyze the particular situation to decide whether the "exigent circumstances" exception applies. In computer network cases, as in all others, the answer is absolutely tied to the facts.

In determining whether exigent circumstances exist, agents should consider: (1) the degree of urgency involved, (2) the amount of time necessary to obtain a warrant, (3) whether the evidence is about to be removed or destroyed, (4) the possibility of danger at the site, (5) information indicating the possessors of the contraband know the police are on their trail, and (6) the ready destructibility of the contraband. United States v. Reed, 935 F.2d 641, 642 (4th Cir.), cert. denied, 112 S. Ct. 423 (1991).

Under the "exigent circumstances" exception to the warrant requirement, agents can search without a warrant if the circumstances would cause a reasonable person to believe it to be necessary. The Supreme Court has upheld warrantless entries and searches when police officers reasonably believe that someone inside needs "immediate aid," Mincey v. Arizona, 437 U.S. 385, 392-93 (1978), or to prevent the destruction of relevant evidence, the escape of a suspect, or the frustration of some other legitimate law enforcement objective. United States v. Arias, 923 F.2d 1387 (9th Cir.), cert. denied, 112 S. Ct. 130 (1991). The officer's fears need not be correct so long as they are reasonable. See United States v. Reed, supra (proper inquiry is what objective officer could reasonably believe).

Recognizing the strong preference for warrants, courts have suppressed evidence where the officers had time to get a warrant but failed to do so. United States v. Houle, 603 F.2d 1297 (8th Cir. 1979). Some courts have even ruled that exigent circumstances did not exist if the law enforcement officers had time to obtain a warrant by

---

[2] See also United States v. Talkington, 875 F.2d 591 (7th Cir. 1989) (warrantless entry of residence and seizure of counterfeit money was justified since agents knew that (1) the suspects had previously discussed burning money; (2) there was a fire in the backyard; and (3) the agents were confident that residents were not having a cookout).

telephone. United States v. Patino, 830 F.2d 1413, 1416 (7th Cir. 1987) (warrantless search not justified when officer had adequate opportunity to obtain telephone warrant during 30-minute wait for backup assistance; not permissible for agents to wait for exigency and then exploit it), cert. denied, 490 U.S. 1069 (1989).

Additionally, while exigencies may justify the seizure of hardware (i.e., the storage device), this does not necessarily mean that they support a warrantless search. In United States v. David, 756 F. Supp. 1385 (D. Nev. 1991), the court held that although the agent was correct to seize the defendant's computer memo book without a warrant (because the agent saw him deleting files), the agent should have gotten a search warrant before re-accessing and searching the book. The court held the exigencies allowed the agent to take the computer memo book but, once taken, there was time to get a warrant to look inside. Therefore, the seized evidence had to be suppressed. Id. at 1392.

This holding is, of course, analogous to cases which address other kinds of containers. In the David case, the computer book itself was not contraband, instrumentality, fruit, or evidence of crime. It was, instead, a small file cabinet, a locked box, a container of data. The agent was not interested in the hardware but in the information inside. As the cases make clear, authority to seize a container does not necessarily authorize a warrantless search of the container's contents. See Texas v. Brown, 460 U.S. 730, 750 (1983) (Stevens, J., concurring) (plain view justified seizure of party balloon but additional justification was required to open balloon without warrant). Courts have suppressed warrantless searches when the defendant still had a reasonable expectation of privacy in the contents of the container. See United States v. Turk, 526 F.2d 654 (5th Cir.) (although seizure of tape was proper, playing taped conversation of private telephone communication was not), cert. denied, 429 U.S. 823 (1976); Blair v. United States, 665 F.2d 500 (4th Cir. 1981).

Agents must always remember, however, that electronic data is perishable. Humidity, temperature, vibrations, physical mutilation, magnetic fields created by passing a strong magnet over a disk, or computer commands (such as "erase *.*" or "format") can destroy data in a matter of seconds. Thus, the exigent circumstances doctrine may justify a warrantless seizure in appropriate cases.

D. BORDER SEARCHES

The law recognizes a limited exception to the Fourth Amendment's probable cause requirement at the nation's borders. Officials may search people and property without a warrant and without probable cause as a condition of crossing the border or its "functional equivalent." United States v. Ramsey, 431 U.S. 606 (1977), cert. denied, 434 U.S. 1062 (1978). Both incoming international baggage (United States v. Scheer, 600 F.2d 5 (3d Cir. 1979) and incoming international mail at the border are subject to search without a warrant to determine whether they contain items which may not lawfully be brought into the country. Border searches or international mail searches of diskettes, tapes, computer hard drives (such as laptops carried by international travelers), or other media should fall under the same rules which apply to incoming persons, documents, and international mail.

On the other hand, the border search exception to the warrant requirement probably will not apply to data transmitted electronically (or by other non-physical methods) into the United States from other countries. For example, if an individual in the U.S. downloads child pornography from a foreign BBS, a warrantless search of his home computer could not be supported by the border search exception. In such cases, it is difficult to find a "border" or its functional equivalent as data travels over international telephone lines or satellite links. What seems clear, however, is that once data has been received by a computer within the United States, that data resides in the country and has passed beyond the border or its functional equivalent. Because the justification for the border search exception is grounded on the sovereign's power to exclude illegal articles from the country, that exception no longer applies once such articles (in this case electronic data) have come into the country undetected.

E. CONSENT SEARCHES

Agents may search a place or object without a warrant or, for that matter, without probable cause, if a person with authority has consented. Schneckloth v. Bustamonte, 412 U.S. 218, 219 (1973). This consent may be explicit or implicit. United States v. Milan-Rodriguez, 759 F.2d 1558, 1563-64 (11th Cir.) (telling police where to find a key constitutes implicit consent to a search of the locked area), cert. denied, 474 U.S. 845 (1985), and cert. denied, 486 U.S. 1054 (1988).

Whether consent was voluntarily given is a question of fact which the court will decide. United States v. Scott, 578 F.2d 1186, 1189 (6th Cir.), cert. denied, 439 U.S. 870 (1978). The burden is on the government to prove that the consent was voluntary, United States v. Price, 599 F.2d 494, 503 (2nd Cir. 1979), and, in making its decision, the court will consider all the facts surrounding the consent. Schneckloth, supra, at 226-7; United States v. Mendenhall, 446 U.S. 544, 557-8 (1980). See generally United States v. Caballos, 812 F.2d 42 (2d Cir. 1987). While no single aspect controls the result, the Supreme Court has identified the following important factors: the age of the person giving consent; the person's education, intelligence, mental and physical condition; whether the person was under arrest; and whether he had been advised of his right to refuse consent. Schneckloth, supra, at 226.

In computer crime cases, several consent issues are likely to arise. First, did the scope of the search exceed the consent given? For example, what if a target consents to a search of his machine, but the data is encrypted? Does his consent authorize breaking the encryption scheme? Second, who is the proper party to consent to a search? Does a system administrator have the authority to consent to a search of a file server containing the files of all the system users?

1. Scope of the Consent

A person who consents to a search may explicitly limit this consent to a certain area. United States v. Griffin, 530 F.2d 739, 744 (7th Cir. 1976). When the limits of the consent are clearly given, either at the time of the search or even afterwards, agents must respect their bounds. In Vaughn v. Baldwin, 950 F.2d 331 (6th Cir. 1991), the plaintiff dentist had voluntarily turned over records to the IRS. The IRS agent kept the records for months and refused several informal requests for their return. Plaintiff then formally, in writing, revoked his consent to the IRS, which still kept the records to make copies. Finally, plaintiff sued and the IRS returned the originals but kept the copies. The court found that the IRS had violated the Fourth Amendment. Although the IRS was entitled to copy the records while they lawfully had them, they could not keep the records once plaintiff revoked his consent. Moreover, considering the long period of time that the IRS held the documents, the court rejected the argument that once the plaintiff demanded return of his documents the government should be entitled to retain them for a reasonable period for copying.

Consent may also be limited implicitly. In United States v. David, 756 F. Supp. 1385 (D. Nev. 1991), the court held that while the defendant had consented, pursuant to a cooperation agreement, to share some of the information contained in his hand-held computer memo book, his attempt to prevent agents from seeing the file password constituted a limit on his consent. Although the agent did nothing wrong by leaning over defendant's shoulder to watch him enter the password, the government clearly exceeded the implicit limits of David's consent when agents used the password to read the whole computer book without David's permission. For a more extensive discussion of encryption issues, see "Encryption," infra [].

2. Third-Party Consent

a. General Rules

It is not uncommon for several people to use or own the target computer equipment. If any one of those people gives permission to search for data, agents may generally rely on that consent, so long as that person has authority over the computer. In these cases, all users have assumed the risk that a co-user might not just discover everything in the computer but might also permit law enforcement to discover the "common area" as well.

In <u>United States v. Matlock</u>, 415 U.S. 164 (1974), the Supreme Court stated that one who has common authority over premises or effects may consent to a search even if the absent co-user objects. In an important footnote, the Court said that "common authority" is not a property law concept but

> rests rather on mutual use of the property by persons generally having joint access or control for most purposes, so that it is reasonable to recognize that any of the co-inhabitants has the right to permit the inspection in his own right and that the others have assumed the risk that one of their number might permit the common area to be searched.

<u>Id.</u> at 171 n.7.

Extending this analysis, a third party with common authority may consent even if he is antagonistic toward the defendant. One could even argue that sharing access to a common premises with an unsympathetic person would objectively increase the risk of disclosure, and thus reasonable expectations of privacy actually diminish. This is especially true where the consenting individual agrees to a search of common premises to exculpate himself from the defendant's criminal activity. <u>See</u> 3 W. LaFave, <u>Search and Seizure: A Treatise on the Fourth Amendment</u> § 8.3(b) at 244-45 (2d ed. 1987). <u>See also</u> <u>United States v. Long</u>, 524 F.2d 660 (9th Cir. 1975) (wife in fear of her husband could still consent to a search of the jointly owned house even though she had moved out and he had changed the locks).

Where two or more people enjoy equal property rights over a place, they may still have exclusive, private zones within the shared premises. Housemates with separate bedrooms, spouses with private areas or containers, and housemates with separate directories on a shared computer may reasonably expect to own that space alone. But when do these individual expectations overcome another's common authority over premises or property? Although there is no bright line test, courts will generally regard a defendant's claims of exclusive control in this situation with some skepticism. <u>See</u> <u>Frazier v. Cupp</u>, 394 U.S. 731, 740 (1969).

Even so, courts may honor claims to privacy where the defendant has taken some <u>special steps</u> to protect his personal effects from the scrutiny of others, and others lack ready access. 3 W. LaFave, <u>supra</u> § 8.3(f), at 259-60. In <u>United States v. Block</u>, 590 F.2d 535 (4th Cir. 1978), the Fourth Circuit held that a mother's authority to permit police officers to inspect her 23-year-old son's room did not include his locked footlocker in the room. The court stated that the authority to consent to search

> cannot be thought automatically to extend to the interiors of every discrete enclosed space capable of search within the area. . . . Common experience . . . teaches all of us that the law's "enclosed spaces"--mankind's valises, suitcases, footlockers, strong boxes, etc.--are frequently the objects of his highest privacy expectations, and that the expectations may well be at their most intense when such effects are deposited temporarily or kept semi-permanently in public places or in places under the general control of another.

<u>Id.</u> at 541.

In a footnote, however, the <u>Block</u> court noted that not every "enclosed space" within a room is exempt from the reach of the authorized search area. A rule of reason applies, one that considers the circumstances "indicating the presence or absence of a discrete expectation of privacy with respect to a particular object: whether it is secured, whether it is commonly used for preserving privacy, etc." <u>Id.</u> at n.8. <u>Cf.</u> <u>United States v. Sealey</u>, 830 F.2d 1028,

1031 (9th Cir. 1987) (spousal consent valid because sealed containers were not marked in any way that would indicate defendant's sole ownership). Thus, creating a separate personal directory on a computer may not sufficiently mark it as exclusive, but protecting that separate directory with a secret password may "lock the container." In that event, if law enforcement analysts search the directory by breaking the password (because the co-user who consented to the search did not know that password), a court would probably suppress the result.

Matlock did not address whether a consent search is valid when police have reasonably, but mistakenly, relied upon the consent of someone who appeared to have common authority over the premises, but in fact did not. In Illinois v. Rodriguez, 497 U.S. 177 (1990), however, the Supreme Court held that a consent search is valid when police are reasonable in thinking they have been given authorized consent. The Court cautioned, however, that police cannot simply rely upon someone at the scene who claims to have authority if the surrounding circumstances indicate otherwise. If such authority is unclear, the police are obligated to ask more questions. Determining who has power to consent is an objective exercise, the Court stated, and the test is whether the facts available to the police officer at the moment would warrant a person of reasonable caution to believe that the consenting party had authority over the premises. Id. at 2801.

b. Spouses

Under the Matlock "common authority" approach, most spousal consent searches are valid. Although spouses who create exclusive areas may preclude their partners from consenting to a search, that circumstance will be unusual. Indeed, spouses do not establish "exclusive use" just by being the only one who uses the area; there must be a showing that the consenting spouse was denied access. 3 W. LaFave, supra p. 11, § 8.4(a), at 278. In United States v. Duran, 957 F.2d 499, 504-5 (7th Cir. 1992), for example, the defendant and his wife lived on a farm with several outbuildings. The wife consented to the search of a building which she believed defendant used as a private gym, but the police found marijuana plants inside. The court emphasized the presumption that the entire marital premises are jointly held and controlled by the partners, and said this presumption can be overcome only by showing that the consenting spouse was actually denied access to the area in question.

With spouses, as with roommates, the Rodriguez "reasonable belief" rule (see "General Rules," supra []) allows investigating agents to draw reasonable conclusions, based upon the situation they encounter, about who has authority to consent. In the absence of objective evidence to the contrary, agents will be reasonable in presuming that spouses have authority to consent to a search of anything on the marital property. Illinois v. Rodriguez, supra.

c. Parents

In some recent computer crime cases the perpetrators have been relatively young and, even if no longer legally minors, have resided with their parents. Under the Matlock rationale, it is clear that parents may consent to a search of common areas in the family home. Additionally, with regard to minor children, the courts have found parents to hold superior rights in the home and "even rather extraordinary efforts by the child to establish exclusive use may not be effective to undermine the parents' authority over their home, including rooms occupied by the child." 3 W. LaFave, supra p. 14, § 8.4(b), at 283. Therefore, if parents consent to a search and seizure of floppy disks or passwords locked in the minor child's room, that consent should be upheld.

The issue becomes more complicated, however, when the sons and daughters who reside with their parents are adults. In these situations, courts may reach the opposite result when, as a practical matter, the adult child has established an exclusive area in the home that the parents have respected. Id. at 285. See discussion of United States v. Block in "General Rules," supra [].

d. Employers

Employers may be either public (i.e., government) or private. The distinction is important because government employers, unlike private employers, are bound by the Fourth Amendment. In construing the reach of the Fourth Amendment into the workplace, the Supreme Court has held that government employers may search employee offices, without either a warrant or the consent of the employee, when the search is administrative in nature; that is, it is work-related (e.g., the supervisor needs to find a case file) or involves work-related misconduct. O'Connor v. Ortega, 480 U.S. 709 (1987).

The Court found that government employees can have a reasonable expectation of privacy even though the physical area is owned by the government. Id. at 717 (specifically rejecting a contention made by the Solicitor General that public employees can never have a reasonable expectation of privacy in their place of work). The realities of the workplace, however, suggest that an employee's expectation of privacy must be reduced to the degree that fellow employees, supervisors, subordinates, guests, and even the general public may have access to that individual's work space. Recognizing that government agencies could not function properly if supervisors had to establish probable cause and obtain a warrant whenever they needed to look for a file in an employee's office, the Supreme Court held that two kinds of searches are exempt. Specifically, both (1) a non-investigatory, work-related intrusion and (2) an investigatory search for evidence of suspected work-related employee misfeasance are permissible without a warrant and should be judged by the standard of reasonableness. Id. at 725-6.

Even so, the Court made clear that "[n]ot everything that passes through the confines of the business address can be considered part of the workplace context. . . ." Id. at 717. For example, the contents of an employee's purse, briefcase, or closed luggage do not lose their private character just because the employee has brought them to work. Thus, while the circumstances may permit a supervisor to search in an employee's desk for a work-related file, the supervisor usually will have to stop at the employee's gym bag or briefcase. This analysis may have interesting implications for "containers" like floppy disks, which certainly may be either work-related or private, depending on the circumstances. It will probably be reasonable for employers to assume that floppy disks found at an office are part of the workplace, but there may be cases where a court will treat a floppy disk as if it were a personal container of private items.

Of course, there may be some government agencies where employees do consent (either expressly or tacitly) to searches of even private parcels because of the nature of the job. For example, employees with security clearances who work with classified material may expect that their purses, briefcases, and other bags may be inspected under certain circumstances. The factual variations on this "reasonable expectation" theme are endless, and are tied absolutely to the details of each case.

The O'Connor Court did not address the appropriate standard to be applied when a government employee is being investigated for criminal misconduct or breaches of other non-work-related statutory or regulatory standards. Id. at 729. In a case involving employee drug testing, at least one court has noted, in dicta, that "[t]he government may not take advantage of any arguably relaxed 'employer' standard for warrantless searches. . .when its true purpose is to obtain evidence of criminal activity without complying with the more stringent standards that normally protect citizens against unreasonably intrusive evidence-gathering." National Federation of Federal Employees v. Weinberger, 818 F.2d 935, 943 n.12 (D.C. Cir. 1987). Therefore, it would appear that whenever law enforcement is conducting an evidence-gathering search, even if the search is to take place at a government office, agents must either obtain a warrant or fall within some generally recognized exception to the warrant requirement. Appropriate consent from a third party is, of course, one of those exceptions.

Generally speaking, an employer (government or private) may consent to a search of an employee's computer and peripherals if the employer has common authority over them. Agents and prosecutors must consider whether, under the facts, the employee would expect privacy in those items and whether that expectation would be objectively reasonable. Relevant factors include whether (1) the area/item to be searched has been set aside for the employee's exclusive or personal use (e.g., does the employee have the only key to the computer or do others have access to the data); (2) the employee has been given permission to store personal information on the system or in the area to be searched; (3) the employee has been advised that the system may be accessed or looked at by others; (4) there have been past inspections of the area/item and this fact is known to the employee; and (5) there is an employment policy that searches of the work area may be conducted at any time for any reason. And when the employer is the federal government, another factor is (6) whether the purpose of the search was work-related, rather than primarily for law enforcement objectives. See generally O'Connor, 480 U.S. at 717 (employee's expectation of privacy must be assessed in the context of the employment relationship).

There are currently no cases specifically addressing an employer's consent to search and seize an employee's computer (and related items). But there are cases that discuss searches of an employee's designated work area or desk. For example, the Seventh Circuit has upheld the search of a hotel room that served as a welfare hotel's business office after the hotel owner consented. United States v. Bilanzich, 771 F.2d 292 (7th Cir. 1985). The room searched was used by the defendant/manager of the hotel for hotel business, the hotel's books were stored there, and the room was also used by doctors and welfare officials when they visited residents. The manager kept the key to the room. In affirming the manager's theft and forgery convictions (based in large part on documents seized from the business office/hotel room), the Seventh Circuit found that the hotel owner had the requisite control over and relationship to the business office to consent to its search. The court rejected the manager's argument that she had sole control over the business office because she generally had the key, finding that the owner could request access to the room at any time, that the room was shared with others (visiting physicians and welfare officials), and that the items sought were business records (e.g., welfare checks that the manager had forged). Thus, the manager did not have exclusive control over the area nor was it for her personal use. In addition, the purpose of the search was "employment related," since the manager was defrauding the employer and the customers.

In United States v. Gargiso, 456 F.2d 584, 587 (2d Cir. 1972), the Second Circuit upheld the search of a locked, wired-off area in the basement of a book company--a search to which the highest official of the book company then on the scene (the company's vice president) had consented. The defendant, an employee of the book company, objected to the search. Both the defendant and the vice president had supervisory authority over the area searched, and both also had keys to the area, as did other company personnel. The court found that the vice president's control over the area was equal to that of the employee's, making the consent effective. The vice president had sufficient control over the area to permit inspection in his own right and the employee had assumed the risk that the vice president would do so.

In Donovan v. A.A. Beiro Construction Co., Inc., 746 F.2d 894, 900 (D.C. Cir. 1984), the D.C. Circuit found the D.C. Government's consent to a search conducted by OSHA inspectors of a D.C. construction site effective against one of the contractors. The site was a large, multi-employer area surrounded by a chain link fence with no interior fences separating the various contractors' work areas. There was considerable overlap and interaction among the various contractors and their employees. The Court found that the defendant/contractor had no reasonable expectation of privacy in the area searched, because it was a common construction site shared by many. Thus, the defendant/ contractor had assumed the risk that anyone with authority at the site would permit inspection of the common construction area.

In an earlier case, United States v. Blok, 188 F.2d 1019 (D.C. Cir. 1951), the D.C. Circuit affirmed the reversal of a petty larceny conviction of a government employee, finding that the search of the employee's desk violated the employee's right of privacy. The court found that the employee had exclusive use of the desk and a reasonable expectation of privacy in it. Her employer's consent to a police search of the desk did not make the search reasonable. There was no policy putting employees on notice that they should not expect privacy in their desks. Nor was the search conducted by the employer for employment purposes (e.g., searching for a file). "It was precisely the kind of search by policemen for evidence of a crime against which the constitutional prohibition was directed." Id. at 1021 (quoting the district court). Thus, the employer's consent was ineffective because the area searched was for the employee's exclusive and personal use (factor number 1 above); the purpose of the search was not work-related (factor number 6 above); and there was no policy putting the employee on notice that her desk might be subject to search (factors number 3 and 5 above). Significantly, the O'Connor Court cited Blok with approval. O'Connor, 480 U.S. at 719.

In Williams v. Philadelphia Housing Authority, 826 F. Supp. 952 (E.D. Pa. 1993), aff'd mem., 27 F.3d 560 (3d Cir. 1994), the court rejected a state employee's challenge to the seizure of a computer disk by his supervisor. During a leave of absence, the plaintiff's supervisor had entered his workplace and removed a computer disk that contained work-related documents as well as personal items. The court reasoned that, under O'Connor v. Ortega, 480 U.S. (1987), employers are granted wide latitude to enter employees' offices for work-related reasons. Here, the superior was acting in her official capacity in retrieving the disk, the employee was asked to clear the office of any personal property, and the search was no broader than necessary to retrieve the work-related files from the disk. Thus, the court held that the plaintiff had failed to allege facts sufficient to state a claim for a violation of his Fourth Amendment rights. Williams, 826 F. Supp. at 954.

See Ohio v. Chubb, No. 70648, 1997 WL 10142, at *1 (Ohio App. 8th Dist. Jan. 9, 1997) (unpublished decision) (describing briefly an administrative search of a state employee's computer pursuant to an internal investigation that led to indictments for Theft in Office and Unauthorized Access to a Computer System based on the original investigative file).

e. Networks: System Administrators

Case law demonstrates that the courts will examine the totality of the circumstances in determining whether an employee has a reasonable expectation of privacy or whether an employer shares authority over the employee's space and can consent to a search. But applying this employer-consent case law to computer searches can become especially troublesome when the employee's computer is not a stand-alone container, but an account on a large network server. The difficulty is a practical one. In the physical world, individuals often intuitively understand their rights to control physical space and to restrict access by others because they can observe how everyone uses the space. For example, with filing cabinets, employees can see whether they are located in private areas, whether others have access, whether the cabinets are locked, and who has the keys. While explicit company policies certainly help to clarify the situation, employees can physically observe company practices and will probably conclude from their observations that certain property is or is not private.

By contrast, in an electronic environment, employees cannot "see" when a network administrator, supervisor, or anyone else accesses their data. They cannot watch the way people behave with data, as they can with a file cabinet, and deduce from their observations the measure of privacy they ought to expect. As a practical matter, system administrators can, and sometimes do, look at data. But when they do, they leave no physical clues which would tell a user they have opened one of his files. Lacking these physical clues, some users who are unfamiliar with computer technology may falsely but honestly believe that their data is completely private. Will the courts hold this false belief to be one that society is prepared to recognize as reasonable? Will the courts still find it reasonable, even when a user knows that there are such people as system administrators who are responsible in some fashion for operating and securing the entire network? If so, do users who actually understand the technology and the scope of a system operator's access to data have a lesser expectation of privacy and fewer Fourth Amendment protections than users who are not so well informed? And what happens in the years ahead as our population becomes increasingly computer literate?

Of course, these search and seizure questions are not limited to computer networks in the workplace. Universities, libraries, and other organizations, both public and private, may operate computer networks on which users store data which they consider private--either partly or completely. If those networks provide services to the public, they will be controlled by the provisions of 18 U.S.C. § 2702, which limits the situations in which a service provider may release the contents of qualifying electronic mail. (For a detailed discussion of this statute, see "STORED ELECTRONIC COMMUNICATIONS," infra.) But for material which falls outside this statute, the Fourth Amendment analysis discussed above will still apply.

Prosecutors who face these issues at trial should be ready to argue that reasonable network users do, indeed, understand the role and power of system operators well enough to expect them to be able to protect and even restore their files. Therefore, absent some guarantees to the contrary, reasonable users will also expect system administrators to be able to access all data on the system. Certainly, if the system has published clear policies about privacy on the network or has even explained to users that its network administrators have oversight responsibility and control, this will support the position that a system operator's consent to a search was valid. But if the network and its users have not addressed these issues and the situation is ambiguous, the safest course will be to get a warrant. (Of course, if the system administrator does have authority to access and produce a user's files and simply will not do it on request, agents should use a subpoena.)

If agents choose to apply for a warrant and are concerned that a target/user will delete his data before they can execute the search, the agents should consider asking a cooperating system operator to make and keep a backup of the target's data, which they can later procure under the warrant or subpoena. The circumstances of each case will dictate the wisest approach, but agents and prosecutors should explore all these questions before they just ask a system administrator to produce a user's files.

F. INFORMANTS AND UNDERCOVER AGENTS

As in other types of investigations, it is often helpful to use informants or undercover agents to develop evidence. In some cases, of course, they may be of limited value (e.g., a case involving a lone hacker). Additionally, as a matter of policy, there may be restrictions on the type of undercover activities in which agents may engage. For example, the FBI does not access bulletin boards simply to view board activities when there is no reason to believe the board is involved in criminal activity.

Generally speaking, however, the law allows informers to read material on electronic bulletin boards if they have the sysop's permission, explicit or implicit, to access the material on the board. Many BBSs, for example, have parts of the board which are open to the public and which require no password or identification for access. Other boards may have isolated directories, known as sub-boards, that are open only to paying subscribers or trusted members, and those individuals must identify themselves with passwords. Some sysops will ask newcomers to "introduce" themselves and will verify the new user's name, address, and other information before granting access with a password. These introductions should follow the same rules that undercover work has traditionally observed. Law enforcement agents need not identify themselves as such, but they must confine their activities to those that are authorized: they should not break into sections of the board for which they have not been given access. Indeed, the Ninth and Tenth Circuits have both written, in dicta, that an undercover participant must adhere scrupulously to the scope of a defendant's invitation to join the organization. United States v. Aguilar, 883 F.2d 662, 705 (9th Cir. 1989), cert. denied, 498 U.S. 1046 (1991); Pleasant v. Lovell, 876 F.2d 787, 803 (10th Cir. 1989). Thus, an informant or undercover agent must not exceed his authorized access, and having been granted access to some "levels" of the board does not give him permission to break into others.

III. SEIZING HARDWARE

Depending on the facts of the case, the seizure of computer hardware itself can be justified on one of three theories without regard to the data it contains: (1) the hardware is itself contraband; (2) the hardware was an instrumentality of the offense; or (3) the hardware constitutes evidence of an offense. Of course, in many cases, hardware may be seizable under more than one theory. For example, if a hacker uses his computer to insert viruses into other systems, his computer may constitute both an instrumentality of the offense and evidence admissible in court.

As noted above under DEFINITIONS (supra), hardware is defined as the physical components of a computer system such as the central processing unit (CPU), keyboard, monitor, modem, and printer.

A. THE INDEPENDENT COMPONENT DOCTRINE

We must highlight once again that computer systems are really a combination of connected components (often by wire but increasingly by wireless means). To say that the government has probable cause to seize a "computer" does not necessarily mean it has probable cause to seize the entire computer system (i.e., the computer and all connected peripheral devices). Indeed, each component in a computer system should be considered independently.

In a strictly corporeal world, this doctrine is easy to understand and apply. For example, suppose a defendant stole a television and placed it on a television stand that he lawfully owned. Agents with a warrant for that television would not seize the stand, recognizing that the two items are easily separable and that there is, simply put, no justification for taking the stand.

With computers, the roles of the different attached components are not always separable and it is more difficult to think in such concrete terms. For example, agents with a warrant to seize a target's workstation may discover that the workstation is nothing more than a dumb terminal, and that all the evidence is in the server to which the dumb terminal is connected by wire.

Nonetheless, it is simply unacceptable to suggest that any item connected to the target device is automatically seizable. In an era of increased networking, this kind of approach can lead to absurd results. In a networked environment, the computer that contains the relevant evidence may be connected to hundreds of computers in a local-area network (LAN) spread throughout a floor, building, or university campus. That LAN may also be connected to a global-area network (GAN) such as the Internet. Taken to its logical extreme, the "take it because it's connected" theory means that in any given case, thousands of machines around the world can be seized because the target machine shares the Internet.

Obviously, this is not the proper approach. The better view is to seize only those pieces of equipment necessary for basic input/output (i.e., the computer itself, plus the keyboard and monitor) so that the government can successfully execute the warrant. When agents prepare warrants for other devices, they should list only those components for which they can articulate an independent basis for search or seizure (i.e., the component itself is contraband, an instrumentality, or evidence). Certainly, the independent component doctrine does not mean that connected devices are exempt; it only requires that agents and prosecutors articulate a reason for taking the item they wish to seize. For example, if the defendant has sent letters to the White House threatening the President's life, agents should explain, as a basis for seizing the target's printer, the need to compare its type with the letter. Additionally, there may be other times when the government should seize peripherals that do not contain evidence but, again, there must be a separate basis for the seizure. See, e.g., "Seizing Hardware and Documentation so the System Will Operate at the Lab," infra.

B. HARDWARE AS CONTRABAND OR FRUITS OF CRIME

1. Authority for Seizing Contraband or Fruits of Crime

Federal Rule of Criminal Procedure 41(b)(2) authorizes warrants to seize "contraband, the fruits of crime, or things otherwise criminally possessed." The rationale behind such seizures is to prevent and deter crime. See Warden v. Hayden, 387 U.S. 294, 306 n.11 (1967). Often the fruits of crime and objects illegally possessed will also constitute evidence of a crime, so that they also can be seized to help apprehend and convict criminals (see "HARDWARE AS EVIDENCE OF AN OFFENSE," infra).

2. Contraband and Fruits of Crime Defined

The fruits of crime include property obtained by criminal activity, United States v. Santarsiero, 566 F. Supp. 536 (S.D.N.Y. 1983) (cash and jewelry obtained by use of a counterfeit credit card), and contraband is property which the private citizen is not permitted to possess, Warden v. Hayden, supra; Aguilar v. Texas, 378 U.S. 108 (1964) (narcotics). Even plans to commit a crime may constitute contraband. Yancey v. Jenkins, 638 F. Supp. 340 (N.D. Ill. 1986).

Of course, many objects which are fruits of crime or illegally possessed are innocent in themselves and can be possessed by at least certain persons under certain conditions. See, e.g., United States v. Truitt, 521 F.2d 1174, 1177 (6th Cir. 1975) (noting that a person legally can possess a sawed-off shotgun if it is properly registered to its owner, though its lawful possession is rare). A court reviewing a seizure under Rule 41(b)(2) will examine whether the circumstances would have led a reasonably cautious agent to believe that the object was a fruit of crime or was illegally possessed. For example, the seizure of jewelry as a fruit of crime in Santarsiero was upheld because a reliable informant had told officers that the suspect had boasted of using counterfeit credit cards to purchase jewelry. 566 F. Supp. at 544-45.

Certainly, there are instances where computer hardware and software are contraband or a fruit of crime. For example, there have been several recent cases involving the theft of computer equipment. Additionally, hackers have been known to penetrate credit reporting companies, illegally obtain credit card numbers, and then order computer equipment with these illegal access devices. In such cases, the equipment that they receive is a product of the fraud and should be seized as such.

C. HARDWARE AS AN INSTRUMENTALITY OF THE OFFENSE

1. Authority for Seizing Instrumentalities

Federal Rule of Criminal Procedure 41(b)(3) authorizes warrants to seize the instrumentalities of crime; that is, "property designed or intended for use or which is or has been used as the means of committing a criminal offense." The historical justification for the government's ability to seize instrumentalities of crime is the prevention of their use to commit future crimes. See Warden v. Hayden, 387 U.S. 294, 306 n.11 (1967); United States v. Boyette, 299 F.2d 92, 98 (4th Cir.) (Sobeloff, C.J., dissenting), cert. denied, 369 U.S. 844 (1962).

2. Instrumentalities Defined

An instrumentality of an offense is any machinery, weapon, instrument, or other tangible object that has played a significant role in a crime. See, e.g., United States v. Viera, 569 F. Supp. 1419, 1428 (S.D.N.Y. 1983) (sophisticated scale used in narcotics trafficking and blacklight used in counterfeiting currency). Where the object itself is innocent in character, courts will assess its role in the crime to determine whether it was an instrumentality. Compare United States v. Markis, 352 F.2d 860, 864-65 (2d Cir. 1965) (telephone used to take bets by operators of illegal wagering business was an instrumentality because it was integral to the criminal enterprise), vacated without opinion, 387 U.S. 425 (1967), with United States v. Stern, 225 F. Supp. 187, 192 (S.D.N.Y. 1964) (Rolodex file was not instrumentality where it contained names of individuals involved in tax fraud scheme). As stated by the Southern District of New York:

> Not every article that plays some part in the commission of the alleged crime is a means of committing it. . . . Although it is not necessary that the crime alleged could not have been committed but for the use of the article seized, after a consideration of all the circumstances it must appear that the article played a significant role in the commission of the crime alleged.

Stern, 225 F. Supp. at 192 (emphasis in original).

Before the Supreme Court's decision in Warden v. Hayden, 387 U.S. 294 (1967), courts held that seizable property included instrumentalities, but did not include mere evidence. See generally 3 Wright & Miller, Federal Practice and Procedure: Criminal 2d § 664 (1982). In practice, however, judges were reluctant to suppress useful pieces of evidence at trial, preferring instead to interpret the term "instrumentality" broadly enough to encompass items of evidentiary value. For example, the district court in United States v. Robinson, 287 F. Supp. 245 (N.D. Ind. 1968), upheld the seizure of the following items, all of which connected the defendant to the murder of a federal narcotics agent, as "instrumentalities" of the crime and not "mere evidence": a pair of shoes, a shirt, a jacket, handkerchiefs, spent shell casings, and wet washcloths. Such legal gymnastics were abandoned when the Supreme Court held, in Hayden, that the Fourth Amendment principally protected privacy rights, not property rights, and secured "the same protection of privacy whether the search is for 'mere evidence' or for fruits, instrumentalities or contraband." Hayden, 387 U.S. at 306-07.

Although items that are evidence of crime may now be seized along with instrumentalities, fruits, and contraband, this historical perspective is important for understanding why some early decisions may have categorized evidentiary items as instrumentalities. Moreover, the distinction between "an instrumentality" and "mere evidence" remains critical in computer crime cases because it may determine the government's ability to seize hardware. If a computer and all its peripherals are instrumentalities of a crime, the warrant should authorize the seizure of these items. But if we are seeking the computer only for the documents (mere evidence) it contains, it may be more difficult to justify the seizure or retention of hardware.

Applying the independent component doctrine to the rule permitting seizure of instrumentalities will, in most cases, not be difficult. For example, if an individual engaging in wire fraud printed out thousands of phony invoices on his home computer, it would be reasonable to take the computer, monitor, keyboard, and printer. If the individual electronically mailed these invoices to his victims, it would also be appropriate to seize his external modem (if the modem were internal it would, of course, be seized when the agents took the computer itself). If, instead of using electronic mail, he used a conventional fax machine, it would be reasonable to seize the fax as it, too, would have played a significant role in the commission of the offense.

A case from the Northern District of New York provides a helpful example of hardware as an instrumentality of an offense. The defendant in United States v. Lamb, 945 F. Supp. 441, 462 (N.D.N.Y. 1996) argued that the computer equipment had been improperly seized during a child pornography case on the theory that only the material on the hard drive, and not the computer, could be seized as either the instrumentality or the fruit of the crime. The court explicitly rejected this theory, asserting that the computer was the instrumentality of the offense because it might have been the computer that facilitated the sending and receiving of the images.

Computer equipment can be an instrumentality of the offense even where it is less intimately associated with the offense. In United States v. Real Property & Premises Known as 5528 Belle Pond Drive, 783 F. Supp. 253 (E.D. Va. 1991), aff'd on other grounds, U.S. v. Campbell, No. 92-1104, 1992 WL 332255 (4th Cir. Nov. 16, 1992), the

Eastern District of Virginia held that a computer, monitor, printer, keyboard, and related accessories found during a search of property for marijuana were properly seized and forfeited to the government under 21 U.S.C. § 881(a)(2) as being equipment used for manufacturing, processing, delivering, importing, or exporting any controlled substance under the statute. During the search for drugs, officers found a computer printout that detailed the growing characteristics of the marijuana plants. The same file was also stored on the defendant's computer. The court held that "[b]ecause storing marijuana-growing data in a computer is use of the computer in manufacturing a controlled substance in violation of 21 U.S.C. § 841(a)(1), the court finds that the defendant computer is forfeitable to the government under 21 U.S.C. § 881(a)(7)." Real Property, 783 F. Supp. at 256.

In Ohio v. Amvets, No. 93 CA 50, 1994 WL 116174 (Ohio Ct. App. April 6, 1994) (unpublished decision), a forfeiture case regarding the seizure of computer equipment allegedly involved in gambling operations by the Amvets and Elks Lodge, the appellate court overruled the judgment of the trial court and held that although the primary purpose of the computer may not have been gambling, the computer was used to make betting odds, to maintain information as to amounts still owed by pool participants, and to otherwise keep track of the gambling operations. As such, the court held that the computer equipment was properly classified under the state forfeiture statute as an instrumentality of the offense.

D. HARDWARE AS EVIDENCE OF AN OFFENSE

    1. Authority for Seizing Evidence

In 1972, Federal Rule of Criminal Procedure 41(b) was amended to authorize seizing "mere evidence" of a crime. In relevant part, the Rule now states: "A warrant may be issued under this rule to search for and seize any (1) property that constitutes evidence of the commission of a criminal offense. . . ."

    2. Evidence Defined

A physical item is evidence if it will aid in apprehending or convicting a person who has committed a crime. The evidence seized need not be admissible at trial.

Courts will evaluate a seizure under this test according to what a reasonable person would believe under the circumstances, and law enforcement officers will not be judged after-the-fact on how helpful the seized evidence actually was in apprehending or convicting a suspect. See Andresen v. Maryland, 427 U.S. 463, 483 (1976) (holding that the "trained special investigator reasonably could have believed" the seized evidence could be used to show criminal intent); United States v. Truitt, 521 F.2d 1174, 1176-78 (6th Cir. 1975) (holding that a reasonably cautious police officer could have believed under the circumstances that a sawed-off shotgun, although legal if registered, was incriminating evidence).

Of course, simply because an item is "evidence of a crime" does not mean that other restrictions may not apply. Law enforcement officials should be aware of other limits imposed by the Constitution, statutes, and regulations upon the seizure of evidence. See, e.g., Guidelines on Methods of Obtaining Documentary Materials Held by Third Parties, 28 C.F.R. §§ 59.1-.6 (governing the application for search warrants for documentary evidence held by non-suspect third parties).

Although computers commonly contain evidence, sometimes they are evidence. If an extortionist sent a letter to his victim with unique print characteristics (e.g., the top half of the letter "W" was missing), his daisy-wheel printer would constitute evidence which could be seized.

E. TRANSPORTING HARDWARE FROM THE SCENE

Whether a computer is seized as contraband, an instrumentality, or evidence, it is important to transport it properly. With some simple computers, moving the equipment is a straightforward proposition. But computer systems are becoming so increasingly complex and diverse that it is harder than ever for technically untrained agents to avoid mistakes. These Guidelines cannot possibly substitute for the expertise that comes from special training courses in seizing, searching, and preserving electronic evidence. Indeed, the discussion that follows is meant only as introduction and orientation to these issues, and not as a comprehensive guide to all the technical contingencies which may arise during a search. The team for a computer-related search should, if possible, include at least one technically trained agent to act as a leader in these areas. Clearly, as complex computer systems become increasingly common, law enforcement agencies will need more trained agents at almost every crime scene. In the meantime, the following discussion may help prosecutors and investigators to anticipate the problems which can confront them.

First, agents must protect the equipment from damage. Second, to the extent they are transporting information storage devices (e.g., hard drives, floppy disks), improper handling can cause loss of data. Third, it may be impossible to make the system work in the field office, laboratory, or courtroom if the seizing agents did not carefully pack and move the computer system so that it can be successfully reassembled later.

Before the search begins, the search leader should prepare a detailed plan for documenting and preserving electronic evidence, and should take time to carefully brief the entire search team to protect both the identity and integrity of all the data. At the scene, agents must remember to collect traditional types of evidence (e.g., latent fingerprints off the keyboard) before touching anything. They must remember, too, that computer data can be destroyed by strong magnetic fields. (Low density magnetic media is more susceptible to such interference than high density media.) Last, some computer experts will not examine evidence if anyone else has already tried to search or manipulate the data. Their chain-of-custody and integrity-of-evidence procedures will not allow them to examine the computer if its original crime-scene seal has been broken.

The agents executing the actual search must take special precautions when disassembling and packing computer equipment. This careful approach protects not only the hardware items, but also the integrity and accessibility of the data inside. Before disconnecting any cables, it is helpful to videotape or photograph the site (including the screen, if possible, and all wiring connections) and prepare a wiring schematic. This will document the condition of the equipment upon the agents' arrival and show how the system was configured. Agents should disconnect all remote access to the system (e.g., unplug the telephone cord, not the power cord, from the modem) and disconnect network cables from the servers so that no one can alter or erase information during the search. Investigators need to accurately label each cable and the device and port to which the cable connects before disconnecting anything. It is a good idea to attach tags at every connection point on every cable to record all relevant information. It is especially important to label every vacant port as "vacant" so that there is no confusion later. (If vacant ports are not labeled, it is impossible for an expert to tell whether the unlabeled port was in fact vacant, or whether an important label simply fell off.) Once this is done, agents are ready to disassemble, tag and inventory the equipment.

Investigators must determine which drives, disks, and other magnetic media need to be protected. If a hard disk drive is being moved, they must insure that the read/write heads are secured to prevent damage. Some systems secure (park) the heads automatically whenever the machine is not in use, but other systems may require that a specific command be executed or that the heads be secured mechanically. The manufacturer's operating manual should specify the proper procedure for each system.

Agents should protect floppy disk drives according to manufacturer's recommendations. Some suggest inserting a new diskette or piece of cardboard in the drive slot; others do not. (As with hard drives, each manufacturer's instructions may be found in the system manual). Investigators must also label diskettes (either individually or in groups), mark them as evidence and place them in non-plastic evidence containers.

Agents must be conscious of static electricity buildup during the execution of the warrant since static electricity can "zap" a disk and damage data. So can degaussing equipment (an electronic appliance that creates a strong magnetic field and can be used to effectively erase a magnetic tape or disk). A well-known story in law enforcement circles involves a hacker who allegedly magnetized his metal door frame, thus creating a magnetic field that erased magnetic media as agents carried it through the doorway. This story has not been verified and, even if true, such an event is unlikely to occur now because high density media is not easily disrupted by magnetic fields. Nonetheless, a device to measure magnetic fields (a compass or, even better, a gaussmeter) can determine whether such fields exist and, as a general rule, agents should avoid placing magnetic media near any strong magnetic field. Magnetic fields may be created by telephones, radio transmitters, and photocopiers. Additionally, although magnetic media has often been taken through airport metal detectors and X-ray machines without damage, it is wiser not to take magnetic media through these devices. (It is the motor driving the conveyor belt on the X-ray machine, not the fluoroscope itself, that creates the magnetic field which causes the damage.)

Transporting agents should keep all hardware and software in dust-free, climate-controlled environments. Computer-related evidence is sensitive to heat and humidity and should not be stored in the back seat or trunk of a car without special precautions. Temperature extremes may render magnetically stored evidence unreadable, and various types of contamination can damage electronic equipment. A safe range for storing magnetic media is between 40°-90°F and 20%-80% humidity, free of dust and tobacco smoke.

See Ohio v. Redd, No. CA93-12-019, 1994 WL 178451 (Ohio Ct. App. May 9, 1994) (unpublished decision) (discussing disassembly and reassembly of computer, and approving sufficiency of evidence derived in part therefrom, without discussing the merits of the search).

IV. SEARCHING FOR AND SEIZING INFORMATION

A. INTRODUCTION

Hardware searches are not conceptually difficult. Like searching for weapons, the items sought are tangible. They occupy physical space and can be moved in familiar ways. Searches for data and software are far more complex. For purposes of clarity, these types of searches must be examined in two distinct groups: (1) searches where the information sought is on the computer at the search scene and (2) searches where the information sought has been stored off-site, and the computer at the search scene is used to access this off-site location.[3]

In some cases, the distinction is insignificant, and many topics covered in this section apply equally to both types of searches. On the other hand, there are certain unique issues that arise only when the computer is part of a network. For example, since Fed. R. Crim. P. 41(a) requires that a search warrant be issued by a court in the district where the property is located, agents may have to get a second warrant in another district if the target has sent data to a distant computer. See "Describing the Place to Be Searched," infra.

Although "property" is defined in Federal Rule of Criminal Procedure 41(h) to include "documents, books, papers and other tangible objects," (emphasis added), courts have held that intangible property such as information may be seized. In United States v. Villegas, 899 F.2d 1324, 1334-35 (2d Cir.), cert. denied, 498 U.S. 991 (1990),

---

[3] Any home PC can be connected to a network simply by adding a modem. Thus, in any case where a modem is present, agents should consider the possibility that the computer user has stored valuable information at some remote location.

the Second Circuit noted that warrants had been upheld for intangible property such as telephone numbers called from a given phone line and recorded by a pen register, conversations overheard by means of a microphone touching a heating duct, the movement of property as tracked by location-monitoring beepers, and images seized with video cameras and telescopes. The court in Villegas upheld a warrant which authorized agents to search a cocaine factory and covertly take photographs without authorizing the seizure of any tangible objects. But see United States v. Johns, 948 F.2d 599 (9th Cir. 1991), cert. denied, 112 S. Ct. 3046 (1992) (a "sneak and peek" warrant executed without giving notice to the defendants that the search had occurred violated Rule 41(d)).

B. INFORMATION AS CONTRABAND

The same theories which justify seizing hardware--contraband or fruit of crime, instrumentality, or evidence--also apply to seizing information. See "Authority for Seizing Contraband or Fruits of Crime," supra. Because individuals often obtain copies of software in violation of copyright laws, it may be appropriate to seize that software as well as any documentation (such as photocopied software manuals) because they are likely to be illegally obtained. (Software producers may allow a purchaser to make a backup copy of the software bought, but these copies may not be disseminated because of copyright laws.) Lists of telephone card access codes and passwords for government computer networks may also be considered contraband, because their possession is prohibited by statute if the possessor has the requisite mens rea. 18 U.S.C. § 1029(a)(3), 18 U.S.C. § 1030(a)(6).

C. INFORMATION AS AN INSTRUMENTALITY

Rule 41(b) broadly defines what may be seized as an instrumentality: any "property designed or intended for use or which is or has been used as the means of committing a criminal offense." Fed. R. Crim. P. 41(b)(3). This includes both tangible and intangible property. See United States v. Villegas, in "INTRODUCTION" to Part IV, supra. Thus, in some cases, informational documents and financial instruments which have been used in the commission of an offense may be seized as instrumentalities of crime. Compare Abel v. United States, 362 U.S. 217, 237-9 (1960) (documents used in connection with suspect's illegal alien status were instrumentalities, including phony birth certificates, bank records, and vaccination records) with Application of Commercial Inv. Co., 305 F. Supp. 967 (S.D.N.Y. 1969) ($5 million in securities were not instrumentalities where the government suspected improprieties with an $18,000 brokerage account and the securities were at most "incidental" to the offense).

Likewise, investigators should seize objects if they are "designed or intended for use" as instrumentalities. Fed. R. Crim. P. 41(b) (3). Sometimes an item will obviously fit that description (like software designed to help hackers crack passwords or lists of stolen credit card numbers) but, at other times, it may not be so simple. Even so, as long as a reasonable person in the agent's position would believe the item to be an instrumentality, the courts will probably respect the agent's judgment. This is, after all, the same test used to determine when an object would aid apprehension or conviction of a criminal. See Andresen v. Maryland, 427 U.S. 463, 483 (1976). As such, the particular facts of the case are very important. For example, if an agent investigating the sysop of an illegal bulletin board knows that the board only operates on one personal computer, a second computer sitting in the same room is probably not an instrumentality. But if the agent has heard from a reliable informant that the suspect has boasted about expanding his operation to a second board, that second computer is probably "intended" as an instrumentality, and the agent should take it. Additionally, if the suspect has substantially modified a personal computer to enhance its usefulness for a particular crime (perhaps by installing password-cracking software), an agent might well reasonably believe that the computer and the software was "designed" for criminal activity.

D. INFORMATION AS EVIDENCE

Before the Supreme Court's rejection of the "mere evidence" rule in Warden v. Hayden, 387 U.S. 294, 300-301 (1967), courts were inconsistent in ruling whether records that helped to connect the criminal to the offense were instrumentalities of crime (and thus seizable), or were instead merely evidence of crime (and thus not seizable).

Compare Marron v. United States, 275 U.S. 192 (1927) (approving prohibition agent's seizure of bills and ledger books belonging to speakeasy operators as instrumentalities of crime) with United States v. Lefkowitz, 285 U.S. 452 (1932) (disapproving prohibition agent's seizure of papers intended to solicit orders for illegal liquor). Indeed, several courts have concluded that, when it comes to documents, it is impossible to separate the two categories. See Hayden, 387 U.S. at 302 (stating that the distinction between mere evidence and instrumentalities "is wholly irrational, since, depending on the circumstances, the same 'papers and effects' may be 'mere evidence' in one case and 'instrumentality' in another"); United States v. Stern, 225 F. Supp. 187, 191 (S.D.N.Y. 1964) ("It would be hazardous to attempt any definition [of papers that are instrumentalities of crime and not mere evidence]; we shall not."). Now that evidence of crime may be seized in the same way as instrumentalities of crime, it is useful to acknowledge that, in most instances, documents and other information connecting the criminal to his offense should be viewed as evidence of the crime, and not as instrumentalities. For example, in United States v. Lindenfield, 142 F.2d 829, 830-32 (2d Cir.), cert. denied, 323 U.S. 761 (1944), the prescription records of a doctor who illegally prescribed morphine to "patients" were classified as evidence, not as instrumentalities.

The prescription records in Lindenfield illustrate the sort of document that may be seized as evidence: records that reveal the operation of the criminal enterprise over time. Other examples include the customer lists of narcotics traffickers, telephone bills of hackers who break into computer networks, and plans for the fraud or embezzlement of corporate and financial targets. This documentary evidence may be in paper or book form, or it may be stored electronically in a computer or on a backup tape. As with other types of evidence, documents may be seized if they aid in showing intent and the absence of mistake on the suspect's part, even though they may not relate directly to the commission of the crime, but to some other similar transaction instead. See Andresen v. Maryland, 427 U.S. 463, at 483-84 (1976) (approving seizure of documents about a second transaction because they showed criminal intent and absence of mistake in the first transaction).

1. Evidence of Identity

Evidence of a crime also includes various types of identification evidence. For example, courts have recognized that clothing seen worn by a criminal during the commission of the offense constitutes evidence of the crime, because it helps to tie the suspect to the crime. See, e.g., United States v. Korman, 614 F.2d 541, 547 (6th Cir.) (approving the seizure of a green ski jacket as both evidence of and an instrumentality of the crime), cert. denied, 446 U.S. 952 (1980).

Documents that incriminate a suspect's co-conspirators also may be seized as evidence because they help identify other involved parties and connect them with the suspect. See, e.g., United States v. Santarsiero, 566 F. Supp. 536, 544 (S.D.N.Y. 1983) (approving the seizure of the suspect's notebook in a counterfeit credit card investigation where others were working with or purchasing cards from him, and the notebook contained telephone numbers that the investigating officers could reasonably believe would help in identifying and connecting others with the suspect's crimes). In many computer crimes, we have found that hackers work jointly and pool hacking information. In these cases, telephone records may prove this connection. Moreover, agents may seize evidence that helps identify the occupant of a home or office connected to the crime, where the home or office is used regularly by more than one person. See, e.g., United States v. Whitten, 706 F.2d 1000, 1008-09 (9th Cir. 1983) (approving the seizure of telephone books, diaries, photos, utility bills, telephone bills, personal property, cancelled mail, keys, rent receipts, deeds, and leases that helped establish who owned and occupied premises used for a large scale narcotics operation, where the premises were used by more than one person and the warrant authorized seizing items "indicating the ownership or occupancy of the residence"), cert. denied, 465 U.S. 1100 (1984). As with houses and offices, computers are often used by more than one person, and this sort of evidence may help establish just who used the computer or computers to commit the crime.

Network operators exercise considerable control and authority over data and information stored on their systems. In United States v. Lamb, 945 F. Supp. 441 (N.D.N.Y. 1996), the defendant was charged with multiple related violations of the child pornography statutes. During the course of its investigation, the government signed on to America Online and obtained files depicting children engaged in explicit sexual conduct from an individual using various screen names. Pursuant to a search warrant, AOL matched the defendant's identity to the previously-obtained screen names and provided copies of all files in the defendant's account. The court denied the defendant's challenge to the scope of the warrant and ruled that the specific information in the warrant, in connection with information about the broader investigation, logically would lead to the conclusion that evidence of child pornography trafficking would be found at America Online's headquarters. Lamb, 945 F. Supp. at 456.

More specifically, the government had been able to trace the identity of the defendant through the screen names contained in his e-mail messages. Each mail message contained the screen name of the AOL subscriber who first uploaded the pornographic image to the system, the screen names to whom it was forwarded, the date and time of transmission, and the title of the image file. A Grand Jury subpoena to AOL had confirmed that the screen name for some of the transmissions belonged to the defendant. A trap and trace on the defendant's home number confirmed he was logged on to AOL. Based on this electronic trail, the court found that the warrant was properly issued. Lamb. 945 F. Supp. at 441.

2. Specific Types of Evidence

a. Hard Copy Printouts

Any information contained in a computer system may have been printed out by the target of the investigation. Finding a printed copy may be valuable for a number of reasons. First, a printout may display an earlier version of data that has since been altered or deleted. Second, in certain electronic environments (such as bulletin boards), individuals may claim to lack knowledge about what information is electronically stored in the computer (e.g., a bulletin board operator may disavow any knowledge that his board contained illegal access codes that were posted and downloaded by others). Finding printed copies in someone's possession may negate this defense. Third, the printouts may tie the crime to a particular printer which, in turn, may be seizable as an instrumentality (e.g., the printouts may reveal that extortionate notes were printed on a certain printer, thus warranting seizure of the printer).

b. Handwritten Notes

Finally, agents should be alert for notes in manuals, on the equipment, or in the area of the computer. These may provide critical keys to breaking passwords, finding the file or directory names of important data, operating the hardware or software, identifying the suspect's electronic or telephone connections with co-conspirators and victims, or finding login names or accounts.

E. PRIVILEGED AND CONFIDENTIAL INFORMATION

1. In General

Warrants to search computers which contain privileged information must meet the same requirements as warrants to search for and seize paper documents under similar conditions; that is, the warrant should be narrowly drawn to include only the data pertinent to the investigation, and that data should be described as specifically as possible. See, e.g., Klitzman v. Krut, 744 F.2d 955 (3d Cir. 1984). Since a broad search of computers used by confidential fiduciaries (e.g., attorneys or physicians) is likely to uncover personal information about individuals who are unconnected with the investigation, it is important to instruct any assisting forensic computer experts not to examine files about uninvolved third parties any more than absolutely necessary to locate and seize the information described in the warrant.

a. Doctors, Lawyers, and Clergy

Federal law recognizes some, but not all, of the common law testimonial privileges. Fed. R. Evid. 501. Indeed, Congress has recognized a "special concern for privacy interests in cases in which a search or seizure for. . . documents would intrude upon a known confidential relationship such as that which may exist between clergyman and parishioner; lawyer and client; or doctor and patient." 42 U.S.C. § 2000aa-11(1)-(3). At Congress's direction, see 42 U.S.C. § 2000aa-11(a), the Attorney General has issued guidelines for federal officers who want to obtain documentary materials from disinterested third parties. 42 U.S.C. § 2000aa-11. Under these rules, they should not use a search warrant to obtain documentary materials believed to be in the private possession of a disinterested third party physician, lawyer, or clergyman where the material sought or likely to be reviewed during the execution of the warrant contains confidential information on patients, clients, or parishioners. 28 C.F.R. § 59.4(b). A search warrant can be used, however, if using less intrusive means would substantially jeopardize the availability or usefulness of the materials sought; access to the documentary materials appears to be of substantial importance to the investigation; and the application for the warrant has been recommended by the U.S. Attorney and approved by the appropriate Deputy Assistant Attorney General. 28 C.F.R. § 59.4(b)(1) and (2).

United States v. Stewart, No. Crim. A. 96-538, 1997 WL 189381 (E.D. Pa. April 16, 1997) (unpublished decision), illustrates how law enforcement agents can protect the confidentiality and privacy of the targets of searches, while still gaining access to pertinent evidence. In Stewart, agents sought to search and seize computer equipment as part of a fraud investigation. Already having determined that the co-targets of the investigation were represented by attorneys and that one was an attorney himself, the agents executing the search received briefings on attorney-client issues, where they were instructed not to remove any documents received from attorneys or regarding legal representation. Following the seizure of the computer equipment, a computer expert duplicated the computer files, and the computers were returned. An uninvolved Assistant United States Attorney reviewed the seized documents for any potential attorney-client privilege problems. The court upheld the seizure of the computer evidence over the defendant's overbreadth objection, but reserved judgment regarding attorney-client privilege on only one document.

b. Publishers and Authors

Additionally, Congress has expressed a special concern for publishers and journalists in the Privacy Protection Act, 42 U.S.C. 2000aa. Generally speaking, agents may not search for or seize any "work product materials" (defined by statute) from someone "reasonably believed to have a purpose to disseminate to the public a newspaper, book, broadcast, or other similar form of public communication." 42 U.S.C. § 2000aa(a). In addition, as an even broader proposition, government officers cannot search for or seize "documentary materials" (also defined) from someone who possesses them in connection with a purpose to similarly publish. 42 U.S.C. § 2000aa(b). These protections do not apply to contraband, fruits of a crime, or things otherwise criminally possessed. 42 U.S.C. § 2000aa-7.

Although this provision may seem, at first blush, to have a somewhat limited application for law enforcement, it has emerged as a frequent issue in computer searches. Because even a stand-alone computer can hold thousands of pages of information, it is common for users to mix data so that evidence of crime is commingled with material which is innocuous--or even statutorily protected. And as a technical matter, analysts sometimes cannot recover the electronic evidence without, in some manner, briefly searching or seizing the protected data. Moreover, this problem becomes exponentially more difficult, both legally and practically, if the target computers are part of a network which holds the work of many different people. The larger the network and the more varied its services, the harder it is to predict whether there might be information on the system which could arguably qualify for statutory protection. (This complex area of the law is discussed in detail at "THE PRIVACY PROTECTION ACT, 42 U.S.C. § 2000aa," infra. It is critical that prosecutors and agents read this section and the statute with care before undertaking a search which may intrude on protected materials.)

2. Targets

If the person who holds the documents sought is not "disinterested" but a target of the investigation, the rules are understandably different. In those cases, agents may get a warrant to search the files for confidential information (regardless of whether that information is technically "privileged" under Federal law), but the warrant should be drawn as narrowly as possible to include only information specifically about the case under investigation.

When the target of an investigation has complete control of the computer to be searched (such as a stand-alone PC), it may be difficult to find all the evidence without examining the entire disk drive or storage diskettes. Even in situations like these, it may be possible to get other people in the suspect's office to help locate the pertinent files without examining everything. When a computer must be removed from the target's premises to examine it, agents must take care that other investigators avoid reading confidential files unrelated to the case. Before examining everything on the computer, analysts should try to use other methods to locate only the material described in the warrant. Finally, as experts comb for hidden or erased files or information contained between disk sectors, they must continue to protect the unrelated, confidential information as much as possible.

3. Using Special Masters

In rare instances, the court may appoint a special master to help search a computer which contains privileged information. See, e.g., DeMassa v. Nunez, 747 F.2d 1283 (9th Cir. 1984). A neutral master would be responsible to the court, and could examine all the documents and determine what is privileged. If the court appoints a master, the government should ask for a neutral computer expert to help the master recover all the data without destroying or altering anything. In cases like these, the computer expert needs detailed instructions on the search procedures to be performed. In no event should the target of the search or his employees serve as the master's computer expert.

F.   UNDERSTANDING WHERE THE EVIDENCE MIGHT BE: STAND-ALONE PCs, NETWORKS AND FILE-SERVERS, BACKUPS, ELECTRONIC BULLETIN BOARDS, AND ELECTRONIC MAIL

1. Stand-Alone PCs

When searching for information, agents must not overlook any storage devices. This includes hard drives, floppy disks, backup tapes, CD-ROMs[4], WORM drives[5], and anything else that could hold data. In addition, notwithstanding the high-tech nature of computer searches, investigators must remember basic evidentiary techniques. If identification is an issue, they should look for fingerprints or other handwritten notes and labels that may help prove identity. If data is encrypted, a written copy of the password is clearly important.

a.   Input/Output Devices: Do Monitors, Modems, Printers, and Keyboards Ever Need to Be Searched?

Prosecutors must always keep in mind the independent component doctrine (see "THE INDEPENDENT COMPONENT DOCTRINE," supra); that is, there must be a basis for seizing each particular item. If agents are only searching for information, it may be senseless to seize hardware that cannot store information.

---

[4] CD-ROM stands for Compact Disk - Read Only Memory. Much like a compact disk for music, it allows the user to search for and read information without being able to alter it.

[5] WORM stands for Write Once Read Many. The user can write large amounts of information to a platter (a large disk); but once written, the platter can only be read, not altered.

That said, it is important to remember that information can be retrieved from many hardware devices, even those not normally associated with a storage function. Generally speaking, input and output (I/O) devices such as keyboards, monitors, and printers do not permanently store data. Most data is stored on devices such as hard drives, CD-ROMs, and floppy disks. By contrast, I/O devices are used to send data to, and receive data from, the computer. Once the computer is turned off, I/O devices do not store information. For example, when a computer is turned off, the information on the screen is lost unless it has been saved to a storage device.

However, there are significant exceptions to this general rule. A trained computer specialist, using specialized techniques, may find data or other evidence even on I/O devices. The following list is not all-inclusive, but rather offers some examples of I/O devices that may provide useful evidence even after they have been turned off.

(1) Laser printers -- It may be possible to search for images of the last page printed on laser printers. This technique requires planning because the expert must examine the printer <u>before it is moved</u>. If this type of evidence may be needed, a computer expert must be ready at the scene with the necessary equipment. Additionally, paper containing information may still be inside a laser printer due to a paper jam that was not cleared.

(2) Hard disk print buffers -- Some laser printers have five- or ten-megabyte hard drives that store an image before it prints, and the information will stay on the drive until the printer runs out of memory space and writes over it. One example of a printer that may have an internal hard drive is the Qume 1000 Color Printer. An expert would be able to search the hard drive for information sent to and stored by that printer.

(3) Print Spooler Device -- This device holds information to be printed. The spooler may be holding a print job if the printer was not ready to print when the print command was given (e.g., the printer was not turned on or was out of paper). This device should be handled at the scene since the information will be lost when power is disrupted.

(4) Ribbon printers -- Like old typewriter ribbons, printer ribbons contain impressions from printed jobs. These impressions can be recovered by examining the ribbon.

(5) Monitors -- Any burning of the screen phosphorus may reveal data or graphics commonly left on the screen.

(6) Keyboards -- Although they do not normally store information, some unusual keyboards are actually computer workstations and may contain an internal diskette drive.

(7) Hard Cards -- These appear to be a typical function board but they function like a hard disk drive and store information.

(8) Scanner -- Flatbed type scanners may have hard paper copy underneath the cover.

(9) Fax machines -- Although some kinds of stand-alone fax machines simply scan and send data without storing it, other models can store the data (e.g., on a hard drive) before sending it. Significantly, the data remains in the machine's memory until overwritten. Some fax machines contain two or more megabytes of memory--enough to hold hundreds of pages of information.

b. Routine Data Backups

Even on stand-alone systems, computer users often make backup copies of files to protect against hardware failure or other physical disruptions. If the computer has any sort of failure which destroys the original copy of data or programs (e.g., a hard disk failure), the data can then be restored from the backups. How often backups are made is solely up to the user. As a practical matter, however, most computer-literate users will back up data regularly since mechanical failures are not uncommon and it is often difficult and time-consuming to recreate data that has been irretrievably lost. Backup copies can be made on magnetic tape, disks, or cartridges.

2. Networked PCs

Increasingly, computers are linked with other computers. This can be done with coaxial cable in a local area network, via common telephone lines, or even through a wireless network, using radio frequency (RF) communications. Due to this interconnectivity, it has become more important than ever to ascertain from sources or surveillance what type of system agents will encounter. Without knowing generally what is there before the search, investigators could end up with nothing more than a "dumb terminal" (no storage capability) connected to a system which stores the files in the next county or state. It would be akin to executing a search warrant for a book-making operation on a vacant room that only has a phone which forwards calls to the actual operation site. During the planning stage of a search, the government must consider the possibility of off-site storage locations.

The following are systems or devices which make it possible for a suspect to store data miles, or even continents, away from her own computer:

FILE SERVER: A file server is a computer on a network that stores the programs and data files shared by the users of the network. A file server acts like a remote disk drive, enabling someone to store information on a computer system other than his own. It can be located in another judicial district from the target machine.

ELECTRONIC MAIL: Electronic mail provides for the transmission of messages and files between computers over a communications network. Sending information in this way is similar in some ways to mailing a letter through the postal service. The messages are sent from one computer through a network to the electronic address of another specific computer or to a series of computers of the sender's choice. The transmitted messages (and attached files) are either stored at the computer of the addressee (such as someone's personal computer) or at a mail server (a machine dedicated, at least in part, to storing mail). If the undelivered mail is stored on a server, it will remain there until the addressee retrieves it. When people "pick up" e-mail from the mail server, they usually receive only a copy of their mail, and the stored message is maintained in the mail server until the addressee deletes it (some systems allow senders to delete mail on the server before delivery). Of course, deleted mail may sometimes be recovered by undeleting the message (if not yet overwritten) or by obtaining a backup copy (if the server was backed up before the message was deleted).

ELECTRONIC BULLETIN BOARD SYSTEMS (BBS): A bulletin board system is a computer dedicated, in whole or in part, to serving as an electronic meeting place. A BBS computer system may contain information, programs, and e-mail, and is set up so that users can dial the bulletin board system, read and leave messages for other users, and download and upload software programs for common use. Some BBSs also have gateways which allow users to connect to other bulletin boards or networks. A BBS can have multiple telephone lines (so that many people can use it at the same time) or a single line where a user's access is first-come, first-served. BBSs can have several levels of access, sometimes called "sub-boards" or "conferences." Access to the different conferences is usually controlled by the system operator with a password system. A single user may have several different passwords, one for each different level or conference. A user may store documents, data, programs, messages, and even photographs in the different levels of the BBS.

A bulletin board system may be located anywhere telephone lines go. Therefore, if a suspect may have stored important information on a BBS, a pen register on the suspect's phone may reveal the location of these stored files. Agents must be careful, though, because sysops have been known to forward incoming calls through a simple phone in one spot to their BBS computers somewhere else. Sometimes these calls hop between houses, and sometimes, between jurisdictions. Investigators cannot assume that the phone number called by the suspect is always the end of the line.

VOICE-MAIL SYSTEMS: A voice-mail system is a complex phone answering machine (computer) which allows individuals to send and receive telephone voice messages to a specific "mailbox" number. A person can call the voice-mail system (often a 1-800 number) and leave a message in a particular person's mailbox, retrieve messages left by other people, or transfer one message to many different mailboxes in a list. Usually, anyone can leave messages, but it takes a password to pick them up or change the initial greeting. The system turns the user's voice into digital data and stores it until the addressee erases it or another message overwrites it. Criminals sometimes use voice mailboxes (especially mailboxes of unsuspecting people, if the criminals can beat the mailbox password) as remote deaddrops for information which may be valuable in a criminal case. Voice mailboxes are located in the message system computer of the commercial vendor which supplies the voice-mail service, or they can be found on the computer at the location called. Voice mail messages can be written on magnetic disk or remain in the computer's memory, depending on the vendor's system.

Of course, all networked systems, whether data or voice, may keep routine and disaster backups.

  a. Routine Backups

Making backups is a routine, mandatory discipline on multi-user systems. On larger systems, backups may be created as often as two to three times per working shift. Usually backups are made once per day on larger systems and once per week on smaller ones. Backups are usually stored in a controlled environment to protect the integrity of the data (e.g., locked in a file cabinet or safe). The system administrators will usually have written procedures which set out how often backup copies will be made and where they will be kept. Backups for large systems are often stored at remote locations.

  b. Disaster Backups

These are additional backups of important data meant to survive all contingencies, such as fire, flood, etc. As extra protection, the data is stored off-site, usually in another building belonging to the business or in rented storage space. It would be unusual to find the disaster backups near the routine backups or original data. Again, these copies can be stored on diskettes, magnetic tape, or cartridge.

G. SEARCHING FOR INFORMATION

  1. Business Records and Other Documents

Obtaining records from a multi-user computer system raises certain issues that are uncommon in the paper world. When dealing with papers stored in filing cabinets, agents can secure the scene and protect the integrity of the evidence by physically restricting access to the storage container and its papers. Electronic records are, of course, easier to alter or destroy. More important, such alteration or destruction may occur while the agent is looking at a copy of the document on a workstation terminal. Therefore, it is important to control remote access to data while the search is being conducted. This can often be done by prohibiting access to the file or file server in question, either by software commands or by physically disconnecting cables. This should only be done by an expert, however, because altering the system's configuration may have significant unintended results.

If the system administrator is cooperating with investigators, the task becomes much easier, and agents should use the least intrusive means possible to obtain the data (e.g., a request, grand jury subpoena, or administrative subpoena). Of course, if the entire business is under investigation or there is reason to believe that records may be altered or destroyed, a search warrant should be used.

2. Data Created or Maintained by Targets

Targets of criminal investigations, particularly computer crimes, may have data on a multi-user computer system. Where the target owns or operates the computer system in question, it is safest to use warrants, although subpoenas may be appropriate in the right case.

Where the target does not control the system but merely has data on it, the sysop may be willing to provide the requested data assuming he has the authority to do so. Never forgetting the legal restraints of 18 U.S.C. § 2702 (see "Stored Electronic Communications," infra), the sysop can, as a practical matter, probably retrieve the needed data rather easily. Ordinarily, a multi-user computer system will have specific accounts assigned to each user or groups of users. While the various "users" may not be able to get into each others' files, the system operator (like a landlord with passkeys) can usually examine and copy any file in the computer system. (Typically, the sysop has what is called "superuser" authority or "root" access.)

Some systems, by their rules, may prohibit the system managers or operators from reading files in specific data areas or may expressly limit the purposes for which sysops may exercise their access. In those cases, sysops may insist on a court order or subpoena. If, on the other hand, users have consented to complete sysop access in order to use the system, a request to the sysop for the information may be all that is required. In either event, rarely will it be wise for investigating agents to search large computer systems by themselves. Without the sysop's help, it may be difficult (if not impossible) for agents to comb a multi-user computer system the way they search file cabinets for paper records.

When using a subpoena with a future return date, agents should specifically ask for the computerized records as they exist at time of service, and state clearly that service of the subpoena obliges the recipient to preserve and safeguard the subpoenaed information by making a copy. Investigators should explain that even if the recipient contests the subpoena, he must not only copy the data "as is," but must also confirm to the agent that the copy has been made. The subpoena should also say that failure to preserve the subpoenaed information may subject the recipient to sanctions for contempt. In some circumstances, a "forthwith subpoena" may even be appropriate. If all this is not done, the data may be altered or erased--deliberately, accidentally, or in the normal course of business--before the return date on the subpoena.

In United States v. Lamb, 945 F. Supp. 441, 461 (N.D.N.Y. 1996), the appellant contended that because agents did not execute the search on his house until five months after the last known transmission of child pornography, the warrant was stale. The court, however, disagreed, basing its decision on the changes in the way people store information on computers. The court stated that "[t]he declining costs and increasing capacity and availability of computer storage devices convinces many users to buy more hardware rather than delete old files." Id. at 461. The court held that due to this change in the way people store computerized information, the magistrate had sufficient information to find that computer image files of child pornography might be retained even longer than hardcopy child pornography.

3. Limited Data Searches

Once analysts have determined the operating system and have taken precautions to protect the integrity of the data, they will select tools to aid in the search. Using specially designed software called "utilities" will greatly help, because analysts can tailor the search to look for specified names, dates, and file extensions. They can scan disks for recently deleted data and recover it in partial or sometimes complete format. They can also identify and expose hidden files. In some cases, analysts may find files that are not in a readable format; the data may have been compressed to save space or encrypted to control access to it. Here again, utility packages will help recover the data. In designing the data search, they might use a variety of utilities. Some are off-the-shelf software available from most computer retailers. But utility software can also be custom-made, especially designed to perform specific search functions that are specified in standard laboratory procedures. Obviously, agents should rely upon experts for this kind of analysis. (See APPENDIX C [not included] for a list of federal sources for experts.)

There are several reasons why analysts will probably want to do a limited rather than a complete search through the data. First of all, the law in general prefers searches of all things--computer data included--to be as discrete and specific as possible. Second, the warrant may specify particular files, directories, or sub-directories, or certain categories of data. Finally, even if the facts of a case give an analyst free rein to search all the data, the economies of scale usually require a more systematic approach. At the least, analysts should plan for a methodical inventory of directories and sub-directories and prepare to document all the steps taken in the search. Because data is so easy to alter or destroy, analysts must have a careful record so that their efforts can be re-created for a court. In examining the data, analysts will probably have to do some sorting--examining things that could be relevant and by-passing the unrelated items. Only rarely will they be allowed to or even want to read everything on the computer system being searched. Even so, caution is advised, because directory headings and file names may often be misleading.

In addition to searching by file, sub-directory, or directory, the power of the computer allows analysts to design a limited search in other ways as well. Computer experts can search data for specific names (like names of clients, co-conspirators, or victims), words (like "drugs," "tax," or "hacking"), places (either geographic locations or electronic ones), or any combination of them. As legal researchers know, if the keyword search is well defined, it can be the most efficient way to find the needle in the haystack. But unless analysts are working from a tip and know how the data is organized, there will probably be some trial and error before they can find the key words, names, or places. In addition, technical problems may complicate a keyword search. For example, encryption, compression, graphics, and certain software formatting schemes may leave data difficult to search in this fashion.

In the list of files contained in a directory or sub-directory, there will be other kinds of information that may indicate whether a particular file should be searched. The names of files in a directory often carry extensions that indicate what sort of file it is or what it does. These file extensions are often associated with common applications software, such as spreadsheets (that could hold accounting data), databases (that can have client information), word processing (which could hold any sort of alphanumeric text), or graphics. There will also be a date and time listed for every file created. Although this information can easily be altered and may be misleading, in some cases it may accurately reflect the last time the file was revised.

Further, the kind of software found loaded on a computer may reveal how the computer has been used. If there is communications software, for example, the computer may have been used to send incriminating data to another computer system at another location. A modem or other evidence of remote access should also tip off the searcher to this possibility, which may expand the investigation and create a need for a new warrant. For example,

the original search may disclose phone bills indicating frequent long-distance calls to one particular number. If a call to this number reveals a modem tone, then further investigation would be warranted.

Clearly, the person conducting a computer search should have high-level technical skills to ensure success. Moreover, a well-meaning investigator with amateur skills could inadvertently, but irretrievably, damage the data. When in doubt, rely only on experts.

4. Discovering the Unexpected

    a. Items Different from the Description in the Warrant

The Fourth Amendment requires specific descriptions of the places, people, and things to be searched as well as the items to be seized. Specificity has two aspects--particularity and overbreadth. "Particularity" is about detail: the warrant must clearly describe what it seeks. "Breadth" is about scope: the warrant cannot include items for which there is no probable cause. Together, the particularity and breadth limitations prevent general searches of a person's property. Thus, generic classifications in a warrant are acceptable only when a more precise description is not possible. In Re Grand Jury Subpoenas, 926 F.2d 847, 856-7 (9th Cir. 1991).

Despite defense objections, the court upheld the seizure of computer disks not named in the warrant in United States v. Musson, 650 F. Supp. 525, 532 (D. Colo. 1986). The warrant in that case authorized agents to seize various specific records, and the court reasoned that because of the changing technology, the government could not necessarily predict what form the records would take. See also United States v. Reyes, 798 F.2d 380, 383 (10th Cir. 1986); United States v. Lucas, 932 F.2d 1210, 1216 (8th Cir.), cert. denied, 112 S. Ct. 399 (1991). In these days, the safest course is always to assume that particular, clearly described "records" or "documents" may be in electronic form and to provide for this possibility in the warrant. (See "SAMPLE COMPUTER LANGUAGE FOR SEARCH WARRANTS," APPENDIX A.)

Other courts, however, have suppressed the results of search warrants which broadly covered electronic "records" in form, but were too vague about their content. In Application of Lafayette Academy, Inc., 610 F.2d 1 (1st Cir. 1979), the court struck a warrant which expressly authorized the seizure of computer tapes, disks, operation manuals, tape logs, tape layouts, and tape printouts. Although the warrant specified that the items must also be evidence of criminal fraud and conspiracy, that limit on content was not sufficiently particular to save the evidence. Id. at 3. See also Voss v. Bergsgaard, 774 F.2d 402, 404-5 (10th Cir. 1985).

In some instances, officers who did not expect to encounter computerized evidence may need to search and seize evidence in electronic form. In United States v. Sprewell, No. 89-50571, 1991 WL 113647 (9th Cir.) (unpublished decision), cert. denied 502 U.S. 885 (1991), LAPD officers seized a personal computer along with programs and disks. These items were taken to the police station where a computer specialist found files that contained evidence of narcotics sales. The defendant challenged the admission of the computer evidence on the grounds that the police exceeded the scope of the warrant because it specified evidence of pay and owe sheets and did not include computer records, despite the police detective's purported knowledge of the presence of the computer from a previous search. The court, however, upheld the search, finding that the warrant's description of "tally sheets or pay and owe sheets" was sufficiently particular to justify the seizure of the computer: "A computer is 'by its nature a device for recording information.' . . . An officer searching for pay-and-owe sheets could reasonably expect to find them within the memory of a computer." Sprewell, 1991 WL 113647 at *4, (quoting United States v. Gomez-Soto, 723 F.2d 649 (9th Cir.) (holding that failure of warrant to specify microcasettes as object of search does not invalidate warrant), cert. denied, 446 U.S. 977 (1984)).

In United States v. Sissler, No. 1:90-CR-12, 1991 WL 239000 (W.D. Mich. Aug. 30, 1991) (unpublished decision), aff'd, 966 F.2d 1455 (6th Cir. 1992), cert. denied, 506 U.S. 1079 (1993), police were authorized by warrant to search and seize records of drug transactions maintained by the defendant. In addition to documents, the police seized nearly 500 computer disks and a personal computer. The defendant challenged the warrant as overbroad and the seizure of the computer disks as outside the scope of the warrant because it merely described the items to be seized as "documents." The court rejected this argument, holding that, "[t]he police were permitted to examine the computer's internal memory and the disks since there was every reason to believe that they contained records whose seizure was authorized by the warrant." Sissler, 1991 WL 239000 at *4.

In City of Akron v. Patrick, 1982 WL 5049 (Ohio Ct. App. 1982), the defendant, convicted of gambling and operating a gambling house, appealed his conviction on the ground that, inter alia, the police illegally searched and seized two home computers. Pursuant to a valid warrant, the police entered the defendant's home, where they saw a computer screen which showed the words, "Advanced, Declined, Unchanged." Recognizing these terms to be consistent with gambling based on daily stock quotations, the police officers summoned a police computer expert, who confirmed that the computers were being used in conjunction with a gambling operation. The computers and diskettes were then seized.

The defendant moved to suppress the computer evidence because it was not specifically named in the search warrant. The search warrant had authorized the search and seizure of phones, U.S. currency, and gambling paraphernalia. The court held that although the computer equipment was not specifically identified in the warrant, the police officer had the authority to seize the computer because its incriminating nature as gambling paraphernalia was readily apparent to the officer from the display on the monitor.

b. Encryption

If agents have authority to search the data in a computer or on a disk and find it has been encrypted, how should they proceed--both legally and practically?

Although an encrypted computer file has been analogized to a locked file cabinet (because the owner is attempting to preserve secrecy), it is also analogous to a document written in a language which is foreign to the reader. As both of these metaphors demonstrate, the authority granted by the warrant to search for and seize the encrypted information also brings the implied authority to decrypt: to "break the lock" on the cabinet or to "translate" the document. Indeed, a warrant to seize a car and its contents implicitly authorizes agents to unlock it.

Of course, the rule may be different if the search is based upon consent. A court might well find that a target who has encrypted his data and has not disclosed the necessary password has tacitly limited the scope of his consent. In that case, the better practice is to ask explicitly for consent to search the encrypted material, as well as for the password. If the target refuses, agents should obtain a warrant for the encrypted data.

In United States v. David, 756 F. Supp. 1385 (D. Nev. 1991), the defendant was cooperating with the government by giving them drug-dealing information from encrypted files in his computer memo book. During one interview, the agent learned the defendant's password by standing over his shoulder and watching as he typed it. Later, when the defendant stopped cooperating and started destroying information in the notebook, the agent seized it and used the defendant's password to access the remaining information. The court reasoned that the agent's learning the password was like his picking up the key to the container. When the defendant withdrew his consent to give more information from the memo book, the act which required a warrant was looking inside the container-- whether locked or unlocked--not the acquisition or even the use of the key. If the agent did not have authority to search the data, then knowing the password would not confer it. Id. at 1391. Conversely, if the agent does have a warrant for the data, she may break the "lock" to search it. For more comment on the consent issues in the David case, see the discussion at "Third-Party Consent," supra.

As a practical matter, getting past the encryption may not be easy, but there are several approaches to try. First of all, the computer crime lab or the software manufacturer may be able to assist in decrypting the file. Investigators should not be discouraged by claims that the password "can't be broken," as this may simply be untrue. Some can be done easily with the right software. If that fails, there may be clues to the password in the other evidence seized--stray notes on hardware or desks; scribbles in the margins of manuals or on the jackets of disks. Agents should consider whether the suspect or someone else will provide the password if requested. In some cases, it might be appropriate to compel a third party who may know the password (or even the suspect) to disclose it by subpoena (with limited immunity, if appropriate).

c. Deleted Information

In <u>United States v. Scott</u>, 975 F.2d 927 (1st Cir. 1992), a case dealing with the expectation of privacy in shredded documents found in trash bags on public streets, the court, in dicta, discussed the level of privacy created by new technologies, finding that although someone using a secret code or obscure language may have a <u>subjective</u> expectation of privacy even when discarding such materials, this expectation does not elevate to a constitutionally recognized one. The court stated:

> Should the mere use of more sophisticated "higher" technology in attempting destruction of the pieces of paper grant higher constitutional protection to this failed attempt at secrecy? We think not. There is no constitutional requirement that police techniques in the detection of crime must remain stagnant while those intent on keeping their nefarious activities secret have the benefit of new knowledge. A person who prepares incriminatory documents in a secret code (or for that matter in some obscure foreign language), and thereafter blithely discards them as trash, relying on the premise or hope that they will not be deciphered (or translated) by the authorities could well be in for an unpleasant surprise if his code is "broken" by the police (or a translator is found for the abstruse language), but he cannot make a valid claim that his subjective expectation in keeping the contents private by use of secret code (or language) was reasonable in a constitutional sense.

<u>Scott</u>, 975 F.2d at 930.

In <u>Pennsylvania v. Copenhefer</u>, 587 A.2d 1353, 526 Pa 555 (1991), the appellant claimed that the recovery and seizure of documents he mistakenly thought he had deleted from his computer was an impermissible intrusion on his expectation of privacy under the Fourth Amendment. During the investigation of a kidnapping and murder, the police obtained a warrant to search the appellant's computer. Using special software, the FBI searched the hard drive and recovered a series of drafts of and amendments to the texts of a ransom call, notes, and a twenty-two point plan for the entire kidnapping scheme, which the appellant believed he had deleted.

The appellant argued that even though his computer was seized pursuant to a valid warrant, his attempted deletion of the documents created an expectation of privacy under the Fourth Amendment requiring the police to obtain a second warrant to search the computer for such documents. The court rejected the contention that searching the deleted files violated his Fourth Amendment rights, holding that "a defendant's attempt to conceal evidence of a crime is not synonymous with a legally cognizable expectation of privacy. A mere hope for secrecy is not a legally protected expectation. . . . An attempt to destroy evidence is not equivalent to a legally protected expectation of privacy." <u>Copenhefer</u>, 587 A.2d at 1356.

H. DECIDING WHETHER TO CONDUCT THE SEARCH ON-SITE OR TO REMOVE HARDWARE TO ANOTHER LOCATION

It is possible for analysts to search for electronic evidence in several places: on-site, at an investigative agency field office, or at a laboratory. The key decision is whether to search at the scene or somewhere else, since an off-site search will require packing and moving the property and may constitute a greater intrusion on the property rights of the computer owner/user.[6] In addressing this issue, it is necessary to consider many factors such as the volume of evidence, the scope of the warrant, and the special problems that may arise when attempting to search computers.

---

[6] If hardware is going to be removed from the site, refer to the suggestions on packing and moving hardware, in "TRANSPORTING HARDWARE FROM THE SCENE," <u>supra</u>.

Although it may, practically speaking, be necessary to remove the computer in order to search it, that logistical reality does not expand the theoretical basis of probable cause. This is a completely separate issue, and agents must not write broad warrants simply because, in reality, it will be necessary to seize the entire filing cabinet or computer. Rather, they should draft the warrant for computer records as specifically as possible (akin to a search warrant for papers in a file cabinet) by focusing on the content of the record. Then, as a separate logical step, they should address the practical aspects of each case: whenever searching data "containers" on site would be unreasonable, agents should explain in the affidavit why this is true and ask for permission to seize the containers in order to find the relevant documents. (See "DRAFTING A WARRANT TO SEIZE INFORMATION: Describing the Items to be Seized," infra.) (If the particular computer storage devices which contain the evidence may also hold electronic mail protected by 18 U.S.C. § 2701, et seq., see "STORED ELECTRONIC COMMUNICATIONS," infra. If they may contain material covered by the Privacy Protection Act, 42 U.S.C. § 2000aa, see "THE PRIVACY PROTECTION ACT," infra.)

1. Seizing Computers Because of the Volume of Evidence

Since any document search can be a time-consuming process, cases discussing file cabinet searches are helpful. Although not technically complex, it can take days to search a file cabinet, and courts have sustained off-site searches when they are "reasonable under the circumstances." The key issues here are: (1) how extensive is the warrant and (2) what type of place is to be searched.

a. Broad Warrant Authorizes Voluminous Seizure of Documents

In determining whether agents may take documents from the scene for later examination, they must consider the scope of the warrant. When the warrant directs agents to seize broad categories of records, or even all records (because the suspect's business is completely criminal or infected by some pervasive, illegal scheme), then it is not difficult to argue all papers and storage devices should be seized. In these cases, courts have supported the carting off of whole file cabinets containing pounds of unsorted paper. United States Postal Service v. C.E.C. Services, 869 F.2d 184, 187 (2d Cir. 1989); United States v. Sawyer, 799 F.2d 1494, 1508 (11th Cir. 1986), cert. denied sub nom. Leavitt v. United States, 479 U.S. 1069 (1987). "When there is probable cause to seize all [items], the warrant may be broad because it is unnecessary to distinguish things that may be taken from things that must be left undisturbed." United States v. Bentley, 825 F.2d 1104, 1110 (7th Cir.), cert. denied, 484 U.S. 901 (1987). In such cases, it is not necessary to carefully sort through documents at the scene to insure that the warrant has been properly executed.

This rationale has been extended to computers. In United States v. Henson, 848 F.2d 1374 (6th Cir. 1988), cert. denied, 488 U.S. 1005 (1989), agents searched several used car dealerships for evidence of an interstate odometer roll-back scheme. The warrant authorized agents to seize, among other things, "modules, modems and connectors, computer, computer terminals, hard copy user documentation pertaining to files and/or programs, cables, printers, discs, floppy discs, tapes, vendor phone numbers, all original and backup tapes and discs, any other informational data input, all vendor manuals for hardware and software, printouts. . . ." Id. at 1382. The warrant did not require on-site sorting, and the defendants later accused agents of going on a "seizing frenzy." The court, however, sustained the search, observing that the extensive seizures were authorized by the warrant, and the warrant was broad because so was the criminality. The court relied on the rule of reasonableness in concluding that officers were right not to try to sort through everything at the scene.

Since the extensive seizure of records was authorized by the terms of the warrant, it was inevitable that the officers would seize documents that were not relevant to the proceedings at hand. We do not think it is reasonable to have required the officers to sift through the large mass of documents and computer files found in the Hensons' office, in an effort to segregate those few papers that were outside the warrant.

Id. at 1383-4 (emphasis added).

Although the Henson defendants argued that agents seized items not covered by the warrant, this did not invalidate the search. As noted by the court,

> A search does not become invalid merely because some items not covered by a warrant are seized .... Absent flagrant disregard for the limitations of a search warrant, the items covered by the warrant will be admissible.

Id. at 1383 (citations omitted). See also United States v. Snow, 919 F.2d 1458, 1461 (10th Cir. 1990).

The Eleventh Circuit expressed a similar rule of reasonableness in United States v. Wuagneux, 683 F.2d 1343, 1353 (11th Cir. 1982), cert. denied, 464 U.S. 814 (1983). In Wuagneux, a dozen agents searched the records of a business for a day and a half, and seized between 50,000 and 100,000 documents (approximately one to two percent of those on the premises). Defendants complained that the agents should not have removed whole files or folders in order to take a particular document, but the court disagreed: "To require otherwise 'would substantially increase the time required to conduct the search, thereby aggravating the intrusiveness of the search,'" citing United States v. Beusch, 596 F.2d 871, 876-7 (9th Cir. 1979). The Eighth Circuit reached the same conclusion in Marvin v. United States, 732 F.2d 669 (8th Cir. 1984), where agents searched a clinic for financial information related to tax fraud. The agents seized many files without examining the contents at the scene, intending to copy and sort them later. Although the agents seized some files that were completely outside the warrant, the district court's remedy, upheld on appeal, was to order return of the irrelevant items. The agents' decision not to comb through all the files at the scene, the court noted, was "prompted largely by practical considerations and time constraints." Id. at 675. Accord Naugle v. Witney, 755 F. Supp. 1504, 1516 (D. Utah 1990) (Removing an entire filing cabinet, including items not described in the warrant, was reasonable since the alternative would require officers to remain on the premises for days, a result less reasonable and more intrusive.)

b. Warrant Is Narrowly Drawn but Number of Documents to Be Sifted Through Is Enormous

The more difficult cases are those in which the sought-after evidence is far more limited and the description in the warrant is (and should be) more limited as well. "When the probable cause covers fewer documents in a system of files, the warrant must be more confined and tell the officers how to separate the documents to be seized from others." United States v. Bentley, supra, at 1110.

The problem of the narrowly drawn, tightly focused warrant is illustrated by United States v. Tamura, 694 F.2d 591 (9th Cir. 1982). Because agents knew exactly what records they sought at a particular business, they were able (and it was reasonable for them) to draft the warrant very specifically. But it was much easier to describe the records than to find them, especially when the company employees refused to help. In the end, the agents simply took all the records including eleven boxes of computer printouts, 34 file drawers of vouchers, and 17 drawers of cancelled checks. Unlike most other cases that address these issues, this court faced a seizure where most of the documents taken were outside the warrant. It concluded, therefore, that "the wholesale seizure for later detailed examination of records not described in a warrant is significantly more intrusive, and has been characterized as 'the kind of investigatory dragnet that the Fourth Amendment was designed to prevent.'" Id. at 595 (citations omitted). Although the court found reversal was not compelled (because the government had been "motivated by considerations of practicality"), it also found this a "close case." Their advice for law enforcement is concrete:

> In the comparatively rare instances where documents are so intermingled that they cannot feasibly be sorted on site, we suggest that the Government and law enforcement officials generally can avoid violating Fourth Amendment rights by sealing and holding the documents pending approval by a magistrate of a further search, in accordance with the procedures set forth in the American Law

Institute's Model Code of Pre-Arraignment Procedure. If the need for transporting the documents is known to the officers prior to the search, they may apply for specific authorization for large-scale removal of material, which should be granted by the magistrate issuing the warrant only where on-site sorting is infeasible and no other practical alternative exists.

Id. at 595-6 (footnote omitted).

Several cases have upheld the constitutionality of seizing entire computers based on the volume of evidence to be searched. In United States v. Schandl, 947 F.2d 462 (11th Cir. 1991), cert. denied 504 U.S. 975 (1992), agents seized a computer disk containing a Bible home study course pursuant to a warrant authorizing the search and seizure of, inter alia, ". . . computer disks, and/or any other computer memory storage devices, plus computer mainframe which operates the memory storage devices relating to any financial transactions." The defendant moved to suppress the evidence resulting from the search on the ground that the agents exceeded the scope of the warrant. The court affirmed the district court's order upholding the removal of the items from the defendant's house, stating that "it might have been far more disruptive had the agents made a thorough search of each individual document and computer disk before removing it from [the defendant's] home and office. To insist on such a practice 'would substantially increase the time required to conduct the search, thereby aggravating the intrusiveness of the search.'" 947 F.2d at 465-66 (quoting United States v. Wuagneux, 848 F.2d 1374, 1353 (11th Cir. 1982), cert. denied, 464 U.S. 814 (1983)).

In United States v. Yung, 786 F. Supp. 1561 (D. Kan. 1992), the court held that the seizure of files outside the scope of the warrant did not invalidate the entire search. Because the court concluded that the videotapes and computer files specifically listed in the warrant could not be individually viewed during the search, the court found that the officers acted in "good faith" in attempting to stay within the boundaries of the warrant. Accordingly, the extensive seizure of certain types of items, such as computer disks, "was prompted largely by practical considerations and time constraints." 786 F. Supp. at 1569 (citing Marvin v. United States, 732 F.2d 669, 675 (8th Cir. 1984) (upholding seizure of entire files that contained information outside the scope of the warrant)).

In United States v. Stewart, No. Crim. A. 96-583, 1997 WL 189381 (E.D. Pa. April 16, 1997) (unpublished decision), pursuant to a valid warrant, police seized several computers along with related accessories. A police computer expert then copied the files and returned them to the defendant. Over the defendant's challenge, the court held that such a procedure was proper and did not violate the Fourth Amendment. The court reasoned that searching all files on the hard drives and diskettes at the scene of the crime is often not practical for the agents executing a warrant. Therefore, agents' seizing voluminous computer files was a permissible search technique.

In United States v. Lamb, 945 F. Supp. 441, 458-59 (N.D.N.Y. 1996), the Court of Appeals held that because a warrant issued for a child pornography investigation articulated probable cause to believe that stored files contained evidence of the crime, the warrant properly authorized the search and seizure of the disks containing the incriminating files. The language of the warrant did not limit investigators to seizing specific graphic files because the actual contents of a computer file usually cannot be determined until it is reviewed with the appropriate application software on a computer. The court elaborated, stating that:

"[e]ven when the filename is known ahead of time, it would rarely if ever be possible to know if the data in the file contains child pornography, without viewing it on a monitor. . . . In these circumstances it is unreasonable to require the executing officers to identify which files actually contain child pornography and which do not in AOL's Virginia headquarters. The task may be more properly performed by a government computer technician at an FBI lab or office." Lamb, 945 F. Supp at 458 n.10.

In <u>Ohio v. McGuire</u>, No. 16423, 16431, 1994 WL 700082 (Ohio App. 9 Dist. 1994) (unpublished decision), the police executed a warrant authorizing the search and seizure of, <u>inter alia</u>, "one (1) computer system, computer disks, VCR tapes containing scenes of sex acts." The court upheld the search and seizure of more than seventy-eight computer disks (which contained both personal and business records) stating that "[g]iven the fact that contents of a computer disk are not readily apparent from mere observation, the police were justified in seizing all defendant's computer disks in order to fully review their contents to determine if they were evidence of the crimes that defendant had allegedly committed." <u>McGuire</u>, 1994 WL 700082 at *9.

c. Warrant Executed in the Home

When a search is conducted at a home instead of a business, courts seem more understanding of an agent's predilections to seize now and sort later. In <u>United States v. Fawole</u>, 785 F.2d 1141, 1144 (4th Cir. 1986), ten agents had searched the defendant's home for three and a half hours removing, among other things, 350 documents. Almost half of those papers were in a briefcase, which the agents seized without sorting. Although many things in the briefcase were outside the scope of the warrant, the court found that, under the circumstances, the seizure did not amount to a general, exploratory rummaging in a person's belongings.

Even more extensive were the seizures in <u>United States v. Santarelli</u>, 778 F.2d 609 (11th Cir. 1985). In that case, agents searched the home of a suspected loanshark, confiscating the entire contents of a four-drawer file cabinet. In the end, they left with eight large boxes of items which they inventoried at the local FBI office. When the defendant objected to this process, the court strongly disagreed:

> Given the fact that the search warrant entitled the agents to search for documents . . .it is clear that the agents were entitled to examine each document in the bedroom or in the filing cabinet to determine whether it constituted evidence. . . . It follows that Santarelli would have no cause to object if the agents had entered his home to examine the documents and remained there as long as the search required. The district court estimated that a brief examination of each document would have taken several days. Under these circumstances, we believe that the agents acted reasonably when they removed the documents to another location for subsequent examination. . . . [T]o require an on-premises examination under such circumstances would significantly aggravate the intrusiveness of the search by prolonging the time the police would be required to remain in the home.

<u>Id.</u> at 615-6 (citations omitted).

d. Applying Existing Rules to Computers

Clearly, the <u>Tamura</u> court could not have anticipated that the explosion in computers would result in the widespread commingling of documents. While computers are often set up with directories and subdirectories (much like a file cabinet is set up with file folders), many users put data on disks in random fashion. Thus, a particular letter or file could be anywhere on a hard disk or in a box of floppies.

Most important, all of the file-cabinet cases discussed above implicitly rely on the premise that "documents" are readily accessible and ascertainable items; that any agent can find them and (unless the subject is quite technical) can read, sort, and copy those covered by warrant. The biggest problem in the paper cases is time, the days it takes to do a painstaking job. But computer searches have added a formidable new barrier, because searching and seizing are no longer as simple as opening a file cabinet drawer. When agents seize data from computer storage devices, they will need technical skill just to get the file drawer open. While some agents will be "computer literate," only a few will be expert; and none can be expert on every sort of system. Courts have not yet addressed this reality.

In the meantime, search warrant planning in every computer case should explore whether agents will ask for off-site search authority in the warrant application.

2. Seizing Computers because of Technical Concerns

a. Conducting a Controlled Search to Avoid Destroying Data

The computer expert who searches a target's computer system for information may need to know about specialized hardware, operating systems, or applications software just to get to the information. For example, an agent who has never used Lotus 1-2-3 (a spreadsheet program) will not be able to safely retrieve and print Lotus 1-2-3 files. If the agent entered the wrong computer command, he could unwittingly alter or destroy the data on the system. This sort of mistake not only alters evidence, but could create problems for the system's owner as well. Since it is the government's responsibility to recover evidence without altering data, the safest course is to rely on experts working in controlled environments.

Additionally, savvy computer criminals may know how to trip-wire their computers with "hot keys" or other self-destruct programs that could erase vital evidence if the system were examined by anyone other than an expert. For example, a criminal could write a very short program that would cause the computer to demand a password periodically and, if the correct password is not entered within ten seconds, it would destroy data automatically. In some cases, valuable evidence has been lost because of the way the computers were handled. Therefore, this concern may make it doubly important to remove the computers, unless an expert determines that an on-site search will be adequate.

Quite obviously, some computers (such as large mainframes) are not easily moved. And some defendants will no doubt argue that if the government can search a mainframe computer on site, it can search PCs on site as well. Even so, the test should not be what is arguably possible, but rather what is the most reasonable, most reliable, and least intrusive way to search each system. The fact that mainframes may pose unique problems should not lead courts to adopt impractical rules for other searches.

In sum, there is ample authority to justify removing computer systems (or the relevant parts of them) to a field office or laboratory in order to search them for information. This is especially true where the warrant is broad, an on-site search will be intrusive, or technical concerns warrant moving the system to a lab. This will not always be the case, however, and agents and their experts should explore searching on site (or making exact copies to search later) whenever it is appropriate. Before agents ask for authority to seize any hardware for an off-site data search, they should analyze the reasons and set them out clearly for the magistrate.

In Mahlberg v. Mentzer, 968 F.2d 772 (8th Cir.), cert. denied, 506 U.S. 1026 (1992), the plaintiff brought a § 1983 action against a police officer, claiming that the officer had violated the plaintiff's Fourth Amendment rights by seizing approximately 160 computer disks along with instruction manuals, directory printouts, and library books pursuant to a warrant that had listed only two computer programs as objects of the search.[7] Judgment was entered for the defendant after a jury trial, and the plaintiff's motion for a new trial was denied. On appeal, the Eighth Circuit considered the question of whether the seizure of items not listed on a warrant violated the subject's Fourth Amendment rights when the officer believed that the diskettes and computers were "booby-trapped" to destroy the evidence. In affirming the district court, the Eighth Circuit held that the finding that the officer's legitimate concern that the disks may have been "booby trapped" to erase themselves if examined on the defendant's home computer, combined with the officer's testimony that he believed the manuals and printouts were related to

---

[7] Plaintiff's motion to suppress these items was granted in the plaintiff's criminal trial. The reasons for the suppression, however, were not discussed in the civil case.

criminal activity, justified the seizure of the disks and related manuals, printouts, and books for later review away from the scene of the search.

b. Seizing Hardware and Documentation so the System Will Operate at the Lab

With an ever-increasing array of computer components on the market--and with existing hardware and software becoming obsolete--it may be impossible to seize parts of a computer system (e.g., the CPU and hard drive) and operate them at the laboratory. In fact, there may be times when agents will need to seize every component in the computer system and later have a laboratory computer specialist determine whether or not each piece can be returned. Many hardware incompatibilities exist (even within a given computer family such as IBM-compatible PCs), and the laboratory experts may need to properly re-configure the system back at the lab in order to read data from it.

Peripherals such as printers and special input and display devices may be necessary to operate and display certain software applications. Agents should attempt to learn as much about the system to be searched as possible so that appropriate seizure decisions can be made. If certain peripherals must be seized to insure that the data can be retrieved from storage devices, this should be articulated in the warrant affidavit and covered in the warrant. Then an expert should examine the seized equipment as soon as practicable to determine whether the peripheral devices need to be retained. This approach relies completely on the facts of each case. It will seem reasonable and temperate when the I/O devices seized are essential, but not when the items seized are commercially available and the only justification for the seizure/retention is convenience and not necessity. If in doubt, agents should seek permission to seize the peripherals, and then insure a prompt review at the lab.

Similarly, when agents search and seize a computer system, they should ask for authority to seize any documentation that explains the hardware and software being seized. Documentation found at the scene may be a key in re-assembling the computer, operating it, or using the software on the machine properly. If the computer's user is experienced, he may have customized the software, and the documentation may be required to retrieve data. Although a computer lab may have or be able to obtain many standard varieties of documentation, some of it may not be easily available for purchase. As with hardware or software, the documentation should not be seized unless needed and, if seized, should be returned when no longer required.

I. EXPERT ASSISTANCE

1. Introduction

Federal law explicitly provides for the use of experts while executing search warrants. 18 U.S.C. § 3105 states that:

> [a] search warrant may in all cases be served by any of the officers mentioned in its direction or by an officer authorized by law to serve such warrant, but by no other person, except in aid of the officer on his requiring it, he being present and acting in its execution.

18 U.S.C. § 3105 (1997) (emphasis added).

While planning is important to the success of any search, it is critical in searching and seizing information from computers. Agents should determine, to the extent possible, the type of computer involved, what operating system it uses, and whether the information sought can be accessed by, or is controlled by, a computer literate target.

Answering these questions is key, because no expert can be expert on all systems. Mainframes, for example, are made by various companies (e.g., IBM, DEC, Cray) and often run unique, proprietary operating systems. Even the PC market offers significantly different hardware/software configurations. Although the most common desk-top computer is an IBM or IBM-compatible system, it runs a range of operating systems including DOS (with or without Windows), OS/2, and UNIX. Apple Computers are also popular and run their own unique operating system.

Computer literate targets may attempt to frustrate the proper execution of a search warrant. For example, an ingenious owner might have installed hidden commands that could delete important data if certain start-up procedures are not followed. If this might be the case, experts will take special precautions before the search: they will, for example, start (or "boot") the computer from a "clean" system diskette in a floppy drive, not from the operating software installed on the system. These hidden traps, as well as passwords and other security devices, are all obstacles that might be encountered in a search.

In sum, since computer experts cannot possibly be expert on all systems, it is important to have the correct expert on the scene. Knowing the type of computer to be searched, and the type of operating system being used, will allow the appropriate expert to be selected. This, in turn, will streamline the search process, since the expert may be familiar with the software and file structures on the target machine.

In Ohio v. Sevfence, No. F-96-001, 1997 WL 89100 (Ohio Ct. App. 1997) (unpublished decision), a police officer presented a warrant to the appellant for the search of his business for stolen computer parts. Because the officer was "computer illiterate," he demanded that the appellant produce the items in the warrant. The court held that requiring the appellant to produce the items in the warrant violated his Fifth Amendment right against testimonial conduct and ruled that the computer evidence must be suppressed. Although the state had tried to justify the seizure by arguing that there was a high probability that the items enumerated on the warrant would have been found by the executing officer in the absence of the appellant's assistance, the court rejected this "inevitable discovery" theory. Instead, the court held that, based on the fact that (1) the officer admitted he was "computer illiterate," (2) the warrant did not specify the serial numbers of the equipment to be seized, and (3) there was a large quantity of computer equipment at the search location, there was not a high likelihood that the officers would have inevitably discovered the stolen goods.

2. Finding Experts

Most situations will require an expert to retrieve, analyze, and preserve data from the computers to be searched. Oftentimes the job may not be so complex: the records may be stored with a standard brand of software using the DOS (Disk Operating System) format. Some of the most common software programs are WordPerfect (for text), Lotus (for spreadsheets), and dBase (for databases). If it is more complicated than this, however, only an expert in the hardware and software at hand should do the work.

To determine what type of expert will be needed, agents should get as much information about the targeted system as possible. Sources like undercover agents, informants, former employees, or mail covers can provide information about the system at the search site. Once the computer systems and software involved have been identified, an appropriate expert can be found from either the federal or private sector. Ultimately, the expert must use sound scientific techniques to examine any computer evidence.

a. Federal Sources

The best place to find an expert may be in the investigating agency itself. Many federal agencies have experienced people on staff who can help quickly when the need arises, and the list at APPENDIX C [not included] provides contact points for various agencies. If the investigating agency lacks an expert in the particular system to be searched, other federal agencies may be able to assist. The trick, of course, is to find the expert while planning for the search and not to start looking after the agents execute the warrant. Prosecutors must allow time to explore the federal network and find the right person.

APPENDIX G

Most of the federal agencies that routinely execute search warrants for computer evidence have analysts at central laboratories or field experts who can search the seized computer evidence. Many of them will also work on evidence from other federal or state agencies as time permits. It is important to call early to get specific instructions for handling the evidence, and these experts can provide other technical assistance as well. For example, there are many kinds of software (both government and private) which will help process evidence, break passwords, decrypt files, recover hidden or deleted data, or assist investigators in other important ways. Because these utilities are constantly changing, it is important to consult with experts who have them and know how to use them.

Each agency organizes its computer experts differently. For example, the Computer Analysis and Response Team (CART) is a specialized team within the central FBI Laboratory in Washington, D.C., that examines various types of computer evidence for FBI agents nationwide. The IRS, on the other hand, has about seventy decentralized experts, called Seized Computer Evidence Recovery (SCER) Specialists who work in controlled environments across the country. Almost every IRS District has at least one SCER Specialist, and many have two. The Drug Enforcement Administration's forensic computer experts are also experienced in all phases of computer operations related to criminal cases, including data retrieval from damaged media and decryption. The United States Secret Service has approximately twelve special agents who are members of the Electronic Crimes Special Agent Program (ECSAP). These agents are assigned to field offices on a regional basis and are trained in the area of computer investigations and computer forensics. (For a list of federal sources for computer experts, see APPENDIX C [not included].)

b. Private Experts

Whatever the source of a private expert, the affidavit should ask permission to use non-law-enforcement personnel during the execution of the search warrant. The issuing magistrate should know why an expert is needed and what his role will be during the search. Agents must carefully monitor the expert to insure that he does not exceed the limits described in the search warrant. Certain experts--those not familiar with the judicial system--are not likely to be expert on how to execute a search warrant, protect chain-of-custody, or resolve search issues that may affect the evidence's admissibility at trial. Thus, a private expert should be paired with an experienced agent every step of the way. In addition, the expert's employment contract should address confidentiality issues, and include a nondisclosure clause and a statement of Privacy Act restrictions. If the contracting agency is the IRS, pay special note to Internal Revenue Code provisions at 26 U.S.C. § 6103, which address rules for confidentiality and nondisclosure of tax return information.

(1) Professional Computer Organizations

Many professional computer organizations have members who are experts in a wide variety of hardware and software. Computer experts from the government are a good source for finding a private expert, for the organizations and contacts between them change almost as fast as the technology. Also, one advantage of using a professional organization as the source of an expert is that these organizations usually have members who work routinely with federal or state law enforcement and are therefore familiar with handling evidence and testifying.

(2) Universities

Another source for experts is a university, especially for high-tech crimes involving rare kinds of hardware or software. The academic environment attracts problem-solvers who may have skills and research contacts unavailable in law enforcement.

(3) Computer and Telecommunications Industry Personnel

In some cases, the very best expert may come from a vendor or service provider, particularly when the case involves mainframes, networks, or unusual systems. Many companies such as IBM and Data General employ some experts solely to assist various law enforcement agencies on search warrants.

(4) The Victim

Finally, in some circumstances, an expert from the victim organization may be the best choice, especially if the hardware configuration or software applications are unique to that organization. Agents and prosecutors must, of course, be sensitive to potential claims of bias. Many relevant issues, such as estimates of loss, may pose a considerable gray area. Even if the victim-expert is completely dispassionate and neutral in her evaluation, her affiliation with and loyalty to the victim organization may create a bias issue later at trial.

3. What the Experts Can Do

a. Search Planning and Execution

Agents and prosecutors who anticipate searching and seizing computers should include a computer expert in the planning team as early as possible. Experts can help immeasurably in anticipating the technical aspects of the search. This not only makes the search smoother, it is important information for designing the scope of the warrant. In particular, if agents can give the expert any information about the target's specific computer system, the expert may be better able to predict which items can be searched at the scene, which must be seized for later analysis, and which may be left behind.

Further, if the computer system is unusual or complex, technical experts can be invaluable help at the scene during the search. Particularly when evidence resides on computer networks, backup tapes, or in custom-tailored systems, the evidence will be safest in the hands of an expert.

The courts have specifically upheld the use of experts when carrying out searches and seizures of computer equipment. In United States v. Schwimmer, 692 F. Supp. 119 (E.D.N.Y. 1988), in an investigation for racketeering, conspiracy, and tax evasion, federal agents obtained a warrant authorizing them to search a bank's premises and the offices of the bank's counsel. Seizure was permitted of "books and records" including computer tapes related to special deals concerning the bank. Additionally, the warrant authorized the assistance of a private computer expert to operate the bank's computer terminals. The defendant challenged the execution of the warrant, in part because it was executed by a private computer expert. The court ruled, however, that "the assistance of this individual, however, was specifically permitted by the warrant pursuant to statutory authority." Schwimmer, 692 F. Supp. at 126-27 (citing 18 U.S.C. § 3105).

In Florida v. Wade, 14 Fla. L. Weekly 1071, 544 So.2d 1028 (Fla. Dist. Ct. App. 1989), the appellant challenged the use of computer experts who were employed by the victim corporation to help identify the stolen computer equipment listed in the search warrant. The court held that in exceptional circumstances such as these, it is proper to use computer experts, including those employed by the victim corporation, to assist in the execution of a warrant. Here, the court found that because the stolen property was of a technical nature not generally familiar to law enforcement officers, the use of computer experts was permissible.

b. Electronic Analysis

The experts will examine all the seized computer items (so long as they are properly preserved and sealed) and will recover whatever evidence they can. Most forensic computer examiners will perform at least the following:

(1) make the equipment operate properly; (2) retrieve information; (3) unblock "deleted" or "erased" data storage devices; (4) bypass or defeat passwords; (5) decipher encrypted data; and (6) detect the presence of known viruses.

The data to be searched can consist of hundreds or even thousands of files and directories. In some cases, there will be evidence in most of the files seized, and in others, only a small fraction of them. Once the analyst has protected the original data from change, she must begin to search for the relevant material.

A good first step is to print out a directory of the information contained on a hard drive or floppy disk. Directories give valuable information about what is in the files, when they were created, and how long they are. Of course, analysts will not entirely trust file names, as hackers have been known to hide highly incriminating material in files with innocuous names and misleading dates.

Once the analyst has printed a directory, he will probably log onto the hard or floppy drive and look at each file, noting on the printed directory (or a separate log sheet if available) the type of information in each file and whether it appears relevant. Relevant files can be copied onto a separate disk or printed out in hard copy. It is a good idea always to review files from bit-stream copies (which record each separate bit of information, including hidden files) or in "read only" mode so that the reviewer can read the document but cannot edit it. This way, the agents can later testify that the seized material could not have been mistakenly altered during the review. Of course, there is more than one "right way" to analyze electronic evidence, and experts must deal with the circumstances of each case. Ultimately the analyst must adhere to sound scientific protocols in recovering and examining computer-related evidence, and keep clear and complete records of the process.

c. Trial Preparation

Computer forensic experts can help prosecute the case with advice about how to present computer-related evidence in court. Many are experienced expert witnesses and they can (1) help prepare the direct case; and (2) anticipate and rebut defense claims. In addition, computer experts can assist prosecutors in complying with the new federal rules pertaining to expert witnesses, Fed. R. Evid. 16(a)(1)(E) and 16(b)(1)(C), effective December 1, 1993. Under these rules, the government must provide, upon request, a written summary of expert testimony which it intends to use during its case in chief. There is a reciprocal requirement for the summary of defense expert witness testimony, as long as the defense has requested a summary from the government, and the government has complied.

d. Training for Field Agents

Before a computer case ever arises, experts can train agents and prosecutors about computer search problems and opportunities. They can teach investigators how to preserve and submit computer evidence for examination, and many will also provide field support as time permits.

V. NETWORKS AND BULLETIN BOARDS

A. INTRODUCTION

Electronic Bulletin Board Services (BBSs) are computers set up to serve in the electronic world as places where users can post and read messages--much like traditional bulletin boards. In addition, however, a BBS may also permit users to communicate via private electronic mail, to engage in "chat sessions" (real-time conversations where the "speakers" talk by using their keyboards instead of their voices), to upload and download files, and to share information on topics of common interest (e.g., a newsletter on stamp collecting). A sysop runs the bulletin board, and BBS users access it with their computers over regular telephone lines.

Some bulletin boards, known as "pirate bulletin boards," are maintained for illegal purposes such as distributing copyrighted software, credit card numbers, telephone access codes, and pornography. A BBS dedicated to phone fraud is also called a "phone phreaker board," and those which distribute child pornography and adult obscenity are called, not surprisingly, "porn boards." The illegal material on these boards is not protected by the First Amendment since such items are "fruits of crime" and "contraband" and do not convey any thought, opinion, or artistic expression. Nor can these operations claim some sort of "press protection" for publishing these items, since the Constitution does not shield the press against laws of general applicability. In short, the First Amendment is not a license to commit crimes. See Securities and Exchange Commission v. McGoff, 647 F.2d 185 (D.C. Cir.), cert. denied, 452 U.S. 963 (1981); Cf. Pell v. Procunier, 417 U.S. 817, 833-5 (1974) (the right to speak and publish does not carry an unrestrained right to gather information; a prison may restrict the press's access to its inmates in accord with the state's legitimate incarceration policy objectives).

Computers often contain information and works that are subject to at least some degree of protection under the First Amendment. In searches and seizures where materials protected by the First Amendment are the object of the search, courts review Fourth Amendment issues with heightened care. "Fourth Amendment protections become the more necessary when the targets of official surveillance may be those suspected of unorthodoxy in their political beliefs." United States v. United States Dist. Court, 407 U.S. 297, 314 (1972). The courts have extended heightened Fourth Amendment protections to all works covered by the First Amendment. "When the contents of a package are books or other materials arguably protected by the First Amendment, and when the basis for the seizure is disapproval of the message contained therein, it is especially important that [the Fourth Amendment's warrant] requirement is scrupulously observed." Walter v. United States, 447 U.S. 649, 655 (1980). Further, "the constitutional requirement that warrants must particularly describe the 'things to be seized' is to be accorded the most scrupulous exactitude when the 'things' are books, and the basis for their seizure is the ideas which they contain." Stanford v. Texas, 379 U.S. 476, 485 (1965).

In United States v. Kimbrough, 69 F.3d 723 (5th Cir. 1995), cert. denied, 116 S. Ct 1547 (1996), the defendant challenged the validity of warrants which in a child obscenity investigation allowed the search and seizure of "commercial software and manuals, hardware, computer disks, disk drives, monitors, computer printers, modems, tape drives, disk application programs, data disks, system disk operating systems, magnetic media-floppy disks, CD ROMs, tape systems and hard drives, other computer related operational equipment, and other similar materials . . . ." The defendant contended that the warrants were unconstitutional on their face because, considering that many of the items were "presumably protected speech," the warrants failed to sufficiently specify with particularity the items to be seized. The court rejected this argument noting that the language of the warrants properly limited the executing officers' discretion by informing them what items were to be seized.

In United States v. Layne, 43 F.3d 127 (5th Cir. 1995), the defendant challenged a warrant authorizing the search and seizure of "assorted pornographic videotapes; assorted pornographic magazines," on the ground that the warrant enumerated items protected by the First Amendment. The Fifth Circuit, however, rejected this claim, holding that although the Supreme Court has required a heightened showing of particularity under Marcus v. Search Warrant, 367 U.S. 717, 732 (1961), this level of particularity is only required where there is a danger of prior restraint. In this case, the Fifth Circuit found that the items to be seized were not being seized on the basis of their content; instead, they were being seized because they corroborated a victim's testimony. Further, the court held that a warrant authorizing the search and seizure of material depicting children under the age of 16 engaged in "sexually explicit conduct" was particular enough to limit an officer's discretion. See United States v. Hurt, 808 F.2d 707 (9th Cir.) cert. denied, 484 U.S. 816 (1987).

It gets more complex, however, because many bulletin boards are not devoted solely to illegal activities, but are hybrid boards: they contain both illegal and legal material. To complicate matters further, the legitimate material on the board (or stored on the same computer which runs the board) may be statutorily protected. For example, some private electronic mail may be covered under 18 U.S.C. § 2701, et seq., Stored Wire and Electronic

Communications. (For further discussion, see "STORED ELECTRONIC COMMUNICATIONS," infra). Even more difficult, some material may be specifically protected from search and seizure by a complex statute called the Privacy Protection Act, 42 U.S.C. § 2000aa. In order to understand the scope and intricacy of this statute and how it might apply to computer searches, it helps to begin with the case which prompted it.

B. THE PRIVACY PROTECTION ACT, 42 U.S.C. § 2000aa

The development of the Internet has changed both the scope and coverage of the Privacy Protection Act ("PPA). As an ever-increasing number of computers become connected to this global network, almost any computer may be a repository of information being prepared for electronic publication. Before executing a search warrant on a computer that might contain files protected by the PPA, agents and prosecutors are strongly encouraged to carefully review the facts of the case and the status of the law in this area. If questions arise, prosecutors and agents are always welcome to contact the Computer Crime and Intellectual Property Section (202-514-1026).

1. A Brief History of the Privacy Protection Act

On April 9, 1971, nine police officers in California responded to Stanford University Hospital to disperse a large group of demonstrators. The demonstrators resisted, and they ultimately attacked and injured all nine officers. Two days later, on April 11, The Stanford Daily, a student newspaper, carried articles and photographs devoted to the student protest and the clash between these protestors and the police. Believing that The Stanford Daily might possess additional photographs that would identify other protestors, the police sought and obtained a search warrant to search the newspaper's offices.

A month after the search, The Stanford Daily brought a civil action alleging violations of the First, Fourth and Fourteenth Amendments. In support of their claims, the plaintiffs alleged that (1) the Fourth Amendment forbade the issuance of search warrants for evidence in the possession of those not suspected of criminal activity and (2) the First Amendment prohibited the use of search warrants against members of the press and, instead, required the use of subpoenas duces tecum. Zurcher v. Stanford Daily, 436 U.S. 547 (1978). The Supreme Court disagreed with both claims, holding that the use of a search warrant, even for the pursuit of "mere evidence," was permitted on both non-suspect third parties and members of the news media.

In response to Zurcher, Congress passed the Privacy Protection Act of 1980, 42 U.S.C. § 2000aa (hereinafter the PPA). The purpose of this legislation, as stated in the Senate Report, is to afford "the press and certain other persons not suspected of committing a crime with protections not provided currently by the Fourth Amendment." S. Rep. No. 874, 96th Cong., 2d Sess. 4 (1980). As the legislative history indicates,

> the purpose of this statute is to limit searches for materials held by persons involved in First Amendment activities who are themselves not suspected of participation in the criminal activity for which the materials are sought, and not to limit the ability of law enforcement officers to search for and seize materials held by those suspected of committing the crime under investigation.[8] Id. at 11.

The PPA protects two classes of materials--defined as "work product materials" and "documentary materials"--by restricting beyond the existing limits of the Fourth Amendment when government agents can get warrants to search for or seize them.

---

[8] The Department had previously promulgated regulations on issuing subpoenas directly to members of the news media or indirectly for their telephone toll records. The regulations also addressed interrogating, indicting, or arresting members of the press. See 28 C.F.R. § 50.10.

It is important to note that, although victims of a search which violates the PPA may not move to suppress the results, the statute does create civil remedies. Moreover, the PPA specifically precludes the government from asserting a good faith defense to civil claims, so in this respect § 2000aa is a strict liability statute.

2. Work Product Materials

In general terms, the first category of protected material covers original work in the possession of anyone (including authors and publishers) who intends (from an objective view) to publish it. In construing this statute, the exact language of the definitions is important. Specifically, "work product materials" are defined in 42 U.S.C. § 2000aa-7(b) as

> materials, other than contraband or the fruits of a crime or things otherwise criminally possessed, or property designed or intended for use, or which is or has been used, as the means of committing a criminal offense, and--

> (1) in anticipation of communicating such materials to the public, are prepared, produced, authored, or created, whether by the person in possession of the materials or by any other person;

> (2) are possessed for the purposes of communicating such materials to the public; and

> (3) include mental impressions, conclusions, opinions, or theories of the person who prepared, produced, authored, or created such material.

When "work product materials" are involved, Title 42, Section 2000aa(a) provides that:

Notwithstanding any other law, it shall be unlawful for a government officer or employee, in connection with the investigation or prosecution of a criminal offense, to search for or seize any work product materials possessed by a person reasonably believed to have a purpose to disseminate to the public a newspaper, book, broadcast, or other similar form of public communication, in or affecting interstate or foreign commerce. . .(emphasis added). . . [unless]

> (1) there is probable cause to believe that the person possessing such materials has committed or is committing the criminal offense to which the materials relate: Provided, however, That a government officer or employee may not search for or seize such materials under the provisions of this paragraph if the offense to which the materials relate consists of the receipt, possession, communication, or withholding of such materials or the information contained therein (but such a search or seizure may be conducted under the provisions of this paragraph if the offense consists of the receipt, possession, or communication of information relating to the national defense, classified information, or restricted data under the provisions of section 793, 794, 797, or 798 of Title 18, or section 2274, 2275 or 2277 of this title, or section 783 of Title 50); or

> (2) there is reason to believe that the immediate seizure of such materials is necessary to prevent the death of, or serious bodily injury to, a human being.

Thus, under § 2000aa(a), there are three situations in which government agents may search for or seize these materials without running afoul of the statute. First, the definition itself specifically excludes contraband or the fruits or instrumentalities of a crime. 42 U.S.C. § 2000aa-7(b). As the drafting Committee noted,

[t]hese kinds of evidence are so intimately related to the commission of a crime, and so often essential to securing a conviction, that they should be available for law enforcement purposes, and, therefore, must fall outside the no search rule that is applied to work product.

S. Rep. 96-874, 96th Cong., 2d Sess. 17, reprinted in 1980 U.S. Code Cong. & Admin. News 3964. In BBS cases, the most common objects of the warrant--stolen access codes, child pornography, and illegally copied software-- would clearly fall within the contraband exclusion, so the PPA would not affect a warrant drawn for these materials.

In addition, as quoted above, the PPA creates two exceptions to the general prohibition against seizing "work product." One excepts situations in which life and limb are at stake. The other applies when (1) the work product is evidence of crime, and (2) the person who possesses the materials probably committed it. Even so, this evidence-of-crime exception does not apply if the particular crime "consists of the receipt, possession, communication or withholding of such material. . ." unless the work product was classified or restricted, and the offense is specifically listed in the PPA. 42 U.S.C. § 2000aa(a)(1) and (b)(1). This general evidence-of-crime exception was intended to

> codify a core principle of this section, which is to protect from search only those persons involved in First Amendment activities who are themselves not implicated in the crime under investigation, and not to shield those who participate in crime.

H.R. Rep. No. 1064, 96th Cong., 2d Sess. 7. To trigger the exception, however, law enforcement officials are held to a higher-than-usual requirement: they must show probable cause to believe the person who holds the evidentiary materials is a suspect of the crime--the same showing of cause required for an arrest warrant. S. Rep. No. 874, 96th Cong., 2d Sess. 11, reprinted in 1980 U.S. Code Cong. & Admin. News 3950, 3957.

It may, of course, be difficult to invoke this evidence-of-crime exception, particularly at early stages of the investigation. As the Supreme Court noted in Zurcher (and a number of commentators have reiterated since), a search warrant is often most useful early in an investigation when agents have probable cause to believe there is evidence on the premises, but are not ready to arrest any particular person. See Zurcher v. Stanford Daily, 436 U.S. at 561; Testimony of Richard J. Williams, Vice President, National District Attorney's Association, in Hearing before the Committee on the Judiciary, United States Senate, 96th Cong., 2d Sess. on S. 115, S. 1790, and S. 1816 (Mar. 28, 1980) Serial No. 96-59, at 152-3.

The receiving-stolen-property exemption--which prevents agents from using the evidence-of-crime exception when the crime is receipt, possession, communication, or withholding of the same work product materials--was included to prevent law enforcement officials from classifying work product as "stolen goods" to justify seizing it. The Committee report gave as its primary example the case of a reporter who receives an under-the-table copy of a corporate memo discussing a defective product. Knowing the report to be stolen, the reporter might be guilty of receiving or possessing stolen property and thus unprotected by the PPA.

> The Committee believed that it would unduly broaden the suspect exception to use the reporter's crime of simple "possession" or "receipt" of the materials (or the similar secondary crimes of "withholding" or "communicating" the materials) as a vehicle for invoking the exception when the reporter himself had not participated in the commission of the crimes through which the materials were obtained.

H. Rep. No. 1064, 96th Cong., 2d Sess. 7 (emphasis added). In light of Congress's stated concern, perhaps this counter-exception does not apply when anything more than simple possession is involved: that is, possession is combined with the mens rea necessary to constitute some other offense (e.g., possession with intent to defraud). See 18 U.S.C. § 1029(a)(3) (making it a crime to "knowingly and with intent to defraud" possess fifteen or more devices which are counterfeit or unauthorized access devices); 18 U.S.C. § 1030(a)(6) (making it a crime to "knowingly and with intent to defraud" traffic in any password or similar information through which a computer may be accessed without authorization).

3. Documentary Materials

In addition to protecting work product, the PPA covers a second, larger class of items called "documentary materials." The statute defines this term in extraordinarily broad fashion--a definition which covers almost all forms of recorded information which are ". . . possessed by a person in connection with a purpose to disseminate to the public a newspaper, book, broadcast, or other similar form of public communication. . . ." 42 U.S.C. § 2000aa(b) (emphasis added). Specifically, "documentary materials" encompass

> materials upon which information is recorded, and includes, but is not limited to, written or printed materials, photographs, motion picture films, negatives, video tapes, audio tapes, and other mechanically, magnetically or electronically recorded cards, tapes, or discs, but does not include contraband or the fruits of a crime or things otherwise criminally possessed, or property designed or intended for use, or which is or has been used as, the means of committing a criminal offense.

42 U.S.C. § 2000aa-7(a).

As with "work product materials," the statute excludes from the definition of "documentary materials" any items which are contraband or the fruits or instrumentalities of a crime. 42 U.S.C. § 2000aa-7(a). Further, the two exceptions to the work-product search prohibition, discussed above, also apply to searches for documentary materials: they may be searched and seized under warrant in order to (1) prevent death or serious injury; or (2) to search for evidence of crime held by a suspect of that crime. (This last exception includes all its attendant internal exemptions, examined above, relating to crimes of possession or receipt.)

Additionally, the PPA allows agents to get a warrant for documentary materials under two more circumstances found at 42 U.S.C. § 2000aa(b):

(3) there is reason to believe that the giving of notice pursuant to a subpena duces tecum would result in the destruction, alteration, or concealment of such materials; or

(4) such materials have not been produced in response to a court order directing compliance with a subpena duces tecum, and--

    (A) all appellate remedies have been exhausted; or

    (B) there is reason to believe that the delay in an investigation or trial occasioned by further proceedings relating to the subpena would threaten the interests of justice.

In drawing these additional exceptions, Congress anticipated some of the factors a court might consider in determining whether relevant documentary materials could be lost to the government. These factors include whether there is (1) a close relationship (personal, family, or business) between the suspect and the person who holds the material, or (2) evidence that someone may hide, move, or destroy it. S. Rep. 96-874, 96th Cong., 2d Sess. 13, reprinted in U.S. Code Cong. & Admin. News 3950, 3959-60.

4. Computer Searches and the Privacy Protection Act

The Privacy Protection Act only applies to situations where law enforcement officers are searching or seizing (1) work product materials possessed by a person reasonably believed to have a purpose to disseminate to the public a newspaper, book, broadcast, or other similar form of public communication; or (2) documentary materials possessed by a person in connection with a purpose to disseminate to the public a newspaper, book, broadcast, or other similar form of public communication. 42 U.S.C. § 2000aa(a) and (b). Before the computer revolution, the statute's most obvious application was to traditional publishers, such as newspaper or book publishers. The legislative history makes clear, however, that the PPA was not intended to apply solely to the traditional news media but was meant to have a more sweeping application. As then-Assistant Attorney General for the Criminal Division Phillip B. Heymann testified:

> While we considered the option of a press-only bill, this format was rejected partially because of the extreme difficulties of arriving at a workable definition of the press, but more importantly because the First Amendment pursuits of others who are not members of the press establishment are equally as important and equally as susceptible to the chilling effect of governmental searches as are those of members of the news media.

H. Rep. No. 1064, 96th Cong., 2d Sess., Transcript of Statement on File, at 4.

With the widespread proliferation of personal computers, desktop publishing, and BBS services, virtually anyone with a personal computer and modem can disseminate to other members of the public (especially those who have appropriate hardware and software) a "newspaper. . .or other similar form of public communication." Thus, the scope of the PPA may have been greatly expanded as a practical consequence of the revolution in information technology--a result which was probably not envisioned by the Act's drafters.

Before searching any BBS, therefore, agents must carefully consider the restrictions of the PPA, along with its exceptions. Additionally, they should include any information bearing on the applicability of this statute (and its many exceptions and sub-exceptions) in the warrant affidavit. That said, it is also important to recognize that not every sysop who possesses information necessarily has an intent to disseminate it to the public. Nor is every BBS engaged in a "similar form of public communication."

    a. The Reasonable Belief Standard

When addressing work product materials, the statute, by its terms, only applies when the materials are possessed by a person "reasonably believed" to have a purpose to disseminate to the public a newspaper, book, broadcast, or other similar form of public communication." 42 U.S.C. § 2000aa(a). In non-computer contexts, the courts have concluded that it is not enough just to possess materials a professional reporter might possess. In addition, there must be some indication the person intended to disseminate them. In Lambert v. Polk County, Iowa, 723 F. Supp. 128 (S.D. Iowa 1989), for example, the plaintiff Lambert captured a fatal beating on videotape. Police investigating the incident seized the tape from Lambert and, shortly thereafter, Lambert contracted to sell the tape to a local television station. After the police refused to relinquish the tape, the television station and Lambert sued for injunctive relief claiming, among other things, a violation of 42 U.S.C. § 2000aa. While the district court granted relief on other grounds, it held that neither the television station nor Lambert was likely to prevail on a 42 U.S.C. § 2000aa claim. The television station was not the aggrieved party, and "there was nothing about the way Lambert presented himself [to the officers] that would have led them to reasonably believe that Lambert's purpose was to make a dissemination of the videotape to the public." Lambert, 723 F. Supp. at 132. But cf. Minneapolis Star & Tribune Co. v. United States, 713 F. Supp. 1308 (D. Minn. 1989) (plaintiffs from whom videotapes were seized at robbery scene were successful in PPA claim because agents apparently had independent knowledge that plaintiffs represented the established media).

The reasonable belief standard was also important in the district court opinion in Steve Jackson Games v. United States, 816 F. Supp. 432 (W.D. Tex. 1993), appeal filed on other grounds, (Sept. 17, 1993). To understand the scope of this opinion, it is important to put it in the context of its facts. In early 1990, the United States Secret

Service began investigating potential federal computer crimes under 18 U.S.C. § 1030. The Secret Service learned that a Bell South computer system had been invaded, and that the computer hackers were attempting to decrypt passwords which would allow them into computer systems belonging to the Department of Defense.

During the course of this investigation, the Secret Service received information implicating an individual who was employed by Steve Jackson Games, a Texas company that published books, magazines, box games, and related products. Steve Jackson Games used computers for a variety of business purposes, including operating an electronic bulletin board system ("BBS"). The Secret Service was informed that the suspect was one of the sysops of the Steve Jackson Games BBS, and that he could delete any documents or information in the Steve Jackson Games computers and bulletin board. Even so, none of the other sysops nor the company itself was ever a suspect in the investigation.

On February 28, 1990, the Secret Service obtained a federal warrant to search the offices of Steve Jackson Games and to seize various computer materials. The warrant covered:

> Computer hardware. . .and computer software. . . and written material and documents relating to the use of the computer system, documentation relating to the attacking of computers and advertising the results of computer attacks. . ., and financial documents and licensing information relative to the computer programs and equipment at [the company's offices] which constitute evidence, instrumentalities and fruits of federal crimes, including interstate transportation of stolen property (18 U.S.C. 2314) and interstate transportation of computer access information (18 U.S.C. 1030(a)(6)). This warrant is for the seizure of the above described computer and computer data and for the authorization to read information stored and contained in the above described computer and computer data.

The Secret Service executed the warrant on March 1, 1990. The agents seized two of thirteen functioning computers, and one other computer that was disassembled for repair. The Secret Service also seized a large number of floppy disks, a printer, other computer components, and computer software documentation. Steve Jackson Games immediately requested the return of the seized materials, but the agency retained most of the materials for several months before returning them. No criminal charges were brought as a result of this investigation.

In May 1991, plaintiffs (Steve Jackson Games; the company's owner and sole shareholder, Steve Jackson; and several individual users of the company's BBS) filed suit against the Secret Service and the United States, alleging violations of the Privacy Protection Act. They also claimed violations of the Stored Electronic Communications Statute, discussed in greater detail at "STORED ELECTRONIC COMMUNICATIONS," infra.

Following a bench trial, the court determined that the defendants had violated the Privacy Protection Act. The court held that the materials seized by the Secret Service (in particular, the draft of a book about to be published) included "work product materials" and "documentary materials" protected by the Privacy Protection Act. The court decided that seizing these materials did not immediately violate the statute, however, because at the time of the seizure, the agents did not (in the language of the statute) "reasonably believe[]" that Steve Jackson Games "ha[d] a purpose to disseminate to the public a newspaper, book, broadcast, or other similar form of public communication. . . ." This was true even though "only a few hours of investigation" would have revealed it. Id. at 440 n.8. However, the court held that a violation did occur on the day after the search when at least one agent learned the materials were protected by the statute and failed to return them promptly.

b. Similar Form of Public Communication

As noted above, the PPA applies only when the materials are possessed by a person reasonably believed to have a purpose to disseminate to the public "a newspaper, book, broadcast, or other similar form of public communication." 42 U.S.C. § 2000aa (emphasis added). Not every BBS will satisfy this standard. For example, a BBS that supplies unauthorized access codes to a small group of phone phreakers is not disseminating information to the public, nor is it engaging in a form of public communication similar to a newspaper. (Of course, the contraband exception will probably also apply in such a case).

The exact scope of the PPA remains uncertain, and the recent opinion in Steve Jackson Games does not clarify the issue. There the court found a cognizable PPA violation arising from the Secret Service's search and prolonged seizure of the successive drafts of a book Steve Jackson was soon to publish. But, just as important, the court did not hold that seizing the Steve Jackson BBS likewise violated the statute. Instead, the court held that "[i]n any event, it is the seizure of the 'work product materials' that leads to the liability of the United States Secret Service and the United States in this case." 816 F. Supp at 441. Indeed, one of the attorneys who represented Steve Jackson Games reached a similar conclusion:

> Though the results in the SJG case were very good on balance, a couple of major BBS issues were left for better resolution on another day. . . . [One issue] is the finding that SJG was a 'publisher' for purposes of the PPA. This holding. . .leaves the applicability of the PPA largely undetermined for other BBS'. Steve Jackson Games was a print publisher, and its computers were used to support the print publishing operation. What about BBS' that publish their information in electronic form only? What about BBS' that do not publish anything themselves in the traditional sense, but host public conferences? The SJG case simply does not give guidance on when a non-printing BBS qualifies as a publisher or journalistic operation for purposes of PPA protection. Rose, Steve Jackson Games Decision Stops the Insanity, Boardwatch, May 1993, at 53, 57.

c. Unique Problems: Unknown Targets and Commingled Materials

Applying the PPA to computer BBS searches is especially difficult for two reasons. First, early in an investigation, it is often impossible to tell whether the BBS sysop is involved in the crime under investigation. But unless agents have probable cause to arrest the sysop at the time of the search, the evidence-held-by-a-target exception in 42 U.S.C. § 2000aa would not apply.

Second, because most computers store thousands of pages of information, targets can easily mix contraband with protected work product or documentary materials. For example, a BBS trafficking in illegally copied software (which, along with the computers used to make the copies, is subject to forfeiture) may also be publishing a newsletter on stamp collecting. If agents seized the computer (or even all the data), the seizure would necessarily include both the pirated software and the newsletter. Assuming the stamp-collectors' newsletter was completely unrelated to the criminal copyright violations and also that it qualified as a "similar form of public communication," the seizure might violate the plain wording of the PPA.

There are, as yet, no cases addressing the status of PPA-protected materials which are commingled with contraband or evidence of crime. However, in construing the Fourth Amendment, the courts have recognized that there is sometimes no practical alternative to seizing non-evidentiary items and sorting them out later. See National City Trading Corp. v. United States, 635 F.2d 1020 (2d Cir. 1980) (space used by a law office and by a targeted business operation was so commingled that the entire suite, really being one set of offices, was properly subject to search); United States v. Hillyard, 677 F.2d 1336, 1340 (9th Cir. 1982) ("Cases may arise in which stolen goods are intermingled with and practically indistinguishable from legitimate goods. If commingling prevents on site inspection, and no practical alternative exists, the entire property may be seizable, at least temporarily."); United States v. Tropp, 725 F. Supp. 482, 487-88 (D. Wyo. 1989) ("Some evidence not pertinent to the warrant was seized. . .only because it had been commingled or misfiled with relevant documents. That evidence was returned. . . . In sum, the search warrant comported with the mandate of the Fourth Amendment and the search conducted pursuant thereto was not unreasonable."). (For a more extensive discussion of commingled materials and off-site searches, see "DECIDING WHETHER TO CONDUCT THE SEARCH ON-SITE OR TO REMOVE HARDWARE TO ANOTHER LOCATION," supra.) Of course, these commingling cases involve the Fourth Amendment, not 42 U.S.C. § 2000aa, and it remains to be seen whether these holdings will apply to the Privacy Protection Act.

5. Approval of Deputy Assistant Attorney General Required

On September 15, 1993, Deputy Attorney General Philip B. Heymann issued a memorandum which requires that all applications for a warrant issued under 42 U.S.C. § 2000aa(a) must be authorized by the Assistant Attorney General for the Criminal Division (AAG), upon the recommendation of the U.S. Attorney or (for direct Department of Justice cases) the supervising Department of Justice attorney.

On December 9, 1993, Jo Ann Harris, the Assistant Attorney General (AAG) for the Criminal Division, delegated this authority by memorandum to the Deputy Assistant Attorneys General of the Criminal Division. There are emergency procedures for expediting the approval in cases which require it. All requests for authorization--emergency or routine--should be directed to the Chief, Legal Support Unit of the Office of Enforcement Operations in the Criminal Division (202-514-0856).

If agents or prosecutors are planning a search and seizure of electronic evidence in a case in which the PPA may apply, we urge them to contact the Computer Crime Unit (202-514-1026) immediately to discuss the investigation and any new legal developments in this area.

6. Liability Under the Privacy Protection Act

The Privacy Protection Act ("PPA") creates a civil cause for damages resulting from a search or seizure of materials in violation of the Act. The PPA states that an aggrieved person shall have a cause of action

(1) against the United States, against a State which has waived its sovereign immunity under the Constitution to a claim for damages resulting from a violation of this chapter, or against any other governmental unit, all of which shall be liable for violations of this chapter by their officers or employees while acting within the scope or under color of their office or employment; and

(2) against an officer or employee of a State who has violated this chapter while acting within the scope of or under color of his office or employment, if such State has not waived its sovereign immunity as provided in paragraph (1).

42 U.S.C. § 2000aa-6(a).

In Davis v. Gracey, 111 F.3d 1472 (10th Cir. 1997), plaintiff brought a civil suit against the city of Oklahoma City, the Oklahoma City Police Department, and the individual officers who had executed a search of a BBS, alleging that the seizure of the computer system which contained shareware intended for future publication, violated the Privacy Protection Act.[9] The police had obtained a warrant that authorized the search and seizure of "equipment, . . . and other paraphernalia pertaining to the distribution or display of pornographic material in violation of state obscenity laws." During the execution the warrant, officers determined that the materials could

---

[9] The plaintiff also alleged that the defendants had violated the Electronic Communications Privacy Act (because the seized system also contained subscriber e-mail) and the Fourth Amendment. See "STORED ELECTRONIC COMMUNICATIONS," infra.

be remotely accessed via the plaintiff's BBS system. As a result, the officers seized the computer equipment used to operate this BBS as an instrumentality of the crime.

The plaintiff asserted that because the computer system contained shareware which the plaintiff planned to "publish" on a forthcoming CD-ROM, the seizure of the computer equipment violated the Privacy Protection Act. Noting that all municipal entities had previously been dismissed from the case,[10] leaving only the police officers in their individual capacities, the district court had granted summary judgment, holding that the defendants were entitled to the "good faith" defense under 42 U.S.C. § 2000aa-6(b) because the officers had relied on a warrant. On appeal, the Tenth Circuit held that it lacked subject matter jurisdiction over the PPA claim. According to the court, a PPA action may only be brought against a governmental entity, unless the applicable state has not waived sovereign immunity. In that event, state employees may be sued in their official capacities. By its terms, however, the PPA does not authorize a suit against municipal officers or employees in their individual capacities. Thus, even though the parties in this action had stipulated to jurisdiction under the PPA, the court dismissed the plaintiff's PPA claim, sua sponte, for lack of subject matter jurisdiction.

In Oklahoma v. One Pioneer CD-Rom Changer, 891 P.2d 600 (Okla. App. 1994), a companion civil forfeiture case to Davis v. Gracey, the owner of the equipment at issue sought to prevent forfeiture of his computer equipment by claiming, inter alia, that the computers in question contained information protected by the PPA. Pursuant to an investigation for distributing obscene material, the police had seized several CD-ROM drives, power supplies, modems, and computers, all of which were connected to a network.

The owner of the equipment contended that because the system contained 500 megabytes of non-obscene software that was to be pressed into a compact disc to be published, the search and seizure violated the PPA's requirement that such publication materials be obtained by subpoena. The owner contended that by not using a subpoena, the police had violated his First Amendment rights. In rejecting this claim, the court held that even if the PPA had been violated, such a violation would not shield equipment seized pursuant to an otherwise lawful search and seizure from forfeiture under state law.

C. STORED ELECTRONIC COMMUNICATIONS

There are special statutory rules protecting some electronic communications in electronic storage. Anyone who provides an electronic communication service or remote computing services to the public, is prohibited by 18 U.S.C. § 2702 from voluntarily disclosing the contents of the electronic communications it stores or maintains on the service. A "remote computing service" means the provision to the public of computer storage or processing services by means of an electronic communications system. 18 U.S.C. § 2711(2).

It is not entirely clear what sorts of electronic communications services will be found to provide "public" service. Generally speaking, "public" means available to all who seek the service, even if there is some requirement, such as a fee. It is probably safe to assume that any service permitting "guest" or "visitor" access is "public." On the other hand, the term should not be read to cover business networks open only to employees for company business. If that business network is connected to the Internet (an extensive world-wide network), it may be part of a "public" system, but this does not necessarily mean that the corporate LAN (local-area network) becomes a "public" service.

There are several important exceptions to § 2702's non-disclosure rule, including (1) a provision under 18 U.S.C. § 2702(b)(3) allowing a person or entity to disclose the contents of a communication with the lawful consent of the originator, an addressee, or the intended recipient of such communication (or the subscriber in the case of a

---

[10] The reason for this dismissal was not provided.

remote computing service), and (2) a provision under 18 U.S.C. § 2702(b)(6) allowing disclosure to a law enforcement agency if the contents were inadvertently obtained and appear to pertain to the commission of a crime.

For the government to obtain access to a "stored electronic communication," it must follow the dictates of 18 U.S.C. § 2703, which sets out different rules depending upon how long the particular communication has been in electronic storage. That section provides that "a governmental entity may require the disclosure by a provider of electronic communication service of the contents of an electronic communication, that is in electronic storage . . .for one hundred and eighty days or less, only pursuant to a warrant issued under the Federal Rules of Criminal Procedure or equivalent state warrant." 18 U.S.C. § 2703(a) (emphasis added). If the information has been stored for more than 180 days, prosecutors may use either a Rule 41 search warrant (without notice to the customer or subscriber) or an administrative subpoena, grand jury subpoena, trial subpoena, or a court order pursuant to 18 U.S.C. § 2703(d) (with notice to the customer or subscriber).

The two terms underlined above merit further discussion. First of all, it is important to note that not all electronically stored communications are covered by this section. The electronic communication must be transmitted on a system that affects interstate or foreign commerce, 18 U.S.C. § 2510(12), and must be in electronic storage. "Electronic storage" means any temporary, intermediate storage of a wire or electronic communication incidental to the electronic transmission thereof or any backup of this communication. 18 U.S.C. § 2510(17).

To understand the importance of this definition, it is critical to know how electronic mail works. Generally speaking, e-mail messages are not transmitted directly from the sender's machine to the recipient's machine; rather, the e-mail message goes from the sending machine to an e-mail server where it is stored (i.e., kept in "electronic storage"). A message is then sent from the server to the addressee indicating that a message for the addressee has been stored. The actual message remains on the server, however, until the addressee retrieves it by having a copy sent to his machine. Often, both the sender and receiver can delete the e-mail from the server.

Section 2703 protects the electronic communication while it is stored in the server in this intermediate state.[11] Once a message is opened, however, its storage is no longer "temporary" nor "incidental to. . .transmission," and it thus takes on the legal character of all other stored data. Therefore, the statute does not apply to all stored communications, such as word processing files residing on a hard drive, even when these files were once transmitted via e-mail.

The other highlighted term--"require the disclosure"--seems to suggest that § 2703 only applies when the government seeks to compel the service provider to produce the electronic mail, not when government agents actually seize it. With this in mind, the statute's cross-reference to Rule 41 is confusing, because Rule 41 authorizes the government to "seize" items, not to "require [their] disclosure." To speak in terms of requiring the disclosure of electronic mail, rather than of seizing it, seems to connote a process of serving subpoenas, not of executing warrants.

On the other hand, Congress may have simply assumed that most system providers would be disinterested in the "search," and that, as a practical matter, the service provider would actually retrieve and turn over to the government those files of suspect-users listed in the warrant. In mentioning Rule 41, Congress may not have been focusing on who would actually do the retrieval, but rather on what level of proof would be required before electronic communications in electronic storage could be procured for a criminal investigation. Therefore, the statute's references to warrants and Rule 41 seem designed to insure that, no matter who actually searches the

---

[11] When a sysop backs up the mail server to protect against system failure, all e-mails stored on the server will be copied. Thus, if the e-mail is later deleted from the server, the backup copy remains. The statute protects this copy as well. 18 U.S.C. § 2510(17)(B).

system, the government will be held to a probable-cause standard--even if the system provider would have been just as willing to honor a subpoena. See H.R. Rep. No. 647, 99th Cong., 2d Sess., at 68 ("The Committee required the government to obtain a search warrant because it concluded that the contents of a message in storage were protected by the Fourth Amendment . . . . To the extent that the record is kept beyond [180 days] it is closer to a regular business record maintained by a third party and, therefore, deserving of a different standard of protection.").

Indeed, it is entirely reasonable to read this statute as Congress's effort to regulate primarily the duties of service providers to protect the privacy of their subscribers in regard to all third parties, including law enforcement. The statute may not have fully contemplated those cases in which the system provider (rather than the subscriber) is, or may be, implicated in the criminal investigation.

In October 1994, Congress amended the Stored Wire and Electronic Communications Act by adding provisions for governmental access to subscriber or transactional information (excluding the content of communications).

Specifically, if the government is acting without the consent of the customer or subscriber, governmental entities must use some compulsory process to obtain subscriber or transactional information. The government may use a subpoena if the material sought is the "name, address, local and long distance telephone toll billing records, telephone number or other subscriber number or identity, and length of service of a subscriber to or customer of such service and the types of services the subscriber or customer utilized. . . ." 18 U.S.C. § 2703(C).

There is, unfortunately, no case law clearly addressing this issue. In a recent civil suit, the government was held liable for seizing electronic mail on an electronic bulletin board service (BBS), even though the agents had a valid warrant.[12] Steve Jackson Games, Inc. v. U.S. Secret Service, 816 F. Supp. 432 (W.D. Tex. 1993), appeal filed on other grounds, (Sept. 17, 1993). In that case, plaintiffs sued following a search by the Secret Service of computers and other electronic storage devices which belonged to the company. (For a more complete description of the facts of the case, see the discussion at "The Reasonable Belief Standard," supra.) One of the computers seized by the Secret Service was the computer used by Steve Jackson Games to operate its BBS. The hard disk of the BBS computer contained a number of private e-mail messages, some of which had not yet been accessed by their addressees. The district court found that the Secret Service read e-mail messages on the computer and subsequently deleted certain information and communications, either intentionally or accidentally, before returning the computer to Steve Jackson Games. Id. at 441. Here, the court held that the Secret Service "exceeded the Government's authority under the statute" by seizing and examining the contents of "all of the electronic communications stored in the [company's] bulletin board" without complying with the statute's requirements for government access. The court's opinion never addressed, however, the interplay between § 2703 and Rule 41, so it sheds no light on the proper interpretation of § 2703(a). In fact, the court never cited § 2703(a) at all. Instead, the court discussed the requirements of § 2703(d), a provision that allows the government to get a court order, upon a showing that the communication sought is relevant to a legitimate law enforcement inquiry, when the communication has been in storage more than 180 days or is held by a remote computing service. (The court did not find how long the searched communications were in storage, but did hold that Steve Jackson was a remote computing service.) Even under this lesser standard--§ 2703(a) requires a search warrant based upon probable cause--the court held that the government's search was improper, noting that the government did not advise the magistrate, by affidavit or otherwise, that the BBS contained private electronic communications between users, nor how the disclosure of the contents of those communications related to the investigation.

---

[12] Pursuant to 18 U.S.C. § 2707(d), a good faith reliance on a court warrant is a complete defense to any civil action. The court summarily rejected the defense, stating that it "declines to find this defense by a preponderance of the evidence in this case." Id. at 443.

On appeal, the Fifth Circuit further addressed the privacy issues raised in the Steve Jackson Games case to decide whether the seizure of a computer, used to operate an electronic bulletin board system and containing private unopened electronic mail, constitutes an unlawful interception under 18 U.S.C. § 2511. The statute defines "intercept" as "the aural or other acquisition of the contents of any wire, electronic, or oral communication through the use of any electronic, mechanical, or other device." 18 U.S.C. § 2510(4).

The Fifth Circuit held that while the interception of electronic communications in transit would violate 18 U.S.C. § 2511(1)(a), that statute does not proscribe the seizure of electronic communications while in "electronic storage" as defined at 18 U.S.C. § 2510(17). Steve Jackson Games v. United States Secret Service, 36 F.3d 457, 461 (5th Cir. 1994). At the same time, the court upheld the district court's determination that the seizure in this case violated 18 U.S.C. § 2701.

The court relied on the decision in United States v. Turk, 526 F.2d 654 (5th Cir.), cert. denied, 429 U.S. 823 (1976), which held that an interception does not occur when the acquisition of the communications is not contemporaneous with their transmission. The appellants argued that Turk did not apply, because that case did not address the situation where the government both acquires the communication prior to delivery of the communication and prevents its delivery. In such an instance, the appellant argued, an interception has occurred.

The court rejected this contention, relying on the integrated structure of § 2510 and § 2701. Congress clearly intended to treat wire communications (human voice) differently from electronic ones in this regard. Although § 2701 treats the unauthorized access of e-mail and voicemail the same (if they were in "electronic storage," as defined), the rules for law enforcement access to these two types are different. Indeed § 2703 explicitly lays out a regime for government's acquisition of stored electronic communications only. Thus, government agents who need to acquire wire communications in electronic storage should look to the wiretap statute rather than § 2703. Differences in the definitions of "wire communication" and "electronic communication" in § 2510 underscore this. "Wire communication," as defined at 18 U.S.C. § 2510(1) also covers those in "electronic storage," while the definition of "electronic communication" does not. "Congress did not intend for 'intercept' to apply to 'electronic communications' when those communications are in 'electronic storage.'" Steve Jackson Games, 36 F.3d at 462.

The District Court for the District of Nevada addressed a similar argument in Bohach v. Reno, 932 F. Supp. 1232 (D. Nev. 1996). In Bohach, two police officers used a police-owned computer-controlled paging system to send communications that later became the subject of an internal affairs investigation. The officers had entered the messages on a police-owned computer terminal that forwarded each message to the police-operated computer paging system, which logged each message and then forwarded a copy to the individual pagers. Internal Affairs recovered the messages in question from the log file on the paging computer.

The plaintiffs brought suit claiming that the department illegally intercepted the messages in violation of 18 U.S.C. § 2511 by recovering them from the log files. Relying on Steve Jackson Games, the court held that, by definition, a communication in electronic storage cannot be "intercepted" under the definition in 18 U.S.C. § 2510(4). Instead, stored electronic communications are governed under 18 U.S.C. §§ 2701-2711. Because 18 U.S.C. § 2701 allows service providers to access communications in electronic storage and the police department was the service provider for the paging service, the court held that neither the department nor its employees could be held liable for violating 18 U.S.C. § 2701.

In Davis v. Gracey, 111 F.3d 1472 (10th Cir. 1997), in addition to claiming PPA violations by Oklahoma City police officers, the plaintiff also claimed that the search and seizure violated 18 U.S.C. § 2701 (see "Liability Under the PPA" supra). In seizing the computer that contained and had distributed obscene images, police incidentally seized approximately 150,000 e-mail messages on the same machine, some of which had not been opened. The plaintiff contended that the officers "obtain[ed] . . . or prevent[ed] authorized access to a[n] electronic communication while it is in electronic storage" within the meaning of 18 U.S.C. § 2701(a).

In making this claim, the plaintiff relied on Steve Jackson Games. The Tenth Circuit, however, distinguished Steve Jackson Games on two separate grounds. First, in Steve Jackson Games, the owner of the seized computer was not a target of the investigation, whereas in Davis, the owner of the BBS was under investigation for distributing and displaying obscene materials. Second, unlike Steve Jackson Games, where the Secret Service read and deleted e-mail messages stored on the seized computers, the officers in Davis did not attempt to read the seized e-mail. Davis, 111 F.3d at 1483.

Having held that the officers did not gain access to or read the seized e-mail, the court addressed whether the incidental seizure of electronic communications, standing alone, is a violation of ECPA. The court assumed, *without deciding*, that the defendants had accessed a stored electronic communication in violation of § 2701. The court held, however, that because the officers relied on a warrant supported by probable cause, the officers were entitled to a "good faith" defense because the seizure of the stored electronic communications was incidental to the execution of the warrant. Davis, 111 F.3d at 1472.

The plaintiff also claimed that the officers executing the search were not entitled to the "good faith" defense because prior to obtaining the warrant, they knew that the same computer system was an e-mail server and did not include this in the warrant affidavit. The court, however, held that as a matter of law the seizure of the e-mail messages fit within a good-faith defense to liability under § 2707(e), which states that "reliance on . . . a court warrant or order, a grand jury subpoena, a legislative authorization, or a statutory authorization . . . is a complete defense to any civil or criminal action brought under this chapter." Even the inference of bad faith while procuring the warrant did not eliminate the officers' ability to rely on a valid warrant supported by probable cause. Davis, 111 F.3d at 1484. In reaching this conclusion, however, the court emphasized that the seized computer system not only contained evidence of crime, it also contained contraband and was itself an instrumentality of crime. As a matter of policy, CCIPS strongly recommends advising magistrates whenever target computer systems are also mail servers. If prosecutors have any questions in this regard, they are encouraged to contact us at (202) 514-1026.

In Tucker v. Waddell, 83 F.3d 688 (4th Cir. 1996), the court held that no governmental liability attaches under 18 U.S.C.§ 2703(c) for the use of improper subpoena. In 1991, police officers in Durham, North Carolina served two improper subpoenas on Cora Tucker's telephone service provider for her subscriber information. (Plaintiff's counsel has advised that the administrative subpoenas were issued without the authorization required by state statute.) Tucker sued the city and the officers under 18 U.S.C. § 2703(c).

Defendants argued successfully that a cause of action does not lie against a government actor under § 2703(c). In accepting this view, the Fourth Circuit relied upon the fact that § 2703(c) "does not expressly proscribe any action by governmental entities or their employees. Rather, § 2703(c) only prohibits the action of [communications] providers . . . . " 83 F.3d at 692.

The Court found this conclusion reinforced by the fact that sections 2703(a) and (b), by contrast, "focus on the conduct of governmental entities." As a result, the Court concluded (in dicta) that government violations of those provisions may give rise to civil liability (citing Steve Jackson Games v. United States Secret Service, 36 F.3d 457, 461 (5th Cir. 1994)) against the government.

In the final footnote of the opinion, the Fourth Circuit held out the possibility that "[a]rguably, it might be possible for a government entity to violate § 2703(c) by aiding and abetting or conspiring in the provider's violation. Id. at 693 n.6. Because Tucker failed to plead either of these theories, her claims were dismissed.

In <u>Oklahoma v. One Pioneer CD-Rom Changer</u>, 891 P.2d 600, 606 (Okla. App. 1994), a companion civil forfeiture case to <u>Davis v. Gracey</u>, the owner of a BBS who was being charged with distributing obscene material, sought to halt forfeiture of his computer equipment by the state by asserting that the computer system seized by the police contained e-mail messages protected by the 18 U.S.C. § 2510 <u>et. seq</u>. The state had originally offered to return the messages as long as this did not compromise its criminal case. The court held that defendant did not make a sufficient showing that the "lawful, physical seizure of computer equipment which was allegedly used to distribute obscene material and which contained private communications in the form of e-mail, constituted an 'interception'" under ECPA.

In most cases, of course, the electronic communications sought will be in storage 180 days or less, and, therefore, may be obtained "<u>only</u> pursuant to a warrant." 18 U.S.C. § 2703(a) (emphasis added). When preparing a warrant to search a computer, investigators should specifically indicate whether there is electronic mail on the target computer. If the agents intend to read those electronic communications, the warrant should identify whose mail is to be read, and establish that those electronic communications are subject to search under Fed. R. Crim. P. 41(b) (Search and Seizure, Property Which May Be Seized With a Warrant).

VI. DRAFTING THE WARRANT

A. DRAFTING A WARRANT TO SEIZE HARDWARE

If a computer component is contraband, an instrumentality of the offense, or evidence, the focus of the warrant should be on the computer component itself and not on the information it contains. The warrant should be as specific as possible about which computer components to seize and, consistent with other types of warrants, it should describe the item to be seized in as much detail as possible, especially if there may be two or more computers at the scene. Include, where possible, the manufacturer, model number, and any other identifying information regarding the device. (For further information, <u>see</u> "SAMPLE COMPUTER LANGUAGE FOR SEARCH WARRANTS," APPENDIX A.)

It may also be appropriate to seek a "no-knock" warrant in cases where knocking and announcing may cause (1) the officer or any other individual to be hurt; (2) the suspect to flee; or (3) the evidence to be destroyed. (<u>See</u> "Seeking Authority for a No-Knock Warrant," <u>infra</u>.)

In computer cases, the evidence is especially perishable, and agents should never underestimate the subjects of the investigation. They may be knowledgeable about telecommunications and may have anticipated a search. As a result, computers and memory devices on telephone speed dialers may be "booby-trapped" to erase if they are improperly entered or if the power is cut off.

In <u>Oklahoma v. One Pioneer CD-Rom Changer</u>, 891 P.2d 600 (Okla. App. 1994), the operator of the BBS contended that the warrant authorizing seizure of the computer equipment was overbroad because it did not describe the networking equipment seized, even though the police knew of its existence. The warrant permitted the police to search the premises for "obscene materials" and specified "equipment, order materials, papers, membership lists, and other paraphernalia pertaining to the distribution or display of pornographic material in violation of state obscenity laws." The appellate court upheld the granting of summary judgment against the owner of the BBS and held that the warrant was as specific as it could be with regard to the officer's knowledge. Furthermore, the equipment and the status messages on the monitor were in plain view to the officers, thus there was an exception to the Fourth Amendment's warrant requirement.

In <u>Massachusetts v. Pasqualino</u>, 3 Mass.L.Rptr. 382 (Mass. Super. 1995), the defendant filed a motion to suppress items seized from his house in a search for stolen computer equipment. Police obtained a warrant that allowed them to search "any room in the house where any computer, or piece of computer, as listed may be concealed from view, including the basement, including a shed located in the backyard as well as any motor vehicle on the property." The defendant claimed that this language did not meet the particularity requirement of the Fourth Amendment because it mostly described the place, not the items, to be searched. Despite the poor drafting, the court upheld the warrant based on the manner in which it was executed; while executing the search, the police relied upon the search warrant affidavit that sufficiently described the items to be seized, checking off each item as they progressed.

In Iowa v. Gogg, 561 N.W.2d 360 (Iowa 1997), a confidential informant has said that a computer, modem, and telephone similar to those stolen from a local business were located at the defendant's residence. The warrant for these items was held invalid (due to lack of probable cause) because there was no showing in the affidavit that the items observed by the informant were unique or unusual. Besides, telephones and computer equipment are often found in homes. "Where items to be seized are not unique, mere similarity to property involved in a crime will not support probable cause." Id. at 366 (citing Iowa v. Seager, 341 N.W.2d 420, 427 (Iowa 1983)).

In Schalk v. Texas, 767 S.W.2d 441 (Ct. App. Tex. 1988), the appellant was found guilty of theft of trade secrets for knowingly copying five separate computer programs that belonged to his former employer. The district attorney obtained a search warrant for the premises of the appellant's new employer. The warrant allowed the search and seizure of all magnetic media tapes, including those bearing a certain brand name and all documents labeled as the first company's trade secrets. Additionally, the warrant specified the access codes and passwords necessary to access the trade secrets. The appellant contended that the search warrant failed to describe the items to be seized with sufficient particularity. The court upheld the validity of the warrant noting that "[t]o describe the 'trade secret' itself in sufficient detail to meet the argument of appellant would be to reveal the precise secret information that was not intended to be revealed." Id. at 453.

B. DRAFTING A WARRANT TO SEIZE INFORMATION

1. Describing the Place to be Searched

Until recently, when a warrant specified where a search was to occur, the exercise was bound by physical laws: agents took objects they could carry from places they could touch. But computers create a "virtual" world where data exists "in effect or essence though not in actual fact or form." The American Heritage Dictionary, (2d ed. 1983).

Rule 41(a) failed to anticipate the creation of this "virtual" world. By its very terms, a warrant may be issued "for a search of property. . .within the district." Specifically, it provides that,

> Upon the request of a federal law enforcement officer or an attorney for the government, a search warrant authorized by this rule may be issued (1) by a federal magistrate, or a state court of record within the federal district, for a search of property or for a person within the district and (2) by a federal magistrate for a search of property or for a person either within or outside the district if the property or person is within the district when the warrant is sought but might move outside the district before the warrant is executed.

Fed. R. Crim. P. 41(a) (emphasis added).

In a networked environment, however, the physical location of stored information may be unknown. For example, an informant indicates that the business where he works has a duplicate set of books used to defraud the Internal Revenue Service. He has seen these books on his computer terminal in his Manhattan office. Based upon this information, agents obtain a warrant in the Southern District of New York authorizing a search for, and seizure of, these records. With the informant's help, agents access his computer workstation, bring up the incriminating documents, and copy them to a diskette. Unfortunately, unbeknownst to the agents, prosecutor, or informant, the file server that held those documents was physically located in another office, building, district, state, or country.[13]

There are, under Rule 41, at least three variations on this problem. First, information is stored off-site, and agents know this second site is within the same district. Second, information is stored off-site, but this second site is outside the district. Third, information is stored off-site, but its location is unknown.

a. General Rule: Obtain a Second Warrant

Whenever agents know that the information is stored at a location other than the one described in the warrant, they should obtain a second warrant. In some cases, that will mean going to another federal district--nearby or across the country. If the data is located overseas, the Criminal Division's Office of International Affairs (202-514-0000) and our foreign law enforcement counterparts can assist in obtaining and executing the foreign warrant. The Computer Crime Unit (202-514-1026) can help in expediting international computer crime investigations.

b. Handling Multiple Sites Within the Same District

Assuming that the server was simply in another office on the same floor, the warrant might well be broad enough to cover the search. Indeed, even with physical searches, courts have sometimes allowed a second but related search to be covered by one warrant. In United States v. Judd, 687 F. Supp. 1052, 1057-9 (N.D. Miss. 1988), aff'd 889 F.2d 1410 (5th Cir. 1989), cert. denied, 494 U.S. 1036 (1989), the FBI executed a search warrant for records at Address #1, and learned that additional records were located at Address #2. Without obtaining a second warrant, and relying only on the first, the agents entered Address #2 and seized the additional records.

The district court framed the question like this: was the partially incorrect description in the warrant sufficient to include both business addresses, which in this case, happened to be in the same building? The court held that since Address #2 was "part" of Address #1, and since they were both used for the business pursuits of the same company, the search was proper. See also United States v. Prout, 526 F.2d 380, 388 (5th Cir.) (search of adjacent separate apartment that was omitted from the warrant was proper), cert. denied, 429 U.S. 840 (1976).

It becomes more problematic when the server is in another building, one clearly not described in the warrant. In situations where a second warrant was not obtained, there is still an argument that remotely accessing information from a computer named in the warrant does not violate Fourth Amendment law. See discussion of United States v. Rodriguez, infra.

c. Handling Multiple Sites in Different Districts

What if, unbeknownst to the agents executing the search warrant, the property seized was located in another district? Although the defense could argue that the court lacked jurisdiction to issue the warrant, the agents executing the warrant never left the district in which the warrant was issued. Moreover, in some cases, it may be difficult, if not impossible, to ascertain the physical location of a given file server and obtain the evidence any other way. In these cases, prosecutors should argue that the warrant authorized the seizure.

---

[13] In this example, the storage of information in an out-of-district server was fortuitous; i.e., a product of the network architecture. In fact, hackers may deliberately store their information remotely. This allows them to recover after their personal computers fail (essentially by creating off-site backup copies). Additionally, if agents seize a hacker's personal computer, no evidence will be found, and the hacker can still copy or destroy the remotely stored data by accessing it from another computer.

If agents have reason to believe the second computer may be in a different district, however, the issue should be addressed with the magistrate. While some courts may strictly construe the language of Rule 41 and require data to be retrieved only from the district where it permanently resides, other courts may follow the logic of the recent Second Circuit case United States v. Rodriguez, 968 F.2d 130 (2d Cir.), cert. denied, 113 S. Ct. 140 (1992). Although that case addressed the issue of "place" under the wiretap statute (18 U.S.C. § 2518) and not under Rule 41, the constraints of the statute were quite similar. ("Upon such application the judge may enter an ex parte order . . . approving interception . . . within the territorial jurisdiction of the court in which the judge is sitting . . . . ")

In Rodriguez, the Second Circuit held that a wiretap occurs in two places simultaneously: the place where the tapped phone is located and the place where law enforcement overhears it. If those two places are in different jurisdictions, a judge in either one can authorize the interception. In this case, the DEA was tapping several phones in New York from its Manhattan headquarters. In addition, they tapped a phone in New Jersey by leasing a phone line from the service carrier and running it to the same New York office from which they monitored all the calls on all the lines. The court cited "sound policy reasons" for allowing one court to authorize all the taps, since all the reception and monitoring occurred in that same jurisdiction.

If the DEA can lease a phone line running from New Jersey to New York in order to consolidate its efforts, courts may also find it completely reasonable to conclude that computer network data searches, like telecommunications interceptions, can occur in more than one place.

In United States v. Denman, 100 F.3d 399, 402 (5th Cir. 1996), cert. denied, 117 S. Ct. 1256 (1997), the Fifth Circuit upheld the legality of a wiretap order issued in one district on phone lines located in another district. The defendant contended that the wiretap evidence should be suppressed because the wiretap order was jurisdictionally defective. Relying on United States v. Rodriguez, 968 F.2d 130 (2d Cir.), cert. denied, 506 U.S. 847 (1992), the court held that for the purposes of Title III, the interception "includes both the location of a tapped telephone and the original listening post, and that judges in either jurisdiction have authority under Title III to issue wiretap orders." The Denman court noted that this interpretation "aids an important goal of Title III, to protect privacy interests, by enabling one judge to supervise an investigation that spans more than one judicial district."

In United States v. Ramirez, 112 F.3d 849, 852 (7th Cir. 1997), the government had obtained, in the Western District of Wisconsin, an order authorizing the wiretapping of a cellular phone line primarily used by a defendant in a drug conspiracy who commuted between his home in Wisconsin and St. Paul, Minnesota where he sold drugs. The listening post was set up in Minnesota. Shortly after setting up the listening post, the government learned that the cellular phone was not being used by the defendant, but was being used by another person who was discussing the drug conspiracy the government was investigating. The defendants challenged the admissibility of the wiretap evidence.

According to Judge Posner, a literal interpretation of 18 U.S.C. § 2518(3):[14]

> would not allow a judge in the Western District of Wisconsin to authorize the interception by a stationary listening post in Minnesota of calls from a cellular phone located in Minnesota, but it would authorize the judge to authorize the interception by a stationary listening post in Minnesota of calls from a cellular phone in the Western District of Wisconsin, by a stationary listening post in

---

[14] This subsection authorizes a district judge to approve a wiretap "within the territorial jurisdiction of the court in which the judge is sitting (and outside that jurisdiction but within the United States in the case of a mobile interception device authorized by a Federal Court within such jurisdiction)."

that district of calls from anywhere, and by a mobile listening post (or other mobile interception device) authorized in the western district but located anywhere in the United States of calls from anywhere. The literal reading makes very little sense. It would mean that if as in this case the listening post is stationary and is for practical reasons located outside the district in which the crime is being investigated and the cellular phone is believed to be located, the government, to be sure of being able to tap the phone if it is carried outside the district (as is it is quite likely to be, given its mobility), must obtain the wiretap order from the district court in which the listening post is located, even though that location is entirely fortuitous from the standpoint of the criminal investigation.

Id. at 852.

Relying on Denman and Rodriguez, the Ramirez court held that it would make far more sense that the term "mobile interception device," for the purposes of 18 U.S.C. § 2518(3), "means a device for intercepting mobile communications." The court, therefore, found that the district court in the Western District of Wisconsin could authorize a wiretap on a cellular phone "regardless of where the phone or listening post was." The court reasoned that to limit the scope of a court order would serve no interest in protecting privacy because "the government can always seek an order from the district of the listening post for nationwide surveillance of cellular phone calls." Id. at 853.

    d. Information at an Unknown Site

Unfortunately, it may be impossible to isolate the location of information. What then? Does a warrant authorizing the search and seizure of one computer automatically allow agents to search and seize any data that it has sent to other computers? If the original warrant does not allow investigators to physically enter another building and search another computer, does it permit them to "go" there electronically, using as their vehicle only the computer that they have been authorized to search? What if the other computer is physically located in another district? Finally, if the warrant does not authorize seizing the off-site data (no matter how it is obtained), are there circumstances under which it could be taken without a warrant?

If agents have reason to believe there is off-site storage but no way to identify the site, they should tell the magistrate. Of course, the standard to use in evaluating a description in the warrant is whether "the description is such that the officer with a search warrant can, with reasonable effort ascertain and identify the place intended." Steele v. United States, 267 U.S. 498, 503 (1925). See also United States v. Darensbourg, 520 F.2d 985, 987 (5th Cir. 1975), quoting United States v. Sklaroff, 323 F. Supp. 296, 321 (S.D. Fla. 1971).

Drawing upon Steele, it may be prudent for the warrant to specifically include any data stored off-site in devices which the subject computer has been configured by its operator to readily access, and which have been regularly used as a component of the subject computer. This is more likely to be upheld if the government has reason to believe the suspect is using an off-site computer and has no way to determine where it is, either geographically or electronically, until the suspect's computer is examined. In such cases, the affidavit should indicate why a complete address is not available, including any attempts that have been made to get the information (e.g., informants, undercover agents, pen registers, electronic or video surveillance) on the subject computer. It will be important to show a clear relationship between the computer described in the warrant and the second computer at the different location. If the second computer is somewhere in the same district, that also holds the second data search closer to the physical terms of Rule 41.

    e. Information/Devices Which Have Been Moved

What happens if the targets: (1) move computers and storage devices (disk drives, floppies, etc.) between two or more districts (e.g., a laptop computer); or (2) transmit data to off-site devices located in another district?

Under Rule 41(a)(2), a magistrate in one district can issue a warrant to be executed in another district provided the property was "within" District A when the warrant was issued. Again, this rule is relatively easy to apply when physical devices are the object of the search. But how does that rule apply to electronic data? If a suspect creates data in District A and uploads[15] that data to a computer in District B, has he "moved" it between districts, thus authorizing a District A magistrate to issue a warrant for a search of the District B computer, even though the District B computer was never physically transported from or even located in District A?

The key to resolving these issues is understanding what agents are seizing. If they are going to seize the computer hardware in District B to get the data, they must get a warrant in District B (after all, the District B computer was never moved). If agents are simply copying data, however, it could be argued that the data uploaded from District A to District B is property that has been moved. Since the item to be seized is data and not its storage device, the "within the district" requirement is fulfilled.

2. Describing the Items to Be Seized

When the evidence consists of information in a computer system, but the computer itself is not an instrumentality of the offense or otherwise seizable, the hardware is simply a storage device. First and foremost, all technical matters aside, searching the computer is conceptually similar to searching a file cabinet for papers. One important difference is that while the storage capacity of a file cabinet is limited, the storage capacity of computers continues to increase. A standard 40-megabyte hard drive contains approximately 20,000 pages of information, and 200+ megabyte drives are already quite common. Therefore, although the computer itself is no more important to an investigation than the old cabinet was, the technology may complicate enormously the process of extracting the information.

Bearing this analogy in mind, if agents have probable cause only for the documents in the computer and not for the box itself, they should draft the warrant with the same degree of specificity as for any other document or business record in a similar situation. For example, the detail used to describe a paper sales receipt (for a certain product sold on a certain date) should not be any less specific merely because the record is electronic.

As with other kinds of document cases, the breadth of a warrant's authority to search through a suspect's computer will depend on the breadth of the criminality. Where there is probable cause to believe that an enterprise is pervasively illegal, the warrant will authorize the seizure of records (both paper and electronic) far more extensively than if probable cause is narrow and specific. "When there is probable cause to seize all [items], the warrant may be broad because it is unnecessary to distinguish things that may be taken from things that must be left undisturbed." United States v. Bentley, 825 F.2d 1104, 1110 (7th Cir.), cert. denied, 484 U.S. 901 (1987). But by the same token, "[w]hen the probable cause covers fewer documents in a system of files, the warrant must be more confined and tell officers how to separate documents to be seized from others." Id. at 1110. See also Application of Lafayette Academy, Inc., 610 F.2d 1 (1st Cir. 1979). There is nothing about the nature of searching for documents on a computer which changes this underlying legal analysis. Each warrant must be crafted broadly or specifically according to the extent of the probable cause, and it should focus on the content of the relevant documents rather than on the storage devices which may contain them.

The difficulties arise when, armed with a narrow and specific warrant, agents begin the search. If agents know exactly what they are looking for (a certain letter; a voucher filed on a particular date), it may be simple enough to state it in the warrant. But because computers, like file cabinets, can store thousands of pages of

---

[15] "Upload" means to transfer data from a user's system to a remote computer system. Webster's, supra. Of course, only a copy is transferred, and the original remains on the user's machine. It may be significant to search for the uploaded data even if the original has been seized. For example, the user may have altered the original.

information, the specific letter may be much easier to describe than to find. Some may argue, with good reason, that the sheer volume of evidence makes it impractical to search on site. (For a more extensive discussion of these issues, see "DECIDING WHETHER TO CONDUCT THE SEARCH ON-SITE OR TO REMOVE HARDWARE TO ANOTHER LOCATION," supra.)

Even so, the volume-of-evidence argument, by itself, may not justify seizing all the information storage devices--or even all of the information on them--when only some of it is relevant. In In Re Grand Jury Subpoena Duces Tecum Dated November 15, 1993, 846 F. Supp. 11 (S.D.N.Y. 1994), the district court applied a similar analysis to a grand jury subpoena for digital storage devices. In that case, the government had subpoenaed the central processing units, hard disks, floppy disks, and any other storage devices supplied by the target corporation ("X Corporation") to specified officers and employees of the corporation. Of course, these storage devices also contained unrelated information, including some that was quite personal: an employee's will and individual financial records and information. When "X Corporation" moved to quash the subpoena, the government acknowledged that searching the storage devices by 'key word' would identify the relevant documents for the grand jury's investigation. Even so, prosecutors continued to argue for enforcement of the subpoena as written, particularly because the grand jury was also investigating the corporation for obstruction of justice. In quashing the subpoena, the judge clearly distinguished between documents or records and the computer devices which contain them:

> The subpoena at issue here is not framed in terms of specified categories of information. Rather, it demands specified information storage devices . . . . Implicit in [an earlier case] is a determination that subpoenas properly are interpreted as seeking categories of paper documents, not categories of filing cabinets. Because it is easier in the computer age to separate relevant from irrelevant documents, [the] ontological choice between filing cabinets and paper documents has even greater force when applied to the modern analogues of these earlier methods of storing information.

Although the judge found that investigating the corporation for "obstruction and related charges indeed justifies a commensurately broader subpoena. . .," he declined to modify, rather than quash, the subpoena at issue because "this Court does not have sufficient information to identify relevant documents (including directory files) . . . ." The court's reference to directory files seems to imply that the directory would necessarily list everything in the storage device--which is, of course, not true. A directory would not display hidden, erased, or overwritten files which could still be recoverable by a computer expert. Perhaps the judge's conclusion might have been different if the government had proceeded by search warrant rather than subpoena. In any case, it is interesting to note that the court, in trying to find a balance, suggested that when a grand jury suspects "that subpoenaed documents are being withheld, a court-appointed expert could search the hard drives and floppy disks."

In Davis v. Gracey, 111 F.3d 1472 (10th Cir. 1997), as described above (see "Liability Under the PPA," supra), the police obtained a warrant to search the business premises of the defendant for pornographic CD-ROMs and "equipment, order materials, papers, membership lists and other paraphernalia pertaining to the distribution or display of pornographic material in violation of state obscenity laws." The warrant did not describe a BBS, which the officers seized after determining that it contained obscene material. The defendant challenged the search and seizure of the BBS, claiming that because the warrant did not define the term "equipment," it was not sufficiently particular. The Tenth Circuit held that because the warrant limited the officers' discretion by authorizing them to search only for "equipment . . . pertaining to the distribution of or display of pornographic materials in violation of state obscenity laws," the computer equipment was legally seized. Id. at 1479. Finally, the court held that although the officers failed to inform the magistrate of the existence of the BBS, the warrant was sufficiently supported by probable cause.

In United States v. Falon, 959 F.2d 1143, 1148-49 (1st Cir. 1992), the First Circuit affirmed an order suppressing the defendant's checkbooks, canceled checks, telephone records, address indexes, message slips, mail, telex and facsimile records, calendars and diaries, memory typewriters, word processors, computer disks, both hard and floppy, and other electronic storage media and unrelated software on the ground that the warrant failed to distinguish between the defendant's personal papers and business documents. The court stated that "when an individual's allegedly fraudulent business activities are centered in his home, the 'all records' doctrine must be applied with caution. . . . [I]t would require extraordinary proof to demonstrate that an individual's entire life is consumed by fraud and that all records found in the home were subject to seizure. Because the warrant failed explicitly to limit these . . . categories of items to the subset directly linked to the alleged fraud, the warrant was to that extent insufficiently particular to meet the requirements of the Fourth Amendment."

The Sixth Circuit upheld an "all records" warrant for the search of a residence in a fraud investigation in United States v. Humphrey, 104 F.3d 65, 69 (5th Cir.), cert. denied, 117 S. Ct 1833 (1997). The warrant included a list of four generic categories of property, all related to financial records, and was supported by a three-page affidavit from the agent. The court held that the search warrant was valid in light of the pervasive nature of the fraud, the considerable overlap of the defendant's business and personal life, and the limitation of the warrant to records of financial transactions.

In United States v. Lyons, 992 F.2d 1029 (10th Cir. 1993), during the course of seizing stolen computer equipment, the FBI also searched and seized the contents of stolen computer disks which were not described in the search warrant. The court held that because the defendant made no attempt to show that he had any rightful claim to the disks, he failed to meet the threshold requirement of demonstrating an expectation of privacy in the property searched. Consequently, the court affirmed the district court's denial of the motion to suppress.

In United States v. Maxwell, 45 M.J. 406 (Ct. App. Armed Forces 1996), agents secured a warrant for a search of America Online's computers to determine the identity of a user suspected of trafficking in child pornography and to secure copies of his e-mail. Before receiving the warrant, AOL programmed its computers to provide the requested information. When the warrant was obtained, however, the defendant's screen name was misspelled as "REDDEL"; however, the search was run using the correct name "REDDE1." Notwithstanding the defendant's contention that a search for the name in the warrant would not have revealed his identity, the court held that the typographical error did not invalidate the warrant.

The defendant also challenged the warrant on the ground that it was overly broad, resulting in a general search prohibited by the Fourth Amendment, because it: (1) included the names of those merely receiving obscenity and child pornography, which is not illegal; and (2) lacked an identifiable "e-mail chain" to conclusively link the copies of the electronic child pornography presented to the magistrate with the separate typed list of screen names provided as an attachment to the warrant application. The court held that it was not a general warrant, because "any attempt to further narrow the field of names to be searched in order to weed out those who might have unknowingly received the illegal materials would have resulted in an advance search of those recipients' mailboxes." Id, at 420.

Finally, the defendant challenged the scope of the search because AOL provided information on his second screen name "ZIRLOC," which was not specified in the warrant. The appellate court held the evidence from that screen name inadmissible, because AOL did not rely on the precise language of the warrant while executing the search. Instead, they provided the information pursuant to their understanding of what the warrant would direct. When AOL learned about the screen name "REDDE1" they determined it belonged to defendant and prepared to produce all e-mail associated with his account, including e-mail sent or received under the account's other screen name, "ZIRLOC." But AOL accounts are often used by more than one member of the same family. The identities within one account are differentiated by using a different screen name for each user. The court thus held that because it was not possible for AOL to determine who actually used the unspecified screen name, the court was "unpersuaded . . . to declare other's expectations of privacy to be forfeited based upon some undefined 'good faith' exception." Id, at 421. The appellate court also rejected arguments that the evidence found under the "ZIRLOC" screen name was admissible under the plain view exception or by the inevitable discovery rule. Id. at 422.

In United States v. Kow, 58 F.3d 423 (9th Cir. 1995), the Ninth Circuit held that a warrant that authorized the seizure of inter alia, "[c]omputers, magnetic floppy disks or diskettes, including 3 ½ inch, 5 1/4 inch, or 8 inch sizes, compact disks, magnetic tapes, including cassettes, cartridges, streaming tape, video tape, hard disk units (with attached control card), magnetic cards, and any other electronic data processing storage medium," was overbroad because it did not specify with particularity which records related to the charged offense. The court ruled that such a general warrant might be appropriate if the government establishes probable cause to believe that the entire business is merely a scheme to defraud or that all the business records are likely to evidence criminal activity. In this case, however, the warrant was not supported by such probable cause. See also United States v. Thomas, 746 F. Supp. 65, 68 (D. Utah 1990) (discussing search that included computer disks in corporate office, holding that warrant must limit search to "particular entity or transaction" in order to be reasonably particular).

In United States v. Hersch, Crim. A. No. 93-10339-Z, 1994 WL 568728 (D. Mass. 1994) (unpublished decision), the court considered whether a warrant for the search and seizure of computer hardware, software, and related equipment amounted to a general search warrant. The defendant filed a motion requesting an evidentiary hearing under Franks v. Delaware, 438 U.S. 154 (1978), to challenge the affidavits that supported a warrant to search his offices. The defendant claimed that the initial warrant and affidavit lacked the requisite particularity under the Fourth Amendment. The court held that because of the "nature" of computer equipment and data, the scope of seizure necessarily must be broad. Furthermore, in this particular case, the complex scheme under investigation required the seizure of the entire computer system in order to piece the scheme together. (citing Andresen v. Maryland, 427 U.S. 463, 481 n.10 (1976)).

The court in United States v. Stewart, Crim A. No. 96-383, 1997 WL 189381 (E.D. Pa. 1997) (unpublished decision), addressed whether the description of the items set forth in the warrant was so broad that it constituted a general exploratory warrant in violation of the Fourth Amendment. The warrant at issue allowed the search and seizure of "[a]ll computer hardware and software containing any [evidence of racketeering, mail and wire fraud, and money laundering], including, any computer hardware and/or software necessary to access this data and any operating manuals and software guides necessary to access this data." The court upheld this warrant, holding that this restriction acted as a sufficient limitation on the scope of the warrant.

In United States v. Lacy, -- F.3d --, 1997 WL 378104 (9th Cir. 1997), the Ninth Circuit further addressed the specificity requirement for warrants. On appeal from a conviction for possession of child pornography, the defendant argued that the warrant was too general because it authorized the seizure of his entire computer system. The Ninth Circuit distinguished the Kow decision, stating that, unlike the Kow case, the affidavit in the present case established probable cause to believe that the entire system would contain evidence of criminal activity. Although both the warrant in Lacy and the warrant in Kow described the computer equipment in generic terms and subjected it to a blanket seizure, the court held that, in the instant case, no more specific description of the computer equipment sought was possible.

In New York v. Loorie, 165 Misc.2d 877, 630 N.Y.S.2d 483 (Monroe Cty. Ct. 1995), police seized a computer, a backup drive, and several dozen floppy disks, pursuant to a valid warrant that authorized the police to search for and seize "any and all computers, keyboards, Central Processing Units, external drives and/or internal drives, external and internal storage devices such as magnetic tapes and/or disks or diskettes." After seizing the computer equipment, the police examined the contents of the computer's internal drive and the floppy disks. The court rejected appellant's contention that the police exceeded the scope of the warrant by examining the contents of the computer's internal drive and the floppy disks. The court stated that United States v. Ross, 456 U.S. 798, 829-22 (1982), and its progeny established the principle that where a search warrant authorizes the seizure of records, the police can search whatever type of container might reasonably contain such records.

In Washington v. Riley, 121 Wash.2d 22, 846 P.2d 1365 (1993), a long distance telephone company observed that the company's general phone card access number was being repeatedly dialed at 40-second intervals.

After connection, a different 6-digit code was entered, followed by the same long distance number. The company recognized this activity as characteristic of a "hacker" attempting to obtain customer's 6-digit access codes which could then be used to make long-distance calls. The long distance company contacted the local phone company which traced the repeated calls to the defendant.

Based on this information, the police secured a warrant which authorized the seizure of "any fruits, instrumentalities and/or evidence of a crime, to-wit: . . . information stored on hard or floppy disks, personal computers, modems, monitors, speed dialers, touchtone telephones, electronic calculators, electronic notebooks, or any electronic recording device."

The defendant claimed that the warrant was overbroad because it did not specify what crimes were being investigated or otherwise limit the scope of the search by reference to particular items to be seized. The Washington State Supreme Court held that the warrant was facially overbroad and therefore invalid because the warrant failed to sufficiently limit the scope of the search, nor did it state the crime under investigation. When the nature of the underlying offense precludes a descriptive itemization of the items to be seized, generic classifications, like the ones used for this warrant, are acceptable. In such an instance, however, the search must be circumscribed by reference to the crime under investigation. In this instance, the warrant authorized broad categories of material to be seized and was not limited by reference to any specific criminal activity. The court thus held the warrant to be invalid.

In Florida v. Wade, 14 Fla. L. Weekly 1071, 544 So.2d 1028 (Fla. Dist. Ct. App. 1989), the appellants challenged a warrant authorizing the search and seizure of "computer equipment and business records which is [sic] being kept and used in violation of the Laws of the State of Florida" as overbroad. The court upheld the warrant, stating that such a description accompanied by a lengthy affidavit of probable cause sufficiently limited the scope of the search.

In Louisiana v. Tanner, 534 So.2d 535 (Ct. App. La. 1988), police obtained a warrant that authorized officers to search an office and seize "a copy of the 'Cosmos Revelation' software disc, . . . on a floppy disc, and other computer related software and copies of computer printouts bearing the name 'First Page Beepers.'" While executing the warrant, officers found manuals, but not the specified disk. The program bearing the proper serial number was found on a computer's hard drive. The officer made a copy of the program from the hard drive, and seized the manuals, computer keyboard, terminal, and numerous related documents.

The defendant claimed that the warrant was overbroad. The warrant authorized the officers to seize a copy of the disk identified by serial number and other computer related software and copies of computer printouts bearing the name of the business. The court found that the warrant was not overbroad because it limited the officers' discretion by authorizing only the search and seizure of related software bearing the name "First Page Beepers."

In Pennsylvania v. McEnamy, 667 A.2d 1143 1149 (Pa. Super. Ct. 1995), the court held that a second warrant to search the memory chip of a validly seized cellular telephone was unnecessary. The court reasoned that "the memory chip in a cellular phone is analogous to the memory chip of a personal computer in that both simply store information," and it has long been held that a warrant authorizing the seizure of a personal computer authorizes reproduction of the documents stored within.

3. Removing Hardware to Search Off-Site: Ask the Magistrate for Explicit Permission.

Because the complexities of computer data searches may require agents to remove computers from a search scene, agents and prosecutors should anticipate this issue and, whenever it arises, ask for the magistrate's express permission. Obviously, the more information they have to support this decision, the better--and the affidavit should set out all the relevant details. It will be most important to have this explicit permission in the warrant for those cases where (as in Tamura, supra) agents must seize the haystack to find the needle.

If the original warrant has not authorized this kind of seizure, but the agent discovers that the search requires it, she should return to the magistrate and amend the warrant, unless exigencies preclude it.

4. Seeking Authority for a No-Knock Warrant

a. In General

Under 18 U.S.C. § 3109, an agent executing a search warrant must announce his authority for acting and the purpose of his call. See, e.g., United States v. Barrett, 725 F. Supp. 9 (D.D.C. 1989) ("Police, search warrant, open up"). This knock-and-announce requirement, although statutory, has been incorporated into the Fourth Amendment, United States v. Bustamante-Gamez, 488 F.2d 4, 11-12 (9th Cir. 1973), cert. denied, 416 U.S. 970 (1974), and therefore a statutory violation may also be a constitutional one. United States v. Murrie, 534 F.2d 695, 698 (6th Cir. 1976); United States v. Valenzuela, 596 F.2d 824, 830 (9th Cir.), cert. denied, 441 U.S. 965 (1979). The knock-and-announce rule is designed to reduce the possibility of violence (the occupant of the premises may believe a burglary is occurring), reduce the risk of damage to private property (by allowing the occupant to open the door), protect the innocent (the agent may be executing the warrant at the wrong location), and symbolize the government's respect for private property.

Of course, if no one is present, there is no one to notify, and agents can search the place without waiting for its occupant. United States v. Brown, 556 F.2d 304 (5th Cir. 1977). The knock-and-announce requirement also does not apply when the door is open. United States v. Remigio, 767 F.2d 730 (10th Cir.), cert. denied, 474 U.S. 1009 (1985). It is unclear whether the rule applies to businesses, as different courts have reached different conclusions. Cf. United States v. Agrusa, 541 F.2d 690 (8th Cir. 1976) (§ 3109 applies to businesses), cert. denied, 429 U.S. 1045 (1977), with United States v. Francis, 646 F.2d 251 (6th Cir.) (§ 3109 applies only to dwellings), cert. denied, 454 U.S. 1082 (1981).

After knocking and announcing, agents must give the occupants a reasonable opportunity to respond, although exigent circumstances may justify breaking in without an actual refusal. Compare United States v. Ruminer, 786 F.2d 381 (10th Cir. 1986) (break-in authorized where police waited five seconds and saw people running in house), with United States v. Sinclair, 742 F. Supp. 688, 690-1 (D.D.C. 1990) (one- to two-second delay, even with noise inside, was insufficient to warrant break-in).

Moreover, exigent circumstances may justify forcible entry without "knocking and announcing" at all. Circumstances are exigent if agents reasonably believe that giving notice to people inside could cause (1) the officer or any other individual to be hurt; (2) a suspect to flee; or (3) the evidence to be destroyed. Additionally, investigators need not knock and announce when it would be a "useless gesture" because the people inside already know their authority and purpose.

b. In Computer-Related Cases

In many computer crime cases, the primary concern will be preserving the evidence. Technically adept suspects may "hot-wire" their computers in an effort to hide evidence. Although there are many ways to do this, two more common practices involve "hot keys" and time-delay functions. A "hot key" program is designed to destroy evidence, usually by overwriting or reformatting a disk, when a certain key is pressed.[16] Thus, when officers knock at the door and announce their presence, the subject of the search can hit the key that activates the program. A time-delay function is a program that monitors the keyboard to determine whether the user has pressed any key.

---

[16] Of course, the fact that this occurs does not mean the evidence cannot be salvaged. Experts can often recover data which has been deleted or overwritten.

If no key is pressed within a certain period of time, such as 30 seconds, the program activates and destroys data. A target may, therefore, answer the door slowly and attempt to delay the agent's access to the machine.

These problems, which may be present in every computer crime investigation, are not, standing alone, sufficient to justify dispensing with the knock-and-announce rule. Most courts have required agents to state specifically why these premises or these people make it either dangerous or imprudent to knock and announce before a search. See United States v. Carter, 566 F.2d 1265 (5th Cir. 1978) (someone inside yelled "It's the cops" and the agent, who had a warrant to search for heroin, heard running inside), cert. denied, 436 U.S. 956 (1978); United States v. Stewart, 867 F.2d 581 (10th Cir. 1989) (collecting cases). But cf. United States v. Wysong, 528 F.2d 345 (9th Cir. 1976) (mere fact that police knew defendant was trafficking in an easily destroyable liquid narcotic created exigent circumstance that justified entry without knocking and announcing).

In short, most cases hold that agents must have some reasonable, articulable basis to dispense with the knock-and-announce requirement. Moreover, in light of the salutary purposes served by the rule, they should have very good reasons before deviating from it. In appropriate cases, however, a no-knock warrant should be obtained. In deciding whether to seek a no-knock warrant, agents should consider, among other things: (1) what offense is being investigated (is it a narcotics case where the subjects may be armed, or is it non-violent hacking?); (2) is there information indicating evidence will be destroyed (in one recent hacker case, the targets talked about destroying evidence if raided by the police); (3) the age and technical sophistication of the target; and (4) whether the target knows, or may know, he is under investigation.

VII. POST-SEARCH PROCEDURES

A. INTRODUCTION

As noted above, the government is permitted to search for and to seize property that is contraband, evidence, or an instrumentality of the offense. The law does not authorize the government to seize items which do not have evidentiary value, and generally agents cannot take things from a search site when their non-evidentiary nature is apparent at the time of the search.

With computer crimes, however, it is not always possible to examine and separate wheat from chaff at the search location. There may be thousands of pages of data on the system; they may be encrypted or compressed (and thus unreadable); and searching computers frequently requires expert computer skills and equipment. All these factors contribute to the impracticality of on-site processing. Accordingly, agents will often seize evidentiary materials that are mixed in with collateral items. (See "DECIDING WHETHER TO CONDUCT THE SEARCH ON-SITE OR TO REMOVE HARDWARE TO ANOTHER LOCATION," supra.)

For several reasons, it is important to separate evidence (and contraband, fruits, and instrumentalities) from irrelevant items. First, as noted above, the law does not generally authorize seizing non-evidentiary property. But to the extent agents sort and return these materials after a search, the courts are less likely to require that large amounts of data be sorted at the scene. Put another way, if law enforcement authorities routinely retain boxes of property that are not evidence, the courts surely will become less sympathetic in those cases where it is, in fact, appropriate to seize entire systems and analyze them later at the lab.

A second reason to promptly sort seized evidence is that the process will help to organize the investigation. Agents and prosecutors will obviously want to focus on the evidence when preparing complaints or indictments. Getting a handle on the items that advance the case will help agents assess quickly and accurately where the case should go. As much as overbroad seizures offend the law, they are just as bad for the investigation. Investigators should cull out the things that do not help the case right away to avoid endlessly sifting through unimportant materials as the investigation progresses.

Procedures for sorting, searching, and returning seized items will depend in part upon the type of evidence involved. There are, however, certain basic concepts that apply across the board. The basics include the following.

B. PROCEDURES FOR PRESERVING EVIDENCE

1. Chain of Custody

Computer evidence requires the same chain of custody procedures as other types of evidence. Of course, the custodian must strictly control access and keep accurate records to show who has examined the evidence and when. (For a further discussion of this issue, see "EVIDENCE: Chain of Custody," infra.)

2. Organization

As with other parts of the investigation, the sorting process should be as organized as possible. If there are only a few agents involved, each with discrete tasks, the job is likely to be quick and efficient. Many agents, unsure of their tasks, are more likely to misplace or overlook evidence. An organized review process, which is part of a larger, well-briefed search plan, is also easier to describe and defend in court.

3. Keeping Records

Agents should always document their investigative activities. This allows other agents and attorneys to keep track of complex investigations, and will help the case agent reconstruct the sorting process at a later time if necessary. A log should be kept that describes each item seized, whether it was examined, and whether it contained evidence.

When items are returned, a receipt should set out: (a) a clear description of the item, (b) the person who received it (with a signature and identification), and (c) when the item was released. It often makes sense to return all items at one time rather than to do it piecemeal. Also, it is a good idea to keep photographs of the property returned in order to avoid disputes.

4. Returning Seized Computers and Materials

Once agents have removed the computer system from the scene, an expert should examine the seized material as soon as practicable. This examination may be conducted by a trained field office agent, a special agent sent to the field office for this purpose, or by a properly-qualified private expert. Some agencies may require that the computer system be shipped to a laboratory. Each agency should establish and follow a reasonable procedure for handling computerized evidence.

Once the analyst has examined the computer system and data and decided that some items or information need not be kept, the government should return this property as soon as practicable. The courts have acknowledged an individual's property interest in seized items, and the owner of seized property can move the court for a return of property under Fed. R. Crim. P. 41(e). That remedy is available not only when the search was illegal, but also if the person simply alleges a "deprivation of property by the Government." In Re Southeastern Equipment Co. Search Warrant, 746 F. Supp. 1563 (S.D. Ga. 1990).

Agents and prosecutors must remember that while a computer may be analogous to a filing cabinet for the agents who search it, it is much more to most computer users. It can be a data processor, graphics designer, publisher, and telecommunications center. Courts will no doubt recognize the increasingly important role computers play in our society, and the public's extensive reliance on these computers to support the way we live and do business. As a result, law enforcement should be prepared to look carefully at the circumstances of each case and to seize computers only as needed, keeping them only as necessary.

a. Federal Rules of Criminal Procedure: Rule 41(e)

While computer-owners may be especially eager for return of their hardware, software, data, and related materials, the issue of whether to retain or return lawfully seized property before trial is not unique to computers. Rule 41(e) of the Federal Rules of Criminal Procedure sets out the standards and procedures for returning all property seized during the execution of a search warrant. The Rule, in general, provides that a party who is "aggrieved by an unlawful search and seizure or by the deprivation of property" may file a motion for the return of the property on the ground that the party is entitled "to lawful possession of the property." [17]

A Rule 41(e) motion for return of property can be made either before or after indictment. However, a district court's jurisdiction over a pre-indictment motion is more limited than if the indictment has been returned. Pre-indictment remedies are equitable in nature and must only be exercised with "caution and restraint." Floyd v. United States, 860 F.2d 999, 1003 (10th Cir. 1988). The Tenth Circuit, the only Circuit to address this issue, held that two conditions must be satisfied before a district court may assume jurisdiction over a pre-indictment Rule 41(e) motion: "a movant must demonstrate that being deprived of actual possession of the seized property causes 'irreparable injury' and must be otherwise without adequate remedy at law." Matter of Search of Kitty's East, 905 F.2d 1367, 1371 (10th Cir. 1990).

Because of the paucity of cases in this area, it is very difficult to say what facts will satisfy this two-part test. However, the reported decisions do offer guidance in responding to a request for the return of seized property. The Tenth Circuit in Kitty's East held that the "irreparable injury" element is not satisfied by the threat of an imminent indictment. 905 F.2d at 1371, citing Blinder, Robinson & Co. v. United States, 897 F.2d 1549, 1557 (10th Cir. 1990). The appellate court in Kitty's East upheld the district court's decision to take jurisdiction because the nature of the seized materials--pornographic videotapes--invoked the First Amendment right of free speech. "Although the interests of the commercial speech at issue here may not equate with those of political speech, we agree that the special protections of the First Amendment justified the exercise of equitable jurisdiction in this case." Id. Conversely, the Blinder court rejected the movant's contention that it was irreparably injured by the government's failure to return original documents: "[T]he record strongly suggests that [the movant] is able to operate with photocopies of the documents seized by the government and either has copies or can make copies of all the property that the government seized." Blinder, 897 F.2d at 1557.

Once jurisdiction has been established, Rule 41(e), according to the Tenth Circuit, requires the party to also show that the retention of the property by the government is unreasonable:

> Reasonableness under all of the circumstances must be the test when a person seeks to obtain the return of property. If the United States has a need for the property in an investigation or prosecution,

---

[17] Rule 41(e) does not distinguish according to how the property was used in the offense; thus, a computer used as an instrumentality of an offense (e.g., to duplicate copyrighted software or hack into other systems) is not treated differently for Rule 41 analysis from a computer used as a "storage cabinet" for documents. Of course the government's interest in seizing and keeping the computer in each case is different and, thus, from a realistic standpoint, how the computer was used in the offense is important in determining whether to retain or return it.

its retention of the property generally is reasonable. But, if the United States' legitimate interests can be satisfied even if the property is returned, continued retention of the property would become unreasonable.

Id., quoting Committee Note to 1989 Amendment at 30, 124 F.R.D. at 428.

As described, the Kitty's East court initially held the district court had properly exercised jurisdiction over the motion because of the possibility that the movant's First Amendment rights would be impaired. However, the court then denied the Rule 41(e) motion for the return of the seized property. The court held that Kitty's East failed to demonstrate that it was aggrieved by an unreasonable retention of the property:

> With regard to the videotapes seized, Kitty's has made no argument that the seizure has precluded all exhibition or rental of the videotapes in question. Kitty's First Amendment rights are not sufficiently infringed by the government's seizure for evidence of a few copies of a limited number of videotapes to be 'aggrieved' under Rule 41(e) . . . . Further, return of the videotapes would pose too great a risk of loss of potential evidence. As the Supreme Court has noted, 'such films may be compact, readily transported for exhibition in other jurisdictions, easily destructible, and particularly susceptible to alteration by cutting and splicing critical areas of film.' We hold therefore, that the government's retention of no more than two evidentiary copies of each film is reasonable and does not 'aggrieve' Kitty's under Rule 41(e).

905 F.2d at 1376 (citations omitted).

In United States v. Taft, 769 F. Supp. 1295, 1307 (D. Vt. 1991) the court relied on Kitty's East to deny a motion for the return of two firearms which had been legally seized by the government during the execution of a search warrant. Moreover, the court refused to second guess the government about the evidentiary value of the guns: "[H]aving decided that the government legally seized the two firearms, this court will not opine as to the evidentiary value of the guns in the instant prosecution for cultivation of marijuana."

The decisions addressing Rule 41(e) impose a heavy burden on a party seeking the return of property, including computers, lawfully seized by the government. However, unless there is a reason not to do it, agents should explore giving the computer owner copies of the computer disks seized--even when Rule 41(e) does not require it. This is especially true if the owner needs the data to run a business. Of course, if the information stored on the disks is contraband or if copying the information would jeopardize the investigation, agents should not make copies for the owner.

Similarly, if the owner of a seized computer needs it for business, there may be intermediate solutions. For example, using careful scientific protocols and keeping exacting records, an analyst can make printouts from the hard drives to have "original" records to admit in court. Following the same process, the analyst can then make a mirror image (or "bit-stream") data copy of the hard drives for later analysis. Before returning the computers, agents should explain the printout and copying processes used, and give the defense an opportunity to object to the integrity and admissibility of the printouts and copies at that time. Best practice is to ask the defense counsel to sign an explicit waiver of those issues at the time the computer is returned and to stipulate that printouts and electronic copies will be admissible under Fed. R. Evid. 1001. (For a more extensive discussion of admitting electronic evidence, see "EVIDENCE," infra.) If the defense refuses to concede the accuracy and admissibility of the printouts and copies, the government should keep the computer. (For a form "Stipulation for Returning Original Electronic Data," see APPENDIX A).

The defendant invoked Fed. R. Evid. 41(e) for the return of seized computer equipment in United States v. Stowe, No. 96 C 2702, 1996 WL 467238 (N.D. Ill. 1996) (unpublished decision). The defendant operated a bulletin board system that allegedly trafficked in copyrighted software. While executing a valid search warrant, police seized two networked computers, a mini-tower containing two hard drives, a tower containing three hard drives, a Digital Audio Tape ("DAT") drive, and two CD-ROM drives containing discs. Eighteen months after the seizure of the computer equipment, the defendant filed a Fed. R. Evid. 41(e) motion requesting the return of the computer equipment. The court denied the defendant's motion, holding that the government's asserted interests in retaining the computer equipment outweighed the defendant's interest in having it returned. The retention of the equipment was held to be justified because of several factors: (1) the investigation appeared to be leading to a criminal charges, (2) the volume of work in determining whether particular files were copyrighted, and their retail value, was time consuming, (3) the age and poor condition of the computer equipment was impeding timely progress in the investigation, and (4) by returning the equipment, the government would have been returning stolen goods.

b. Hardware

In deciding whether to retain hardware, agents should consider several factors. Aspects that weigh in favor of keeping hardware include: (1) the hardware was used to commit a crime, was obtained through criminal activity, or is evidence of criminal activity, (2) the owner of the hardware would use it to commit additional crimes if it were returned, (3) the hardware is unique and is either essential for recovering data from storage devices or difficult to describe without the physical item present in court, and (4) the hardware does not serve legitimate purposes. Factors that weigh in favor of returning hardware include: (1) a photograph of the hardware would serve the same evidentiary purpose as having the machines in court, (2) the hardware is an ordinary, unspecialized piece of equipment such as a telephone, (3) the hardware is used primarily for legal purposes, and (4) the hardware is unlikely to be used criminally if returned.

Although the result will depend on the precise facts of each case, some basic principles are clear. Where hardware was used to commit a crime (instrumentality) or is the proceeds of crime (fruit) and it belongs to the suspect, agents should generally keep it. When the hardware clearly is not evidence of a crime (e.g. an electronic wristwatch which turns out to have no memory), it should generally be returned.

The difficult situations arise when hardware was only tangential in the crime, played primarily a non-criminal role, or does not belong to the suspect. In these cases, agents and prosecutors must balance the government's need to retain the original items against the property owner's interest in getting them back. In any case, aggrieved property owners can ask the court to order the government to return even lawfully-seized items. See Fed. R. Crim. P. 41(e).

c. Documentation

Warrants often include computer books, programming guides, user manuals and the like. These items may have evidentiary significance in several ways: they may be proprietary (e.g. telephone company technical manual for employees); they may indicate that software, hardware, or the manuals themselves were obtained illegally; they may be necessary for searching a particular, customized machine also covered by the warrant; or they may contain handwritten notes about how the subject used the machine. In this case, agents should treat the books and manuals as evidence and retain them.

Very often, however, books and manuals are not unique. Most of the time, they will be publicly available user guides without significant handwritten notes. They may be convenient references for investigators, but they do not add anything that could not be commercially purchased. In such cases, Rule 41(e) does not require subjects to supply such equipment or technical information, so these items (if they contain no evidence) should be returned.

d. Notes and Papers

Notes and papers often contain extremely valuable information like passwords, login sequences, and other suspects' telephone numbers or names. Notes also tend to be rather cryptic, so agents will not always know right away what they are. Accordingly, it may be appropriate to retain notes and papers until they can be carefully examined, but agents should return records that are clearly not evidence or instrumentality.

e. Third-Party Owners

The retain-or-return question is particularly delicate when the evidence (usually hardware) belongs to innocent third parties. While the government is clearly entitled to seize evidence no matter who owns it, Rule 41(e) of the Federal Rules of Criminal Procedure recognizes that the property owner may move for return of unreasonably held items. See Fed. R. Crim. P. 41(e) advisory committee note (1989) ("reasonableness under all of the circumstances must be the test when a person seeks to obtain the return of property"). The committee notes further point out that the government's legitimate interests can often be satisfied "by copying documents or by conditioning the return on government access to the property at a future time." Id.

When a third party claims ownership, it is important to evaluate competing claims before deciding what to do. The worst solution is to return property to someone who later turns out <u>not</u> to have been the rightful owner. Thus, whenever it is appropriate to return property, agents must verify ownership with documents or other reliable evidence. If in doubt, it is best to retain the item and let the aggrieved parties assert their various claims in court. This way, the government will not become embroiled in complicated ownership investigations, and will not release property to the wrong party.

VIII. EVIDENCE

A. INTRODUCTION

Although the primary concern of these Guidelines is search and seizure, the ultimate goal is to obtain evidence admissible in court. From the moment agents seize electronic evidence, they should understand both the legal and technical issues that this sort of evidence presents under the Federal Rules of Evidence.

It can be especially confusing to think about digital proof because, both in our current discussions and in early cases, legal analysts have tended to treat "computer evidence" as if it were its own separate, overarching evidentiary category. Of course, in some very practical ways electronic evidence is unique: it can be created, altered, stored, copied, and moved with unprecedented ease, which creates both problems and opportunities for advocates. But in many important respects, "computer evidence," like any other, must pass a variety of traditional admissibility tests.

Specifically, some commentary is not very clear whether admitting computer records requires a "best evidence" analysis, an authentication process, a hearsay examination, or all of the above. Advocates and courts have sometimes mixed, matched, and lumped these ideas together by talking simply about the "reliability" or "trustworthiness" of computer evidence in general, sweeping terms, rather than asking critically whether the evidence was "trustworthy" in all required aspects.

Part of the reason for this is probably that the first computer evidence offered in court was information generated by businesses. Long before most people used computers in their homes, telephone companies and banks were using them to record, process, and report information that their businesses required. Not surprisingly, many of the early decisions link computer evidence with the business records exception to the hearsay rule. Of course, that exception—which is meant to address a substantive hearsay problem—also includes a sort of internal authentication analysis. (Fed. R. Evid. 803(6) requires a showing that a record was made "at or near the time by, or from information transmitted by, a person with knowledge. . .").

But "computer evidence" as we know it today covers the universe of documentary materials, and is certainly not limited to business records. Computer evidence may or may not contain hearsay statements. It will always need to be authenticated in some way. And data that has been produced, processed, and retrieved under circumstances other than the discipline of a business probably will not contain the qualities that make electronic evidence "reliable" as a business record. Even business records, themselves, may require a closer look, depending on what the proponent wants to do with them at trial.

The key for advocates will be in understanding the true nature of each electronic exhibit they offer or oppose: for what purpose and by what process (both human and technological) was it created? And what specific issues of evidence (rules of form? rules of substance?) does that particular electronic item raise?

B. THE BEST EVIDENCE RULE

One of the issues that investigators and lawyers sometimes cite as troublesome in working with electronic evidence turns out, on examination, to be a largely surmountable hurdle: the "best evidence rule." This rule provides that "[t]o prove the content of a writing, recording, or photograph, the original writing, recording, or photograph is required, except as otherwise provided in these rules or by Act of Congress." Fed. R. Evid. 1002.

The impact of this rule is softened considerably by its reference to other rules. Indeed, Fed. R. Evid. 1001 makes clear in two separate provisions that when it comes to electronic documents, the term "original" has an expansive meaning. First of all, Fed. R. Evid. 1001(1) defines "writings and recordings" to explicitly include magnetic, mechanical, or electronic methods of "setting down" letters, words, numbers, or their equivalents. Clearly, then, when someone creates a document on a computer hard drive, for example, the electronic data stored on that drive is an admissible writing. A proponent could obviously offer it to a court by producing the hard drive in court and displaying it with a monitor. But that somewhat cumbersome process is not the only choice. In telling us what constitutes an "original" writing or recording, Fed. R. Evid. 1001(3) says further that "[i]f data are stored in a computer or similar device, any printout or other output readable by sight, shown to reflect the data accurately, is an 'original.'" Thus, so long as they are accurate, paper printouts from electronic storage devices qualify as "originals" under the rule, and there is clearly no evidentiary need to haul computer equipment into a courtroom simply to admit a document--although there sometimes may be tactical reasons for doing so.

But even having set up that inclusive definition of "original" writing, the Federal Rules go much further to relax the common law standard. Fed. R. Evid. 1003 provides that "[a] duplicate is admissible to the same extent as an original unless (1) a genuine question is raised as to the authenticity of the original or (2) in the circumstances it would be unfair to admit the duplicate in lieu of the original." Therefore, unless authenticity or some "unfairness" is at issue, courts may freely admit duplicate electronic documents. "Duplicate" is defined in Fed. R. Evid. 1001(4) as "a counterpart produced by the same impression as the original. . .by mechanical or electronic re-recording. . .or by other equivalent techniques which accurately reproduces (sic) the original." Many investigative agencies analyze data evidence from exact electronic copies (called "bit-stream" copies) made with commercial or custom-made software. So long as the copies have been properly made and maintained, the Federal Rules allow judges to accept these copies (or expert opinions based on them) as readily as the originals.

Thus, the Federal Rules have, despite their nod to the best evidence rule, made way for a lively courtroom use of electronic evidence in all its many forms. Questions of admissibility turn not on whether the data before a court is on a hard drive, a duplicate floppy disk, or a printout of either one. Instead, courts must ask whether the original data is authentic and whether any copies offered are accurate.

C. AUTHENTICATING ELECTRONIC DOCUMENTS

Of course, every time trial lawyers offer any piece of evidence, they must be ready to show that, as the authentication rule, Fed. R. Evid. 901(a), states, "the matter in question is what its proponent claims." Clearly, there are many ways to do this, including the ten illustrations offered by Fed. R. Evid. 901(b).

1. "Distinctive" Evidence

One of the most common methods for authenticating evidence is to show the item's identity through some distinctive characteristic or quality. Indeed, the authentication requirement of Fed. R. Evid. 901(a) is satisfied if an item is "distinctive" in its "appearance, contents, substance, internal patterns, or other distinctive characteristics, taken in conjunction with circumstances." Fed. R. Evid. 901(b)(4). In fact, it is standard practice to use this method to authenticate some kinds of evidence which may now be digitally created, stored, and reproduced. For example, attorneys offering photographs into evidence invariably just ask a "witness with knowledge" (under Fed. R. Evid. 901(b)(1)) whether a particular photo is "a fair and accurate representation" of something or someone. But should the process of authenticating photographs recognize that, with the advent of digital photography, it is now possible to alter an electronic image without leaving a trace? Consider the following example.

Agents and prosecutors were shown a photograph of a body--twisted on the floor, a gaping wound in the chest. Across the room, on the floor, was a large pistol. On the white wall above the victim's body, scrawled in the victim's own blood, were the words, "I'll kill again. You'll never catch me."

Unlike conventional photographs, however, this picture was not created with film, but with a digital camera. The entire picture was made up of binary digits, ones and zeros, which could be altered without detection. So two law enforcement agents, using commercially available software, started rearranging the digits. They "cleaned" the wall, removing the bloody words. They closed the chest wound, choosing instead to have blood trickling from the victim's temple. Last, they moved the gun into the victim's hand. The case was now solved: the report would claim, and the photograph would "prove," the victim committed suicide.

This was, of course, only a demonstration, which took place in the summer of 1991 at a meeting of the Federal Computer Investigations Committee. The Committee had been established by a handful of federal and state law enforcement personnel who were among the first to appreciate how emerging technologies were both providing new opportunities for criminals and creating new challenges for law enforcement officials. For this group, the point of this demonstration was apparent: not only could ordinary photographs not be trusted in the same old way to be reliable, but an ordinary agent might be duped if he or she were not technologically astute enough to realize the potential for sophisticated digital alteration. The key, of course, is that there is no negative, and the alteration leaves no tracks.

Nor will these authenticity problems be limited to photographs. For example, some package delivery services now allow recipients to sign for their packages on a hand-held device which creates a digital copy of the recipient's signature. Although this makes it easy to transfer the information to a computer, it also enables the computer to recreate the signature. If the hand-held device measures and records the pressure applied by the signer and if the computer reprints that signature with an ink-based printer, the computer-generated copy will look absolutely authentic--even to the author.

Despite these examples, there will be many times when electronic evidence--whether photographs or documents--will indeed be identifiable based on distinctive characteristics alone. An eyewitness can just as easily identify a digital photograph of a person as he could a conventional photo. The question for both judge and jury will be the witness's ability and veracity in observing and recalling the original person, photo, scene, or document with which he compares the in-court version. The fact that it is possible to alter a photo--for example, to extend the skid marks at an accident scene--is far less significant if the authenticating witness is independently sure from observing the site that the skid marks were, in fact, ten feet long. Similarly, the recipient of a discarded electronic ransom note may recall the content of the original note well enough to authenticate a printout from the accused's computer.

But to the extent that in-court photos or documents support incomplete or fading witness memories--or even substitute for witness memory altogether--lawyers must realize that "distinctive characteristics" in electronic evidence may be easy to alter, and may not, depending on the circumstances, satisfy a court. What witness can independently verify the distinctive accuracy of long lists of names or numbers? Can he say that a digital photo is "a fair and accurate representation of a crime scene" in all details--no matter how minor they may have seemed at the time? While he will probably be able to remember whether there was a knife sticking out of a body, will he be able to verify the precise location of a shoe across the room? An eyewitness who picked out the defendant at a line-up should be able to look at a photograph of the array and find the defendant again. But can she say for sure, when testifying at a hearing on defendant's motion to suppress an allegedly suggestive line-up, that all the other people in the picture are exactly as she saw them? Has there been no mustache added in this picture, no height or weight changed in any way? And although the recipient of a ransom note may well be able to recall the exact words of the note, will he recall the type face?

It is important to remember that the traditional process of authenticating an item through its uniqueness often carries an unspoken assumption that the thing--the murder weapon, the photo, or the letter, for example--is a package deal. It either is or is not the thing the witness remembers. Thus, if the witness can identify particular aspects of the item with certainty (such as the content of the ransom note), the other aspects (such as the type face) usually follow along without much debate. Of course, there are times, even with conventional photography, when an authenticating witness will be asked about internal details: "When you saw the crime scene at 5:30, were the shoes both on the right side of the room?" In those circumstances, attorneys and judges naturally tend to be more exacting in establishing that the witness can authenticate not only part of the package, but all the parts that matter.

But with digital photography, this rather minor problem of authentication takes on a new life. Depending on the way electronic evidence has been produced, stored, and reproduced, the collection of ones and zeros that constitutes the "package" of the photograph is infinitely and independently variable--not by moving shoes at the crime scene, but by changing any digits at any time before the exhibit photo is printed. Perhaps judges will find themselves admitting digital photographs and documents based on "distinctive characteristics" if a witness with knowledge can identify and authenticate the item in all relevant detail. But that, of course, requires a judge to know in advance which details will be relevant to the case and which are insignificant. If the characteristic that makes the item distinctive is not the same one that makes it relevant, judges might and should be wary about admitting digital evidence in this way. Even if judges are satisfied, attorneys who cross examine an authenticating witness on minute details of digital photographs may affect the witness's credibility with the jury, especially if the attorney shows how easily the evidence could be altered.

One of the potential solutions to this problem which arises from the nature of electronic evidence may actually be electronic: digital signatures. The Digital Signature Standard, proposed by the National Institute of Standards and Technology (NIST) in the Department of Commerce, would allow authors to encrypt their documents with a key known only to them. Assuming the author has not disclosed his password to others, this identifying key could serve as a sort of electronic evidence seal. In that event, the signature would be just the kind of distinctive characteristic the rules already recognize.

For the time being, however, most computer evidence can still be altered electronically--in dramatic ways or in imperceptible detail--without any sign of erasure. But this does not mean that electronic evidence, having become less distinctive, has become any less admissible. It simply may require us to authenticate it in other ways.

2. Chain of Custody

When prosecutors present evidence to a court, they must be ready to show that the thing they offer is the same thing the agents seized. When that evidence is not distinctive but fungible (whether little bags of cocaine, bullet shell casings, or electronic data), the "process or system" (to use the language of Fed. R. Evid. 901(b)(9)) which authenticates the item is a hand-to-hand chain of accountability.

Although courts generally have allowed any witness with knowledge to authenticate a photograph without requiring the photographer to testify, that may not suffice for digital photos. Indeed, judges may now demand that the proponent of a digital picture be ready to establish a complete chain of custody--from the photographer to the person who produced the printout for trial. Even so, the printout itself may be a distinctive item when it bears the authenticator's initials, or some other recognizable mark. If the photographer takes a picture, and then immediately prints and initials the image that becomes an exhibit, the chain of custody is just that simple. But if the exhibit was made by another person or at a later time, the proponent should be ready to show where the data has been stored and how it was protected from alteration.

3. Electronic Processing of Evidence

When data goes into computers, there are many methods and forms for getting it out. To the extent that computers simply store information for later retrieval, a data printout may qualify as an original document under Fed. R. Evid. 1001(3). Where the computer has merely acted as a technological file cabinet, advocates must be ready to authenticate the in-court version of the document as genuine, but the evidentiary issues (at least those connected to the computer) do not pertain to the substance or content of the document.

But in many cases, attorneys want to introduce evidence that the computer has not only stored, but has also processed in some fashion. If the computer, its operating system, and its applications software have reorganized the relevant information--by comparing, calculating, evaluating, re-grouping, or selectively retrieving--this processing has altered at least the form of the information, and probably the substance as well.

The fact that the computer has changed, selected, or evaluated data naturally does not make the resulting product inadmissible, but it does require another analytical step. The computer processing itself often creates a new meaning, adds new information--which is really the equivalent of an implicit statement. If an advocate wishes to introduce this processed product, he usually offers it for the truth of the conclusion it asserts. For example, when the telephone company compiles raw data into a phone bill for a subscriber, the bill is literally a statement: "The following long distance calls (and no others) were placed from your phone to these numbers on these days and times."

If the computer has created a hearsay statement by turning raw evidence into processed evidence, its proponent should be ready to show that the process is reliable. Computers process data in many different ways by running programs, which can be commercially or privately written. Any of these programs can contain logical errors, called "bugs," which could significantly affect the accuracy of the computer process. And even if there is no error in the code, a technician may run the program in a way that creates a false result. For example, a particular computer search program may be "case sensitive," which means that the upper- and lower-case versions of any given letter are not interchangeable. If an author working in WordPerfect (a popular word-processing program), searches a document for the word "Evidence," the computer will not find the word "evidence," because the letter "e" was not capitalized. What does it mean, then, when the computer reports that the word was "not found"? Under what circumstances should a computer's conclusion be admissible in court?

Consider a failure-to-file tax case. If a prosecutor asks the IRS to search its databanks to see whether a taxpayer filed a return in a particular year, the IRS may give her two very different products. If the taxpayer filed electronically, the IRS can produce either an original document from its computers (a printout of the filing) or an admissible duplicate in the form of an electronic copy. In that case, the IRS computers simply acted as storage cabinets to hold and reproduce the information that was entered by the taxpayer. Tax return in; tax return out.

But if, on the other hand, the IRS searches its databanks and finds nothing, the IRS's negative report is clearly a hearsay statement which results from a computer process--the electronic search for the taxpayer's tax return. The hearsay rule (Fed. R. Evid. 803(10)) allows the absence of a public record to be shown by testimony "that diligent search failed to disclose the record. . . ." But testimony in what form? Will the negative computer report suffice, or should the technician who ran the search testify? Must the technician explain not only what keystrokes he entered to conduct the search, but also establish the error-free logic of the program he used? Must he know not only that the program searches for both lower-and upper-case versions of the taxpayer's name, but also exactly how it accomplishes that task? While the absence of a record is often admitted in evidence, prosecutors can expect that as attorneys become more computer-literate, defense counsel will raise new challenges in this area. Indeed, the accuracy or inaccuracy of the IRS's negative report rests on many different components, including the reliability (both human and technical) of the computer process.

Certainly, the mathematical validity of any program is a question of fact--a question which the opponent of a piece of processed evidence should have an opportunity at some point to explore and to contest. Similarly, the methods and safeguards involved in executing the program must also be fair ground for analysis and challenge. While it would clearly be both unnecessary and burdensome to prove every step of a computer process in every case, courts must also be ready to look behind these processes when the facts warrant. As lawyers and judges learn more about all the variables involved in creating evidence through computer processing, this area may become a new battleground for technical experts.

D. THE HEARSAY RULE

Most agents and prosecutors are familiar with the business records exception to the hearsay rule. Fed. R. Evid. 803(6). Generally speaking, any "memorandum, report, record, or data compilation" (1) made at or near the time of the event, (2) by, or from information transmitted by, a person with knowledge, is admissible if the record was kept in the course of a regularly conducted business activity, and it was the regular practice of that business activity to make the record.

A business computer's processing and re-arranging of digital information is often part of a company's overall practice of recording its regularly conducted activity. Information from telephone calls, bank transactions, and employee time sheets is regularly processed, as a fundamental part of the business, into customer phone bills, bank account statements, and payroll checks. Logic argues that if the business relies on the accuracy of the computer process, the court probably can as well.

This is different, however, from using a company's raw data (collected and stored in the course of business, perhaps) and electronically processing it in a new or unusual way to create an exhibit for trial. For example, banks regularly process data to show each account-holder's transactions for the month, and most courts would readily accept that monthly statement as a qualifying business record. But may a court presume a similar regularity when the same bank runs a special data search for all checks paid from the account-holder's account over the past year to an account in Switzerland? In this case, even though the report was not made at or near the time of the event, the document is probably admissible as a summary under Fed. R. Evid. 1006. That rule allows courts to admit a "chart, summary, or calculation" as a substitute for "voluminous writing, recordings, or photographs." Nonetheless, other parties still have the right to examine and copy the unabridged original data, and to challenge the accuracy of the summary. Of course, this also opens the way to challenges of any computer process which created the summary.

In most other respects, of course, the hearsay rule operates with computer evidence exactly as it does with any other sort of evidence. For instance, statements for purposes of medical treatment, vital statistics, or statements against interest may all qualify as exceptions to the hearsay rule, whether they are oral, written, or electronic. Clearly, an electronic statement against interest must also be authenticated properly, but it does not fail as hearsay. Conversely, a correctly authenticated electronic message may contain all sorts of hearsay statements for which there are no exceptions.

The key is that computer evidence is no longer limited to business records, and the cases that carry that assumption are distinguishable when advocates work with other kinds of electronic evidence. But even with business records, a trial lawyer well versed in the technological world who knows how to ask the right questions may find that the "method or circumstances of preparation indicate lack of trustworthiness," under Fed. R. Evid. 803(6), to such a degree that a court will sustain, or at least consider, a challenge to the admissibility of the evidence. Computers and their products are not inherently reliable, and it is always wise to ask, in any particular case, what computers do and how they do it.

IX. APPENDICES

APPENDIX A: SAMPLE COMPUTER LANGUAGE FOR SEARCH WARRANTS

IT IS ESSENTIAL to evaluate each case on its facts and craft the language of the warrant accordingly. Computer search warrants, even more than most others, are never one-size-fits-all products. The following paragraphs are a starting point for recurring situations, but may be adjusted in infinite ways. If you have any questions about tailoring an affidavit and warrant for your case, please call the Computer Crime Unit at 202-514-1026 for more suggestions.

Your affiant knows that computer hardware, software, documentation, passwords, and data security devices may be important to a criminal investigation in two distinct and important respects: (1) the objects themselves may be instrumentalities, fruits, or evidence of crime, and/or (2) the objects may have been used to collect and store information about crimes (in the form of electronic data). Rule 41 of the Federal Rules of Criminal Procedure permits the government to search and seize computer hardware, software, documentation, passwords, and data security devices which are (1) instrumentalities, fruits, or evidence of crime; or (2) storage devices for information about crime.

1. Tangible Objects

a. Justify Seizing the Objects

Explain why, in this case, the tangible computer items are instrumentalities, fruits, or evidence of crime--independent of the information they may hold.

Your affiant knows that [subject's] regional offices concertedly and systematically supplied various specialized computer programs to its individual local offices. These computer programs were designed to manipulate data in ways which would automatically add a few pennies to the amount billed to customers for each transaction. By using this specially designed program in its computers, the [subject] was able to commit a pervasive and significant fraud on all customers which would be very difficult for any one of them to detect.

* * * * * * *

or

* * * * * * *

Your affiant knows that [subject] accessed computers without authority from his home by using computer hardware, software, related documentation, passwords, data security devices, and data, more specifically described as follows: [ ].

* * * * * * *

and

* * * * * * *

As described above, the [subject's] computer hardware, software, related documentation, passwords, data security devices, and data were integral tools of this crime and constitute the means of committing it. As such, they are instrumentalities and evidence of the violations designated. Rule 41 of the Federal Rules of Criminal Procedure authorizes the government to seize and retain evidence and instrumentalities of a crime for a reasonable time, and to examine, analyze, and test them.

b. List and Describe the Objects

The tangible objects listed below may be named and seized as the objects of the search when they are, themselves, instrumentalities, fruits, or evidence of crime. Depending on the facts of the case, the list may be long or very short. The affidavit should describe the specific tangible objects with as much particularity as the facts allow. The following paragraphs are designed to be expansive and all-inclusive for those cases in which the government has probable cause to search and seize all computer hardware, software, documentation, and data security devices (including passwords) on site. However, most cases will call for a much more limited list.

(1) Hardware

Computer hardware consists of all equipment which can collect, analyze, create, display, convert, store, conceal, or transmit electronic, magnetic, optical, or similar computer impulses or data. Hardware includes (but is not limited to) any data-processing devices (such as central processing units, memory typewriters, and self-contained "laptop" or "notebook" computers); internal and peripheral storage devices (such as fixed disks, external hard disks, floppy disk drives and diskettes, tape drives and tapes, optical storage devices, transistor-like binary devices, and other memory storage devices); peripheral input/output devices (such as keyboards, printers, scanners, plotters, video display monitors, and optical readers); and related communications devices (such as modems, cables and connections, recording equipment, RAM or ROM units, acoustic couplers, automatic dialers, speed dialers, programmable telephone dialing or signaling devices, and electronic tone-generating devices); as well as any devices, mechanisms, or parts that can be used to restrict access to computer hardware (such as physical keys and locks).

(2) Software

Computer software is digital information which can be interpreted by a computer and any of its related components to direct the way they work. Software is stored in electronic, magnetic, optical, or other digital form. It commonly includes programs to run operating systems, applications (like word-processing, graphics, or spreadsheet programs), utilities, compilers, interpreters, and communications programs.

(3) Documentation

Computer-related documentation consists of written, recorded, printed, or electronically stored material which explains or illustrates how to configure or use computer hardware, software, or other related items.

(4) Passwords and Data Security Devices

Computer passwords and other data security devices are designed to restrict access to or hide computer software, documentation, or data. Data security devices may consist of hardware, software, or other programming code. A password (a string of alpha-numeric characters) usually operates as a sort of digital key to "unlock" particular data security devices. Data security hardware may include encryption devices, chips, and circuit boards. Data security software or digital code may include programming code that creates "test" keys or "hot" keys, which perform certain pre-set security functions when touched. Data security software or code may also encrypt, compress, hide, or "booby-trap" protected data to make it inaccessible or unusable, as well as reverse the process to restore it.

2. Information: Records, Documents, Data

For clarity, most "information" warrants need one paragraph listing all the kinds of evidence they seek (content). Then they need a separate paragraph detailing all the various forms this evidence could take, so it is clear that all forms apply to all records. Most warrants will need another section (in appropriate cases) explaining why agents need to seize data storage devices for off-site searches. It may also be necessary to ask the magistrate for permission to take some peripheral hardware and software even though it does not directly contain evidence.

a. Describe the Content of Records, Documents, or other Information

If the object of the search is information which has been recorded in some fashion (including digital form), it is important to begin with the content of the record and not with its form. Depending on the case, the probable cause may be limited to one very specific document or extend to every record in a wholly criminal enterprise. Describe the content of the document with the same specificity and particularity as for paper records.

Based on the facts as recited above, your affiant has probable cause to believe the following records are located at [the suspect's] residence and contain evidence of the crimes described:

A letter dated July 31, 1991 from [the suspect] to his mother.

Tax records and all accompanying accounts, records, checks, receipts, statements, and related information for tax year 1991.

Lists of illegal or unauthorized access codes or passwords, including (but not limited to) telephone, credit card, and computer access codes.

All records relating to [the suspect's] drug trafficking, including (but not limited to) lists of customers and related identifying information; types, amounts, and prices of drugs trafficked as well as dates, places, and amounts of specific transactions; any information related to sources of narcotic drugs (including names, addresses, phone numbers, or any other identifying information); any information recording [the suspect's] schedule or travel from 1988 to present; all bank records, checks, credit card bills, account information, and other financial records.

b. Describe the Form which the Relevant Information May Take

If you know the records are stored on a computer or in some other digital form, you should limit the scope of the search to digital records. If you cannot determine in advance the form of the records (or if the records are in several different forms) the following language is a starting point. BUT BE SURE TO ELIMINATE ANYTHING WHICH DOES NOT APPLY TO YOUR CASE. Once again, because cases which have nothing else in common may all have digital evidence, the following list is extremely broad. For example, in child pornography or counterfeiting cases, the non-digital evidence may be photographs, films, or drawings. But in drug cases, tax cases, or computer crimes, the agents may not be searching for graphics or other pictures.

The terms "records," "documents," and "materials" include all of the foregoing items of evidence in whatever form and by whatever means such records, documents, or materials, their drafts, or their modifications may have been created or stored, including (but not limited to) any handmade form (such as writing, drawing, painting, with any implement on any surface, directly or indirectly); any photographic form (such as microfilm, microfiche, prints, slides, negatives, videotapes, motion pictures, photocopies); any mechanical form (such as phonograph records, printing, or typing); any electrical, electronic, or magnetic form (such as tape recordings, cassettes, compact discs, or any information on an electronic or magnetic storage device, such as floppy diskettes, hard disks, backup tapes, CD-ROMs, optical discs, printer buffers, smart cards, memory calculators, electronic dialers, Bernoulli drives, or electronic notebooks, as well as printouts or readouts from any magnetic storage device).

c. Electronic Mail: Searching and Seizing Data from a BBS Server under 18 U.S.C. § 2703

In some situations, you may know or suspect that the target's computer is the server for an electronic bulletin board service (BBS). If you need to seize the computer, the data on it, or backups of the data, consider the applicability of 18 U.S.C. § 2703. (See "STORED ELECTRONIC COMMUNICATIONS," supra.) If the statute applies and there is or may be qualifying e-mail on the computer, consider whether the government has probable cause to believe that all or any of it is evidence of crime.

Your affiant has probable cause to believe that [the suspect's] computer operates, in part, as the server (or communications center) of an electronic bulletin board service ("BBS"). This BBS [appears to] provide[s] "electronic communication service" to other persons, and [may] contain[s] their "electronic communications," which may have been in "electronic storage" on [the suspect's] computer for less than 180 days (as those terms are defined in 18 U.S.C. § 2510). The affiant is aware of the requirements of Title 18 U.S.C. § 2703 describing law enforcement's obligations regarding electronic communications in temporary storage incident to transmission, as defined in that statute.

(1) If All the E-Mail Is Evidence of Crime

If the whole BBS is dedicated to criminal enterprise (such as a specialty "porn board" or "pirate board"), the facts may support searching and seizing all the e-mail, including the electronic mail which qualifies under the statute.

[Your affiant, as an undercover subscriber and user of (the suspect's) BBS network, has learned that it is dedicated to exchanging illegal copies of computer software and stolen access codes among users. All users are asked to furnish pirated software products and active access codes (phone cards, credit cards, PBX codes, and computer passwords) in return for the privilege of illegally downloading from the BBS other illegal software or codes they may choose. Your affiant has used the electronic mail services of the BBS, and knows that the subscribers use it primarily to share information about other sources of illegal software and about how to use stolen access codes and computer passwords. Thus, your affiant has probable cause to believe that any electronic mail residing on the system contains evidence of these illegal activities.]

(2) If Some of the E-Mail is Evidence of Crime

If you have probable cause to believe that there will be evidence of crime in the e-mail of some users and not others, the affidavit and warrant should distinguish and describe which will be searched and seized and which will not. In most cases like this, the government will be focusing on the electronic communications of the suspect/ sysop's co-conspirators. The affidavit should identify the particular individuals, if possible (by name or "hacker handle"), so that data analysts will know which e-mail to search and which to leave unopened. In some cases, the government may have probable cause to search e-mail from some "sub-boards" of the BBS, but not from others. In other cases, the magistrate may allow the government to run "string searches" of all the e-mail for certain specified key words or phrases. There are too many variations in these cases to draft useful models, but the wisest course is to address this issue in the affidavit and set out a search and seizure plan which the magistrate can approve. Please call the Computer Crime Unit (202-514-1026) for more specific assistance.

(3) If None of the E-Mail Is Evidence of Crime

In some cases, the suspect's criminal uses of his computer are quite separate from and coincidental to his using it as the server for a BBS. For example, a sysop who runs a legal bulletin board from his home may also use the same computer to store personal copies of child pornography, or records of his drug-dealing business, or a death-threat letter to the President of the United States. None of these criminal uses has anything to do with the legal (and perhaps statutorily protected) private electronic communications of his BBS subscribers--except for the fact that they reside on the same computer system. And even when this computer system clearly is an instrumentality of the suspect/sysop's crime, the government may be obliged to protect the unrelated, qualifying e-mail of innocent third parties and set it aside, unopened. In any event, the government should consider and address this issue with the magistrate and devise a plan which will work in the case at hand. Call the Computer Crime Unit for more help.

d. Ask Permission to Seize Storage Devices when an Off-Site Search Is Necessary

Based upon your affiant's knowledge, training and experience, and consultations with [NAME AND QUALIFICATIONS OF EXPERT], your affiant knows that searching and seizing information from computers often requires agents to seize most or all electronic storage devices (along with related peripherals) to be searched later by a qualified computer expert in a laboratory or other controlled environment. This is true because of the following:

1) The volume of evidence. Computer storage devices (like hard disks, diskettes, tapes, laser disks, Bernoulli drives) can store the equivalent of thousands of pages of information. Additionally, a suspect may try to conceal criminal evidence; he or she might store it in random order with deceptive file names. This may require searching authorities to examine all the stored data to determine which particular files are evidence or instrumentalities of crime. This sorting process can take weeks or months, depending on the volume of data stored, and it would be impractical to attempt this kind of data search on site.

2) Technical requirements. Searching computer systems for criminal evidence is a highly technical process requiring expert skill and a properly controlled environment. The vast array of computer hardware and software available requires even computer experts to specialize in some systems and applications, so it is difficult to know before a search which expert is qualified to analyze the system and its data. In any event, however, data search protocols are exacting scientific procedures designed to protect the integrity of the evidence and to recover even "hidden," erased, compressed, password-protected, or encrypted files. Since computer evidence is extremely vulnerable to inadvertent or intentional modification or destruction (both from external sources or from destructive code imbedded in the system as a "booby trap"), a controlled environment is essential to its complete and accurate analysis.

e. Ask Permission to Seize, Use, and Return Auxiliary Items, as Necessary

In cases where you must seize hardware, software, documentation, and data security devices in order to search and seize the data for which you have probable cause, ask the magistrate's permission in the affidavit. The language which follows is general and will be most applicable to computers which are not part of an extensive network. Of course, if you have specific information in your case to support seizing auxiliary items (e.g., the computer hardware is rare; the operating system is custom-designed), cite those factors rather than using the general description which follows.

Based upon your affiant's knowledge, training and experience, and [NAME AND QUALIFICATIONS OF EXPERT], your affiant knows that searching computerized information for evidence or instrumentalities of crime commonly requires agents to seize most or all of a computer system's input/output peripheral devices, related software, documentation, and data security devices (including passwords) so that a qualified computer expert can accurately retrieve the system's data in a laboratory or other controlled environment. This is true because of the following:

The peripheral devices which allow users to enter or retrieve data from the storage devices vary widely in their compatibility with other hardware and software. Many system storage devices require particular input/output (or "I/O") devices in order to read the data on the system. It is important that the analyst be able to properly re-configure the system as it now operates in order to accurately retrieve the evidence listed above. In addition, the analyst needs the relevant system software (operating systems, interfaces, and hardware drivers) and any applications software which may have been used to create the data (whether stored on hard drives or on external media), as well as all related instruction manuals or other documentation and data security devices.

If, after inspecting the I/O devices, software, documentation, and data security devices, the analyst determines that these items are no longer necessary to retrieve and preserve the data evidence, the government will return them within a reasonable time.

f. Data Analysis Techniques

Data analysts may use several different techniques to search electronic data for evidence or instrumentalities of crime. These include, but are not limited to the following: examining file directories and subdirectories for the lists of files they contain; "opening" or reading the first few "pages" of selected files to determine their contents; scanning for deleted or hidden data; searching for key words or phrases ("string searches").

3. Stipulation for Returning Original Electronic Data

In some cases, you may want to return data storage devices which contain original electronic evidence to the suspect and keep "bit-stream" or "mirror-image" copies for processing and for use at trial. For example, the suspect may be a large business which employs many innocent people and which needs its computers and data in order to run the business and pay the employees. If you do wish to return the equipment and data before trial, consider using some version of the following stipulation to avoid evidentiary issues. Of course, whether the copies are, indeed, "exact" copies is a question of fact, and the defense will have to satisfy itself that the government's copying process was accurate. But if, after exploring the issue, the defense refuses to sign a stipulation and cannot be satisfied about the reliability of the duplicates, you will probably need to keep the originals. (See "Returning Seized Computers and Materials," supra, and "EVIDENCE," supra.) (For a form stipulation, see below.)

UNITED STATES DISTRICT COURT

In the Matter of the Search of:

_____

STIPULATION OF THE PARTIES

It is hereby stipulated and agreed between

and

as an individual and as an agent for

that:

(1) the electronic information contained on the [Bernoulli 90-MB disk, number _____] is a complete, exact, and accurate duplicate of the electronic information contained on [the hard drive of an IBM personal computer, serial number _____] [the hard drive of a personal computer identified as "Fred's" by an evidence tag attached to the top of the CPU cover, said personal computer bearing no serial number or other identifying information] [a floppy disk marked with an evidence sticker as "item number _____, and bearing the initials "_ _ _"]; which computers/floppy disk were/was seized from _____ on _____, 199_, by agents of the _____.

(2) the electronic information contained on the [Bernoulli 90-MB disk, number _____] accurately reproduces the original data described above as of _____, 199_.

_____
Assistant U.S. Attorney

_____
Defendant

_____
Agency

_____
Attorney

TABLE OF STATUTES AND RULES

TABLE OF STATUTES AND RULES

TAB–2   [February 1999]

TABLE OF CASES

INDEX

References are to sections

A

ACCESS CONTROL LIST AS EVIDENCE, § 2.10

ADMISSIBILITY OF EVIDENCE

    In general, § 8.01 et seq.
    Animations (*see* Computer-generated visual evidence)
    Authentication (*see* Authentication of evidence)
    Best evidence rule (*see* Secondary evidence rule)
    Charts (*see* Computer-generated visual evidence)
    Diagrams (*see* Computer-generated visual evidence)
    Graphs (*see* Computer-generated visual evidence)
    Hearsay rule (*see* Hearsay rule)
    Presentations at trial (*see* Computer-generated visual evidence)
    Simulations (*see* Computer-generated visual evidence)

ANIMATIONS, USE OF (*see* Computer-generated visual evidence)

ANONYMOUS RE-MAILER DEFINED, § 1.03[B]

ARCHIVE AS EVIDENCE, § 2.18

ASCII defined, § 1.03[B]

ASYMMETRIC ENCRYPTION (*see* Encryption)

ATTORNEY-CLIENT PRIVILEGE AS LIMITATION ON DISCOVERY, § 5.02

AUDIT TRAIL

    Authentication of evidence, audit trail as basis for, § 8.02
    Definition, § 1.03[B]
    Evidentiary value, § 2.09

AUTHENTICATION OF EVIDENCE

    In general, § 8.01 et seq.
    Admission of party, direct examination for authentication on, § 10.08[A]
    Audit trail as basis for authentication, § 8.02
    Business records, §§ 10.07, 10.08[B]
    Ciphers as basis for authentication, § 8.03[B]
    Computer-generated visual evidence, authentication issues of, § 11.09
    Direct examination, authentication by, §§ 8.06, 10.08
    Electronic signatures as basis for authentication, § 8.03[C]
    E-mail as basis for authentication, § 8.03[C]
    Encryption as basis for authentication, § 8.03
    Intermediary transmission as basis for authentication, § 8.04
    Password as basis for authentication, § 8.03
    Private key encryption as basis for authentication, § 8.03[B]
    Public key encryption as basis for authentication, § 8.03[C]
    Qualifying authenticating witness, § 10.05

[February 1999]

E

P

PARTITION defined, § 1.03[B]

PASSWORD
  Authentication of evidence, password as basis for, § 8.03
  Computer use policy, form for, § 7.06

PC defined, § 1.03[B]

PCMCIA
  Definition, § 1.03[B]
  Memory cards as evidence, § 2.17

PDA (*see* Personal digital assistants)

PEER-TO-PEER NETWORK (*see* Networks)

PERIPHERALS
  Definition, § 1.03[B]
  Memory as evidence, § 2.19[C]

PERSONAL DIGITAL ASSISTANTS
  Definition, § 1.03[B]
  Evidentiary value, § 2.16

PLAIN TEXT defined, § 1.03[B]

POSTINGS AS EVIDENCE, § 2.12[E]

PRESENTATIONS AT TRIAL (*see* Computer-generated visual evidence)

PRESERVATION REQUESTS AND ORDERS (*see* Spoliation of evidence)

PRIVACY RIGHTS
  In general, § 7.01 et seq.
  Common law rights, § 7.02
  Computer use memo, § 7.07
  Computer use policy, § 7.05 et seq.
  Constitutional rights, § 7.03
  Electronic Communications Privacy Act of 1986, § 7.04, Appendix C
  E-mail use policy, § 7.05
  Employee privacy rights, § 7.01
  Invasion of privacy, § 7.02

PRIVATE KEY ENCRYPTION (*see* Encryption)

PROGRAM FILES AS EVIDENCE, § 2.07

PROPRIETARY INFORMATION AS LIMITATION ON DISCOVERY, § 5.04

PROTECTIVE ORDERS
  In general, § 3.12
  Stipulation for order protecting confidential material, § 5.07

PROXY defined, § 1.03[B]

PUBLIC KEY ENCRYPTION (*see* Encryption)

PUBLIC RECORDS, INSPECTION OF (*see* Freedom of Information Act, Public Records Act)

INDEX